P9-CMA-893

The Arts of Top Management:

A McKinsey Anthology

The Arts of Top Management

A McKinsey Anthology

Edited by Roland Mann

McGraw-Hill Book Company

New York · St. Louis · San Francisco · Mexico · Panama
Toronto

Published simultaneously with a U.K. edition
in which the Introduction and Chapters 2 and 4 vary.

Library of Congress Catalog Card Number 75-128413

07-045197-4

1234567890 MAMM 7543210

Contents

Introduction   ix
    Marvin Bower

Part One. Shaping corporate strategy   1

1. Three strategies for successful growth   4
    J. ROGER MORRISON

2. Controlling postmerger change   12
    FREDERICK WRIGHT SEARBY

3. Britain's quiet managerial revolution   22
    J. ROGER MORRISON

4. Put the board of directors to work!   29
    E. EVERETT SMITH

5. Leadership style and organizational achievement   40
    ROBERT P. NEUSCHEL

Part Two. Organizing for effectiveness   51

6. Organization: the harness to help people pull together   53
    MARVIN BOWER

7. Reorganizing for results   66
    D. RONALD DANIEL

8. Organizing a worldwide business   79
    GILBERT H. CLEE AND WILBUR M. SACHTJEN

9. New concepts in overseas investment   94
    PETER P. GABRIEL

Part Three. The profit-improvement discipline   109

10. Can companies plan their profits?   111
    JON R. KATZENBACH

v

11. Rediscovering profits in manufacturing   118
    JOHN M. UPDEGRAPH, JR. AND BURTON C. PERSON

12. Profit improvement as a way of corporate life   133
    RICHARD F. NEUSCHEL

Part Four. Managing executive manpower   143

13. The new manager: a man for all organizations   146
    GILBERT H. CLEE

14. The coming scramble for executive talent   157
    ARCH PATTON

15. Compensation and the executive career cycle   169
    GEORGE H. FOOTE

16. Executive development—new perspective   178
    ROBERT K. STOLZ

17. Motivating tomorrow's executives   192
    ARCH PATTON

18. A demanding environment: the role of compensation   205
    ARCH PATTON

Part Five. Market and distribution strategy   213

19. Managing the product life cycle   216
    DONALD K. CLIFFORD, JR.

20. Keys to better product planning   227
    B. CHARLES AMES

21. Marketing planning for industrial products   237
    B. CHARLES AMES

22. Shaping distribution channels to your needs   251
    A. L. MCDONALD, JR.

23. Physical distribution: forgotten profit frontier   263
    ROBERT P. NEUSCHEL

Part Six. Harnessing the technological explosion   277

24. The future impact of technology on management   280
    ALCON C. COPISAROW

25. Strategies for a technology-based business   290
    H. IGOR ANSOFF AND JOHN M. STEWART

26. The successful innovators 308
    DAVID B. HERTZ

27. R & D as a partner in world enterprise 317
    DAVID B. HERTZ

28. The promise of project management 326
    JOHN M. STEWART

Part Seven. Management sciences and the computer 339

29. Unlocking the computer's profit potential 341

30. Risk analysis in capital investment 354
    DAVID B. HERTZ

31. Business logistics for better profit performance 369
    ALAN H. GEPFERT

32. Management information: the myth of total systems 380
    C. RIDLEY RHIND

About the authors 392

Acknowledgments 399

Index 401

Introduction

Marvin Bower*

One day in 1935, while serving as a management consultant to the dominant company in its industry, I asked the chief executive how his company had attained its position of leadership. With no hesitation, he told me, in just about these words: "We make it our business to study the consumer, determine his needs and attitudes, and then develop a product that he will prefer to anyone else's. We don't copy our competitors—they copy us. And by the time they catch up, we are ready with something better."

The power of this simple strategy has been proved many times over since 1935, and for most industries its relevance will be even greater in the years ahead. There are two reasons to expect this: first, competition is growing more acute in most industries; second, strategic corporate planning is the most effective way to cope with competition. During the next decade, strategic planning will become better understood and more broadly and effectively applied in industrial, commercial, and financial firms—and, indeed, in nonbusiness organizations as well.

It is relatively easy for the management consultant to forecast management trends a decade ahead in his own field. The beginnings of any trend are clear to him that far in the future because his clients, typically the most successful companies in their industries, are usually about ten years ahead of the crowd. He need only observe what is going on, help think through and develop new concepts, policies, and programs, and then help managers to apply them.

Far from being proprietary, advanced management methods are almost always readily available for adoption. Indeed, their originators and developers usually push them hard; and in the United States, at least, the companies that pioneer in their practical application are surprisingly generous and candid in sharing their experience with others, even including their own competitors.

To be sure, the management consultant is more likely to be present at the birth and early development of a new method than at its conception.

* Mr. Bower, a Director of McKinsey & Company, Inc., was Managing Director from 1950 to 1967. He is the author of *The Will to Manage* (McGraw-Hill, 1966).

He may occasionally do a piece of original research; more often, he gets in at the developmental and application stages. It is here, at the practical level, that he can be most effective in helping to push back the frontiers of management.

In a sense, the management consultant works in a vast field development laboratory for advanced management methods. He brings new ideas from the frontiers of management—the theoretical "state of the art" and the practice of progressive organizations—and works with client personnel to apply the methods in particular company situations. At all times, his problem-solving discipline is his primary development tool. Whatever his specialized skills, he is a generalist by temperament, conviction, and training, adept at combining his own ideas and experience with those of client managers to develop the methods, programs, and strategies best suited to the particular company.

In McKinsey & Company we have a particular interest in the management methods employed by the chief executive and those who report to him. In effect, we operate a group of top-management developmental and application laboratories in many countries of the world. This *Anthology*, a selection of writings published in recent years by members of our professional staff, is a by-product of these laboratories. The chapters cover a broad range of management topics: strategic planning, organization, profit improvement, managing executives, marketing, managing technology, and computer science. They are not, however, research materials in the usual sense. Almost every chapter deals with workable methods that have been accepted and put into effect by the managements of successful firms.

Each author has written as a practicing management consultant, drawing on his own professional experience in working with leading companies in the United States and Europe. His insights have been deepened by those of the client executives with whom he has worked, and his thinking has been thoroughly tested in practice. Given the nature of the book, the concepts, findings, and approaches embodied in many of these chapters are by now some distance behind the advancing frontier of the "art"; but none of them, I believe, is without practical relevance for the top managers of even the most progressive of today's organizations.

Although three of our European offices are represented on the roster of authors, each of their contributions deals with, or draws heavily on, American management methods. This is because of the virtually universal interest of top managements around the world in acquiring and applying American management know-how. At the same time, several authors have incorporated relevant experience from other advanced economies. In most cases, the approaches discussed are applicable to the operations of a firm in any industrialized economy. Indeed, our recent experience suggests they can be adapted successfully to enterprises in socialist states and developing countries as well.

Along with the massive exportation of American know-how, one of the most striking developments of the past two decades on the international management scene has been the upsurge of scientific techniques and analytical approaches. Science dominates today's new-product technology, is revolutionizing our information technology, and is replacing marketing hunch and intuition by statistical research methods. Behavioral research findings are being applied to organization design and personnel management. And, of course, there is the ever-widening application of operations research, systems analysis, and the whole complex of so-called management sciences. Clearly, management-as-science is very much on the way in.

It would be a mistake, however, to conclude from this that management-as-art is on the way out. Closer examination discloses that the direct impact of science and technology is not uniformly distributed throughout the management structure. It is heaviest at the *functional* and *operational* levels; on the higher levels of management, the ratio of science to art in managing begins to drop off. To be sure, the chief executive and his immediate colleagues in management must understand the new scientific tools in principle, know how they are applied at lower levels, and be able to see how they may be useful in the executive suite. Lacking this sophistication, they will be unable to evaluate the high investments these tools and techniques entail, and unable to apply them in top-management decision making.

The top leaders always seek to bring science to the executive suite whenever it is relevant. They know that creative leadership, judgment, and intuition can be powerfully aided by the latest tools, techniques, and information systems. Creative management seeks constantly to inaugurate advanced methods, and it is our hope that this anthology may serve as an aid and stimulus to such action.

Still, it is well to remember that the top manager is not and never will be purely or even primarily a technologist, applying precise techniques to the solution of rigorously defined problems. Rather he is an artist in the broadest sense: a creative allocator of resources, an orchestrator of diverse technical disciplines for the implementation of strategies designed to achieve objectives geared to the organization's mission.

At the summit there are no formulae. The arts of top management, practiced with ever increasing skill, sophistication, and conceptual contribution, are the whole content of the job. Hence the focus (and the title) of the book.

*   *   *

This collection was planned and put together by my colleague Roland Mann, editor of the *McKinsey Quarterly*. Thanks are due to Alan Harrington, author of *Life in the Crystal Palace* (Knopf, 1959) for his thoughtful and imaginative consulting assistance, and to Carol Mastrosati of McKinsey & Company for coping gracefully and efficiently with an awkward load of administrative and editorial detail.

PART ONE

Shaping corporate strategy

The businessman's field of action has been compared to a chessboard. The comparison is intriguing, but not really apt. If corporate strategy were confined to combinations of a few rigidly prescribed moves, the arts of management would be far easier to master. In reality, a competitive economy practically compels every enterprise to invent new moves of its own, and the scope of the business chessboard is limited only by the imagination and the aggressiveness of the players.

A single theme runs through all the following essays: Corporate success strategies, along with the effective organization of corporate efforts to implement them, can never be reduced to formula. Yet they can and must be formulated within the framework of a sound conceptual approach, solidly grounded in objective fact.

In "Three Strategies for Successful Growth," J. Roger Morrison points to the changing nature of the environmental backdrop against which management decisions must be made. Precise growth goals may be set and vigorously pursued. But management cannot always confidently decree the rate at which the company's products will pass through their life cycles. Still less can it predict the behavior of competition or foresee the vagaries of the economy. Hence, business strategies "must be prepared to change and, if need be, change quickly."

Involved here may be the art of balancing flexibility of response with firmness of purpose. Establish a strong growth philosophy, yet at the same time stay flexible enough so that you can quickly seize unforeseen opportunities. Be ready to move in new directions, but don't be diverted

1

from a sound strategic plan by the glamor of novelty for its own sake. At the same time, beware the dangers of emotional involvement with "old reliable" products that no longer contribute an adequate return on investment.

A unique opportunity to make far-reaching improvements and innovations is presented to a company that has acquired or merged with another. In "Controlling Postmerger Change," Frederick Wright Searby discusses the approaches some managements have used to successfully integrate their acquisitions and take advantage of the opportunities for change in the postmerger period. Searby stresses the need for objectivity in resolving the critical personnel, policy, and procedural problems that are bound to occur. In his words, "Unless the executives of the acquiring company make a real effort to be guided by facts rather than assumptions, preconceptions, or wishful thinking, they will be prone to make decisions that can seriously threaten the success of the joint enterprise."

The need for fact-founded decisions—as opposed to those based on intuition, tradition, or snap judgments—is a theme of Roger Morrison's second contribution, "Britain's Quiet Managerial Revolution." He explores its implications for the practice of a number of management arts that have, until recently, been too often neglected by senior executives in the United Kingdom (and elsewhere). These include setting difficult-to-attain goals that challenge executives up and down the line; delegating responsibility to front-line management rather than reserving all real authority for a few men at the top; pressing for productive change instead of accepting rationalizations and excuses for unproductive policies; keeping a close watch on competitors; and encouraging creative dissatisfaction at all levels in the office and plant.

In "Put the Board of Directors to Work!" E. Everett Smith analyzes a nearly universal problem of management: how to make the board of directors a truly vital force in the strategic direction of the company. It is a complex and thorny problem, but it will yield to a positive and pragmatic attack, the author argues. For the chief executive concerned with strengthening his board of directors, he suggests the outlines of such an approach. It begins with thinking through what should be expected of the board, defining its functions and responsibilities, and determining the information it will need to successfully carry out its role. Then the chief executive can set about attracting capable, independent men to serve as directors with some assurance that their talents will be put to effective use in shaping company objectives and guiding corporate strategy.

In the final analysis, successful implementation of corporate strategy is a human enterprise, strongly conditioned by the temperament and leadership capabilities of one man and bearing, for better or worse, the stamp of his personal style. In "Leadership Style and Organizational Achievement," Robert P. Neuschel surveys the management styles of 11 chief executives whom he has known and closely observed over a period of years. Our present-day business environment has profoundly altered the chief executive's role, Mr. Neuschel believes. His job is "less to make all key decisions himself than to develop an organization and process by which decisions can be made . . . not so much to wield his own decision-making power as to unleash [that] of company personnel down the line . . ." How he resolves the problems of providing strong direction through the subtle arts of participative management is the heart of his style—and, perhaps, the ultimate test of his leadership.

1. Three strategies for successful growth

J. Roger Morrison

The growth of any economy depends on a series of interrelated forces. *Government policy* will inevitably be one of these. The economy's *stage of development*—whether it is developing, such as that of Israel or Brazil; or mature, like that of the United States, the United Kingdom, or Germany—is another. A third force, often unrecognized, is the *impact of management action* on individual companies whose annual reports account in large measure for national industrial advances. In the aggregate, such management policies are not merely important; they may be seen as decisive in determining the country's economic growth rate.

We know beyond a doubt that a well-directed management effort can make a company grow at a faster rate than the general economy or even its own industry. Furthermore, management's drive for growth can cause whole new industries to develop—synthetics and semiconductors being two notable examples. Since these expanded activities, reinforcing one another, work together to build and strengthen the economy, any discussion of management's opportunities to increase national economic growth should consider:

¶ What major growth strategies are available to individual company managements.

¶ What programs management can adopt to open up new fields of action for its company.

To provide a practical framework for these two questions, let us first review the growth strategies employed by some of the more outstanding U.S. and U.K. companies, and then distill from these case histories a number of specific measures that other managements can take.

Growth strategies

Analysis shows that companies reporting exceptional growth, *in terms of earnings per share*, have followed three strategies, either singly or in combination: (1) developing existing products in established fields, (2) adding new products or models to the present line, and (3) entering fields entirely new to the company.

4

GROWTH FROM ESTABLISHED PRODUCTS. An outstanding example of a company that has grown by exploiting its existing product is Coca-Cola. Between 1959 and 1969, Coca-Cola maintained an almost constant growth rate. It increased its earnings by 200 percent, far outstripping the rate achieved by most other companies and that of the U.S. economy as a whole. Until recently (with the introduction of Lo-Cal drinks, etc.) Coca-Cola was virtually a one-product company, and most of its earnings growth appears to have come from aggressive selling of that one product in every corner of the world.

GROWTH FROM NEW PRODUCTS IN ESTABLISHED FIELDS. Relatively few companies can increase their business year after year marketing only one product. Most successful enterprises have followed a different strategy: introducing new products in their fields.

Corporations like IBM and Kellogg, for instance, have done this in order to break through to new uses or markets within their existing businesses—"fragmenting the market" for their products.

In contrast to Coca-Cola, IBM has grown over the years by the systematic introduction of new generations of computers and new types of office equipment. An essential element in this strategy has been the company's conscientious cultivation of each specific end-use market. For example, they have developed not only new computers but also the appropriate software for the problems of individual industries. Thus, they have specialists, sales engineers, and programmers who concentrate on computer applications in banking, insurance, public utilities, etc. These new products and services within existing businesses have allowed IBM to expand its market by fragmentation and enabled the corporation to attain its remarkable record of growth.

Similarly, Kellogg's growth of over 100 percent in ten years seems to have resulted largely from continual introduction of new products in an existing field (cereals), as well as rapid expansion throughout the world. New cereals such as "Special K," with nutritive values designed to appeal to weight-watchers, have allowed the company to tap new segments of the breakfast food market.

GROWTH FROM NEW FIELDS. Some large companies have achieved noteworthy growth records by following the third growth strategy—entry into new fields or businesses. About 20 years ago, W. R. Grace, historically a shipping company with plantations and shipping interests throughout Latin America, recognized that neither shipping nor Latin America offered them adequate earnings growth opportunities. Management decided to diversify into chemicals, and today W. R. Grace has become a major factor in the chemicals industry. The company's earnings growth of 200 percent from 1960 to 1966 came about largely as the result of shifting capital from an established business into a new field of opportunity. Un-

5

fortunately, competitive pressures in chemicals, particularly fertilizers, have resulted in a leveling off of earnings since 1967—but at a substantially higher level than ten years ago.

Bristol-Myers serves as another example of a company that pursued this strategy. Originally a manufacturer of proprietary drugs, the corporation diversified first into the field of ethical drugs and then into the faster growing fields of hair coloring and cosmetics. For a decade now, the company has maintained an earnings growth rate of about 10 percent annually.

In selecting appropriate strategies, one point must be kept in mind: The approaches outlined here may well overlap; in fact most companies actually use a combination of strategies to carry out growth programs over the decades.

Management's task

Achieving a brilliant growth record is not easy; maintaining it is even more difficult. Some companies, though continuing to grow faster than the economy, have been unable to sustain a high rate of earnings growth, and in some instances their total earnings have dropped dramatically. Thus, in 1961 approximately 60 major companies had attained an annual growth rate of 7 to 12 percent over a five-year period. Yet by 1963 half of them had been unable to maintain this rate. At last count only 10 of the remaining 30 had succeeded in sustaining their growth in earnings per share at their 1956–1961 rate.

What, then, must management do to build and maintain a record of exceptional growth? The evidence indicates that managements successful in this endeavor consistently follow five practices:

1. They establish growth goals.
2. They adapt their strategies to changes in economic and business conditions.
3. They keep alert to the advantages of entering new fields ahead of the competition.
4. They evaluate opportunities in new fields on the basis of facts rather than personal opinions.
5. They are quick to dump losing products or businesses and put the capital to better use.

SETTING GROWTH GOALS. Top management must demonstrate at the outset that growth is not merely a pious hope to be discussed at annual meetings but a prime corporate objective. This means establishing growth goals for each of the company's business activities, demanding results, and refusing to settle for mediocre performance. Almost without exception, the top managements of superior growth companies display this dedication. It is reflected in their objectives, their incentive compensation, their decisions on allocation of financial resources, and their evaluation of executives.

Some years ago the chairman of a U.K. food products company determined to double the enterprise's sales and profits in the next five years. To meet this objective, his managers found they would have to bring out twice as many successful new products during the period and increase productivity by 12 percent per year (versus 5 percent historically). They therefore completely reorganized their new product development effort and launched programs for accelerated mechanization of labor-intensive processes. These measures have already started to pay off, and management is well on the way to meeting its five-year objective.

Through a growth philosophy, a company can achieve results that put its competitors in the shade. For example, two large companies in a consumer-product industry have had dramatically contrasting earnings histories. The major difference between the two companies is that Company A—the more successful—has a very tough, strong policy of striving to grow; Company B does not. The top-echelon managers of Company A have been dedicated to an overall goal: The company must grow faster than the economy. They are determined to meet this standard year after year not only because such a program, in their opinion, represents sound business practice, but also to provide fresh opportunities for executives down the line, thus maintaining the vitality of their organization.

¶ Not only has Company A higher goals for return on invested capital than Company B, but its management has also set earnings growth objectives ranging between 4 and 12 percent for each of its businesses.

¶ Company A consciously invests 60 to 70 percent of its capital in businesses and projects that offer growth opportunities above the average for the company as a whole. In contrast, Company B's capital allocations are related to the depreciation and current profitability of its businesses, a practice which has led to reinvestment in some of the older, slower growing affiliates and product lines.

¶ The compensation of Company A's divisional management is based on each division's attainment of both its return-on-investment and growth goals. In contrast, Company B's executives receive bonuses based on the total profitability of the company, regardless of divisional performance.

KNOWING WHEN TO CHANGE STRATEGY. In any industry the basic economic forces of competition, technological change, government policy, etc., are continually changing. Products inevitably pass through a life cycle with an initial growth period, a leveling off at maturity, and eventually a period of decline. A basic commodity such as coal has its own characteristic life cycle; different kinds of cycles can be seen in consumer products (breakfast foods), consumer durables (TV sets), capital equipment (turbo-generators), and so on.

Business strategies must be prepared to change and, if need be, change quickly with the shifting economic environment and the changing product life cycle. In the early years, product design (the conception and innovation phase) may well be the company's most important consideration. In the second stage, skilled marketing and effective control of the dealer network become much more important. In the final stages, operating cost control becomes vital. The company must make sure that it is not "out of phase" in any of these developmental stages. Hence, timely recognition of the need to change business strategy is essential to maintaining growth.

The importance of changing business strategy to adjust to changes in the environment can be easily illustrated. Fifteen to 20 years ago, the American Telephone & Telegraph management recognized that to ensure future growth the company's basic marketing strategy would have to be altered. Since management had virtually achieved the objective of a telephone in every home, it would now be necessary to concentrate on persuading people to increase their use of telephones in every possible way. Consequently, in recent years A T & T has promoted concepts such as telephones in every room, luxury telephones, and special night rates. These tactics have enabled the company to increase telephone usage and maintain earnings growth until very recently.

The U.K. frozen food industry provides another interesting illustration of timely change in business strategy. Until a few years ago, 70 to 80 percent of the industry's growth had come about through the opening of additional retail distribution points by manufacturers. The number of retail shops marketing frozen foods doubled in five years, as did the sales of the total industry. However, in the past four to five years the number of retail outlets has reached economic saturation, and future industry growth must come from increasing sales per existing frozen food cabinet. As a result, the industry shifted its marketing strategy from securing new outlets to helping stores increase their weekly sales of foods. For example, manufacturers launched programs to install display refrigeration and to develop point-of-sale merchandising techniques.

Another striking example of how changed economic conditions require changes in management strategy occurred in the U.S. oil industry. For years, domestic sales had been growing by 6 to 7 percent a year. During this period, management gave priority to finding more oil reserves, since this would produce maximum profits. But in 1956–1957 the growth rate fell off to 3 to 4 percent a year. Most companies thought this was a temporary drop. Instead of concentrating on cost reduction and strengthening their market position—a strategy that (in retrospect) would have been more profitable—they continued to add to refining and producing capacity.

8

The rate of growth continued to decline, and utilization of U.S. refining capacity dropped from almost 98 percent to about 85 percent. Conditions worsened as wholesale prices came under pressure from several crude-rich integrated companies with underutilized refining capacity. These companies adopted a strategy of reaching for additional product sales—at almost any price—to realize profits on the "incremental barrel" of crude oil that they could produce and refine. In consequence, prices dropped, and the industry's return on investment declined from about 15 percent to about 10 percent.

Not every oil company suffered this decline in earnings. At least one management identified the basic changes that were to affect the industry and focused both on reducing costs and on strengthening the company's retail dealer structure (two or three years ahead of its competitors). This corporation was among the first in the oil industry to initiate a manpower freeze. With the basic objective of reducing costs by 20 percent, management followed up the freeze by systematically studying every activity within the company. The retailer/dealer structure was improved by eliminating marginal dealers, by systematically upgrading dealers at high-potential sites, and by launching a new site acquisition program. The company recovered from the industry-wide earnings slump of 1957 much more rapidly than some of its competitors, who took six to seven years to regain even their 1957 earnings position. The story illustrates a very simple point: The management that sees the trend before its competitors will be in the best position to maintain its earnings growth.

RECOGNIZING THE NEED TO MOVE INTO NEW FIELDS. However astutely management changes its business strategy, there will almost certainly come a time when the growth rate in any business will fall off. Most companies must ultimately enter new businesses if they are to continue to grow. For example, all but 10 of the 60 companies mentioned earlier, though they had maintained attractive growth rates for at least seven years, were obliged to move into new businesses in order to keep on growing.

Prompt management recognition of a need for moving into new fields is vital to company growth. Several of the companies we have been discussing previously recorded a dramatic growth followed by an equally dramatic fall in earnings. Had their managements recognized in time the need to move into new lines of business, these earnings drops might have been less severe.

Four years ago, for example, the management of a food products company—recognizing that the growth of their present business would probably slacken in five years—began systematically investigating fresh possibilities. Through a series of acquisitions, the corporation entered several attractive new businesses. The predicted falloff in the growth rate of the original business has begun, but it will probably be cushioned and even-

9

tually offset by the new business enterprises—because management was able to foresee the need for action.

EXAMINING NEW FIELDS BEFORE INVESTING. Not all companies moving into new kinds of business achieve the growth they anticipated; indeed, many have found their earnings actually reduced. Such disappointments nearly always come about because the management has failed to consider these crucial questions:

1. How attractive are the economic characteristics and vitality of the particular field?
2. What marketing, manufacturing, or technological know-how could the company contribute to the new business?

In the United States, chain-saw manufacturing grew a vigorous 8 to 10 percent annually for nearly eight years. One company, observing this attractive field, acquired a chain-saw manufacturer in an attempt to offset the decline of current earnings. After the merger, unhappily, it discovered that the historical growth rate was unlikely to continue. The professional logger market, which comprised about 70 percent of the chain-saw business, was completely saturated; almost every logger had a chain saw. In the future, sales to loggers would be primarily for replacement. Furthermore, the company's particular know-how—skill in selling through hardware stores—could not be applied to the new acquisition. Actually, hardware stores were generally unsatisfactory outlets for chain saws, since most of them would not repair or service the saws, an essential function of the retailer in this business.

The sad part of the story is that the outlook for the industry and the information about the type of retail outlet required could easily have been ascertained prior to the acquisition. Moral: Investigate before you invest.

DROPPING THE LOSERS. Many managements become emotionally involved with their products. They are reluctant to cut out the once "old reliable" products that are now losing money or not contributing an adequate return on investment. If they find themselves obliged to justify perpetuating a failing business or product, they have recourse to the accountant's argument, "It covers overhead."

Often management does not realize that the financial resources *and* management skills needed to shore up a dying business can be employed much more profitably in other fields. For example, one textile company operated in five different segments of the industry. One segment suffered from overcapacity and loss of its markets to synthetics. Return on investment amounted to only 2 percent. A substantial part of top management's time was spent trying to improve this yield by cutting costs, but to little avail. When a new management took over the company, it liquidated this

10

business. The proceeds, invested in other company activities, earned 15 percent without requiring as much top-management effort.

That relatively few companies have been able to maintain an outstanding growth record over a period of years emphasizes the difficulty of the task. Yet the techniques of managing steady growth are not obscured by forbidding mysteries. The record shows that it can be managed—many times over.

2. Controlling postmerger change

Frederick Wright Searby

Along with a small array of glittering successes and a handful of dismal failures, the recent wave of mergers and acquisitions has produced a multitude of underachievers—mergers which simply have not worked out as well as they should have.

The number of mergers falling into this category is hard to determine with any precision, since the underachievement is often masked by growth of the combined company in a strong economy. But the phenomenon of the semi-failure, or half-success, is common enough to call for explanation. And its costs, both to stockholders and in aggregate to the U.S. economy as a whole, are heavy enough to lend urgency to the question of how its causes can be avoided.

Consider the example of two successful retail chains with complementary product lines, which were attracted by the potential synergistic effects of pooling their buying and product design capabilities as well as by the cost advantages of combining their administrative staffs and facilities. They merged, and sales of the combined company grew slowly and steadily. A success story? Not quite. Ten years after the merger, the chains were still separate businesses. No product skills had been interchanged; each maintained its own processing equipment; they were still competing with each other for shopping center space. And earnings were still bumping along at the level of a decade earlier.

Management of change

Conventional wisdom usually puts the blame for such failure on poor premerger planning, and certainly there is considerable risk in improvised strategy and careless appraisal of acquisition candidates. But recent evidence suggests there is another factor, no less vital to success or failure, that merger-minded managements are too prone to overlook. A study of 69 acquisitions by John Kitching led him to conclude that "the key variable for success . . . is not superior strategy; it is the managers of change, who can take an unplanned acquisition whose resources are related only indirectly to those of the parent company and make a success of it."[1]

Change is certain after a merger—not evolutionary change, but sudden, often traumatic change. This is most apparent when the new partner is being fully integrated into a centralized enterprise. But even if the acquired company is to be an autonomous subsidiary, new reporting relationships are created, new corporate goals and obligations are assumed, and changes affecting both the acquired company and the acquirer are inevitable.

The problems inherent in sudden change are aggravated when the change is being imposed by strangers, as it is in the postmerger period. The resulting apprehensions, misunderstandings, suspicions, and resentments make a successful transition especially difficult to effect. At the same time, however, the postmerger period offers almost unparalleled opportunities for far-reaching improvements and innovations. Whether these opportunities will be realized depends almost entirely on management's effectiveness in planning and managing change.

We can easily see why postmerger management is becoming ever more critical to the success of acquisition programs. As price tags on acquisitions get heftier, would-be acquirers find fewer and fewer opportunities for immediate financial advantages such as increased earnings per share, higher return on equity, substantial tax loss carry-forwards, or the obtaining of disposable assets at an attractive price. The rising premiums demanded by sellers can only be justified by what happens after the merger to increase profitability or reduce the initial investment. This means that more and more merger-minded companies will be on the lookout for partners that offer longer range business advantages.

We can expect to see more companies undertake mergers or acquisitions solely to obtain executive talent or technical expertise. Others will seek to capitalize on their own or their partner's special strengths—for example, by utilizing one company's direct sales muscle to move the products of both, by gaining access to new distribution channels, or by obtaining a favorable raw material position. Still others will plan to lower production and distribution costs by combining facilities, eliminating middleman profit, improving distribution patterns, or obtaining production economies of scale.

Among other business advantages that will be sought are opportunities to broaden the product line, to gain preeminence in a market, to smooth out seasonal or cyclical fluctuations, or to minimize risk by branching out from a single industry or geographic area.

Obviously, capitalizing on these opportunities is a matter not of financial legerdemain but of skillful and strong-minded postmerger management.

[1] "Why Do Mergers Miscarry?" *Harvard Business Review*, November–December 1967, p. 98.

13

What lessons can be distilled from the experience—good and bad—of companies in postmerger management? What problems are characteristic of the postmerger period? What approaches have companies found useful in seizing the unique opportunities for change?

It is difficult to generalize on postmerger problems when premerger circumstances and the intent of merger partners vary so widely. Nevertheless, it is possible to set forth some broad guidelines that will be applicable to the management of postmerger change in most situations.

A complex task

Too many acquisitions go sour from the start simply because the acquiring management has failed to realize the size and complexity of the job it has taken on. "Taking hold" of an acquired company right after the merger is both a massive and a delicate assignment. Too often it is neglected because of the natural tendency to relax once the merger is legally consummated and the usual premerger hassles have faded into memories.

To put the postmerger job into perspective, we can summarize some of the more important tasks that must be carried out in most postmerger situations:

1. EFFECTING THE MERGER:
   Complete legal arrangements (e.g., new corporate charters, transfer of title on assets).
   Designate agents of the new corporation for suppliers and vendors.
   Change corporate signs and logos.
   Prepare the necessary public relations releases.
2. MAINTAINING MOMENTUM IMMEDIATELY AFTER THE MERGER:
   Clarify reporting relationships.
   Ensure the continuity of credit lines and insurance.
   Make financial authorizations.
3. BRINGING THE NEW ORGANIZATION INTO THE CORPORATE STRUCTURE:
   Install a reporting system for the new company.
   Consolidate financial reporting, press relations, and stockholder communications.
   Review compensation and personnel policies of the acquired company.
   Consolidate tax return preparation.
   Review accounting practices and policies, and develop a new audit program.
   Eliminate activities not appropriate to a division.
4. REALIZING SHORT-TERM PROFIT-IMPROVEMENT POTENTIAL:
   Consolidate the headquarters staffs.
   Close down unnecessary facilities.
   Eliminate redundant executive positions and unproductive personnel.

Centralize volume leverage functions (e.g., purchasing, insurance, data processing).

Cut unnecessary frills (e.g., cars, planes, club memberships).

Consolidate banking relationships.

5. REALIZING LONG-TERM PROFIT-IMPROVEMENT POTENTIAL:

Integrate operations (e.g., raw materials, manufacturing, distribution, marketing).

Transfer technologies and methods.

One writer has estimated that a modest amount of integration between two partners may involve 2,000 changes and 10,000 major, nonroutine decisions.[2] This estimate does not seem exaggerated if we consider that 400 separate steps were required in the critical path program used by the Pennsylvania and New York Central railroads merely to consolidate their equipment maintenance functions.

Many large companies underestimate the time required to merge with a smaller company. The demands of the postmerger period do not fluctuate greatly with the size of the acquired company. The history of oil company acquisition efforts in the late 1950s testifies to the disproportionate amount of time that executives of large companies can spend on minimergers.

Successful practices

The successful performance of an acquired company can be just as important to an enterprise as is, say, getting a new plant or process on-stream. But how many managers give the same amount of thought and attention to ensuring the success of an acquisition as they do to building a new plant?

The practices that appear to have been used successfully to cope with the complex task of managing the large-scale change required following merger can be divided into three major areas—organization, leadership, and timing—each of which deserves special attention.

ORGANIZATION. Perhaps the most critical step for ensuring successful postmerger management is to provide the full-time, talented manpower that the job warrants. Mergers cannot be carried out on a part-time basis.

One organizational move that has been used with considerable success is the appointment of a merger manager—a highly capable executive who is assigned responsibility for planning and overseeing the execution of all postmerger changes. Ordinarily, he spends most of his time during the first year or so at the acquired company's headquarters. He reports to the chief executive officer of the surviving business, is relieved of other responsibilities, and is given substantial authority for recommending postmerger changes and total control over implementing them.

[2] Forrest D. Wallace, "Some Principles of Acquisition," in *The Corporate Merger*, edited by William Alberts, University of Chicago Press, Chicago, 1966.

Obviously, in order to be effective, the merger manager must have the trust of the chief executive officer, and he must have a clear understanding of how the parent company gets decisions made, both formally and informally.

It is the merger manager's job to help plan and control postmerger change by identifying needed action, sequencing steps, and monitoring the pace of change so it stretches (but does not overpower) the organization. This will give the chief executive time to determine the ultimate organization structure and to select individuals to fill key positions.

The merger manager becomes a clear symbol of leadership over the merged organization. He is the unmistakable answer to the critical question of the postmerger period, "Who's in charge here?" He acts as an on-the-scene representative of the chief executive officer to ensure that the decisions necessary to sustain business momentum are made during the uncertainty and confusion immediately following the merger, to defend the rights of the acquired organization, and to gather intelligence on candidates for key executive slots.

Further, he is charged with preventing "take-over" attempts or intramural wars between staff departments having the same responsibilities (e.g., data processing, credit, public relations, treasury), and with controlling the operations of the new partner.

Companies in the oil, transportation, and aerospace industries have used a merger manager to help effect their mergers. Other organizational alternatives that have been used successfully include merger coordinators and merger committees. Whatever organizational device is used, it is absolutely essential that (a) highly qualified personnel be assigned full time to assist in merger implementation, (b) they have the confidence of the chief executive officer, and (c) they be authorized to cross organization lines.

LEADERSHIP. Immediately following a merger, there is a need for a clear and immediate point of leadership for both the acquired enterprise and the new corporate entity. This seems obvious; yet many mergers have bogged down because of two recurring problems:

¶ The inadequacy of the committee appointed to resolve postmerger questions

¶ Unclear lines between the functional groups of the acquired company and those of the new parent company (e.g., "To whom does the vice president of marketing report?").

The merger manager or merger committee can help establish leadership by becoming a visible point of contact between the parent and its newly acquired organization. Regardless of the organizational device used, a vigorous and constructive atmosphere for change should be created.

To provide leadership for the new acquisition, management needs first to promulgate a written strategy that includes long-range goals for both companies. This strategy can help to develop a positive focus on the future of the new organization. In turn, the focus is helpful in resolving short-term problems and making temporary inconveniences livable. For planning purposes, this strategy should be developed prior to the merger.

The importance of communication with personnel throughout the merged company cannot be overestimated. "Overkill" should be the guideline in both the chief executive's and the merger manager's written communications, meetings with subordinates, and personal appearances throughout the company. These communications should indicate a genuine interest in and commitment to the new acquisition. Being subject to an unknown, distant master is psychologically unsettling and can generate unnecessary resentments. The executive charged with implementation of the merger should be readily accessible to deal with problems that need attention but may otherwise be overlooked.

Many acquisitions are followed quickly by early retirements, resignations, and separation of key personnel. Depending on the quality of the men, these losses can either help or hinder the adjustments that must occur during the postmerger period. In general, however, promoting key people of the acquired company to top jobs that have become open in their organization, or to responsible positions in the parent company, is a healthy move. It can encourage other capable people to remain in the merged organization.

The general company compensation program should be reviewed early in the postmerger period. In most circumstances, the compensation packages of both companies—salary, bonus, options, and fringe benefits—should be rationalized on a common basis. This establishes a one-company atmosphere, eliminates a potential source of divisiveness, and permits intercompany transfers. A common compensation program need not, of course, rule out special compensation features or even separate salary scales which may be desirable in a company with sharply diversified divisions.

As part of this step, *key* managers should be provided with *extra* financial incentives to make the merger work. This may well involve cash outlays in addition to those anticipated in the premerger analysis. But if incentive payments are limited to a few individuals who can really influence profits, their cost will be a small fraction of the total value received.

Finally, a constructive atmosphere for change is fostered by prompt measurement of results. The chief executive, assisted by the merger manager, should measure the new organization's performance in an obvious and personal way—e.g., in oral reviews conducted by the chief executive officer. Thus, it will be clear throughout the total organization that the new management is committed to achieving agreed-to performance. This appraisal will also help to clarify the new company's management style and to create an atmosphere conducive to accomplishment.

17

TIMING. In postmerger management, as in many endeavors, timing is critical. Immediately following a merger, there is a period when people in the new organization expect and perhaps even want change. This is particularly true when the acquired company has a poor earnings record. Some observers suggest a period of "settling in" or "adjustment" before major changes are made, but I believe that—provided the facts are there to support the action—the immediate postmerger period is an ideal time for making changes, including some that have nothing to do with the merger but are simply overdue.

Companies that have a record of successful acquisitions seem to know when to take advantage of the postmerger period to make changes and when to delay, even at some apparent cost. The job of selecting and scheduling changes from among the many that could be made can best be done by a tough-minded individual who knows how to deal with the conflicting pressures implicit in the postmerger situation.

Some necessary major changes in policy or personnel in both companies are obvious even before the merger day. Making these changes early—if the facts are in—is an excellent way to demonstrate new leadership, to exemplify management philosophy, to get people thinking about change, and to reduce the apprehension of waiting for the other shoe to drop. Considerable experience indicates that where personnel changes are required, as many of these changes as possible should be made quickly—just as soon as management has identified and gained the support of the strong executives on whom the future of the acquired company depends.

Special care should be given to personnel issues, since the manner in which they are resolved will tell the acquired organization much about the new management's style. Where possible, a few decisions that clearly favor personnel of the acquired company will foster an atmosphere of cooperation.

Inevitably, certain executives will resist postmerger change and challenge the new leadership. Those who cannot be reoriented to new organizational relationships rather quickly must be eliminated. This is a delicate business, and morale can suffer severely if the executives being separated do not receive fair, tactful treatment. This means provision for fair settlements, job relocation assistance (if needed), and endorsements that give ample recognition to the past services of the separated executives and present their termination in the most favorable light.

Sins of omission

Many mergers—especially those of equals—create an entirely new business enterprise with totally different characteristics from a simple combination of the preexisting businesses. Inevitably, new problems and new opportunities will be generated. In these situations, nothing can be more crucial to realizing the merger's potential than a critical and imaginative reexamination by management of every key area of the business. The greatest sins of postmerger management are sins of omission. For example:

¶ When two service companies with overlapping national sales forces merged, only historical sites and staffing levels were considered in planning both the immediate and the long-term sales organization. The possibility that the new company might benefit from some different sites and staffing levels was never considered.

¶ Similarly, two large manufacturing companies simply consolidated their insurance programs after merger—neglecting for nearly three years the opportunity to take profitable advantage of their new risk characteristics by shifting their insurance strategy.

Postmerger management lends itself to the same management techniques that are used in the day-to-day conduct of company business, including such sophisticated scheduling techniques as critical path method and PERT. As a general approach, however, a simple four-step planning process, used in more elaborate versions throughout most companies, can be immensely helpful:

1. *Specific and realizable objectives should be developed before the merger is consummated.* These objectives, which provide standards for measuring the success of the various operations of the merged companies, should be communicated to the merger partner in advance.

2. *The key variables should be brought under control immediately following the merger.* In any business, a handful of factors exert a decisive influence on profits. The key variables in transportation companies, for example, are operating personnel costs, utilization of equipment and facilities, and development of new customer service programs. These key variables should be identified and examined during the premerger analyses so that management will be able to watch them closely from the day the merger takes place—if need be, via periodic supplementary reports.

3. *Programs should be thoroughly designed to achieve the merger's objectives.* These programs, obviously vital to the success of the merger, usually involve individuals who have the additional responsibility of operating the business.

4. *Controls to measure the results of actual performance against plan should be installed.* These controls can be simple, manually prepared analyses; oral review sessions; or computer-based reports.

Immediately after the merger of two integrated oil companies, for example, management installed revenue, expense, and capital budgets for the remaining three months of the year in which the merger took place. This budgeting process provided a basis for financial planning, established an understanding of what would constitute acceptable performance for the remainder of the year, and gave the acquired company's managers the financial authorizations they needed to sustain the momentum of their operations.

But more important, it gave the chief executive and his merger manager the opportunity to meet and assess key executives in functional departments and major subsidiaries. From the start, this merger has been a conspicuous success.

Importance of objectivity

Perhaps the prime requisite in dealing with the problems and opportunities of the postmerger period is objectivity. Unless the executives of the acquiring company make a real effort to be guided by facts rather than assumptions, preconceptions, or wishful thinking, they will be prone to make decisions that can seriously threaten the success of the joint enterprise.

Important personnel, policy, and procedural issues must receive careful, factual analyses to ensure that all reasonable possibilities are considered and that a fact-based decision is reached. Full-time, qualified people should be assigned to develop the data for these decisions.

Consider personnel decisions, for example. The possible permutations and combinations of job assignments for even a few people can stagger the imagination; in theory, at least, there are two and a half quintillion (2.5×10^{18}) ways of matching up 20 people with 20 jobs. Fortunately, the alternatives for filling most positions are a lot less numerous than this.

However, to ensure that key personnel decisions are made in an orderly and equitable fashion, two steps should be taken, First, for open positions, criteria should be developed to permit objective, fact-based measurement of individuals, as well as subjective evaluation. Second, people available for the positions should be listed, together with biographical data and evaluations by each individual's recent superior. Such lists will allow individuals to be matched with job openings, perhaps by a joint committee from both merger partners.

The real risk in managing the postmerger period is not the danger of a colossal failure but the possibility that the merger will end "not with a bang but a whimper." Considering the high cost of most current mergers, half-successes can be costly indeed.

It can be argued, I think, that postmerger management is the greatest single determinant of success in many corporate acquisition programs.

Obviously, the selection of candidates and the establishment of terms set the range of possible return in most merger circumstances. But the fact is that the leverage exerted by management performance in the postmerger period is immense. And it has yet to be fully recognized—either in the merger literature or, more importantly, in practice.

3. Britain's quiet managerial revolution

J. Roger Morrison

In recent years, criticizing British management has become one of the country's most popular indoor blood sports. Participants in this simple game have commonly used for ammunition four specific charges:

¶ British industry has consistently lost its share of world export markets through lack of aggressive selling, poor deliveries, high prices, and over-concern with the home market.

¶ British productivity, low relative to the United States, has not been increasing as rapidly as that of Continental countries or as fast as U.K. wage rates.

¶ British manufacturing and distribution are too fragmented in many fields to compete with large foreign international concerns (e.g., computers) or to serve domestic markets effectively (e.g., appliances).

¶ British management has not fully recognized the importance of formal training for business.

Obviously the validity of these charges will vary from industry to industry and from one business organization to another. Steps are already being taken by companies, by industry groups, and by the Government to do something about each of these charges. The publicity surrounding these remedial steps fosters a dangerous assumption that they can correct the basic problem of British management. The fact is that they merely attack the symptoms. The cause lies deeper.

For years, many U.K. companies (in common with others throughout the world) have not recognized that *they must manage their business, rather than be managed by it*. Too often management feels that its job is to cope with problems as they arise rather than to anticipate problems and challenges and prepare to deal with them in advance.

Under the pressure of increasing world competition, many major U.K. firms have now come to recognize the need for this basic change in management philosophy. Consequently, their managements have not only begun a concerted attack on the symptoms, but have also, without fanfare, been making fundamental changes in the way they manage their companies. Thus, while carrying on major campaigns to stimulate exports and productivity, they have also been coming to grips with their internal management practices. They have (1) set stretching targets, (2) delegated key responsibilities to middle management, (3) demanded fact-founded decisions, and (4) encouraged a philosophy of constructive dissatisfaction.

Set stretching targets

Until recently, few major U.K. companies established targets covering return on investment, share of market, productivity, etc. If they did, the targets only required maintenance of the status quo and consequently did not extend management to try for greater achievements. In this respect, they could be compared to runners competing in a track meet whose only objective was to equal, rather than better, the previous record. Managements, like athletes, need to be challenged continually to better their past achievements if they are to become champions. Tough goals can have an astonishing impact on profit and efficiency.

Two large British chemical companies I know are similar in product line. Both consistently achieve their financial goals, but one far outstrips the other in profitability, principally because it has set a return-on-invested-capital objective of 25 percent before tax versus the other's 12.5 percent. Thanks to its more challenging goal, the leader is far more efficient in its use of working capital. It boasts higher productivity per worker, and a greater turnover per £1 of plant investment.

Again, a British engineering firm was considering a £7 million investment in a new development project. Although the proposal submitted to the board met the company's customary return-on-investment objective of 12 percent, it was initially turned down by the new chairman, who made it clear he would settle for nothing less than a 25 percent yield. Within a week, the project had been reevaluated and revised to meet the more challenging objective. The reevaluation highlighted many non-essentials (building a new plant rather than using an existing one, excess capacity, unnecessary equipment, etc.) that were eliminated from the more profit-oriented proposal. The 25 percent return on investment was achieved.

Because many top managers have now recognized the importance of challenging their executives, setting up more difficult targets has become a way of life in several British companies. In turn, these hard-to-reach goals have forced management to do a better job in thinking through *how* sales or productivity are going to be increased.

A British electronics manufacturer—faced with the threat of growing low-priced Japanese competition when U.K. tariffs were lowered—set a 50 per-cent-cost-reduction target for its electronic components. Over a three-year period the management substantially surpassed this target. Besides successfully defending its home market, the company is now giving

23

real competition to Japanese component makers in export markets they once had almost entirely to themselves.

Delegate responsibilities

British (and European) management tends to delegate far less responsibility to middle management than U.S. companies. This often seems to be a carryover from the one-man autocracy characteristic of companies during their initial stages of growth. In many companies where directors still are felt to be omniscient, middle and frontline managers have little to do but execute the policies determined on high.

Handicapped for years by uncompetitive costs, the management of one company decided a thoroughgoing investigation was in order. It did not take long before the cause was revealed: ten years earlier, the chairman had decreed—wisely, at the time—that 30 percent of capacity should be reserved to meet unforeseen spurts in demand from the company's major automotive customers. He had since died and market conditions had changed, but no one had thought to reexamine the policy. The production superintendents readily admitted that it no longer made sense to them. "We thought the directors knew best," they said. "We were waiting for them to tell us when to stop following the policy."

Recently there has been a growing shift away from this autocratic type of organization. Many managements now realize that a high proportion of their management resources have been wasted. Furthermore, they have come to understand that front-line management—not higher authority—really determines from day to day whether costs are reduced, deliveries met, and sales increased. This is the logic behind a number of major organizational changes in British companies aimed at delegating greater responsibility to down-the-line management.

The experience of one large multibusiness company illustrates the validity of this approach. Management first divided the company into a series of divisions or profit centers. Each division constituted a separate business with its own products, factories, customers, and competitors. A chief executive had full responsibility for the division's profits and return on investment. Once a division became established, the second step was to define the responsibilities of each top executive within the unit in terms of specific end results on which his performance would be judged. For example, the success of a divisional marketing director is judged on his performance in terms of sales volume, share of market, price, and sales force productivity targets. And this process was repeated all the way down to the lowest level of management.

As a consequence, many more managers all the way down the line are concerning themselves with the substantive problems of the business. And it has become much easier to distinguish the talented executives from the mediocrities at an early stage in their careers.

Demand fact-founded decisions

Until recently, many British executives prided themselves on their ability to make swift—even snap—decisions on matters of great consequence. These decisions were usually justified in high-sounding but empty terms: "In our judgment" . . . "Vitally necessary to maintain our business" . . . "Our experience indicates," and the like. Facts were reserved usually only for decisions of minor consequence—in accordance, be it noted, with C. Northcote Parkinson's Law of Triviality: "Time spent on any item . . . will be in inverse proportion to the sum involved." With the growth of competition and the present rates of technological change, poor decisions inevitably resulted from moves based on mere "judgment" rather than facts. Such decisions, in fact, underlie many problems of British industry: overcapacity, too many production units, loss of export markets, ineffective use of labor resources, and low profitability.

Yet fact-founded decision making does not necessarily require using batteries of computers or sophisticated mathematical techniques. Most mistaken decisions can be traced to the absence of a few simple but vital facts. To avert these mistakes, progressive managements have been following five simple guidelines.

1. BEWARE OF THE BOOKKEEPERS. Over the years accountants and their jargon have often exercised a mesmerizing effect on management decision makers. For example, the expression "underabsorbed overhead," has confused some managements to the point that they operate their factories to "absorb overhead" rather than to make profits. For years, a major British engineering concern had been maintaining a large fabricating plant next to its main works. The plant consistently lost money, but it was kept in operation because of its contribution to the overhead of the main works. When objective analysis revealed this contribution to be only £50,000 a year, the company took action. It shut down the fabricating plant, freed £3 million in working capital, and—not surprisingly—managed to increase its return on investment.

2. REMEMBER THE CUSTOMER. During the consumer and industrial product shortages of the 1950s and early 1960s, British manufacturers could sell all they produced. Product, market, and pricing decisions could be arrived at without extended analysis of customers' needs. But the days of the sellers' market have long vanished. And management must now make increasingly sophisticated assessments of customers' requirements to prevent expensive failures.

One British industrial equipment manufacturer was puzzled by a persistent decline in the export and domestic sales of one of its leading lines, which had been redesigned only recently at a cost of £250,000. Subsequent market assessment revealed the main problem with the machine: since most of the products made on the machine had short production runs, its lengthy setup time tended to cancel out the advantages of its faster production rate. With the equipment redesigned once more to meet the need for a shorter setup time the company made major inroads on its competitors, both at home and overseas.

3. HISTORY DOES NOT REPEAT. Far too often managements base their market projections on a continuance of historical growth rates. Yet, if anything can be certain, it is that historical growth patterns will not automatically be repeated—especially with a worldwide buyers' market. Because too few companies recognize this, overcapacity typically builds up in an industry after its growth rate has slackened. For example, one British company's £15 million expansion program was based on the projection of an 8 percent industry growth. But by the time the expansion program was completed, changing consumer patterns and competition from new materials had caused a slackening of the industry's growth to 3 percent. This could have been foreseen from a factual analysis of the market.

4. LOOK OUT FOR COMPETITORS. Many managements do not consider the possible reaction of competitors to their decisions. New products are often introduced on the assumption that they will capture the market, but to management's surprise, competitors quickly copy the original idea, soon regaining their share of the total market.

5. WATCH THE POUNDS, NOT THE PENCE. Many U.K. companies have exerted meticulous control over minor items of expenditure, ranging from rules on who should travel first class to detailed reviews by main boards of capital expenditure items under £25,000. In contrast, most managements do not establish *effective* controls over major expenditures by evaluating whether their major capital expenditures actually have achieved planned results. The managements demanding a factual basis for decisions that involve major expenditures have often received an unexpected bonus in the form of speedier decision making. Previous methods had left ample room for argument and discussion because each executive had his own opinion. Insistence on facts quickly narrows the issues to be discussed and discourages time-consuming debate based on individual executives' experience, which may be 10 or 15 years out of date.

Encourage constructive dissatisfaction

One of the subtlest but most fundamental changes brought about by the quiet revolution has been a shift on top management's part from the "I'm all right, Jack" posture of former years to an active encouragement of

26

constructive dissatisfaction among company executives. The difference between these attitudes may in fact be highlighted by visits to two U.S. companies. In the first, the management—down to the sales managers and shop superintendents—spent a great deal of its time pointing out what could be improved *and* how it was planning to do so. The comments covered a wide variety of new ideas, including design, marketing, production, and research. The search for means to improve performance went on—even though the factory was already one of the most modern and efficient in the industry, and the market position was outstanding.

In contrast, the management of the second company spent all its time describing in detail present methods of operation and why they were the best. Several managers justified their current practices by saying, in effect: "We've been doing it this way for 20 years, so it must be right." Yet their factories and offices showed signs of age and neglect, and there seemed little indication that current management had ever *factually* evaluated the soundness of current policies and practices. The two companies presented a striking contrast in atmosphere. In the management canteen of the one, new ideas were criticized in minute detail and usually rejected. In the other, new ideas were seized upon eagerly and improved in the course of discussion. This is the difference between decay and vitality.

Many companies pay lip service to the need for encouraging creativity and innovation in every aspect of their business. Few have given practical recognition to this need or built it into their basic management philosophies. Yet a questioning approach, a constructive dissatisfaction with the status quo, inevitably characterizes the successful company. And to the managements of such companies this attitude will be more important to long-term profitability and vitality than any product, process, or market know-how.

For example, a president of General Motors, in testifying before a United States Senate Subcommittee, once said, "Our approach to problems . . . is really an attitude of mind. It might be defined as bringing the research point of view to bear on all phases of the business. This point of view is never satisfied with things as they are. It assumes that everything and anything can be improved. I have tried to think of a single term to describe this attitude and I think perhaps the closest is *the inquiring mind.*"

Creating a constructive dissatisfaction with the status quo may at first appear to be an academic concept. Yet, when properly applied and encouraged, it makes the difference between the average and the outstanding performer in an industry. This may be illustrated by the experience of the more vital of the two U.S. companies described above. Each year its management prepares a profit-improvement program. The savings that result from this plan, covering all aspects of the business, have allowed the company to offset the pressure of wage and raw material price rises for seven years, thereby outstripping its competitors in growth in earnings per share and return on investment.

Recognizing the realities

The root cause of the deterioration in Britain's world competitive position has been the failure of British executives to manage their businesses rather than be managed by them. The absence of hard-to-reach goals, the unwillingness to involve middle management in decision making, the excessive use of "judgment" rather than facts in arriving at decisions, and the absence of a philosophy of constructive dissatisfaction have inevitably deadened the thrust and drive needed for success in increasingly competitive world markets. But many British companies, perhaps the majority, have now come to recognize this need for change in their management practices and have already started to achieve tangible results. The question remains whether managements will be able to carry out the quiet revolution rapidly enough to make a major contribution to strengthening Britain's economic position. The change can hardly be too rapid.

4. Put the board of directors to work!

E. Everett Smith

The classic definition of the corporation in our economy, as given by Chief Justice Marshall, is "An artificial being invisible and intangible and existing only in contemplation of law." The "artificial being," however, is short one critical faculty—the ability to think. Therefore, its business must be *managed* and its affairs *directed*.

What is the distinction between managing and directing? What are some of the principal roadblocks to proper functioning of the board of directors? How can the operation of the board be improved? In short, how can the board be made into a more effective force in ensuring the health and continuity of the corporate system?

This problem is of concern to every company. And since every company is in a different stage of development and operates in different circumstances from all other companies, each board represents a slightly different problem from all other boards.

Under the law, the board of directors alone has all the power in the corporation. It can delegate to management the implementation of as much responsibility and authority as it sees fit, but it cannot avoid the ultimate responsibility and accountability to the stockholders.

Unfortunately, however, in most companies the board has become more and more a legal fiction in practice. Its role as a vital organ of the business has deteriorated, and in many cases it has been deposed by operating management.

Excuses for weakness

There are many reasons for the lack of attention and the confusion surrounding the role and function of the board of directors. Some of these reasons are superficial, but they tend to cloud the more profound and deepseated issues, and therefore should be examined.

NO CLEAR PATTERN. One such reason is that there is no clear pattern of board operations because each undertaking is in a different stage of transition ranging all the way from the firm managed by an owner-executive to the publicly held and professionally managed corporation.

29

On the one extreme, the owner-executive may fill the legal requirements of the board by staffing it with employee-officers. At the opposite end of the spectrum, a few enterprises have developed full-time board members divorced from all operating responsibility. In between, one can find any number of variations in size, composition, and manner of functioning. Thus, proponents of any particular point of view concerning the board function can easily support their belief with numerous examples of successful enterprises that at least outwardly appear to follow their concepts.

Now, the fact of tremendous variety is true, as we all know. But it should not lead us to think that "anything can be right" in patterns of board operations. I shall return to this point later.

The practical divorce of ownership from control that has taken place and the rise of the institutional investor further add to the confusion over the board's responsibility. Also, we have witnessed revolutionary changes in the concept of the social, political, and economic responsibilities of the corporation. These responsibilities present a challenge to the board, but they have only recently emerged, and directors' obligations to harmonize them have not yet been clearly defined either by custom or by law.

NO WILLING OUTSIDERS. Another area of confusion relates to the much-discussed question of how to get able men who are willing to serve. I suggest that this is a smoke-screen topic. In fact, we have many able men on boards who are not being effectively used, so that there is a tragic waste of talent. If a company has not clearly thought out the function of the board and structured it accordingly, the members can be expected to be confused and feel that they are wasting their time; it is natural that they consider themselves as merely a group of advisers. To make matters even more difficult, they probably have business or social relationships with the chief executive. This tends to make them reluctant to put themselves in the role of prosecuting attorneys by asking searching questions and digging in to satisfy themselves as to the general health and continuity of the business.

An additional problem is that the usual outside member of a board is often by vocation a top executive in his own company. Thus, his training and experience are in exercising power rather than in rendering advice, counsel, and judgment. These are two completely different skills and are not frequently found in the same individual. It is my own frank opinion that often a director, being an executive in his own right, is fully conscious of the danger of interfering with another executive's program. When this problem is added to the confusion over the powers reserved to the board, it is no wonder that the average board member is unsure of his proper function.

NO INDEPENDENT INSIDERS. Up to this point I have been referring to outside members of the board and disregarding the large number of companies that have boards composed solely of employee-officers. This has been intention-

30

al. I firmly believe that anyone who digs deeply into the responsibilities of the board and wants to make it a vital organ of the business will come to the conclusion that a strictly inside board—a board of operating managers —cannot fill that role. Men who meet once a month to pass on their own action during the other 29 or 30 days, men working for and naturally beholden to a strong chief executive, will certainly absorb his point of view and find it embarrassing, if not extremely difficult, to differ with him in board meetings. Men who must live with their fellow executives from day to day are certainly not ideal members of a truly effective board.

It is easy to turn to insiders because of their ready availability and knowledge of the business. But it is not necessary. Sometimes we *delude* ourselves into thinking it necessary because of the superficial difficulties just mentioned. Or we justify the action by pointing to exceptional circumstances where men have worn two hats successfully, and digress into discussions of the proper makeup of the board—how many outsiders and how many insiders. Personally, I think that all this is merely a way to postpone facing up to the real issue of making the board a functioning and effective organ. The first step in this process is to begin to inject people who can bring a fresh viewpoint, who are not subordinate to the chief executive, and who will act as independent judges.

The real problems

So much for the surface problems that tend to cloud this subject. Let us turn now to the more profound reasons why the board is one of management's most poorly used assets. There are at least two; and they are closely related.

LACK OF INTEREST. The first big problem, in my opinion, is a real lack of recognition in management circles of the proper role of the board and the tremendous contribution it can make to the success of the business. The general erosion of the function (and the vast number of relatively ineffective boards) has caused people to view it as a necessary but impotent nuisance to be hurried through as quickly and painlessly as possible. Perhaps the growing ranks of professional managers have been so preoccupied with the necessity of building in new management techniques and with the pressures of day-to-day operating problems that they have not had time to recognize the need for and unique value of the board.

It is true that in periods of crisis most boards ultimately face up to their responsibilities. In most cases, however, the board takes action only after much harm has been done to the enterprise—harm that could have been avoided with alert, aggressive action.

It is ironic that we in this country who have done so much to further the art of management should have so neglected such a vital area as the job of directors. Almost every other management function has received much detailed, painstaking attention, and new concepts and methods have been developed. In addition, each of these functions has its "high priests" who are dedicated to improving their particular phase of management and developing an understanding of its importance and relationship with other phases of the business. But not so in the case of the board. The management literature about it is pitifully brief and strikingly devoid of any real depth or new concepts.

So it is not surprising that there is little real recognition of the need for a truly effective board and an absence of pressure to obtain one.

RELUCTANT CHIEF EXECUTIVE. The second basic problem lies in this fact: for all practical purposes the board is a creature of the chief executive. He alone can structure it in terms of his attitude toward its function, the types of problems brought before it, and the manner in which material is presented to it. As a practical matter he can, although not always without difficulty, change the makeup of the board and select new members.

In the final analysis, I believe the basic cause for the decline of the board is the fact that many chief executives are not really convinced they want a strong and independent group of directors. I realize that this is not a popular statement; but based on the privilege of considerable observation, I do believe it is an accurate expression of the problem in many companies. And is it not a natural situation? After all, the chief executive has fought long and hard to reach his position of power. Is it not normal and natural for him to tend to avoid critical review of his stewardship?

Also, it is to be expected that he should regard outsiders, however capable, as being inadequately informed about company problems and therefore not really qualified to direct his operating team. And how is he likely to feel about the immense time demands involved in keeping directors well informed about company policies, plans, and procedures?

Consciously or unconsciously, therefore, the chief executive generally will look for a rubber-stamp board.

As a result, the one individual whom we should expect to be—and who is in a position to be—the spokesman for a strong board has strong motives to avoid the subject and be satisfied with the status quo. This is not meant critically. But to be realistic, we must face the forces at work.

Is it therefore futile to tackle this problem? Are we beaten before we start? I do not think so. I am confident that a great many corporation executives throughout a wide range of industries are fully aware of the changes that are taking place. They are conscious of the many responsibilities placed on large enterprises in our society. And they are, in my opinion, about to take on the next challenge: to revitalize the function of the board of directors.

Forces for change

Why should a chief executive, faced with all the difficulties and conflicts I have mentioned, attempt to construct an independent group over which he will have relatively little control and to whom he will be responsible? One reason is the deep drive of executives to seek ways of improving all phases of management. This drive has focused belatedly on the board, but attention has turned to that area now.

In the words of one executive:

> You've got to have a cabinet. A man who is in a tough executive post has got to be able to call together a group of his associates, his colleagues, his subordinates, and sound out his plans, thrash them out when they are in half-baked form. But, in addition, I believe very strongly that he needs to take one more step if you are going to have the proper safeguards, and that is the job of proving his point to an independent group that are damn good judges, who have not been participants in the plans, but who stand aside and judge. They interfere in no way with the management, but they are judges. I think that if that element is lacking, you are always in danger.

Or, as another executive put it, "Any chief executive should have the full authority, but should have that privilege of going before a board and of defending his practice."

Notice particularly the use of the word "privilege." It carries with it the idea that every chief executive has both the right and responsibility to be judged. It also implies that while failure to use the board as a free constituency may appear to buy time and protect the executive, his real strength in difficult times lies in being sure that the independent board has all the facts and shares in the basic decisions. This commits it to support the chief executive and thus strengthens his position. Referring to this view, still another executive observed, "If you can walk into a group that are your judges and say, 'Now gentlemen, this is my program,' let them attack it, and you defend it; and when you finally come out of there, they say it's all right that you go—then you go with confidence. But you've got to have that element—if it's lacking, you're in a damned difficult spot."

Another reason why I think that top management will find answers to the problems of the board is the growing awareness that in the long term the corporate system as we know it depends for its existence on public confidence. If our corporations are not well run in the total sense of having a good harmonization of all the interests involved, the public will not continue to believe that they are functioning in the general public interest. And if that day comes, the politicians will be only too ready to find a different way of handling things.

This longer term problem is amplified by the rapid trend toward larger and larger enterprises, which will probably continue and perhaps accelerate because of the economics of technological development. Certainly history teaches us that the public sooner or later distrusts size, whether it be in the church, the state, monopolies as in the age of Theodore Roosevelt, financial interests, or in the labor unions. Such distrust centers around the fear of too much power being granted to individuals without adequate checks and balances.

In the case of our artificial being, the soulless corporation, it is becoming more and more obvious that the stockholder with his vote is becoming one of the "last of the Indians" and that management and the board can be self-perpetuating institutions. As a result, distrust could rise even more rapidly than in the case of monopolistic and powerful groups such as labor unions, which have outwardly a better public relations posture. In the long run, therefore, American management must evolve a better system of checks and balances to satisfy the public interest. This probably means some major innovations over and beyond the present system.

All of this adds importance to the immediate problem of strengthening the board of directors. If constructive steps can be taken to improve company operations today, management may well be able to buy time and public confidence so that it can work out better long-term solutions.

Improving performance

As for improving current board performance, our first task is to try to identify areas where the average board fails to fulfill its basic purpose. This is not easy to do when a company is going along successfully, for the workings of the board and its relationship with management are not evident to outsiders. Weaknesses in the board become apparent only when a company falls from competitive grace and major problems come to the surface. Since the acid test of any management function is whether it is effective in maintaining the competitive posture of the enterprise, perhaps we can spotlight board failings by looking at some common features of companies that are in poor health.

One such sign of a weak board is that the weaknesses and condition of the enterprise are clearly evident to the trade—customers, competitors— and even to people within the organization long before they are faced by the board. This suggests that the board is not an independent group but is dominated by the chief executive or by officer-employees. In any event, the lack of independence effectively puts the blinders on the board to problems that are fairly obvious.

A second common aspect is the apparent failure on the part of the board to really understand the key profit-making factors in the industry and then evaluate the company in terms of these factors. For example, the important factors in the chemical industry are entirely different from those, say, in the automobile industry. Yet, frequently boards are supplied with routine operating statements that do not pinpoint the key elements controlling the company's success. In such cases it is unrealistic to expect the board to concentrate on the vital matters that spell success for the company, since it lacks the information that enables it to judge.

A third common aspect of declining companies might be called "ingrownness." It takes many different forms, such as the lack of cross-fertilization of ideas or the absence of new ideas and failure to utilize new management techniques, but it generally results from long association of people who think alike. The worst thing about "ingrownness" is that younger key executives brought up in this surrounding have no background of experience that enables them to compare their manner of operating with progressive competition. Consequently, they develop the same attitudes, pass them along in time to their juniors—and management is in a vicious circle. It may be necessary, therefore, to bring in outsiders with fresh viewpoints to turn the situation around.

I believe that the foregoing characteristics will be found in one form or another (though not necessarily together) in a wide range of companies that are in trouble. They make a very convincing case for a truly independent board, one that is thoroughly familiar with the company and the economic environment in which it operates, is well supplied with adequate information to evaluate results, and is capable of injecting fresh viewpoints and ideas into the management.

What, then, can be done by the chief executive who wants to create an effective board and make real use of it? Obviously, I shall have to discuss the answers in somewhat general terms, because each company has an entirely different set of conditions, but we can profit from the experience of men who have taken specific steps in this area.

I suggest that the first and basic step for the chief executive is to really think through what he expects of the board. This means that he must develop clear convictions about the board's responsibilities and the manner in which he believes they can be carried out. He is the one who is going to live with the directors, and he knows best of all the needs of his company and its particular situation. He should also think through the functions of the various committees of the board—particularly the executive committee, if there is one, and its relationship to the operating management.

One of the more helpful ways of beginning this job is to define the functions that can best be performed by the board and then eliminate functions currently performed which duplicate the area of operating management's responsibility. For example, if the chief executive believes that the board is essentially responsible for the overall welfare and continuity

35

of the business, as distinct from day-to-day operating responsibilities, then he should carefully screen out all matters that do not concern either long-range objectives or key profit areas.

Having thought through the responsibilities of the board, the chief executive should next reduce them to writing. There is no greater challenge to clear thinking than the necessity to put one's thoughts in writing; also, the ideas will have to be clearly communicated both to the board and to management.

At the same time he is doing this, the chief executive should review the agenda and material coming before the board. He should eliminate as much routine and irrelevant data as possible. Nothing is more deadening to a board member than to sit through routine drudgery.

Useful criteria

What are the most important kinds of information that the board needs to perform its function properly? Most businessmen would probably agree that, as a general proposition, the board of a multidivision company should review the record of the whole organization in much the same way as a good management team reviews the accomplishments of its divisional organization. However, I believe that if we compare the standards of performance and measurement criteria used by a well-managed multidivision company with those supplied the average board, we will find an amazing double standard. The company executives are in a far better position to appraise and evaluate division performance.

If we are not to treat the board as an impotent second-class citizen, we must develop specific criteria that it can apply not only to each segment of the business but also to the business as a whole. By criteria I mean material that will really identify in each segment the key factors that control profits and the general health of the business.

In trying to give the board a real picture of the business, such companies as Du Pont, General Motors, and General Electric are among those that have developed useful measurement criteria. Basically, these criteria fall into two general categories.

First are the specific criteria, which are largely of a financial or statistical nature—for instance, position in the industry, share of market, return on investment, return on sales dollar, and inventory turnover. The manner in which such measures are presented can make a world of difference. Many times they merely compare one year or budget with another, so that in effect they use a self-set bogey. There should at least be sufficient figures to highlight significant trends. Here it is important to stress the longer term planning and review function of the board as distinct from management's daily operating responsibilities. Accordingly, the charts and data should throw light on long-run objectives, without necessarily being encumbered by monthly operating statements and reasons for short-term variances, which are essentially management's job.

The second category of criteria largely comprises semi-intangibles. Any business is competitively successful only to the degree that its policies, organizational structure, and people are better than those of the competition. It is this area of evaluation that presents the greatest difficulty and, therefore, the greatest challenge to both the chief executive and the board. My own conviction is that any function or process worth performing can be measured in one way or another. Significantly, top management *is* developing objective measurement standards for decentralized divisions, and the same approach can be taken to the business as a whole.

Of course, in many cases standards will have to be subjective—in making judgments about the promotability of people, for instance, or in deciding how to stimulate executive development. When results can be measured objectively only over long periods of time, the board must draw on its intuition and experience to make periodic appraisals. It can meet and learn about management people by inviting them to make presentations to the board and answer questions in their areas of work, in the course of special studies of management problems undertaken by board committees, and in other ways.

Further measures

Beyond the steps just mentioned, there are many other improvements and innovations which might help board performance. Certainly agenda prepared and distributed well in advance of meetings would help immeasurably. And, by all means, the chief executive should get the important data to the members so that they can do their "homework" and come prepared to ask searching questions. Is anything more destructive to a director's morale than to come to a meeting, be handed a batch of papers containing the agenda and some related data that are completely new to him, and have to shuffle the documents in frustration while motions are being made, seconded, and passed? No wonder potentially capable members lose all interest and turn a deaf ear to the next suggestion that they serve on a board.

Some companies have successfully tried the use of revolving committees of the board that concern themselves with specific functions of the business and, in effect, report to the whole board on their particular segment.

Actually, there are many promising innovations that can be introduced if the chief executive really wants to develop an effective board group. My own experience leads me to believe that once he starts down this road with sincere conviction, he will get lots of help and encouragement from his associates.

37

What about the problem of recruiting and compensating really valuable outside directors? This is the rock on which most discussions about the board founder. To be sure, the problem is difficult, but it is not impossible. I would suggest that we approach it in about the same way as we would the recruiting of a top member of operating management.

To begin with, we should draw up the specifications for the type of man we want and then go on an intelligent manhunt, using all our resources to find him and to make the position attractive to him. We should be especially careful to avoid picking personal acquaintances for the board or recruiting on a *quid pro quo* basis.

In spite of all the discussion as to the near impossibility of persuading a busy executive to serve on a board, I am convinced that the average chief executive, if he is really determined to have a strong board and has taken the trouble to structure it properly, is a good enough salesman to persuade almost anyone he picks out to serve on it.

Perhaps the most effective inducement he can offer is to restructure the board to deal with important long-term problems. For one thing, they are stimulating. For another, a director can get ideas from discussing them that he can carry back to his own business. Finally, while a scrutiny of key problem areas demands a high degree of perceptiveness and good judgment, it is not so burdensome and does not involve the same time pressures as an examination of the minutiae of operating statements and short-term developments.

As to the other old saw that a company cannot compensate a successful executive for board service, I wonder if it really holds up. Suppose we use the same ingenuity that we apply to all other recruiting and compensation problems. Is there any rule that says all board members should receive the same stipend? Each man we approach has a different fiscal and tax status, so why not gear our proposition to suit his particular requirements?

Some companies pay a flat compensation (as distinct from directors' fees) in the range of $10,000 to $20,000. This compensation has no relationship to number of meetings attended. Naturally, such companies feel free to call on directors for consultation—and they fully expect to get their money's worth.

With a flexible and attractive compensation policy, the chief executive has a better chance of landing a top-notch man on his board early in his search. This makes it easier to get another good man, then still easier to get another, and so on—it snowballs.

The chief executive's role

No discussion of reshaping and revitalizing the board function would be complete without calling attention to the related problem of how such a change may affect the chief executive's work load.

The transformation of the board into a free constituency composed of capable independent members means that much more time and care must be taken in preparing for meetings. The policies and programs that could be thrashed out and developed in a management-dominated board must now be worked out ahead of time and presented in such a way as to promote intelligent questioning. The development of criteria and meaningful reports requires real management ingenuity. Also, of course, keeping the members informed of developments, briefing them in advance of scheduled meetings, and preparing agenda that will make meetings constructive and interesting to the members all require time on the part of the chief executive.

Ideally, much of the "care and feeding" of the board could be handled by the chairman. Practically, however, it is too much to suppose that all businesses will be blessed with two such paragons as a top-notch chairman and an excellent president. This means that, in many situations, the full load will fall on the chief executive, whichever title he holds. My point is that, concurrently with strengthening the board, he must find ways of freeing some of his time that in the past has been spent on operating problems. He must structure his own job so that he can devote more attention to the vital tasks of planning and review, rather than being completely occupied with day-to-day fire fighting. Probably this alone would be of real benefit, regardless of the improvement in the board.

As noted earlier, there are no pat answers to the numerous difficulties and problems of making the board effective. Only general approaches can be suggested. Unlike other management functions, such as marketing and controllership, we cannot even pin down specific principles that many people can agree on. This is a perplexing and frustrating area of management, and ideas that apply and work effectively in one undertaking would be out of place in another. In this exciting and dramatic period of terrific change, with all the pressures and forces affecting corporate life, the job of harmonizing the interests of stockholders, directors, management, employees, customers, and the public must be analyzed on a case-by-case basis.

It seems to me that the most fruitful approach is not to try to seek the ultimate answer, but to roll up our sleeves and start making improvements in the present apparatus. This is particularly true where there is clear evidence that the board of directors is not functioning effectively. Perhaps the very first step in trying to improve matters is simply to get management people talking about the problem and interested enough to begin to work out solutions and methods of improvement in their own enterprises.

5. Leadership style and organizational achievement

Robert P. Neuschel

The arts and styles of leadership have always fascinated historians. For centuries chroniclers as well as military men have mused on the generalship of Alexander. Herodotus and Thucydides observed the exercises of command on the battlegrounds of Greece and Asia Minor. From Socrates to Machiavelli, wise men have advised princes on the techniques of conquest.

Thomas Carlyle believed that the course of history was determined by the actions of great men. Many scholars have maintained the opposite view—that the figures we recognize as great happened, for better or worse, to come along at the right time; happened to have the right styles to succeed during the particular eras in which they achieved fame. Whichever view we hold—that leaders create history, or that historical trends already set in motion create the appropriate leaders—clearly individual style is a vital ingredient of all leadership: whether on the battlefield, in the conduct of government affairs, or in any kind of business, large or small.

There are probably as many styles of leadership as there are leaders. Almost by definition, those who manage the efforts of other men display supremely individualistic traits. Yet in a general way we may note certain characteristics of leadership duplicated over and over. In our own experience at one time or another each of us may have met with counterparts of classic models, present-day descendants exhibiting the bravado of a Genghis Khan, the calm mastery of a Caesar, the drive and purpose of a Bismarck, the dignity and statesmanlike qualities of a Robert E. Lee, or the eloquence and valor of a Churchill.

Taking these variations into account, what may be described as the aim, the foremost purpose, of the leaders I have mentioned? It is, I think, to *unleash the full power of their organizations*. Leadership releases energy in the rank and file by means of personal impact: whether in government, an army, a corporation, or any sort of business or team effort. A leader's successful style, we may say, becomes the complete expression of the man, giving strength and enthusiasm to his subordinates and reinforcing their desire to do well. This style is more than his characteristic way of involving himself in the common enterprise and making his expectations known to his subordinates. Style is pace, flair, commitment. It shapes a president's technique of organizing company-wide energies down the line. It determines how well he exercises and delegates authority to obtain results.

In every field of action, successful styles vary widely. To cite a military example, during World War II allied forces moved into Europe under two extremes of command: the bold and fiery direction of General Patton and, in contrast, the quietly effective leadership of General Omar Bradley. Similarly, the calm overview of General Dwight D. Eisenhower balanced the flamboyant style of General Montgomery. All of these commanders scored repeated victories, each pursuing his goals in his own distinctive way.

American business leadership styles have also presented dramatically contrasting approaches to success. A century ago it was considerably easier than it is now for uninhibited captains to dominate their companies' performance. The great industrial leaders, Vanderbilt, Carnegie, and Rockefeller, were men with visions and large designs all their own. The technology at their command could, for the most part, be comprehended by founder management. Marketing procedures were simpler. New developments arrived in leisurely fashion; the instantaneous relay of information by radio, television, and computer was still decades in the future. Hence, the company president took charge of a more nearly controlled environment, and was often able to stamp the organization in his own image. Operations down to the junior executive level tended to reflect the chief's personal and often idiosyncratic philosophy.

Style and the new forces

Today, even with founder management increasingly being replaced in American industry by cadres of professional managers, presidential style still continues to play an exceedingly important role in a company's success. But the chief executive's role has been altered by four revolutionary forces which have had an unprecedented impact on methods of business management across the nation.

The first of these trends has been the rapidly accelerating *democratization of society*. From the end of feudalism in the fifteenth century, the story of Western man has been one of growth or development away from the rule of the few toward democratic modes of action. The tendency, of course, has been blocked and reversed many times, but in general we may observe the democratic idea gaining momentum following the Industrial Revolution, until today it is recognized, even by its opponents, as the strongest force in the world. In simplest terms, this idea informs each man that he has the right to try; that within the framework of order he is by no means obliged to know his place; that he may advance according to his ability, and enjoy in all kinds of enterprise the right of participation. The result, so far as the conduct of American business is concerned, has been not merely a growing desire but a demand, voiced loud and clear by down-the-line managers and staff specialists, for a meaningful role in company planning and a real opportunity to contribute importantly to decision making. These management voices cannot be ignored. Their determination to be heard has become a fact of corporate life that inevitably exerts a moderating influence on presidential style, no matter how extreme and individualistic.

The second revolutionary force reshaping top management practices has been the *information explosion* that since the end of World War II has transformed the international industrial scene almost beyond recognition. Breakthroughs continue to proliferate in virtually all the sciences (including the science of management). Technological developments follow upon one another so rapidly that in many fields no sooner does a product reach the mass market than it can almost automatically be assumed to be obsolescent, with refined and improved models about to leave the drawing board. Information that 50 or even 25 years ago might have taken months to assemble—allowing company presidents and their advisers a relatively comfortable lead time in which to arrive at important decisions—today becomes available to the top manager (and to his competition) within days, hours, or even—thanks to the computer—within minutes.

Ultimately, to be sure, the chief executive must take responsibility for the go-ahead decision. If he tends to excessive dominance, he may still ignore or override the recommendations of his staff. But in our day he will do this at greater peril than ever before. First, since he cannot possibly maintain a sure grasp of the multiplying specialties under his command, he runs an acute risk of being wrong. Second, if he persistently overrides his subordinates and generally refuses them meaningful participation in company planning, they will be likely to leave him for positions of greater opportunity. To maintain his dominating style can cost him his best men—hardly a good sign for the company's future.

Several centuries ago a diligent and well-educated person might hope to acquaint himself with a large part of the world's useful knowledge. In our era an executive will be hard put to keep up with the literature that covers even *one* field of study essential to the proper management of his company. Faced with today's new technology, the most vigorous and authoritative chief executive must learn to know what he does not know and be prepared to curb his natural self-assertiveness—even if this means accommodating himself to the loss of some authority.

A third force for change modifying present-day styles of executive leadership may be identified as the *economics of scale* or simply the growing phenomenon of "bigness." Accelerating production and mass marketing over recent years have combined to generate businesses of enormous size. One impressive indicator is revealed in a recent *Fortune* report on 500 leading corporations. In a 14-year period from 1954 to 1968, the 100th largest company expanded from $303 to $1,026 million (239 percent!), and the 500th from $49 to $144 million (no less than 194 percent). The corporation heading the list (General Motors) grew from $9 to $23 *billion*, an increase of 156 percent. This spectacular growth represents not only a growth in sales and income but also an increase in the numbers and kinds of business activities in which these corporations have become engaged. In short, diversification built on top of growth will unavoidably have the effect of broadening middle-management powers of decision making. By the same token, it will further reduce the number of decisions the president alone can reach in any one of the many businesses in which his corporation competes.

The fourth trend which has altered techniques of leadership in recent decades has been *the worldwide expansion of business opportunity*, based in large measure on an insatiable demand for consumer goods among all income groups. The proliferation of product lines may be seen in many major industries—automotive, beverage, frozen foods, pharmaceuticals, to name only a few. In these circumstances the chief executive of a corporation finds himself charged with directing operations that may take place in a dozen different industries or markets, each with its own unique requirements for success.

Beyond this, a large percentage of American businesses have expended considerable talent and money to tap foreign markets. Consider, for example, that U.S. private investment in overseas operations moved from $11.8 billion in 1950 to $37.1 billion in 1962 and $64.8 billion in 1968. Thus, in addition to his myriad duties at home, the company president will likely cross and re-cross the ocean many times in order to keep track of developments on the other side of the world. But he cannot spend his life on airplanes. Much of the time, therefore, he will be thousands of miles from his foreign managers and the overseas administration of his company. In these areas—there can be no way around it—the direct impact of his leadership will be felt only intermittently.

Decline of the autocrat

If the new forces I have cited combine to limit presidential authority in various ways, does this mean that old-fashioned styles of leadership have been rendered obsolete? To some degree, the answer must be yes. I believe, for example, that in the new theater of business management the days of the autocrat are numbered. But this does not signify that presidential style has gone out of style, nor that it must give way to a colorless and dehumanized system of organizing company activities "by the numbers." On the contrary, the style, the salt of individuality, the sense of purpose that employees detect in their top management may have a more immediately decisive effect on an organization's future than ever before. Everything happens more rapidly now; the effects of all decisions, right or wrong, multiply more quickly and have more lasting consequences.

What is different today, I believe, is the president's *role*. The definition of a chief executive's excellence, the criterion by which we judge him, has evolved in recent years toward a quite new and different concept of business leadership. The president's principal role today is less to make all key decisions himself than to develop an organization and a process by which decisions can be made. Restating my earlier premise, his job is not so much to wield his own decision-making power in impressive fashion as to unleash the decision-making power of company personnel down the line to the lowest executive levels. Thus, although the chief executive's role may have changed, executive style remains all-important. The arts of command and persuasion can never be depersonalized. We cannot have leadership by computer. Presidential style—the way in which the top manager sets out to organize a company's creative energies down the line—gives the enterprise its character and competitive edge; determines its enthusiasm, adaptability and readiness to meet new challenges. It is what gives the company the nerve to grow faster than its industry.

What qualities of a chief executive have the most noticeable effect on the productivity of his organization? Over the past several years I have had the opportunity to carry out an informal study of leadership styles practiced by the presidents of 11 large, profitable companies and a number of their lieutenants. Here are some general observations.

Each of these men in his own way is a strong individualist, with a style different from the others. Each is uniquely his own man. Yet they have qualities in common. Their presidential style, for example, seems to be projected with unusual energy. Some of this extra effort may result from self-discipline, and some from enthusiasm, but my impression is that these executives have simply been endowed with more reserves of sheer physical energy than most people. This may account for a second characteristic observable in most successful company presidents I have known: total commitment to the business. Each has worked at his job with a consuming effort that takes up much of his time and energy.

We may safely predict, I think, that the style of a successful chief executive will, without exception, be an energetic style and that it will compel him to drive himself hard. He will study a great deal to keep abreast of technological developments. In recent years, understanding that his enterprise cannot operate in a vacuum, he will have been involving himself increasingly in outside political, social, and civic activities. Further, in Ernest Hemingway's classic phrase, he will be likely to demonstrate "grace under pressure." A poised style is not everything, of course. A company president may, after all, act with great aplomb and still make bad mistakes. But a talent for swift, cool action when the heat is on clearly remains a hallmark of the successful leader.

Four basic test areas

How, then, can we best predict his overall effectiveness? The presidents whose techniques of leadership I have studied have been most articulate on this point. In many conversations they shared with me their insights into the top manager's job. From these talks and my own observations I have a strong impression that the effectiveness of a president's style is closely related to the degree of force and understanding he brings to bear in four critical areas of management. The chart on the two following pages analyzes the style of five presidents out of the eleven I have studied. It shows in some detail how each performs in certain areas:

HIS LEADERSHIP IMAGE. Observe the way in which he comes across to and gets along with company personnel. He must deal with a variety of administrative talents, professional skills, and scientific disciplines. All of these must work together. Can the president spark people with such widely differing points of view? Can he release their creative enthusiasm, imparting to them a feeling of pride not only in their own efforts but in the company-wide effort as well? How do they instinctively react to his memorandums, his directives, his personal persuasion?

HIS PERFORMANCE STANDARDS AND METHODS OF EVALUATION. This category defines the nature of the demands he places on his people and the stringency with which he requires adherence to them. How hard does he push the organization? What rewards or penalties does he mete out to subordinates according to the quality of their performance?

HIS DECISION-MAKING TECHNIQUES. These are likely to be all-important to his company's long-range effectiveness. No mystique of leadership is involved here. Decisions are the meat and potatoes of executive power, the visible evidence of a top manager's day-to-day competence. Managers as a group make up their minds in very different ways. Before deciding on a course of action, does the president depend on large accumulations of facts and exhaustive research? Does he rely more on his own intuitions and perceptions? Or, perhaps, does he wait for a management consensus to emerge from meetings and discussions?

HIS USE OF AUTHORITY. There are many faces and symbols of authority. Recognized wisdom, usually in an older person, is a prime source of this

Leadership style of five presidents in action

PRESIDENT	LEADERSHIP IMAGE	PERFORMANCE STANDARDS AND EVALUATION
No. 1 60 YEARS OLD $365 MILLION SALES SINGLE PRODUCT FUNCTIONAL ORGANIZATION	Inspires by deep concern for others, apparent sincerity, and unquestioned ethics. Evokes a feeling of deep respect.	Appeals for improved performance but does not make tough, specific demands. Will tolerate mediocrity.
No. 2 45 YEARS OLD $225 MILLION SALES MULTIPRODUCT DIVISIONALIZED ORGANIZATION	Sparks subordinates by questioning mind, youthful energy, ideas, and efforts to "stretch" executives. Considered tough but fair.	Pushes executives to set high standards. Tough evaluator. Will replace mediocrity.
No. 3 63 YEARS OLD $425 MILLION SALES SINGLE PRODUCT FUNCTIONAL ORGANIZATION	Inspires through his own loyalty and devotion to company. Respected for judgment and common sense. Informal and friendly, the "old shoe" type.	Varies between being very demanding and quite permissive. Some standards set but he judges more on "belly feel." When pushed, removes poor performer.
No. 4 61 YEARS OLD $785 MILLION SALES MULTIPRODUCT DIVISIONALIZED ORGANIZATION	Moves by his shrewdness and detailed knowledge of all operating aspects of business. Held in fear and not well-liked.	No formal or general setting of standards. Will "chew out" executives for performance in specific situations, but will tolerate overall mediocre performance.
No. 5 53 YEARS OLD $325 MILLION SALES SINGLE PRODUCT FUNCTIONAL ORGANIZATION	Drives others by the sharpness and toughness of his thinking. Sets the climate by his own drive for perfection. Respected, but not held in affection.	Highly demanding and critical. Generally imposes own standards. Critical evaluator on both results and methods. Highly emotional over tough "people decisions." Will bypass but not fire the mediocre performer.

power. We have the authority of the big stick, and also moral authority; authority arising from performance in the past, or that imposed by a commanding presence and loud voice. Within the framework of a business organization, company presidents may drive lower-echelon executives to superior performance by imposing a regime of fear. Others prefer to exercise authority in subtle, sometimes almost imperceptible ways. The hard-driving and the "soft-line" top manager may each achieve good results. Very possibly, over-long exposure to either technique, without a change, may cause middle-management performance to suffer.

Two more indicators

These, by consensus of the company presidents in my study, are the critical management areas in which a top manager's style may be defined and his performance tested. They are the four elements that most clearly emerge from their introspective comments and their articulated philosophies of management. But my own observations suggest that these basic indicators may no longer suffice to measure a company president's performance in

DECISION-MAKING TECHNIQUES	USE OF AUTHORITY	ATTITUDE ON CHANGE	NATURE OF INVOLVEMENT
Based primarily on experience mixed with some fact and intuition. Will listen, then make decisions. These are rarely challenged.	Permissive on performance. Established mores of organization exert control over operating methods. Rarely exhibits raw authority.	Has experienced little. Is cautious but modestly willing to try change. Becoming more desirous to make changes.	Involved in individual incidents. Follows up on specific events that come to his attention or that he finds of particular interest. Major concern operational.
Fact-based. Discusses decisions in advance with subordinates. Willing to change his mind.	Reasonably permissive within limits of achieving goals. Authority more implied than overtly used.	Seeks change and pushes others. Thorough in programming to carry it out.	Deeply involved in planning, goal setting and evaluation against targets. Has deep understanding of each business; thus has close, frequent contact with each key executive.
Based on mixture of experience, some facts, and much intuitive feel. Unusual mixture of group and unilateral decisions. In group decision making, heavily influences results.	Alternates between being permissive and highly authoritative	Does not seek change, but when thrust upon him will accept and move quickly.	Manages by incident for short-term results. Deeply involved in all aspects of business. Has established formal planning but does not follow in practice.
Heavily weighted on experience. Will listen, but decisions generally unilateral and are not challenged.	Permissive on overall performance but highly authoritative in individual situations where he has particular interest.	Generally resists strongly but is beginning to make changes of substance.	Heavily involved in individual incidents, primarily in areas of own background.
Goes heavily on intuition and long experience. While he does consult with key people, in the main makes most decisions himself and holds fast to them.	Highly authoritative. Strong and positive in viewpoints, which he imposes with force.	Intellectually ready for change, but fearful that organization cannot cope with resulting problems. Fear of mistakes further holds back some change.	Has made strong effort to delegate responsibility widely but continues "over the shoulder" control. Gives much thought to strategy, but also holds on to operations.

today's business arena. Two more, I believe, must be added, and I would even venture a judgment that as qualities essential for top-grade leadership they have come to stand out above all others. These are (1) the president's readiness to seek out and foster change, and (2) the effectiveness of his commitment to what has been called, not always without a sneer, "participative management."

ATTITUDE TOWARD CHANGE. In his provocative book, *Management and Machiavelli,* Antony Jay observes,

> Leadership, especially at the highest levels, is becoming more and more concerned with change. Change has become the dominant concern of top management, and growth plans are geared to projected changes in wealth, technology, demand patterns, birth rate, habit, taste, population distribution, power supply, raw material production, and other such considerations.

Very possibly, the major function of management has become that of managing change. No company president can afford to ignore today's rapid turnover of new development and ideas. Technological unreadiness, we know, can be a prelude to disaster. Equally, the refusal or inability to recognize and adapt to emerging social and economic patterns such as those threatening America's great metropolitan centers today can get a complacent management into trouble in a remarkably short time. In this area, once again, the chief executive sets the company's style and pace. Does he demand change, encourage it, accept a new idea when necessary, or tend to resist it?

I am not concerned here with the pros and cons of any particular change, but rather with top management's overall attitude toward change *per se*. Is concern with change infused throughout the company's managing process? Does it *permeate* the organization? Is planning really—not just in name but in fact—a program for identifying *new* methods of operation, *new* business directions, and carrying them out?

There are three levels of commitment, it seems to me, that a president can reveal in his approach to change.

1. He may resist a fresh approach even when it is thrust upon him. This happens mostly because he refuses to understand the reasons for change or to see what benefits will accrue from it. Often, what he really fears is that he will be unable to cope with its consequences.

2. He may accept a new development once he has been confronted with the need for it. If the challenge to change is sufficiently clearcut he will respond, but he will not seek change and will be unlikely to lead others in new directions.

3. He may—and this is characteristic of the more successful top manager —actively seek out change, both for himself and his organization. Such an executive is restless and ill at ease with the status quo. Not only that, but he manages to transmit this creative discontent to others, inspiring enthusiasm for change down the line.

THE CHALLENGE OF PARTICIPATIVE MANAGEMENT. To what extent does the president encourage independent thinking and decision-making among his subordinates? Years ago the legendary football giant, Jim Thorpe of the Carlisle Indians, became increasingly frustrated when his team's intricate plays came up against a stubborn defense and could make no headway. Finally, late in the game, he commanded his discouraged teammates: "Just give me the ball and follow me!" and ran for a touchdown.

Many business leaders periodically have the same dream: in the face of difficulties to take the ball and run with it, leaving the members of their staff to follow along as best they can. But today such impulsive action is rarely practicable: if attempted in an industrial field of any complexity, it will almost certainly result in unacceptable losses.

What we come down to in the end is a confrontation between a top manager's vigorous style—his natural impulse to lead, not only to call the plays but to run with the ball himself—and the all-important need to unleash the power of making creative decisions throughout the organization. Here a question now presents itself—a question asked repeatedly, in many different ways, by the company presidents with whom I have talked: Is there something at the heart of even the most enlightened and constructive leadership that resists delegation of responsibility? If so, how can the contradiction be resolved?

At this point I am aware of entering an intellectual mine field where paradoxes abound. We are dealing, first, with the nature of the chief executive's personal involvement in his management duties. Our basic assumption has been that presidential style is what makes the company go, and that without strong leadership the company's drive and enthusiasm will go flat. This spirit must come down from the top; it is always the chief executive's job to see that it does. Yet, paradoxically, in today's complex economic and technological environment, high-spirited individualistic leadership is double-edged. The leader's style can both stimulate and interfere with company operations. To put the issue most sharply, presidential achievement can ultimately weaken the capacity for organizational achievement. Significantly, many of the successful presidents with whom I have consulted worry a great deal over this problem, and few have found a satisfactory answer.

Delegating decisions

Each president fights hard but with differing success to keep from heavy involvement in the mechanics of his business. Each one understands intellectually that it would be best for him to delegate as many decisions as possible to executives down the line. Each knows that—tradition to the contrary—the ability to let go of power is the mark of the strong, courageous manager, not of the weak one. It is obvious to all 11 presidents that they are faced with a continuing need to relinquish decision-making capacity down and throughout the organization in order to multiply its power to decide and act. Yet, knowing as they do that the higher an executive goes in an organization the fewer decisions he should make, they still feel inexorably drawn to the decision-making process.

We must remember that in discussing presidents we are dealing with flesh-and-blood human beings, not animated titles stepping out of an organization chart. These men did not arrive at the top management level by relinquishing responsibility to others. Instead, on their way up, they reached for responsibility and rose to the top by handling assignments with skill and energy. It is difficult to ask such a man—particularly a younger president in the prime of life—to leave all but the highest-level decisions to others. We know this type of chief executive. His pleasure, the lifeblood of his style, is to manage through day-to-day involvement down the line, regularly (and possibly too frequently) checking progress in the machine shop, drafting room, and laboratory. Shall he—can he—change the very style that brought him to the top? Yet the paradox persists: sooner or later, for his company's long-range good, the president must prepare to delegate authority to his subordinate managers and specialists.

How difficult this can be! As one president expressed it: "Participative management has a high price in terms of presidential time. But it also demands enormous self-restraint to avoid overinvolvement in decision making. And that's a habit that is frustratingly hard to acquire."

Many presidents have told me they find it far more exhilarating to make today's action-oriented decisions than to think about the company's long-term strategy. In doing the former, the president can be an impressive figure, particularly to the specialists who respond to his enthusiasm and concern over their progress. For them, his drive and purpose will be inspiring. But at the same time, he must guard against reducing lower echelon executives to mere spear carriers. If his style of leadership involves reserving every key decision for himself or a small entourage of deputies, then the organization headed by an inspiring president cannot help suffering a serious loss of vitality.

Clearly, presidents do not manage as well as they know how. Each of the 11 emphasized this point. Each is aware of his responsibility to be a steward of change. Each believes he understands the importance of participative management. The difficulty comes in the doing.

The challenge, I believe, can be simply expressed. The qualities that will enable the top executive of the future to stand out among his fellow presidents are his capacity to perceive meaningful change and spark his people to respond, and his skill in fostering participative management without losing drive and spirit in his leadership style. The president who achieves these qualities will possess the indispensable ingredients for unleashing the full power of his organization.

PART TWO

Organizing for effectiveness

In the large corporation of our day, effective organization is not merely a precondition for the successful implementation of strategy; it is, or should be, a logical reflection of that strategy. And since long-range corporate success is largely determined by the excellence of the fit between the two, few issues concern top management more critically than that of structuring and restructuring the corporate organization. The issue has had its share of attention from scholars and theorists, but their findings offer, at best, no more than guidelines to senior managers confronted by the need to structure, within the context of a shifting economic environment, an immense complex of activities and resources in support of a predetermined set of corporate objectives. Here organization transcends science to emerge as one of the subtlest and most challenging of all the management arts.

In "Organization: The Harness to Help People Pull Together," Marvin Bower examines the art of organization in terms of its effect on the flesh-and-blood individuals who make up the economy. He warns against confusing organizational planning with the drawing up of charts and the definition of formal lines of authority. Rightly understood, organization planning can never be a precise science. It is "a process designed for managing people as they are–with all their fine qualities and their meannesses as well."

Human nature being what it is, no such plan can be perfect. A seriously defective organization structure, however, will almost certainly bring out the worst in everyone–and allow corporate strengths to be sapped by internal frictions. Hence an important criterion of any organization structure: It should hold destructive political and personality conflicts

51

to a minimum, so that they will drain as little as possible from the energies needed to supply the company's forward thrust.

If effective management sparks corporate growth, growth is a frequent forerunner of reorganizations designed to improve corporate performance. Sometimes they accomplish this; too often they do not. "Reorganizing for Results," by D. Ronald Daniel, throws light on some of the pitfalls encountered in planning. Again, we come upon the art of reconciling theory and practice. Skillfully employed, the classic principles of organization can serve as invaluable reference points in designing the right organization plan. But these principles are neither definitive nor sacrosanct. Indeed, there are situations where they ought to be violated. In Daniel's words, "it is as foolish to be bound by past experience as to ignore it."

"Organizing a Worldwide Business," by Gilbert H. Clee and Wilbur M. Sachtjen, studies the growing number of true world enterprises which apply their corporate resources on a global scale rather than operating as domestic companies with interests abroad. The writers are primarily concerned with the organizational alternatives confronting these companies as they conduct their "intense and sophisticated rivalry" around the world. In particular, they examine the variables that should influence the all-important choice of a regional vs. a functional organization structure.

In "New Concepts in Overseas Investment," Peter P. Gabriel takes the measure of an obstacle beginning to loom in the path of world enterprise, and explores the possibility of avoiding it by means of a fresh approach to the concept of overseas investment. The management contract, he suggests, may well be the coming solution to the dilemma of how to reap profits from overseas business without suffering the stigma—and, ultimately paying the penalty—associated with foreign ownership in politically sensitive foreign environments.

6. Organization: the harness to help people pull together

Marvin Bower

One summer afternoon a friend telephoned me about a golf game. He had a twosome and was looking for two more. I accepted, and we spent a minute discussing whom we might get as the fourth. But we did not settle on anyone. Nor did we decide which of us was to get the fourth.

The next day I met another member of the club. He agreed to join us, and I immediately called my friend with the news. But in the meantime he too had invited a guest, so we had one too many. Since my friend could hardly "disinvite" his guest, I called back the member I had invited and told him of our plight. He was most understanding and readily agreed to withdraw. So no harm was done.

Even so, the incident was embarrassing to me, and it could easily have been avoided. All we had needed to do in our first telephone conversation was to follow one of the most fundamental principles of organization: decide who does what—in this instance, who would invite the fourth player.

Importance of good organization

Unfortunately, organizational muddles of much greater consequence take place every day in even the largest and best managed companies. Consequences of the resulting mix-ups and conflicts are duplication, wasted effort, delay, frustration, angry words—or relaxing and letting the other fellow do the job. All this combines to bring about ineffective performance, needlessly high costs, loss of competitive position, low morale, reduced profits, and lost opportunities to develop executives.

Let me recall one more incident that shows the importance of sound organization. It concerns an able man in his early thirties whom I often met as we walked to the same commuting train. He was an executive with a large consumer and industrial goods company.

One morning he told me that he was going to resign his job that day; he had just accepted a new position with a competitor. Why? This was his explanation:

53

In my new job I'll have a better chance to get ahead, and I'll make a little more money. I like the people in the new company. But I also like the people I'm with now. I guess my main reason for taking the new job is the way my present division is organized. As you know, I'm a product manager. I'm held accountable for profits on my line of products, though I'm only in charge of marketing. But procurement happens to be the principal factor in our division's profits. So if the procurement people do poorly, I take the rap—even though I have nothing to say about how they buy or how much inventory we carry.

Actually the chief executive of the whole corporation is the one really responsible for profits on my line, and my line is only one tiny part of our total business. I've done my best to get the setup changed; but all I could get was agreement to let me handle communications more directly instead of going up one line to the top and then down the other.

So I'm going in and break the news to my boss this morning. I plan to tell him the way my job is organized was a major factor in my leaving. But since I'm going with a direct competitor, they'll probably be so busy getting me out of the place by noon that the point won't register.

That product manager may have been a serious loss to his company. Far more serious was the loss of one man to General Motors. Alfred Sloan tells the story in his classic book:

As to organization, we did not have adequate knowledge or control of the individual operating divisions. It was management by crony, with the divisions operating on a horse-trading basis. When Walter Chrysler, one of the best men in General Motors, became a general executive of the corporation, he collided with Mr. Durant over their respective jurisdictions, I believe. Mr. Chrysler was a man of strong will and feeling. When he could not get the arrangement he wanted, he left the corporation. I remember the day. He banged the door on the way out, and out of that bang eventually came the Chrysler Corporation.[1]

Yet organizing has been a much neglected and underrated managing process, more often disdained than respected by business executives. Here are some typical comments I have heard from high-level executives in sizable companies:

"We don't go in much for formal organization around here. We're more interested in people than in boxes on charts."

[1] Alfred P. Sloan, Jr., *My Years with General Motors*, Doubleday and Company, Inc., New York, 1964, p. 27.

"Suppose there *is* some confusion. The strong men will always get along all right, and the others we can't worry much about anyway. Even a good dogfight isn't always bad."

"Formal organization is too restricting. We want every man to feel he can go ahead and do things on his own."

Ralph Cordiner, then president of General Electric Company, put it better than any executive I know of has since:

> You are familiar with the argument that an organization chart consists of little boxes within which the talents of men are confined and within which their capacity for creative and individual effort is smothered. Certainly you can misuse even a well-defined organization structure to achieve such purposes. But equally certain, you do not need to do so.[2]

What organization really is

Fundamentally, organization consists of a planning (i.e., decision-making) process that involves these steps:

1. The work or activities to be performed in order to carry out plans are determined. The things to be done or tasks to be performed become *duties*.

2. These activities are grouped into positions so they can be assigned to an individual, thus becoming *responsibilities*.

3. Next, *authority* is assigned to each position, conferring on the person holding the position the right to carry out the responsibilities himself or to command others to carry them out.

It is useful to recognize the distinction between authority and power. Power may be defined as the ability to get things done—by doing them personally or by commanding or influencing others to do them, with or without authority. A person may have power because he is liked or feared, or because he is respected for his knowledge, judgment, skill, force of personality, seniority, age, or past accomplishments.

Authority, which confers the right to command, helps to build power—to legitimize it. But if a person with authority is not respected, his authority may give him little power.

Power may be, and frequently is, exercised without authority. For example, a politically minded individual without formal authority may attempt to control the activities of others by exploiting their fears and

[2] Ralph Cordiner, "Problems of Management in a Large Decentralized Organization," speech to General Management Conference, American Management Association, June 19, 1952.

55

weaknesses, without having to accept responsibility for his actions. But a good executive who recognizes the value of sound organization and wants to support the management system will not exploit his seniority or popularity in this fashion unless he also possesses the requisite formal authority.

4. The next step in organization planning is to determine *authority relationships* among positions—that is, decide who reports to whom and what kind of authority, if any, the holder of each position may exercise. This will ensure that every person knows who his boss is, who his subordinates are, and what type and extent of authority he is subject to and can exercise.

5. Finally, the *personal qualifications* required for superior performance in each position should be decided. Thus organization planning will be concerned with the duties, responsibilities, authorities, relationships, and personal requirements of positions. This kind of planning harnesses and legitimizes power. It also helps to contain illegitimate power.

Ideal organization structures nearly always have to be modified—simply because ideal people are seldom available. But it is better to accept compromises in an ideal plan than not to have an ideal plan to start from. And usually, less compromise will be needed than expected.

To be sure, an organization plan *is* restrictive. In fact, *all* managing processes are restrictive, just as, in a sense, all guidance is restrictive. If people are to pull together, rather than work at cross-purposes, some harness will be needed.

But the restrictiveness of the management system depends less on the harness itself than on how tightly the reins are held and how frequently and sharply the whip is used. With a soundly developed system of management and good leadership, high-caliber people will work productively and with zest, despite the restrictions of the organization plan.

How organization structure affects performance

In the early days of his administration, President Kennedy had trouble filling an important position in the State Department. As *The New York Times* declared editorially: "The President's difficulty in finding anyone willing and able to take the extremely important post of Assistant Secretary of State for Inter-American Affairs would be ridiculous if it were not so serious."[3] It was reported that about 20 candidates had been considered or approached. The names of two candidates who had actually been offered the post became known, but both had rejected the job. The *Times* editorial continued:

[3] *The New York Times*, June 16, 1961.

Of the probable reasons for their refusal, the main one is the dispersion of authority in the field of Latin-American affairs. The State Department's Inter-American Bureau has been pushed into the background by the White House "task force," headed by Adolf Berle, the two White House aides, Richard Goodwin and Arthur Schlesinger, Jr., and—in some cases like Cuba—by the C.I.A. As a result the State Department staff has become demoralized. How can President Kennedy expect anyone of importance to assume a post in such conditions? At best it will be one of the most difficult and thankless jobs in the Government . . . Mr. Kennedy will obtain the right man when he offers him a position of authority with a clear line of command from the White House through the Secretary of State.'

Corporate chief executives who seek to attract able men to poorly defined positions often have similar difficulties. Able people in any walk of life simply will not accept jobs with inadequate or unclear authority. Based on my observations of executives at work, and on hundreds of confidential interviews with executives at all levels, it is my conviction that any high-caliber man's effectiveness, job satisfaction, and zest for work—from the time he takes his first job until he retires—are vitally affected by the structure of the organization in which he works.

Organization planning will usually be pictured in the form of charts with boxes and lines of authority. But organization planning really deals with the actions, ambitions, emotions, and personal effectiveness of people. Whether or not the actions of individuals have been effectively harnessed largely depends, I believe, on how well the plan of organization has been fashioned, how resolutely managers at all levels follow it themselves, and how consistently they require others to do so.

Organization planning should be a process designed for managing people as they *are*—with all their fine qualities and their meannesses as well. Product managers, Walter Chryslers, and candidates for Assistant Secretary of State all have their pride. Each wants his own clearly defined job: none wants anyone else interfering with his authority. A well-planned structure, therefore, serves to hold personal politics and personality conflicts in check.

Even a perfect organization plan won't control all the imperfections of human nature. But a defective plan can be counted on to bring out the worst in people and to raise costly havoc in the organization. Business executives, like generals and educators, often engage in infighting. And business concerns, like all other organizations, have their political camps and cliques. The mean side of human nature is frequently brought out by a defective organization structure. At least, such a structure stimulates and facilitates infighting and politics.

Organization guidelines

The so-called "principles of organization" have nothing like the proven validity of natural laws. In fact, management authorities still differ among themselves on many of these. Hence, they may better be termed "guidelines"—derived from observation and analysis of how people really act in groups. As such, they serve to lay down a general set of ground rules for determining how best to go about the task of establishing an effective organization structure.

SETTING UP POSITIONS. "A square peg in a round hole" is the cliché often used to describe the man who has failed to perform well in a job. Classic examples are the star salesman who fails as a district sales manager and the outstanding worker who makes a poor foreman. The business losses and the personal heartbreaks that flow from such failures constitute a great waste of human energy. Often the failures are not so much the fault of the man as of poor organizational decisions by management. And often they can be avoided if senior executives understand and follow the elementary guidelines for setting up positions.

The organizing process is basically a matter of assigning work to people. Consequently, organization planning starts with deciding what activities are necessary and then grouping the work—by *type* and *amount*—so that the position or job constitutes an assignment that can be performed effectively by the individual.

Basically the different *types* of work assigned to any position should not be so numerous that it will be hard to fill. That is, the work should be homogeneous enough so there will generally be enough candidates to fill and refill the position without much difficulty. Since most people do not have a wide range of talents, a position calling for an unusual spread of abilities should not ordinarily be created. Even if an unusually talented person may currently be available to fill a poorly set up position, replacements will be difficult to develop, and later on unnecessary reorganization and upset will be likely to result.

The different types of work can be usefully classified in terms of the personal qualifications needed to do the job:

Operating work is generally repetitive, and requires *doing* rather than planning. Therefore, it demands a relatively lower degree of imagination and analytical power.

Analytical work, such as staff assignments performed by engineers, or market and financial analysts, calls for highly developed problem-solving skills. Planning too requires analytical ability.

Technical work involves knowledge of some specialized field, such as engineering, chemistry, accounting, operations research, or electronic data processing. This knowledge must be gained through education and/or job experience.

Creative work, such as scientific research or advertising, requires a high degree of imagination, vision, and the ability to come up with fresh ideas.

Administrative work, from the district sales manager's or foreman's job on up, requires a talent for exercising authority and the capacity to direct and get things done through others.

Leadership, such as that of the president and the director of marketing, must above all inspire others to effective performance.

Even at lower levels, positions usually combine two or more basic types of work. The higher the position, the more varied will be the types of work assigned to it. A highly creative person generally dislikes routine, and if routine tasks are forced on him, rare skills will be wasted. A man efficient at the operating level will not necessarily be a good analyst, administrator, or leader. Thus, a position entailing several different types of work demands a degree of versatility from the individual. Obviously, then, the number of qualified candidates decreases as the range of work assigned to a position increases.

The guidelines for determining *how much* work to assign to a position are inherently less specific. If the proper *types* of work are assigned, the person filling it will be able to turn out more work. Decisions of this kind can best be reached through line managers' observations, and the findings of specialists such as organization analysts and industrial engineers.

Any executive seeking organizational improvement should always be prepared to consider setting up precisely defined new positions—both line and staff. But before such new positions are created, their hidden costs should be weighed as well as the added salaries involved. The bill for supplementary compensation (pension, insurance, hospitalization, etc.) must be carefully examined. So should the costs of office space and secretarial help.

Besides the setting up of new positions, effective organization planning also challenges the value of existing ones. The simple question, "Is this work necessary?" may expose the need for drastic change. An activity that once was necessary may become obsolete as conditions change. For example, technical services established during a new-product introduction may not be needed after the product is well established. In business, the will to manage will not tolerate the luxury of vested interests.

GRANTING AUTHORITY. No position can be soundly established unless its holder has the authority to carry out his duties or responsibilities. Responsibility and authority should go hand in hand. Many companies, both large and small, incorporate in written job descriptions various specific grants of authority: approving capital investment, granting salary increases, hiring people at various levels of salary, signing contracts, retaining lawyers and consultants, etc.

In building a system of management, much depends on distinguishing properly between line and functional authority, and also on understanding the difference between functional authority and staff work.

Line authority gives an executive the right to give direct orders. The line executive controls his subordinates chiefly through discipline (approval or disapproval) and decisions or recommendations on compensation or promotion. His ultimate control, of course, is the right to hire and fire. Awareness of the superior's right to fire is the most powerful negative control in any system of management. The line executive concerns himself with determining the need, time, and place for action and seeing that things get done. He says "Do it," and "Do it *now*."

Line authority descends from the chief executive down through the various management levels, to the lowest level of operating or sales supervisor who directs any subordinates. Functional authority is more subtle, and also less widely understood and used. Yet proper understanding and use of this concept can be of great value in a company of any size. And as companies become larger, more complex, and more subject to the impact of rapid change, the usefulness of this kind of authority increases.

Functional (*sometimes called technical*) *authority* confers the right to see to it that activities in other departments or organizational units are carried on in accordance with the proper technical standards. If line authority is a grant of power, functional authority may be viewed as the authority of knowledge. Just as the holder of line authority says "Do it," and "Do it *now*," the holder of functional authority says "If and when you do it, do it this way—in accordance with this policy or standard."

For example:

1. The controller has functional authority over all accounting procedures in all departments of a company. He prescribes how transactions shall be recorded, and line executives must follow his instructions.

2. The purchasing department sets standards for local purchases made by line departments. If and when they buy parts, supplies, or materials, they must buy to established standards.

3. The personnel department has functional authority to prescribe to line executives how grievances will be handled, what salary ranges will be established, what limitations there may be on dismissals, etc.

4. The public relations department draws up restrictions and guidelines determining what plant managers may discuss with the local press and how they discuss it.

These illustrations point up another important aspect of this concept:

Line executives help enforce *functional* authority by putting their own authority behind it. The chief executive, in effect, commands all line executives to follow and enforce the policies, procedures, and standards of the functional departments. Thus, the functional departments are not merely advisory. They have their own authority, which is backed by line authority.

Functional departments should approach the job of enforcing their policies, standards, and procedures in a spirit of exercising authority, not merely offering advice. That does not mean, of course, that they should be arrogant. Indeed, the most effective functional departments seldom need to resort to a show of authority. Their policies, standards, and procedures ought ideally to be so useful, so sensible, and so persuasively presented that the line departments will be glad to follow and enforce them.

But if it happens that a line manager disagrees with a policy established by one of the functional departments, and the difference of opinion cannot be resolved, it will be referred to the next highest common *line* superior of the executives who differ. For example, a plant manager may disagree with the plant controller. This executive reports to the manager but remains bound to enforce the procedures under dispute, since these have been established in the company controller's department. The plant manager first tries to persuade the plant controller. If that fails, they refer the issue to their respective line and functional superiors, who seek to resolve the issue through discussion. The final decision will be made by the highest common line superior to whom the issue can be appealed—perhaps even the chief executive.

This system of checks and balances has been devised to bring about the best compromise between getting things done quickly and getting them done right—i.e., in accordance with company policies, standards, and philosophy. An overzealous functional executive cannot long hold up important operations since line executives can always convince functional managers or line superiors that the functional guideline is wrong and should be changed, or that an exception should be made.

Parenthetically, a company philosophy that includes an objective, factual approach to resolving issues permits the best use of the checks and balances between line and functional authority. Under such a philosophy, people will try to determine *what* is right, not *who* is right. Persuasion based on facts will always be more effective; in the light of new facts people can change their positions with less damage to their pride.

In summary:

¶ Functional authority provides the means of making technical and specialized knowledge more productive in a company. The importance of this will grow as science, technology, and advanced knowledge of all types become increasingly important to business success.

¶ With proper functional authority behind them, specialists and technicians need not feel like second-class citizens, entirely dependent on their powers of persuasion. At the same time, their knowledge of the checks that line executives can impose on them should keep them from being officious and arrogant—if common sense does not. Consequently, an organization in which functional authority is strong can more easily attract and retain the specialists needed today by virtually every company doing business in a complex environment of rapid technological change.

¶ The system of checks and balances, by providing for appeals up the line, ensures that the line executives are always in command on major issues. The chief executive has the security of knowing that line executives —ultimately responsible for profits—can assert their authority any time they wish. And he knows that issues of enough importance will ultimately be appealed to him if they cannot be resolved at a lower level.

¶ Recognition and exercise of functional authority can provide any company with a powerful competitive advantage by identifying *ideas* that have value and making sure that they are put to work.

Staff activity, properly understood, consists simply of fact-finding, analysis, and the development of advice and recommendations. Unlike the functional department, a staff unit—market research, engineering, legal— *has no authority*. A staff unit cannot *enforce* its recommendations, however valuable they may be. Staff people can only advise and persuade. Line or functional departments receiving this advice may act on it or ignore it.

The term "staff" has commonly been used to cover all activities that are not clearly line work, thus blurring or obliterating the concept of functional authority. This fuzziness is unfortunate because it forecloses an opportunity for competitive advantage.

In several companies that have paid close attention to building management systems, services are charged to the department that uses them. Staff units are expected to make their services so valuable that they develop a line "clientele." Du Pont's engineering department, for example, publishes a booklet to inform executives in the operating departments about the services it has to offer.

Although staff activities have increased greatly in U.S. companies during the past 25 years, additional growth will be needed to cope with the growing size and complexity of companies and with rapidly developing changes in the business environment. Desirable new staff units—such as those involved in formulating long-range company strategy, logistics, and organization planning—will meet with less resistance, and hence are more likely to be successfully established, if management makes clear that they will be strictly advisory.

The "office" concept in organizing

Establishing the idea that each major position should be viewed as an *office* will help substantially to transmit the will to manage throughout the company. This concept is simple and useful. It merely means recognizing each position as a bundle of responsiblity and authority, distinct from the person who holds it. The incumbent *fills* the office—he does not *make* it.

Of course, executives will interpret the limits of the office in accordance with their individual natures. We have dominating and permissive managers.

In most business concerns, the chief executive sets the pace for his administration. Through his style of managing, he expands or contracts the authority of his office. In the way he carves out the scope and performs the job, people throughout the organization come to understand, accept, and expect that the job will be performed that way, and a clear and distinct image of the office of chief executive in that company is built up in people's minds. But the image can change.

In one very large corporation, for example, the president was an extremely dominant individual—a poor delegator but a brilliant and successful decision maker. His successor, on taking over the presidency, was staggered by the number of issues brought to him for decision. He was even more dismayed by the way people hung on his words and reacted to any indication of his opinion as if it were a command. I pointed out to him that the people in the business had simply come to accept the "office" of president as it had been built by his predecessor. I advised him to rebuild the office by gradually delegating more authority to his subordinates. After about three years of the new president's style, the office of president had contracted in scope, but it was still an *office*.

In most companies, unfortunately, positions are not widely enough recognized at lower levels as *offices*. As a rule, every senior position has some acceptance and recognition as an office, but too often each executive below the chief feels that in order to build his own prestige he must widen the scope of the job. Frequently new incumbents are obliged to do battle with other executives to establish authority that clearly should attach to the position, not the man. In these circumstances, the authorities of the position expand or contract from week to week, or even from day to day, as the incumbent gains or loses personal standing with those above him.

Thus, lack of established "offices" makes for a continuing power struggle. As new people enter positions, the others involved wait to see how much support each new executive receives from higher up. Not only are such struggles wasteful; they usually permit the accomplished politician to win power that should not go with the "office." And when a struggle for power or standing becomes extreme, the more capable executives will leave, not wanting to work in an atmosphere where they must constantly be worrying about where they stand.

Consequently, part of building a management system involves building respect for offices up and down the line at all levels. This is done by making it clear that "the way we do things around here" requires every executive—from the chief on down—to build positions and develop men to fill them.

Each executive does this by holding his subordinates accountable for the responsibilities of the position, and supporting them in the exercise of appropriate authority. He should, of course, make it clear to all concerned that he is supporting the authority of the *position*, not the executive as an individual. This approach makes for personal security, minimizes personal and corporate politics, improves performance, and builds *esprit*.

Staffing the structure

Modifying the ideal structure to fit the available people comes almost too naturally in most situations. Unusual responsibilities may be attached to a position because the incumbent has specialized abilities. Again, two jobs may be combined to fit the unusually broad abilities of a particular individual. Or the responsibilities of a position may be narrowed because the man who holds it does not possess all the abilities it requires. In these circumstances, not all the work gets done and part of the "office" tends to atrophy.

In real life as we live it, the ideal individual is almost never available for a given job. Even so, the value of ideal specifications as the basis for selecting people for positions can hardly be overstressed. I recall a chairman and president faced with the task of picking a man to move into the presidency when the chairman retired and the president moved up to chairman. The choice had come down to three outstanding candidates. As they discussed the selection with me, I realized that they were about to reach agreement on one of the three—not, in my opinion, the best-qualified man. I asked them to let me prepare a memorandum outlining the important management problems the president would face during the next ten years, and the personal qualifications he would need for the job.

After a couple of drafts, we reached agreement on the character of the job and personal qualifications needed to fill it well. Then the chairman and the president separately evaluated the three candidates in terms of those qualifications. They quickly decided on a man whom they had been on the point of passing over. He proved to be an excellent choice, and the company has prospered handsomely under his leadership.

Whether the post be that of district sales manager, foreman, or president, the same approach should be followed: Set up a definite position, specify the types of work it demands, define the ideal qualifications for the office, analyze the qualifications of each candidate on the basis of his demonstrated performance, and then match the qualifications for the job as closely as possible to those of the candidates. This approach enforces objectivity and assures consideration of a wider range of candidates.

Organization for organizing

Since organization planning is an all-important management process, any large company or division needs a special staff unit to carry it out. Such a unit can range from a single individual, working part time, to a staff of half a dozen people.

It goes almost without saying that the staff man or the head of the organization planning unit must be someone who enjoys the confidence and support of the chief executive, and should report directly to him or one of his immediate subordinates.

The staff head needs no special experience. He should be a man whom people trust and in whom they feel they can confide. Given intelligence, analytical ability, imagination, and common sense, he can learn organization planning by doing it and studying texts on the side.

Too often the prospect of reorganization brings shudders throughout a company because it is assumed that heads will roll. This attitude is unfortunate. Reorganizing has been one of industrial man's most reliable prescriptions for seizing opportunities and remedying company weaknesses. As a company grows, new positions should be added and existing ones changed—continuous reorganization is both natural and necessary. In a very real sense, reorganization is the mark of a progressive top management's determination to adjust skillfully and dynamically to new internal conditions and an ever-changing environment. Such adjustments can and should be made with consideration for the individual. Indeed, postponing needed reorganization is as bad for the individual as it is for the company—or even worse.

7. Reorganizing for results

D. Ronald Daniel

Even the casual reader of the business press these days can hardly help noticing that organizational change—once a relatively infrequent pheno- menon—has become something very much like a way of life in U.S. industry. Scarcely a day passes without an announcement of some major corporation's decision to subdivide, consolidate, or otherwise restructure itself. And even allowing for management's growing willingness to talk about such moves, it is certain that for every publicly acknowledged organizational realignment a good many others have quietly taken place without publicity.

The visible part of this iceberg seems impressive enough. No fewer than 66 of the nation's top 100 industrial companies reported major organiza- tional realignments to their stockholders over a recent three-year period— an average rate of one change per company every 54 months. There must also be many changes that go unreported. One major restructuring every two or three years is probably a conservative estimate of the current rate of organizational change among the largest industrial corporations. Our firm alone works with over 100 U.S. clients each year on problems that are resolved—at least in part— by changes in organization structure. And solving organization problems has become an even larger part of our practice outside the United States. And neither in the United States nor elsewhere has there been any sign of a leveling off in the immediate future.

Current challenges

Where have these changes been concentrated, and what principal forces have brought them about? Our own experience suggests some answers:

The bigger the company, the more likely it will be to undergo a major change. For instance, in the three-year period I have just cited, 9 of the 10 largest companies, 16 of the top 25, and 27 of the top 50 were among the 66 corporations reporting change to their stockholders.

Commonest among the types of organization change were those relating to international operations, followed closely by the establishment of group vice president positions, consolidation of product divisions into larger units, and rearrangement of marketing functions, in that order.

We find no mystery behind these changes. At least five causes may be identified:

1. The pressures of competition on margins and profits have made an efficient organization structure practically essential. Overlapping departments are being combined, product divisions consolidated, and marginal units eliminated.

2. The internationalization of business has compelled more and more companies to supplant export departments by international divisions, to establish regional management groups, and to restructure corporate staffs.

3. Mergers and acquisitions—rampant in the United States and increasing in Europe—have generated strong pressures for reorganization in parent companies as well as in newly-acquired subsidiaries.

4. New developments in technology—such as the advanced management information systems made possible by recent progress in computer hardware and software—often require new organizational arrangements to realize their ultimate potential for improving corporate performance.

5. Finally, sheer growth compels many companies to amend time-honored organizational arrangements in order to cope with volume increases of as much as 20 percent a year.

Undoubtedly, the talent for planning organizational change wisely, carrying it out effectively, and realizing its benefits promptly has come to be more and more vital to effective, competitive corporate performance. Indeed, the costs of bungling a reorganization, in terms of both dollars and of competitive position, have become more punishing every year.

How well is management equipped for the organizational challenges ahead? And how successfully has it managed organizational change to date?

During recent years, I have had a chance to discuss with hundreds of top executives the concepts, strategies, expectations, and results of several dozen reorganizations. The conclusion appears as inescapable as it is serious: Far too many of these organizational changes fail to produce more vigorous competitive drive, greater profitability, or renewed readiness for future growth.

Indeed, the record shows not only unrealized benefits, but unexpected troubles as well. In company after company organizational change, envisioned as a solution to present difficulties, has only brought new ones. Momentum and continuity have been interrupted; confusion over responsibility and decision-making authority has reigned; and, in some cases. company morale has been seriously damaged.

Pitfalls in planning

Among those companies whose organization changes have misfired, the great majority of fiascoes can be laid to one or more of five errors in organization planning.

1. THEORY AND "PRINCIPLE." Perhaps the most conspicuous mistake has been the tendency to rely too heavily—or, rather, too exclusively—on theory and "principle" in organization design. The so-called principles of organization—those familiar universals dealing with span of control, reporting relationships, and so forth—frequently seem to be invested by organization planners with the authority of moral law. Certain organizational relationships, whatever their apparent practical merits, may be damned because they commit the sin of violating these principles; others seem to be favored mainly because of their theoretical purity.

Actually, of course, most such principles should be viewed as no more than generalizations about what has been observed to work in practice, based on past organizational experience. Derived from experience, they are subject to revision in the light of new experiences and circumstances. Certainly they ought not to be considered sacred; it is as foolish to be bound by past experience as to ignore it.

The principles of organization may be imagined as a double-edged sword. Employed with skill and discretion, they serve to define and refine an organization structure. Applied insistently and inflexibly, they can result in a rigid, bureaucratic organization structure poorly attuned to a company's unique needs.

Blind reverence for principle in organization planning has not been confined to the classical school of thought, which considers organizations as mechanisms for the accomplishment of work. Much the same approach may be taken, with equally unfortunate results, by proponents of more contemporary theoretical approaches such as these:

¶ The behavioral science school, which sees organizations in terms of interacting individuals and groups, takes personal development and satisfaction as its central criteria, and often seeks to remove structural constraints on their fulfillment.

¶ The management science school, which tends to view the organization as a huge man-machine system susceptible to modification in terms of mathematical models.

Both these schools, and others as well, have insights to contribute. But their adherents are so often obsessed with one set of concepts that they deny the value of any insights generated by other approaches.

The ill effects of theory-bound organization planning may be illustrated by this classic example. A well-known airline decided some years ago to reexamine its organization structure. Its chief planner, a fervent believer in delegation of authority and the value of general manager positions for developing executive skills, designed a new geographically decentralized organization for the airline. The plan looked fine on paper, but it failed to recognize the need for centralized decisions on equipment acquisition, route planning, flight scheduling, maintenance and overhaul scheduling, customer service standards, and other key profit elements in air transportation.

For years after the new organization structure was imposed, the regional managers—presumably accountable for profits, but actually unable to function as anything more than public relations coordinators—slowed down critical decisions. Finally, top management, admitting that the new structure had been a mistake, reverted to the airline's traditional alignment of functional departments.

2. IMITATIVE PATTERN. The tendency to reproduce a given organization pattern, simply because it has proved successful for another company, has been another common error in organization planning.

For example, the General Motors concept of profit-accountable product divisions coupled with a policy-making headquarters staff has been copied in countless instances. Admittedly, the concept is broadly applicable. But too many imitators have adopted the form without the substance. Lacking GM's depth of quality manpower and GM's finely tuned planning and control systems, some companies have found their divisionalized structures leading to abdication rather than delegation, and to anarchy rather than accountability.

3. UNCHANGING STRUCTURE. Reorganizations often miscarry because of a simple failure to allow for the dynamics of change. In adopting a new structure, some managements are inclined to assume that the company has achieved its ideal, ultimate form. Actually, the history of any successful enterprise will demonstrate that organization structures can never be permanent. No matter how well-designed its present organization, alterations in a company's human resources, size, geographical scope, environment, or mission can make changes in its structure not only desirable but necessary.

This coin of dynamic evolution has another side—radical changes in organization do tax the momentum and continuity of business. For this reason a prudent phasing of change in a sequence of evolutionary steps, possibly over several years' time, will sometimes be the only way to realize fully the benefits promised by a different organization structure.

A number of years ago, one petroleum company began a succession of organizational moves to form the present structure for its international operations. First the president announced a regional approach to the management of its overseas operations. After two years, the regional management units were moved abroad to place them closer to affiliate operations. Finally, four years later, after several years of intensive and successful work by regional staffs to upgrade affiliate performance, certain regions were organizationally consolidated to simplify the structure.

But for every company that times its moves so carefully, there may be three that reap disillusion by trying to reach ambitious organizational goals overnight.

4. STRUCTURE INCONSISTENT WITH PHILOSOPHY. Still another source of trouble afflicting many organization changes of recent years has been the lack of attention devoted to coordinating the organization structure and the company's philosophy of management. Ideally, structure and philosophy should be mutually reinforcing. At the very least, they must be compatible.

Where they turn out to be in conflict, only frustration can result. Consider an enterprise structured in profit-accountable divisions whose chief executive retains authority on even low-level management appointments. Or an organization with a newly-established international division but still entirely dominated by domestic thinking. Or a company whose top management constantly preaches loyalty to the corporate interest while erecting impregnable organizational walls between functional departments. In all such situations, with philosophy and structure at odds, performance will inevitably suffer.

5. POOR IMPLEMENTATION. A final inadequacy has inhibited the effectiveness of many reorganizations: a lack of respect for the difficulties of implementing change. In some companies I have observed, top management almost seems to have assumed that switching formal reporting relationships—or adding, deleting, and rearranging boxes on the organization chart—would automatically change individual behavior overnight. In reality, established managerial habits usually tend to persist despite new organization charts.

Where organization change has successfully improved company performance, it is a safe bet that considerable thought has been given to the steps involved in creating the new structure—announcing the changes, realigning executive personnel, timing the various moves, and securing the participation of those affected as a means of building understanding, acceptance, and commitment.

Thus, one of the world's largest corporations, embarking on a massive reorganization in the early 1960s, assigned to eight executives the task of working out detailed schedules and explaining the objectives and concepts underlying the new arrangements to the rest of the organization. So that they could do the job properly, these eight top managers were relieved of their regular assignments for six months. Implementation was thorough, and the reorganization "took" with exemplary effect.

Key inputs

Against this background of organizational changes that often fail to achieve promised results, I propose to outline a practical (and proven) approach to the determination of the right structure for any business organization—whether it be an entire enterprise or a department or division.

The best organization structure for a given enterprise is uniquely determined by four different inputs: (1) the requirements for competitive success in the business, (2) the objectives and plans of the enterprise, (3) the "givens" of the present situation, and (4) tested organization theory.

SUCCESS REQUIREMENTS. Alfred P. Sloan, Jr., wrote, "Every enterprise needs a concept of its industry. There is a logical way of doing business in accordance with the facts and circumstances of an industry, if you can figure it out."[1] Careful analysis of the "facts and circumstances" of an industry will often be needed to identify the basic requirements for success—namely, those few things that management must do exceedingly well if the company is to prosper. Some of these requirements are apparent:

¶ In auto making, the maintenance of a strong dealer organization, skillful, well-coordinated model year planning, and effective manufacturing cost control to keep the break-even point low.

¶ In petroleum, well-integrated planning of investment expenditures, and astute management of the logistics network that moves oil from wellhead to the ultimate customer of refined products.

¶ In the soap and detergent business, creative new-product development, effective advertising and promotion, and a sound trade relations program.

But in most instances, not all the success requirements of a company will be as obvious as the examples above. In order to be able to identify and define them with precision, the analyst must evaluate products, markets, and marketing requirements; he must understand the manufacturing processes and the role of technology; he must learn the economics of the business in terms of the behavior of costs, prices, margin levels, capital requirements, and the like; he must appraise environmental forces, including the competitive picture; and he must identify the critical decision-making functions.

Whether the success requirements of a particular business are obvious or elusive, their implications for organization structure can be easy to overlook. This is why they should be defined by formal analysis.

Considered in this light, the success requirements provide insights into

---

[1] *My Years With General Motors*, edited by John McDonald with Catherine Stevens (Garden City, New York, Doubleday & Company, Inc., 1954), p. 58.

important aspects of a company's structure: (1) the soundness of the basic organizational arrangement, (2) the specific activities that must be carried on, and (3) the relative prominence of these activities.

To begin with, success requirements will usually help to define the most effective organization pattern for the company—whether it should be structured along functional, product, or geographic lines, or patterned on some other concept. Thus:

¶ Two important forestry products companies merged. At the time of the merger each had a basically functional organization structure. Promptly the new enterprise began to exhibit some classic symptoms of organizational malfunction—sluggishness in getting new products to market, inertia in the face of new profit opportunities, and a gradual decline in return on investment. Analysis showed that the company was really involved in four separate businesses: logging, wood products, pulp and paper, and packaging. Each of these had its own success requirements, and they were by no means wholly compatible. The company found it advisable to reorganize into four divisions, with two set up on a functional and two on a geographic pattern.

¶ A functionally structured cement company decided that the importance of transportation economics and local market contacts demanded a region-by-region approach to the business. The company restructured itself into geographic divisions with local accountability. Its return on investment has already improved markedly in the two years since the shift.

Few businesses fail to give due organizational prominence to such basic functions as manufacturing, marketing, and finance. But without a clear definition of success factors, certain key activities can easily be overlooked in the organization structure. Thus:

¶ One of the truly critical factors in the performance of a food chain is pricing; no other variable has a greater impact on profitability. One major chain discovered that it had in effect no real pricing function because the activity was fragmented among dozens of people in the organization. In the course of an organizational overhaul, each geographic division established a two-man pricing staff to analyze competitors' price strategies, to suggest different approaches to pricing (including store displays and feature advertising), and to work with stores in troubled trading areas where competitors' prices were especially low.

¶ A study of success requirements for an international farm equipment company showed that new-product development was pivotal: It provided the basis for keeping franchised dealers healthy and permitted premium prices by keeping products out of the "me-too" category. Accordingly, the company, whose lead time to bring new models to market had been dangerously long, set up special organization arrangements designed to ensure that the new-product function was really doing its job. Activities that had been informally coordinated among sales, manufacturing, engineering, and research were made the responsibility of a corporate new-product development staff. Already, the lead time has been sharply cut.

Clearly defined success requirements also shed light on the relative prominence of key activities. One sometimes hears it said, in connection with a particular company: "That's an old-line manufacturing business," or "To get ahead in XYZ you really have to come up the sales route." Often a study will reveal that these functional emphases, historical in origin and perpetuated by habit, are now in conflict with today's realities.

Thus, many airlines have come to consider passenger service as paramount in distinguishing a line and, hence, in building revenues. They reason that, since government regulation has equalized prices and made most routes competitive, a customer's selection will usually be based on the quality of reservation service, baggage handling, food service, equipment cleanliness, stewardess service, and so on—functions that have historically been buried deep in other departments. Some lines have therefore consolidated all of these functions into a single passenger service department, under the direction of a senior executive, in order to give them new cohesion and importance.

Again, oil companies have long had supply and distribution departments. But some companies, recognizing the logistics function as crucial for profits, have upgraded S & D—once a clerically staffed expediting and balancing group—to a far more important, professionally managed coordinating agency for the company's entire physical distribution operation. Its mission is to create the best possible overall logistics system and to prevent the suboptimization of profits in individual segments of the system.

In both of these examples, analysis of success requirements gave new organizational prominence to already established activities—with rewarding results.

OBJECTIVES AND PLANS. Although their importance would appear self-evident, the objectives and plans of the enterprise have been completely ignored in many reorganizations—perhaps because of the temptation to regard organization structure as an end in itself rather than as a tool.

Every company has been organized to achieve a particular goal. Structure is designed as a means to this end, and changed ends often call for changed means. Thus, companies that formulate new objectives will often find that supporting organizational moves are needed.

For example, a chemical coatings company, ambitious to enter new fields, recently established a commercial development function as a first step. This department, free from day-to-day operating responsibilities, is a careful blend of individuals with technical and marketing skills. Its mission: to identify promising market opportunities and decide what arrangement—self-development, licensing, acquisition, or some other—will be the best means of building the required technology. This unit will manage fledgling new ventures until they can be turned over to the stewardship of a division or be set up on their own.

A diversified machinery company in the Midwest decided to push aggressively into international markets, particularly in Europe. Its export division, selling modest amounts of equipment produced in the United States by over a dozen divisions of the corporation, would have impeded rather than facilitated direct manufacturing investments and intensified marketing activities on the Continent. Accordingly, the company developed a regional organization for Europe with a carefully defined role vis-à-vis the domestic product divisions. At a later stage, this company plans to dismantle its strong regional staff and give its product divisions worldwide responsibility.

Again, General Foods determined several years ago to greatly strengthen its trade franchise. The company adopted a new organizational concept. It consolidated the physical distribution and order-taking activities of all its product divisions into a single distribution sales service division. This move has greatly facilitated the attainment of General Foods' trade franchise objectives.

Analysis of a company's success requirements and its objectives and plans will usually permit the *ideal* structure to be defined with some confidence. But the *ideal* structure and the *right* structure are only rarely one and the same. To bridge the gap between them, another critical input must be taken into account.

RANGE OF "GIVENS." This key input includes the entire range of "givens" that add up to the enterprise's current situation. The givens that will influence organization design are (1) the company's structure, (2) style of leadership, (3) managerial processes, and (4) manpower resources. Together, they define the position from which any changes must begin. Any or all of them may call for modifying the *ideal* structure into some different form more feasible to attain and more likely to be successful.

Is the current organizational structure clearly defined? How well do top and middle management understand it? How closely has it been adhered to? It will not be unusual to find one structure documented on a chart, while a shadow organization—consisting of quite a different set of informal relationships—actually operates in practice. The existence of such shadow organizations must be recognized in planning and designing any reorganization. In some instances they must be neutralized; in others, it will be possible to capitalize on them.

Every chief executive projects a style of leadership to his organization. This style or way of operating, often reinforced by other members of the top-management group, becomes one component of a company's management philosophy. It reveals itself in personal characteristics—assertiveness or reserve, conservatism or flamboyance, and so on—that others in the company tend to emulate. It also appears in the way a chief executive manages: his concept of staff work, his view of risk-taking, approach to decisions, feelings about planning, and so forth. These often intangible factors can greatly influence the design of the right structure for an organization. Ideally, the leadership style and the organization structure should effectively reinforce each other.

By what sort of managerial processes has the company been directed? How plans have been developed, budgets created, decisions made, control effected, and performance appraised—all must be considered in developing the right structure for a company.

Often, executive behavior can be modified faster, more easily, and more productively by changing the processes rather than the organization structure. Thus, an organization study of the headquarters staff of an international rubber company suggested that new approaches to planning and control were much more likely than structural changes to achieve the desired results—namely, greater profit contribution from the corporate staffs to the operating units. A careful review and overhaul of the company's planning and control mechanisms led to significantly improved performance while preserving the existing structure intact.

In contrast, a change in structure may be designed primarily to strengthen a management process. Thus, another international organization, a multiproduct chemical company, sought to accelerate management development—one of its most basic needs—by improving performance evaluation. Problems of shared responsibilities and ambiguous authority arising from the previous functional setup were largely eliminated by moving to a product division setup and giving general managers genuine profit accountability.

What about the company's manpower resources? The quality, depth, and age and experience distribution of management personnel must also be evaluated in defining the right organization structure. Changes geared to capitalize on an individual's talents may be appropriate. In a number of companies, organization changes have been planned over a period of three to five years, matching the structural shifts to the current state of executive resources.

For example, a multibillion-dollar company wanted to separate top-level policy making from its day-to-day administration, but found it could not do so because of a shortage of senior executive talent. After rejecting the possibility of outside recruiting, the chairman and the president decided they would have to share both roles until three group vice presidents could be developed within the company. Four years later, the shift was successfully made, and operations assigned to the group vice presidents.

Another company, having decided to move from a functional to a regional structure, discovered that it would need seven strong general managers to assume a significant degree of delegated authority. Since they were not available, the company sensibly conserved its limited talent for a number of years by retaining its functional structure, meanwhile developing some younger executives. It has now successfully regionalized its operations.

TESTED THEORY. Once the right structure has been clearly defined, principles of organization can usefully be applied. As suggested earlier, the word "principles" can easily be misunderstood. Far from being provable laws with universal applicability, they constitute no more than a set of ground rules distilled from experience.

Among the most unassailable is the general rule that authority and responsibility should go together. One without the other often leads to confusion and friction in organizational relationships. Yet were it not for challenges to this principle two of today's most successfully applied organization concepts would never have evolved.

The *product* manager in a consumer package goods company has substantial responsibility, but usually little outright authority. He must secure the success of his product in terms of market share and profit contribution. But he lacks decision-making power over the activities of several essential contributors to this success—the sales force, manufacturing plants, physical distribution operations, and so forth.

In contrast, the *project* manager, most commonly found in aerospace and construction companies, possesses specifically delegated authority—often without commensurate responsibility.[2] He will not be responsible for the engineering of a new system or plant; even so, in order to keep his project on schedule or under estimate, he frequently makes unilateral decisions that can have a profound impact on engineering soundness.

Both of these concepts violate the letter of a supposedly inviolable principle.

But my point is not that the principles of organization must be put down as worthless. Rather they ought to be challenged, applied with discretion, and never used to build the "permanent" foundation of an organization. In too many companies I have seen them used in an overly authoritative manner to scrutinize the established organization for supposedly improper structural arrangements and to rationalize proposed changes—an approach that tends to result in a rigid, oversimplified, and bureaucratic structure ill-suited to the complexity of the enterprise or its real business needs. Yet, turning this around, I have seen the principles used in a number of highly successful reorganizations simply to check out contemplated organization changes for common-sense defects.

[2] See Section VII, Chapter 3.

In short, the more pragmatic approach I am describing first builds the theoretical basis of the organization structure on an analysis of success requirements, objectives, and plans, tempered by allowance for present conditions. Then the resulting structure is reviewed in the light of accepted organization principles. Where the structure is at odds with the principles, the reasoning behind the structure should be reexamined for possible weaknesses. Where weaknesses are discovered, the structural arrangement will be reconsidered; where none are found, it will, of course, be allowed to stand.

Management philosophy

The approach to organization problems described thus far has been tied to an important complementary idea: No change in organization structure should be implemented until its consonance, or lack of consonance, with the enterprises's management philosophy has been evaluated.

A division manager I talked with recently put it more pungently. "The form and substance of this corporation are out of whack," he said. "On the surface, you'd think we had autonomous product divisions. But the way the man upstairs wants to run things, our divisionalized setup is a fiction."

If organization structures are designed to guide individuals and groups in an enterprise toward doing things in a certain way, then we should make sure that other points of influence on behavior are not defeating the purpose of the structure. Whether tacit or explicit, a philosophy of management can be just as strong an influence as the organization structure itself.

By management philosophy, I mean the beliefs, attitudes, values, and supporting actions that condition the way in which an enterprise is run. It comprises attitudes and values relating to such matters as these;

Location of decision-making authority. Has the company been committed to a GE-like concept of decentralization, or is authority tightly held at the top?

Individual vs. group action. Are decisions "syndicated"? In particular, do committee arrangements dominate? Or has personal accountability been considered all-important?

Volume vs. profit. What has been the fundamental measure of accomplishment in the company? Sheer size? Return on investment, *à la* Du-Pont? Or earnings per share? Indian Head Mills leaves no doubt on this score. In one of its annual reports, the company's chief executive wrote: "The principal objective of the directors and management of Indian Head Mills is to increase the intrinsic value of the company's common stock. To do this requires expansion of operating power per common share."

Character of personnel policies. Are managers ever recruited from outside? What have been the criteria for promotion? Is incentive compensation employed? Does seniority outweigh ability? Is the basic personnel philosophy one of paternalism, toughness, or something in between?

Holding company vs. operating company. Have the company's departments, divisions, subsidiaries, and affiliates been regarded simply as investments, or are they tightly managed and controlled in the interest of the total corporation?

Executive leadership. What about the prevailing managerial style? How assertive, autocratic, dominant is it? How passive, democratic, supportive?

Facts vs. intuition. How do facts stack up against executive "judgment" and "experience" when major decisions are at stake?

Free wheeling vs. formality. Are original thinkers and mavericks encouraged or repressed? Has the atmosphere been charged with easygoing permissiveness or made heavy with protocol? Do people say what the boss wants to hear or what they think?

A company's philosophy inevitably exerts a powerful influence on organization. It generally evolves over many years. Reflecting the personal convictions of top management, it will not be subject to ready modification. But even if its basic nature remains essentially the same over a long period, some of its peripheral characteristics can be changed. On occasion the success requirements of the business may call for a readjustment in some elements of the philosophy, just as they may dictate a modification in structure.

For example, the company involved in several different businesses will not only have to structure itself into product divisions but will also have to adopt a philosophy of decentralized decision making. Again, the company in an industry with rapidly changing technology cannot safely give precedence to seniority if its veteran executives fail to keep pace with technical advances.

Mutual adjustment of corporate philosophy and organization structure appears to be a hallmark of the most successful reorganizations. Without it the impact of structural changes on managers' behavior may be negligible. In contrast, a company whose philosophy and organization structure turn out to be mutually reinforcing possesses a powerful means for effecting constructive change.

8. Organizing a worldwide business

Gilbert H. Clee and Wilbur M. Sachtjen

Over the last ten years, growing numbers of major companies in the United States and around the world have committed themselves to full-scale, long-term participation in the intense and sophisticated rivalry of global enterprise. Increasingly, the tempo and character of international competition are being determined by management decisions in a growing group of true world enterprises. Headquartered in London, Brussels, Tokyo, or New York, these companies no longer plan their strategy in the manner of domestic companies with interests abroad. Instead, they apply their corporate resources on a global scale to exploit growth and profit opportunities wherever they may be found in the world.

In undertaking the commitment to world enterprise, businessmen have found themselves confronting a whole new range of problems. If managing a domestic business is complex, managing an international enterprise will be infinitely more so because of the many new variables bearing on crucial management decisions. Consequently, organizational structures and relationships that may have worked smoothly for an export-oriented domestic company soon show signs of strain when management begins to wrestle with problems like these:

¶ What kind of relationship should we establish between domestic and foreign operations to enable the more experienced domestic companies to give effective technical and functional guidance to the less advanced overseas subsidiaries? What incentive can we offer the domestic companies to provide this guidance, particularly if we lack majority control?

¶ What position should we take with respect to local ownership participation? Do we need the tight control that only 100 percent or majority ownership will provide? Or can we operate successfully as a minority partner when and where this is the only way to achieve our objective?

¶ How do we develop a flow of managerial manpower with the background, technical capability, and breadth of perspective to function effectively in different national environments?

¶ How do we develop a system for planning and control that will (1) coordinate objectives, strategies, and action programs for all worldwide activities, and (2) provide an information flow to keep key executives informed about our progress?

At the outset, it should be noted that no two world enterprises pass through the same organizational stages in the same way. No two arrive at precisely the same organizational pattern. Nor should they. Companies and circumstances both differ.

Among the major U.S. companies committed to investment abroad, three basic organizational structures have evolved in response to growing pressures, and enough experience has now been accumulated to permit some meaningful evaluation of them. Each of the structural patterns— subject, of course, to many variations and modifications—has its own distinctive rationale. Each offers advantages for companies in particular situations and at particular stages in their transition to world enterprise.

These basic organizational patterns are:

1. Variants of the traditional *international division* structure, all displaying a shift of responsibility for policy and worldwide strategic planning to the corporate level.

2. The *geographic* structure, replacing the international division with line managers at the top-management level who bear full operating responsibility for subsidiaries in assigned geographic areas.

3. The *product* structure, replacing the international division with executives at the top-management level who bear worldwide responsibility for development of individual product groups.

International division structure

In some companies, responsibility for broad policy and strategic planning of overseas operations—once in the hands of an international division or actually carried out by affiliates acting independently—has shifted to executives at the corporate level without significant change in the formal structure. Operational responsibilities, such as running the overseas plants and developing markets in individual foreign countries, continue to be handled by the subsidiaries and affiliates, with corporate or international division assistance given as required. The international division headquarters may continue to coordinate export sales from the U.S. operation to foreign affiliates and export markets. But it may also function as a coordinating "middleman" between production facilities anywhere in the world and the corporation's complex of worldwide markets.

The Alpha Corporation,[1] a giant automobile manufacturer, approached the problems of managing a world enterprise without any major departure

[1] Throughout this article, fictitious names have been assigned to the companies whose organizational structures are discussed. Otherwise, no facts have been altered.

80

from the international division structure. But within that framework its managerial setup underwent important shifts over the years.

During the lifetime of Alpha's founder, its foreign affiliates were handled more in the fashion of personal investments than as extensions of the U.S. operation. To be sure, the founder and a few corporate officers maintained close contact with the foreign affiliates. But in practice—beginning in the late 1920s, when they were given control of foreign sales and assembly— the two big foreign manufacturing affiliates had been making virtually all the key decisions regarding overseas activities.

In 1948, three years after taking command of the company, Alpha's new chief executive turned his attention to international opportunities and problems. Aware that a potentially huge car and truck market was almost certain to emerge in postwar Europe, he realized that this market could never be won with high-cost U.S. and Canadian output. To wage an effective competitive battle, European production bases would be required. And this, he reasoned, meant tighter operating control over the big foreign manufacturing affiliates, which were hardly prepared to exploit in an effective, coordinated way the massive opportunities that would soon be developing.

For more than 20 years, these two subsidiaries had been virtually auto- nomous companies with strongly entrenched local managements, exercising ownership control over all the other foreign affiliates. But the new chief executive made it clear that he wanted ownership control of *all* foreign activities to rest in the United States, with broad policy and strategic planning for the international activities emanating from a single U.S. office.

Therefore, in addition to supplying the foreign affiliates with technical and management skills to help them recover from the havoc of World War II, corporate headquarters began increasingly to assume control of key management decisions for these foreign operations.

Two years before corporate headquarters "reached out" for control of the foreign affiliates, an international division had been set up in New York to channel and coordinate the dealings between the domestic corporation and its foreign companies. From 1948 on, however, decisions on policy and strategic planning for the overseas operations were in- creasingly made directly by top corporate management. Responsibilities of the international division were mainly confined to coordinating overseas activities, providing advice and assistance to its foreign companies, developing markets in individual countries, and channeling output from producing affiliates to distributors in areas without assembly facilities.

Practically speaking, Alpha continues to be a domestically oriented company. The most urgent pressures and preoccupations of corporate headquarters executives involve meeting competition on the domestic front, not overseas. And Alpha's foreign expansion plans are also heavily influenced by the international strategy of its most powerful domestic competitor. Moreover, there has been a discernible tendency to fill key positions in the international division with seasoned domestic managers.

Meanwhile, the overseas activities are being carried on within an increasingly apparent framework of corporate policy and strategy. Corporate headquarters exercises fairly strong worldwide control over all products and planning, and the individual foreign units are functioning much more like operating entities than like the autonomous companies they were in the past. Under this arrangement, the international division has responsibility for running the overseas plants, determining minor product modifications from country to country, and increasing penetration in individual markets. At the same time, though, the overseas operating units retain considerable flexibility. A manager responsible for sales development in a particular market, for example, is free to explore the opportunities for obtaining vehicles from plants outside his area more economically.

Another example of the long-time use of the international division pattern in an important world enterprise is Beta, Inc., a large manufacturer of computers and other business machines. Beta's top management has always devoted a great deal of attention to worldwide problems and opportunities. For many years, the overseas activities have been grouped together in a separate corporation, quite apart from Beta's domestic divisions. Historically, this international corporation has operated with considerable autonomy, though most major product-development activity has emanated from the U.S. divisions.

Unlike Beta's domestic operations, which are laid out along product and functional lines, the operations of the international corporation have been organized on a geographic basis. The range of products sold by any one geographic unit in the international corporation is limited only by the local markets' state of development and by local import policies. Some of Beta's foreign units have manufacturing facilities to turn out part of the product line, but they depend on the domestic manufacturing operations for items not in heavy demand overseas.

As Beta's international operations have expanded—in many areas reaching a level of development comparable to that of its domestic divisions—management has felt a growing need for worldwide policy determination, for effective global product strategy, and for the development of better ways to meet the needs of individual users on a worldwide basis. In response, the corporate staff, which has long had worldwide functional responsibilities, now devotes an increasing share of its time and effort to overseas activities.

How can a company such as Alpha alter long-standing management decision-making patterns for its foreign operations so thoroughly without

82

making major changes in its basic organizational pattern? Why has Beta's management continued to favor the international division form—while setting worldwide policy and controlling the approval of worldwide operating plans at the corporate level? And why do other companies as deeply committed in worldwide activities as these two sometimes prefer to retain the international division form?

Analysis indicates that their preference may be based on one or more of five reasons:

1. Formal organizational changes sometimes threaten to disrupt delicate working relationships. This will be true particularly in long-established overseas subsidiaries under strong, well-entrenched local managements accustomed to running their operations without interference. In this situation, it may be desirable to avoid major organizational realignments while seeking closer coordination between domestic and overseas activities or strengthening corporate control of worldwide policy and strategy. The same considerations are likely to apply where the parent company lacks majority control.

2. Top management may believe that the foreign activities will receive better direction with an international division than with some other organizational form. Under an international division pattern, the overseas operations (particularly individual subsidiaries) can benefit from extra management attention, which may be needed in the early stages of developing a particular line of business abroad. Later on, a different organizational structure may prove more appropriate.

Where the domestic operations are many times larger than those overseas and where corporate management finds it difficult to persuade a diverse group of domestic divisions to devote adequate attention to their overseas counterparts, the international division form has a good deal of merit. Multiple-product-line companies have the option of organizing the international division on a product—rather than a geographic—basis, thereby encouraging a closer liaison with domestic divisions.

The international division recommends itself with special force when broad-scale international activities are relatively new to a company and when most members of senior operating management lack experience with worldwide problems. Later, as overseas interests become more important to the company and top management gains assurance in handling global problems, a shift in the organizational pattern may become desirable.

3. Because top management views domestic performance as the primary measure of success, the company's key executives may be domestically oriented even though they participate in policy and strategy formulation for the overseas activities. As long as it achieves tight and effective financial control, top management generally has little inclination to tamper with the existing organizational framework.

4. The company may have worked out special ways—peculiar to its own situation—of deriving the key benefits from another organizational pattern without relinquishing the international division form. If so, it has no compelling motive to make a purely structural realignment.

5. Finally, the company may not have enough trained, capable executive personnel to staff a truly worldwide organization effectively.

The international division form can become troublesome when a company's overseas activities shift significantly from primary emphasis on "exporting" to development of a network of "subsidiary" operations at many points on the globe. Under these circumstances, too strong an international division can hamper corporate direction of worldwide activities. Ironically, the more independent an international division becomes, the more it tends to insulate corporate management from overseas problems and opportunities.

For a worldwide company with a reasonably diverse product line, the international division form may impede management's efforts to mobilize the resources of the total company toward accomplishing global objectives. Even with superb coordination at the corporate level, global planning for individual products or product lines is carried out at best awkwardly by two "semiautonomous" organizations—the domestic company and the international division. To add a series of country (or area) managements makes the problem still more difficult.

Geographic structure

The second basic organizational form that has emerged as companies evolve toward functioning world enterprises is the geographic structure. This assigns operational responsibility for geographic areas of the world to line managers, with corporate headquarters retaining authority for worldwide strategic planning and control. (Strategic planning, in this context, includes such critical decisions as what businesses to engage in, the nature of the basic product line, and the location of major facilities. Adaptation of the basic product to meet local needs is, in contrast, an area activity.)

In the geographic form of organization, which has replaced the international division form today in many companies—both single-product-line and multiple-product-line—the home country has become simply one of a number of world markets. Producing and selling operations are grouped into geographic units. Sometimes the make-and-sell operations in a particular geographic unit are self-contained, with most or all of the company's output in a given area sold locally. Then again, there may be a substantial flow of semifinished parts or fully assembled units from one area to another.

In the geographic form, responsibility for all products in a particular area will be assigned to a single line executive who reports to corporate management. Policy, strategic and logistic planning, and major product development are handled at the corporate level.

Three examples will serve to illustrate the emergence of the geographic structure in varying circumstances.

The geographic form has been commonly used by companies with relatively homogeneous product lines—such as pharmaceuticals, farm implements, soft drinks, home appliances, or packaged food products—sold in similar end-use markets around the world.

Some years ago Gamma, Ltd., a huge international farm equipment manufacturer whose operations had been organized along regional lines, adopted an organizational structure built around a series of largely self-contained marketing and manufacturing *operations* units. This grouping is not regional; that is, not divided into broad areas (North America, Latin America, or Europe). Rather, it centers on important individual markets (the United Kingdom, France, Germany, the United States, and Canada). Supplementing these operations units, an *export marketing* group takes charge of sales in parts of the world where Gamma has no manufacturing operations.

Longer range corporate strategy—determination of the basic worldwide product line, decisions on major facilities, and changes in the logistic product flow from production sources to markets—is set at corporate headquarters. But these decisions are heavily influenced by operations unit judgments and recommendations. Each unit assumes responsibility for determining the product lines best suited to its local markets. Besides directing the logistic flow of components and completed machines between countries, corporate-level executives coordinate the operations unit product planning. They also make strategic decisions on the nature of basic Gamma product development. Then managers at the local level carry out the engineering and product development modifications needed to meet market requirements.

Less commonly, the geographic form has also been used by organizations with reasonably diverse product lines. One example is the Delta Company, a widely diversified manufacturing and services organization, which utilizes a distinctive regional organizational pattern. Four area managers (North America; Latin America; Europe/Middle East/Africa; and Far East/Pacific) have full responsibility for day-to-day operations of all Delta units within their geographical assignments. Regional offices for both North American and Latin American operations are located in New York; for Europe, in Brussels; and for the Far East, in Hong Kong. Individual country organizations in more than 30 nations report to these regional headquarters.

Since, for decades, much of its activity had been carried on overseas,

Delta was able to move into the area form with unusual speed. Some years ago, foreign operating companies, previously more or less autonomous, were drawn together for tighter control and closer coordination. Corporate headquarters quickly took on ultimate responsibility for long-range worldwide strategic planning, and began to exert much tighter direction over the foreign companies. Now both short-and long-range plans are developed locally, reviewed at the area manager level, then submitted to corporate management for review and approval. Thus, although planning clearly reflects local needs and requirements, corporate headquarters can closely control capital investment and make other strategic decisions.

The Delta Company has a special need for local identification in some of its operating fields. Much of its manufacturing output goes to local governments and telephone companies. For this reason, Delta's individual country organizations must try to avoid the appearance of foreign control. Moreover, their products must be adapted to meet varying local requirements and specifications. Its area/country type of geographic organization has proven well-suited for this purpose, enabling Delta to fit its sales efforts and product specifications closely to local market needs.

Another kind of business enterprise employing the geographic concept has been the international oil company. Key decisions on concessions, refinery scheduling, and tanker fleet management are logically made on a centralized basis, with geographic units operating within that framework. Worldwide exploration has been essentially a corporate activity, as are major investment decisions such as building new refineries and pipelines. Moreover, the supply and distribution function—which works out the worldwide logistic flow of crude to an international complex of refineries, terminals, and markets—can be carried out effectively only on a centralized basis.

Understandably, in different oil companies the geographic structure takes varying forms. In one, for example, the area manager exercises true line responsibility for operations in his geographic area. In another, the area manager functions essentially as a coordinator, with instructions emanating from strong functional departments at corporate headquarters. But despite such variations the formal division by geographic areas has been a common organizational feature.

Companies successfully employing the geographic organizational structure seem to share two significant characteristics:

1. The great bulk of sales revenue is derived from similar end-use markets.

2. Local marketing requirements are critical.

The geographic organizational form has been well suited to coping with these problems, since variations from market to market in a centrally developed basic product can be dealt with at close range. Normally, such adjustments require only modest technological skills that can easily be provided at the area level or below. When greater skills are needed, they can be supplied from corporate headquarters.

The geographic pattern also works well when the product is highly standardized but techniques for penetrating local markets differ. For example: A major soft-drink maker ended the separation of its international and domestic operations, placing worldwide direction of marketing, finance, and research at the corporate level. To strengthen their contact with corporate management, the overseas operations were organized into geographic divisions. Each division is headed by an experienced area manager located at corporate headquarters.

The tasks of coordinating product variations, transferring new ideas and techniques from one country to another, and achieving the best possible logistic flow of product from source to worldwide markets frequently prove difficult for companies using the geographic organizational form. This is particularly true of those marketing a line of many diverse products.

One organizational response, though by no means a universally satisfactory one, has been to create a unique type of product manager at the corporate level. This executive is assigned worldwide responsibilities for particular products or product lines. He follows the progress of his assigned products everywhere in the world, acting as an "exchange desk" to transfer successful developments from area to area and recommending worldwide strategy for individual products with respect to broad markets and basic design changes. Under this arrangement the corporate product manager's purpose in the organizational structure is easy to describe; in actual practice, however, his operating relationships with line area managers have frequently proven to be ambiguous.

Product structure

The third basic organizational pattern, more recent in origin than the other two, assigns worldwide responsibility to product group executives at the top management level. Under this structure, all product activity in a given geographic area is coordinated through area specialists at the corporate staff level.

Overall goals and strategies for the enterprise as a whole and for each product group are set at corporate headquarters. Within these corporate guidelines, strategic plans are drawn up by the product group executives for review and approval by top management. Each product group, therefore, has primary responsibility for planning and controlling all activities for its products on a worldwide basis. Staff officers at the corporate level provide functional guidance (financial, legal, technical, and so on) to the worldwide product organizations.

This pattern may be found at Epsilon, Inc., whose diverse product line includes man-made fibers, organic intermediates, and plastic resins. By no means a stranger to international operations, Epsilon established operations in Mexico in the mid-1940s and in Canada in the late 1940s and early 1950s. With substantial foreign business, ambitious plans for further international activities, and a diverse, technologically complex product line, Epsilon soon outgrew the capabilities of its existing organizational pattern and sought a more appropriate form.

The geographic structure offered no real advantages. Practically all of Epsilon's foreign operations were in the Western hemisphere. Its products drew on a wide range of complex technologies and went into many different end-use markets. These complexities, top management believed, would seriously overtax either the geographic pattern or an international division form of organization.

The product form promised to be a more appealing alternative. Most importantly, Epsilon had a group of relatively strong domestic operating companies, each one capable of providing essential technological and marketing leadership to present and future affiliates. To be sure, there were reasons to hesitate:

¶ First, the big domestic divisions had historically maintained relatively little contact with their foreign counterparts. Hence, most of the executives who would be logical choices to assume worldwide product responsibility had acquired only modest experience with foreign operations and problems.

¶ Second, Epsilon's ambitious expansion program had already begun to tax the executive group, and it was not certain whether under the product form the international activities would receive the attention they would require.

But since the promise of the product organizational form clearly outweighed these considerations, Epsilon decided to adopt the new pattern.

The transition was eased by establishing an export sales organization to operate in markets where the parent company had no production facilities. At the outset, Epsilon set up export sales as a strong operating unit, since the various world product groups lacked much international orientation and needed a good deal of assistance. But as soon as individual managers in the operating divisions acquired experience, responsibility for export sales was to be transferred to the appropriate product group. In effect, export sales would function as a "wasting" international division.

Since Epsilon's large and diversified domestic operations overshadow those of their foreign counterparts, the new group organizations have been built around the domestic companies. At the heart of each worldwide group is the domestic operation. The group executive serves as the principal communication link between the corporate operations committee (Epsilon's top decision-making body) and the individual foreign subsidiaries and affiliates within his product group. Each product group has an international vice president who acts as a deputy with as much responsibility for managing the group's foreign operations as his management group chooses to assign. Functional and technical advice is provided by appropriate staff at the domestic operating company level or the corporate level.

To coordinate the various product-group activities in major world markets, Epsilon has set up area managers at the corporate staff level. Each is responsible for keeping corporate management and the product groups informed about economic, political, and social developments in his assigned geographic area. He is also responsible for identifying potential investment opportunities in his area, and for stimulating and assisting strategic planning by both corporate and product-group management. He is also charged with developing an *area* plan for all Epsilon's products in a given geographic area to complement the worldwide product planning of the groups. But, as is the case with the worldwide product manager function within the geographic structure, this area responsibility within the product form has often proved easier to describe than to put into effective operation.

A number of international oil companies active in the petrochemical business have adopted another form of the basic product organizational pattern. This consists of two worldwide groups—one petroleum and one chemical—operating with considerable autonomy under top corporate management. In one such company, petroleum operations have been organized geographically, with all strategic and logistic decisions controlled at the corporate level. Contrastingly, its chemical operations have generally been divided into worldwide product groups.

A large non-U.S. electrical equipment manufacturer, Zeta, Ltd., one of the oldest world enterprises, has evolved a unique kind of product organizational structure, embodying some features of the geographic form.

Each of Zeta's so-called product divisions is responsible for planning the development of its product line throughout the world. In short, each product division acts much as a "worldwide product manager"—thus ensuring that measures are taken to penetrate important world markets for its particular product line.

But these product groups differ from those at Epsilon in that they do *not* have worldwide operational responsibility. First, the Zeta product divisions bear manufacturing responsibility only for operations in the home country. Second, although assigned certain responsibilities for marketing on a worldwide basis—such as in export markets where no production facilities exist—the product divisions must sell their products largely through the national subsidiary companies, which have primary responsibility for planning and managing *all* of Zeta's businesses in their assigned countries. Once a subsidiary company undertakes production of an item, for example, it assumes full responsibility for marketing it as well. Thus, the product divisions, which have no line authority over the subsidiary companies, review relevant parts of the subsidiaries' operating plans—but ultimate approval of all plans rests with top corporate management.

One limitation of the geographic form is its inherent awkwardness when diversified product lines, or lines of technological complexity, must be sold to various end-use markets. In contrast, the product organization seems made to order for these situations. For instance, when:

1. *The company's product line is widely diversified and the range of products goes into a variety of end-use markets, using quite different marketing skills and distribution channels.* Bulk chemicals, for example, are sold on a specification basis to industrial users around the world, while synthetic fibers require a highly-specialized merchandising capability to reach from textile manufacturers to ultimate consumers.

2. *High shipping costs, tariffs, or other considerations dictate local manufacture of the product, and a relatively high level of technological capability is required.* Compare the technological support that is required for the local production of a new plastic with that required for the production of a standard product, such as bar soap, that can be manufactured with comparatively little difficulty.

At Epsilon, the product organization has brought foreign operations into close contact with the latest technology in every product field. The foreign management units have been tremendously stimulated by this contact and also by the knowledge that their parent organization is really alert to local problems and needs.

Perhaps the most important challenge faced by companies adopting the product organization will be the risk involved in turning worldwide product responsibility over to executives whose working experience has been largely domestic. These managers may either lack sufficient understanding of international problems or be disinclined to devote enough attention to them. Nor will the problem be confined to the corporate and product group level. It also applies to key functional managers within the domestic operating companies, who may also be called upon to exercise judgment on international problems and to provide leadership in overseas business activity.

In the multiproduct company—for which the product structure has the strongest appeal—this problem has generally been more serious than in the predominantly single-product business (automobile, oil, and others) whose top management is invariably involved to some degree in worldwide planning for the total enterprise. In the diversified company, top management cannot plan effectively for each business; instead the prime responsibility for direction must be divided into manageable assignments.

Another difficulty inherent in the product form has been one of coordinating the various product groups' moves in any given part of the world. At Epsilon, where careful provision was made for this situation, there remains the problem of developing satisfactory working relationships —and clearly drawing the lines of responsibility—between the line product group executives and the staff area managers at the corporate level.

Selecting an organizational pattern

Clearly, there can be no one "right way" to organize and manage a large-scale enterprise, particularly one whose operations are worldwide in scope. Successful companies, as we have seen, employ a variety of organizational patterns in managing world enterprises. Yet despite the myriad circumstances affecting any such decision, the choice of organizational pattern has historically been determined by a small number of key variables.

The rapidity with which an emerging world enterprise moves toward a basic organizational structure will inevitably be influenced by its past experience. A company that has operated overseas for decades—one possessing a top management experienced in dealing with worldwide problems, as well as a large cadre of executive manpower able to assume international responsibilities—will approach organizational change very differently from a company newly arrived on the international scene.

Some managements are bold, others cautious. Some make major organizational changes frequently, others only when absolutely necessary. Some set ambitious growth targets, while others move more slowly to expand.

Again, the qualities of key executives differ widely from company to company. At least over the short run, any sound organizational plan must be geared to these variations in the capabilities and personalities of these men.

Perhaps the most significant influence on basic organizational structure will or should be determined by the very nature of the business itself. Certainly a worldwide aggregation of different businesses with different end-use markets and highly technical production processes calls for a pattern quite different from that needed by a single-product world enterprise whose production process is simple and whose marketing requirements are not overly involved.

An enterprise committed to increasing its market position, or diversifying operations on a worldwide scale, can cripple organizational planning by failing to consider *future* objectives and the most desirable strategy to achieve them. Unless it does so, it may find itself with an organization well adapted to today's needs, but hopelessly unsuited to what the company will be tomorrow.

Sound forward planning will always be essential when management determines the rate of international expansion, the strategy by which it will be effected, and the organizational pattern best suited to realize its benefits.

Bringing about fundamental change in a company's basic organizational structure, even in a purely domestic operation, is no easy accomplishment. In a world enterprise, the task takes on special complexities—just as other management problems do. For this reason alone, it would be unwise to pass general judgments on the three broad organizational patterns currently dominant among emerging world enterprises. Even to categorize them as ultimate or transitional forms would presuppose a knowledge of the nature and behavior of world enterprise that we do not as yet possess.

However, one observation does apply with equal force to all the organizational patterns we have examined: *The decisive point in the transition to world enterprise has been top management's recognition that ultimate control of strategic planning and policy decisions must shift from decentralized subsidiaries or division locations to corporate headquarters.* Only in this way can a worldwide perspective be brought to bear on the interests of the entire enterprise.

How tight should that control be? How deeply should top corporate management become involved in planning for the individual businesses? This, once more, depends on the nature of the enterprise.

Below the top decision and control level, the four decisive variables just discussed—company history, management traits, the nature of business, and long-term strategy—stand as the basic determinants of corporate choice in selecting a world organizational pattern. Unfortunately, it can be easy to overlook the fact that only the latter two variables—the nature of the business and long-term strategy—have permanent validity. Indeed, many difficulties encountered by world enterprises can be traced directly to a single mistake—that of allowing the corporation to remain locked in an organizational form originally chosen in the light of company history and the current limitations of management.

Inevitably, these often appear as important constraining factors at the time when organizational change becomes necessary. The requirements they impose may at that time be entirely in harmony with the immediate objectives of the corporation. Yet trouble inevitably arises later, when new corporate objectives and external conditions begin to chafe against the rigidities of a once appropriate organizational pattern. Unless top management is keenly aware of this likelihood, it may continue to cling to the outgrown organizational form until the costs of inaction, in time and unexploited opportunities, have mounted dangerously high.

No company, once embarked on the route to world enterprise, can safely assume that its original organization form will indefinitely meet changing needs. This is why top management needs to periodically appraise its organizational structure, evaluating its compatibility with the nature of the business and with long-term corporate strategy. No top-management responsibility bears more directly on long-term effectiveness and profitability in the world enterprise.

9. New concepts in overseas investment

Peter P. Gabriel

The unprecedented flow of foreign direct investments during the last two decades has made spectacular contributions to the economic restoration of Europe and to the industrialization of many of the developing countries. Spectacular, too, have been the returns realized by the international corporations that undertook the investments. Both kinds of results have fostered the assumption that the growth of international direct capital flows will necessarily continue as long as opportunities for profitable foreign investment abound. Proponents of this view tend to dismiss the increasingly strident concern in host countries about the proliferation of foreign direct investments as an expression of narrow nationalism, political opportunism, or unfortunate ignorance of the economics of international specialization.

But if we examine the conditions a host country must satisfy if it is to continue attracting foreign investments, quite distinct limits to a country's ability to keep its doors open to the foreign investor become apparent. A few basic facts will make the point.

The most fundamental is this: A country's capacity to absorb foreign direct capital inflows will ultimately be limited by its ability to *service* that capital, in terms of current account debits (e.g., dividends) and eventual repatriation of principal. In turn, a country's ability to service the stock of foreign-owned capital will be tied to its ability to generate sufficiently large payments surpluses on other current account items. (Relying on a positive balance in the capital accounts merely puts off the day of reckoning.) This means that if any given rate of increase in the total foreign-owned capital stock is to be sustainable, the country's foreign-exchange availabilities (net of necessary imports and other foreign expenditures deemed essential) must eventually rise in step with the payout to foreign investors.

These relationships can obviously be more easily stated in the aggregate than conclusively sorted out in detail. The "current account" of a country's balance of payments has many components, and "foreign-exchange availabilities" come from many sources. And there are the well-known leads and lags in the balance-of-payments effects of foreign direct investment: Primary capital inflows are followed, before giving rise to dividend outflows, by initially high rates of earnings-reinjection (which, of course raise the host country's *future* liabilities proportionately), before giving rise to dividend outflows.

The standard arguments supporting a sanguine view of the future of conventional foreign direct investments refer to these leads and lags as well as to the effects of foreign investment on the different components of the host country's balance of payments. It is commonly assumed that these effects will, overall, be favorable. According to the argument, foreign direct investments "earn their keep" by increasing the host country's exports or reducing its needs for imports. If a given foreign investment does neither of these things, it tends at least to raise local productivity and to strengthen the host country's international competitiveness, thereby contributing indirectly, in some measure, to the country's foreign-exchange earnings.

The other side of the coin

These arguments seem perfectly true for most foreign direct investments—looked at individually. And yet, the *total* effects of rapidly rising inflows of direct capital from abroad have caused concern in many host countries—not entirely without reason. For even though foreign-owned companies may increase exports, most of their sales will be on the local market, and on these sales there can be no direct foreign-exchange offset to the foreign parent's eventual profit. Similarly, even though the foreign firm may contribute to import substitution as far as finished products are concerned, it may also *raise* imports through dependence on the foreign parent organization for components or semimanufactures. Imports may rise even more as a consequence of the otherwise positive effects of foreign direct investment on local productivity and national income. This result has been especially apparent in the less developed countries, where "marginal propensities to import" tend to be high.

Generalizations on these points appear futile. We find too much diversity in the foreign-investment experience of different countries, as well as in the "portfolio" of foreign-owned investments of any one country. But again, considering direct-investment flows in the aggregate, the overall effect on the balance of payments of recipient countries does not appear to be so favorable as generally assumed.

In an indirect but thoroughly convincing way, the U.S. foreign-investor community itself has supported this contention. Congressional hearings on the Administration's program to curb the outflow of private long-term capital saw witness after witness assert that foreign direct investment, far from *burdening* the U.S. balance of payments, in fact strengthened it. The argument was that total income from direct investments abroad was already outpacing the outflow of long-term capital; that this outflow stimulated a significant portion of current U.S. exports; that the outflow paid for only a third of new direct investments abroad (the rest being financed by re-investment of earnings and local borrowing); and that the volume of profit remittances was bound to increase steeply in the coming years. Since a U.S. surplus on the direct-investment account must be built from the deficit of other countries, one cannot logically advance the foregoing argument without at the same time seeing merit in the concern of those receiving direct capital flows over the mounting liabilities on their own balances of payments.

We may cite other limits on a country's capacity to absorb direct invest-ments from abroad. And though more difficult to quantify, they should be considered just as real and important. These limits are essentially political. Few countries can afford to be indifferent to actual or threatened control of major industries by foreigners. The fact must also be recognized that the more successful the foreign investor, and the larger his holdings become, the more insistently will local business clamor for a "piece of the action." Nor can we ignore the occasional but always well-publicized conflict between the national interests of the host country and corporate policies obeisant to a home government: for example, on the issue of whether a foreign-based subsidiary of a U.S. company should trade with Red China. More often, the conflict occurs between the national interests of the host country and the domestic interests of the foreign parent corporation—as with the issue of where to locate major research and development facilities. All of these actual or potential conflicts *limit* the continued growth of foreign direct investment, in the sense that the more foreign investment there may be in a given country, the more likely it becomes that the composite pressure from such conflicts will result in restrictive action by the host government.

For these reasons, my own view is that, in many countries, both developed and developing, the recent and current growth in direct invest-ments from abroad cannot continue indefinitely. Sooner or later it is bound to run into the economic constraints imposed by the host country's balance of payments and the political constraints imposed by local pressure groups, both private and governmental.

No diminishing returns

Now, all this would not be particularly alarming were there any reason to expect the growth rate or profitability of *individual* foreign investments to decline as the host country's *total* exposure to direct foreign investment approaches its ceiling. But we can observe absolutely no necessary, or even probable, connection between the two. If there were, individual foreign investors would by themselves cut back their commitments, and the ultimate external limits would have no practical significance for the individual firm.

In reality, these limits do have significance: They tend to motivate host governments to take restrictive actions at precisely the point when existing foreign investments are producing their largest yields and available market opportunities are calling for continued expansion. For this is the point at which profit remissions begin to rise, burdening the host country's balance of payments. It is also the point at which aroused local competitors will be likely to enlist their government's support in trying to cut in on the foreign investor's success. And it is the point at which the largest fresh inflows of direct capital from abroad are likely to be attracted, giving ostensible substance to local arguments about foreign colonization.

The restrictions and prohibitions sooner or later brought on by these developments do not usually affect all foreign investments alike. Both the restrictions on the freedom of action of current foreign investors and the prohibitions applied to new entrants will obviously discriminate most against those investments whose nature and form appear least compatible with local interests.

The notion of "compatibility with local interests" can be reduced to a single issue: control of local enterprise by foreign ownership. No country takes exception to the inflow of foreign capital as such (aside from capital movements that interfere with domestic monetary policy). Even less do countries object to the managerial and technical know-how that accompanies corporate investments from abroad. The bone of contention is not the commitment of foreign corporate resources, but the form in which this commitment is made.

Skirting the onus of ownership

This suggests the fundamental requirement that any alternative to the traditional concept of direct investment must meet if it is to escape the objections, and the restrictions, I have just mentioned: Such an alternative must not involve control through ownership by the foreign firm, with its indefinite foreign-exchange liabilities and political costs.

We may affirm this: any company that succeeds in planning and structuring a foreign commitment of its resources so as to obviate the need for ownership has thereby neutralized the essence of the economic and political constraints discussed above. At the same time, as we shall see, such a company will have put itself in a position to take advantage of potentially vast profit opportunities in areas where conventional direct investments will be clearly unworkable: the industries of the Eastern Bloc and the public sector of developing countries.

The central importance of the ownership issue has been increasingly recognized by corporate foreign investors. The growing acceptability of joint ventures with local partners reflects this recognition. A number of more novel approaches, representing (like the joint venture) at least *partial* solutions to the problem, have been tried or are being proposed.

Some corporations have attempted to reduce the onus of foreign ownership of local enterprise by giving nationals the opportunity to invest in the stock of the foreign parent company. The listing of the latter's securities on local exchanges is intended to facilitate such investment. The attractiveness of this approach, from the local standpoint, would appear somewhat doubtful. For the market price and per-share earnings of the parent company's stock reflect neither local capital-market conditions nor, more importantly, the profitability of the local subsidiary. The latter's earnings will have been averaged into the typically far lower returns on the parent's domestic operations. Moreover, in a macroeconomic sense, the offer of parent-company securities as a means of enabling local investors to "participate" in the parent's subsidiary leads to "perverse" capital movements—from places of relative scarcity to places of relative surplus—which is hardly a contribution to local economic growth. In any event, while speculative motives or personal liquidity preferences of local investors will always cause interest in foreign equities, the mere act of making such securities more readily accessible is unlikely to be accepted as a solution to the ownership issue of foreign direct investment.

The regional holding company

A more imaginative approach has been tried or considered by some U.S. firms with extensive direct investments in Europe. This approach calls for consolidating all European operations into a new parent company, based in Europe, that owns and controls all subsidiaries in the area. The new holding company then sells its shares on European exchanges. This plan has important advantages from the standpoint of local interests. Participation is much more direct than in the approach described earlier, and local capital invested in the holding company is more likely to stay "at home." But two problem areas remain. To the extent that the initiator of the holding company retains majority control (some U.S. firms considering this plan have been reported to be intent on retaining absolute control), national criticism of foreign ownership will persist. Moreover, the problem of reaching agreement with local shareholders on the "reasonableness" of management and license fees paid to the original parent can prove to be a thorny one indeed.

A third approach to the ownership issue has been tried. At the time the investment is made, the foreign corporation agrees to sell, within a specified number of years, all or part of its interests to local parties. This approach has been advocated especially in connection with investments in the developing countries. The difficulties of this plan are readily apparent. First, there will be the problem of setting a price for the equity to be transferred. Book value, whether gross or net, may well be rejected as unjust by the foreign investor on the grounds that it fails to allow for the assumption of initial risk. A multiple of earnings is just as likely to be frowned upon by potential local purchasers, who will argue that the initial earnings of the foreign investment reflect monopoly rents made possible by host-government protection against competition from abroad. Whatever the terms of the sale, there will be the additional problem of repatriating the proceeds, since the host country is apt to suffer from chronic foreign-exchange shortages.

None of these three approaches, or their many possible variants, can be called a fully satisfactory solution to the ownership problem of foreign investment. The first two leave unaltered the basic fact of foreign control; the third exacts a price for the relinquishment of ownership that represents at best an undesirable drain on local capital funds or an unrealistic burden on the balance of payments. More important still, none of these approaches can be applied to the rapidly increasing number of profit opportunities provided (a) by government-sponsored projects in the developing countries, and (b) by the searching reappraisal which the entire Eastern Bloc is undertaking of the organization and management of its economies, industries, and enterprises.

Entrepreneurship without capital

An alternative to the traditional form of direct investment that overcomes these limitations has been known as the "management contract." A considerable number of major corporations, both European and American, have already gained experience with contractual arrangements on this general pattern.

Among the most widely publicized contracts have been those signed by Fiat and Renault for the establishment and initial operation of automobile manufacturing facilities in the Soviet Union. Other major European companies, such as I.C.I., Montecatini, and Olivetti, have also entered into contracts for the supply of managerial and technical know-how to Iron Curtain countries. Significant, too, has been the formation of a partnership between the International Basic Economy Corporation (IBEC), controlled by the Rockefeller brothers, and Tower International, Inc., of Cleveland, to promote U.S. private business participation in industrial projects in Eastern Europe. Projects reportedly being undertaken or planned include the building and operation of hotels and of rubber, glass, and aluminum plants.

99

As far as management contracts in developing countries are concerned American business probably has the edge over European companies. Such arrangements involving U.S. firms are already in effect in countries as diverse as Chile, Ethiopia, Nigeria, Pakistan, and Turkey. Industries involved include steel, agricultural implements, chemicals, electronics, hotels, commercial aviation, and oil exploration and drilling.

In a few cases the returns to the management contractor have been limited to fixed and/or profit-variable cash fees and royalties. More often, significant additional returns are realized through the sale of equipment to the contract venture, and through long-term purchase or supply agreements covering raw materials or component parts. Other benefits typically cited by management contractors include the gain of valuable experience and reputation, obtaining a toehold in new markets on a relatively riskless basis, or securing nonmonetary concessions such as distribution franchises.

The device by which a corporation manages an enterprise in which it has no ownership interests in effect separates the *capital-risk bearing* from the *managerial and technical* elements of entrepreneurship. The services rendered under such an arrangement may be likened to the administrative and technical functions that a corporation performs in operating a subsidiary or affiliate set up by direct investment. In other words, the management contract goes far beyond the common "technical services" and "know-how" agreements. These require the existence of a functioning enterprise at the receiving end. The management contract *creates* such an enterprise.

So defined, the management contract makes available to host countries the benefits accompanying foreign direct investment without raising the issue of foreign ownership of local industry. Similarly, the management contract limits the host country's liabilities from the import of foreign resources to the period during which these are deemed essential to the local economy. From the standpoint of the foreign corporation, the management contract eliminates the risk of property seizure by host governments, since no title to property is obtained by the foreign firm. For this reason, the arrangement appears particularly suitable to associations between foreign private and local public enterprises. It thus permits the application of foreign corporate skills to situations where conventional direct investment is impractical or impossible.

A close look at this arrangement raises two basic questions. In a direct investment, ownership of the receiving enterprise, and hence control in proportion to the degree of ownership held, is both absolute and indefinite. In contrast, under a management contract, the extent of control by the management contractor will be explicitly qualified and its duration limited. Is a corporation likely to be willing to employ its supposedly scarcest resource—management—in a situation where its managerial freedom would seem to be subject to significant limitations, and where the corporation's tenure as manager might be relatively short-lived, or in any event cancellable?

A second major question relates to the possible effects of separating capital and management in establishing and operating an enterprise by means of a management contract. The contract principal, or project owner, provides the required capital resources and assumes the attendant risks. The management contractor in turn administers these resources for a fee and possibly other considerations. Will a corporation supply services of the same quality to an enterprise in which it does not have a capital stake as it would to an enterprise in which it *has* risked capital?

Let us consider, first, the question of the willingness of a corporation to enter into a management contract—i.e., to commit its capabilities to an enterprise it does not control by ownership.

As a general proposition, that willingness will obviously depend on the *objectives* of the supplying firm. Conventional foreign direct investments still commonly assume that the investor's objective in going abroad will be to achieve higher returns on his assets than he can realize at home. But extensive research on corporate foreign investment motives has shown that this assumption is almost meaningless, if not outright misleading.[1] Investment decisions tend to serve considerably more specific purposes—as for example, to create outlets for domestic production; to find and maintain foreign sources of supply; to establish tie-ins with existing foreign operations, and to prevent competitors' inroads on market positions gained through exports.

Control without ownership

As many international corporations discovered in operating joint ventures, most of these purposes can be attained without control by majority ownership of the local enterprise. The ability to make all major technical decisions will often suffice to render production processes, or output generally, dependent on the equipment, component parts, or other goods supplied by the parent organization. Similarly, if the objective is to secure a source of supply, possession of unique distribution channels or outlets can give the international corporation an adequate measure of monopsonistic control

[1] See, for example: J. N. Behrman, "Direct Private Foreign Investment: Nature, Effects, and Methods of Promotion," in R. F. Mikesell (ed.), *U.S. Private and Government Investment Abroad*, Eugene, Oregon, 1962; W. G. Friedmann and G. Kalmanoff, *Joint International Business Ventures*, Columbia University Press, New York, 1961; R. D. Robinson, *International Business Policy*, Holt, Rinehart and Winston, New York, 1964, Chapters 3, 4 and 5; and Y. Aharoni, *The Foreign Investment Decision Process*, Harvard University Division of Research, Graduate School of Business Administration, Boston, 1966.

over the venture in question. In other words, *functional* control over an enterprise does not necessarily require ownership. It can be achieved as effectively through dependence of that enterprise on the services supplied by the other firm.

But there remains an important distinction between control by ownership and control by management. The distinction is basically a legal one. It relates to the *temporal* dimension of control. Ownership gives the investor definite property rights in the receiving enterprise. These may be used to reinforce and to perpetuate whatever control the investor exercises through the essentiality of his managerial and technical contribution. The management contract, on the other hand, explicitly limits the duration of the relationship between resource supplier and resource recipient. However long the association may endure, the contract and any extensions will be for finite terms.

If this constitutes the essential distinction between management contracts and conventional direct investments, we may generalize that, as long as the investment objectives of the foreign firm assume or can be adapted to a finite time horizon, one of the major conditions for the firm's willingness to enter into a management contract will be fulfilled.

This time factor must be seen in proper perspective. The researches mentioned earlier in connection with foreign direct investment decisions suggest that most international corporations, particularly when investing in the developing countries, tend to plan on the basis of payback periods of five years or less. In effect, the special risk premiums commonly attached to expected rates of return on foreign investments frequently originate in planning horizons that lie well within the likely duration of a management-contract relationship.

Second-best management?

Now let us turn to the second consideration—the scope and quality of the managerial and technical resources a foreign firm would be likely to supply under a management contract. According to the conventional view, proper development and administration of a project require that the managing company have a financial stake in it. At first blush, this view seems to make a lot of sense. A company will assign its best managerial and technical talent wherever a part of the corporate substance is at stake. When no such interests are involved, the residue of lesser capabilities are likely to be deployed. Similarly, it seems easier to make a decision to pull out when nothing but a recall of company personnel will be required than in situations where abandonment of a project involves writing off substantial financial assets.

However sensible this viewpoint appears to be, analysis of foreign-investment decision making leads to an opposite conclusion. Let us first take up the question of whether a direct financial stake is in fact an indispensable underpinning to genuine commitment to a foreign venture. Then let us consider the matter of the relative quality of managerial and technical resources likely to be supplied under a management-contract arrangement.

So far as the first question is concerned, one of the more comprehensive surveys of foreign-investment practice has revealed that companies seem prone to "regard their foreign earnings much as a man does his winnings at a racetrack, in that they are much more willing to utilize them than fresh dollar capital for additional foreign investment."[2] This suggests that a company's loyalty to assets committed abroad is often, however irrationally, less marked than its loyalty to domestic capital investments—especially when the funds invested abroad issue from a pool of foreign earnings. In other words, in terms of reinforcing a company's commitment to a foreign venture, the relative strength of foreign-held assets, *in themselves*, may decline in measure as the initial investment "pays for itself" once or several times over.

More important still, conventional direct investment involves more than an *initial* decision to invest capital. Continued, genuine commitment to the venture and to its expansion in response to local market opportunities will generally demand continued infusion of both know-how *and* capital. If the venture is profitable and growing, additional financing may call for a decision "only" to reinvest profits rather than to repatriate them. Just as likely, however, additional foreign-currency investment will be required, especially in countries where foreign-exchange shortages make it difficult to convert local currency to pay for essential equipment, parts, materials, etc., that must be imported. If the venture has been incurring losses, then financing will almost certainly take the form of additional investment by the parent organization. The point is that conventional direct investment constitutes an *indissoluble compound of continual financial and "intangible" (managerial and technical) commitments.* In order to maintain its initial stake in the project, the resource-supplying corporation continually has to make decisions about additional investments which will almost inevitably be required.

If this is so, the value of a financial interest—from the standpoint of strengthening management's determination to stick with a project even when "the going gets rough"—appears doubtful. Instead, it would seem that the dimmer management's view of the emergency, the more strongly will it be tempted to apply the "sunk-cost" rationale to the investment, and the less attractive the alternative of further capital injections will become.

[2] E. R. Barlow and I. T. Wender, *Foreign Investment and Taxation*, Prentice-Hall, New York, 1955, p. 161.

"Why throw good money after bad?" Since, in a conventional direct investment, corporate intangibles are inseparably joined with corporate capital, a decision to "cut our losses" or "pick up our winnings as long as we're ahead" will result in a pullout not only of the investor's financial assets, but of his managerial and technical resources as well.

Now consider a case where the commitment of the foreign corporation has been limited to intangibles. Here, the direct and indirect benefits from the venture accruing to the resource supplier do not depend on continual recommitment of financial assets owned by the foreign firm (i.e., retained earnings), or on the investment of new capital. Aside from the opportunity costs of the intangibles deployed—which may or may not be perceived by management—the supplying firm can, in an incremental sense, "stay in the game for free." The continued flow of the managerial and technical resources of the foreign corporation will not be dependent on simultaneous *financial* investment.

This reasoning suggests that management's loyalty to a foreign project is not necessarily enhanced by the presence of an initial financial stake. Indeed, because of the continual need for additional finance in a direct investment project, the latter may be more readily abandoned—absolutely or relatively—in times of severe crisis than an undertaking where maintenance of rights to future earnings does *not* require incremental capital injections by the foreign firm, as in the case of a management contract.

Contractor's incentives

Let us now examine the matter of the relative quality of managerial and technical resources likely to be supplied under a management-contract relationship. The question comes down to this: Will the benefits that the resource-supplying firm gains from a management contract be smaller than the benefits associated with a conventional direct investment? Or, more precisely, are these benefits sufficiently smaller to have an adverse effect on the company's incentive to operate the project at least as efficiently as it would if it had an *ownership* interest in the venture?

Research on the management-contract experience of major international corporations indicates that the incentives this arrangement provides are at least as powerful as the incentives perceived in conventional direct investments. Two reasons for this can be discerned. First, just as the expected gains from a direct investment typically go beyond the direct financial payout of the foreign venture, so the benefits from a management contract transcend direct returns in the form of fees. In several of the cases studied, the contract project became an important profit-generating link in the management contractor's total foreign operations. In another case, promotion of product sales from the contractor's domestic plants as well as gains in commercially valuable reputation were cited as benefits reinforcing the company's substantial fee income from the project.[3]

Second, just as with conventional direct investment, the realization by the foreign corporation of the benefits it expects from a management contract tends to be vitally dependent on the success of the contract project itself. That success, in turn, depends on the quality of the services performed by the foreign corporation. Now, if the overall success of the contract project is directly related to the competence of the management and technical know-how supplied by the foreign corporation, and if the actual returns to the supplying firm are contingent on the measure of success attained by the receiving enterprise, then there is no logical reason for a firm to supply a poorer grade of managerial and technical resources under a management contract than it would in the case of a conventional direct investment.

In practical application, the management-contract concept requires considerable sophistication in planning foreign operations and the greatest skill and imagination in negotiations with the local owners of the enterprise. This concept, of course, does not amount to a panacea relevant to *all* projects traditionally undertaken through direct investment. But the growing diversity of projects successfully operated by management contracts suggests that the applicability of the device may be far wider than commonly assumed. In any event, the experience of numerous companies that have entered into management contracts—in the developing countries, Eastern Bloc nations,[4] and increasingly in the public sector of the United States— has clearly demonstrated that the arrangement works.

Indeed, the management contract we have been discussing represents the purest form of the extraordinarily significant current innovation in methods of overseas and even domestic corporate investment. These new methods pose a formidable challenge to the still-prevalent notion of the primacy of the capital component in corporate investment. They put in its place the primacy of the so-called *intangible* component. Besides managerial, adminstrative, and technological resources, this component includes the crucial capabilities specific to the going-concern condition of large-scale enterprise, that is, the ability to attract and deploy high-caliber personnel, access to worldwide procurement facilities and distribution channels, a financially significant reputation, and the instant availability of the accumulated and continually expanding store of intra-firm research and development in products, manufacturing processes, and administrative techniques.

In the traditional view, corporate direct investment involves the assump-

---

[3] See Peter P. Gabriel, *The International Transfer of Corporate Skills*, Harvard University, Division of Research, Graduate School of Business Administration, Boston, 1967.

[4] For a discussion of case examples of management contracts ("co-production" arrangements) in Eastern Europe, see E. Benoit, "Interdependence on a Small Planet," *Columbia Journal of World Business*, Spring 1966.

tion by Company A of certain capital risks in establishing or acquiring Company B. Management of Company B by Company A is considered a right vested in ownership, theoretically extending in perpetuity. The reward that A receives from managing B is primarily an entrepreneurial one for risks taken.

In contrast, the new methods of corporate resource commitment exemplified by the management contract regard management of Company B by Company A as an agreed-upon obligation assumed for a specific period of time. In consequence, the managing firm's reward is primarily a managerial one for services rendered.

Evolution, not revolution

This distinction has an historical parallel. According to many analysts, the most significant development in private business during the first half of this century was the divorce of management from ownership through the rise of the professional manager. Today, most large corporations are administered by executives who have little or no significant ownership interests in the companies they run. Perhaps the most important business development of the second half of our century may prove to be the rise of what I would call, for lack of a better term, "corporate contract management." It is really no more than an extension of the earlier development. Under this new concept, the corporation does not view itself as a direct mobilizer and allocator of capital but as a generator and seller of management capability in the broadest sense.

The new concept supplements, but does not supplant, the traditional economic function of the corporation. Within the total activities of a given firm, the relative importance of the new "management-selling" function vs. the traditional capital-mobilizing and capital-allocating functions will depend on the firm's stage of development and on the maturity of its natural markets. The more developed the firm, the larger and more diversified its inventory of managerial and technical resources is likely to be. Similarly, the more the firm's natural markets mature, the greater the incentive for alternative applications of its resources.

Examples of this new role played by the corporation emerge almost daily. In the United States, more and more companies are entering into contracts with the Federal Government to manage public-sector projects. These range from the management of the Cape Kennedy missile launching site to the operation of Job Corps Training Centers. To mention just a few of the companies involved: Litton Industries, General Dynamics, Westinghouse, International Business Machines, Pan American World Airways.

Roy Ash, president of Litton Industries, described his own company's interest in these opportunities:

We think our country will be better off if there's a heavy involvement of private industry in these public-sector programs. We plan to be in a number of them—economic development, solving water-resources problems, and developing new cities.

Over the years . . . we have developed a systems management capability and are interested in using it in new ways. . . . We think this concept has tremendous potential and many applications. You can think of it as a new kind of technology in itself.[5]

Whatever the potential applications of these new concepts in the United States, their greatest promise may well be abroad. There, imaginative use of these new concepts can yield the largest returns. There, the international corporation, through commitments previously made and positions already established, has the most to lose—and most to gain. There, increasing constraints on the traditional form of corporate investment make the need for innovation most urgent.

These innovations may take the form of the management contract as described here. They may be the sort of "co-production" arrangements about which Professor Benoit writes. They may take the form of the "service contracts" pioneered by international oil companies in producer countries. Such innovations may involve the commitment only of managerial and technical resources, or include a long-term loan to the contract project. They may be strictly bilateral arrangements between an international corporation and a host government, or involve a third party— like the World Bank. They may concern government enterprises in the receiving country or relate to private-sector projects.

The only features common to all these variants of the new approach to corporate investment abroad are, first, that ownership of the resource-receiving enterprise remains in local hands and, second, that the foreign corporation's tenure as manager is limited by agreement—even though successive renewals of the initial contract may make the foreign participation in the project long-lasting indeed.

The increasing acceptance of such arrangements, and their frequently outstanding profitability to all concerned, augur well for the future of the international corporation. There is growing evidence that private international business will make the profound conceptual and practical adaptations that today's environment suggests—and that the environment of tomorrow will make essential.

[5] *Fortune*, September 1966, p. 154.

PART THREE

The profit-improvement discipline

Among the most basic but least understood of the arts of management is that of increasing profits by waging imaginative and relentless warfare on cost and inefficiency. The tendency of managers to feel they are doing a good job of holding down costs is nearly universal. Often, however, it turns out to be unjustified. Cost cutting drives are launched, often with dramatic immediate results. But within a few months the old attitudes and habits gain the upper hand, and presently the fat of superfluous expenses has accumulated once more.

Formal profit planning has been carried through with phenomenal success by some companies and proven a disappointment for others. "Can Companies Plan Their Profits?" by Jon R. Katzenbach gives some reasons why. Profit planning fails, he says, chiefly because of four misconceptions: that it is unrealistic, a job for staff specialists only, does not concern line managers, and cannot be applied to staff functions. "Each of these misconceptions contains a grain of truth, but any one of them can paralyze the profit planning effort. They must be recognized and rooted out if profit planning is to have a real chance of success."

"Rediscovering Profits in Manufacturing" by John M. Updegraph and Burton C. Person develops the implications of consistent profit-mindedness in a single functional area. Their theme: "Imaginative research and hard-hitting marketing can build sales volume, but manufacturing still has by far the greatest impact on how profitable that volume will be." Technological advances, the authors find, seldom bring about a corresponding improvement in the efficiency of manufacturing operations. Yet unduly high manufacturing costs should not be tolerated

when a variety of proven corrective measures are available—some traditional, others involving new analytical techniques.

"Profit Improvement as a Way of Corporate Life," Richard F. Neuschel points out, is the ultimate implication of this approach. If profit improvement is to become a company habit month after month, year after year, management must possess—and demonstrate—"a willingness to challenge everything and anything" in the budget. Profit consciousness must be instilled in every executive. There is, however, no "secret weapon" by which this can be accomplished. The only key is overall company discipline: an atmosphere that prizes objectivity, welcomes change, and rewards accomplishment. There are those who would argue that the creation and maintenance of such a climate is, in the last analysis, the most basic and perhaps the most difficult of all the arts of top management.

10. Can companies plan their profits?

Jon R. Katzenbach

A decade or two ago the approach of many large and prosperous companies to planning was extremely casual. As long as they were "getting somewhere," they didn't worry too much about setting precise objectives. And they seldom attempted to specify routes and timetables to success.

Today things are very different. Most success-minded top managements have firmly committed themselves to the concept of formal planning. They wouldn't consider operating without a plan in the vital functional areas of the business—production, marketing, manpower, finance, even public relations. They do their best to make planning a way of corporate life.

Yet in one crucial area the casual approach to planning remains surprisingly prevalent. When it comes to profits many top executives remain unconvinced of the power of planning. They will agree readily that profit planning may be an exciting concept. They concede its logic. But in practice, they argue, it just doesn't seem to work—"at least not in our business."

But profit planning can and does work dramatically for certain companies. A manufacturer of heavy industrial equipment adopted a profit planning system eight years ago over the initial resistance of many line managers. It took three years for top management to sell the organization on profit planning and work the bugs out of the system. Since then the company has edged well ahead of its competitors in return on investment—and top management gives profit planning the lion's share of the credit.

What explains this contrast? Why does profit planning, capable of such successes, prove such a disappointment in many companies? Observation suggests that the answer lies in four basic misconceptions that handicap profit planning efforts in too many organizations. Briefly, these are the notions (1) that profit planning is unrealistic, (2) that it is a job for staff specialists, (3) that it does not concern down-the-line managers, and (4) that it cannot really be applied to staff functions. Each of these misconceptions contains a grain of truth, but any one of them can paralyze the profit planning effort. They must be recognized and rooted out if profit planning is to have a real chance of success.

Pinning down assumptions

The first misconception assumes profit planning to be an academic exercise in juggling uncertain assumptions. Executives who feel this way make complaints like these:

¶ "The planning department's assumptions are wrong 90 percent of the time. Those boys live in a fog."

¶ "Our judgment is as good as all these graphs and tables, so why bother?"

¶ "We just can't predict the future in our business."

While not all future conditions can be predicted with the same degree of accuracy, this seems hardly a good reason for refusing to try to predict the future at all. Companies whose managements regard profit planning as an academic guessing game are those that have made no real effort to pin down their planning assumptions. Instead, they rely on relatively ambiguous concepts like "rapidly increasing sales," "changing distribution patterns" and "increasing importance of new products." Such assumptions, of course, guide a company nowhere. For meaningful guidance, management needs specific answers to questions that challenge and may even upset previous company policies: By what percentage a year will sales in each product line grow between now and 1975? Exactly how will distribution patterns change? What proportion of profits is going to come from new-product innovation in the industry?

Obviously, planning assumptions must take into account the company's own particular strengths and weaknesses. A company also must assess its position within its industry by determining where it has competitive advantages to exploit and where its competitors have a clear edge.

Management's aim here must be to establish measurable objectives. Many companies, by stating goals in terms that cannot be quantified or challenged, provide the perfect excuse for mediocre performance. Merely aiming for "increased profits" is not enough, and no astute board of directors should accept that kind of "planned" objective. Increase profits? In terms of what measures or standards? How much improvement, by what point in time? What are the assumptions regarding the availability of resources? These questions may sound obvious, but surprisingly they often go unanswered.

Here is a simple test for detecting fuzzy objectives. If the obverse of a stated objective sounds ridiculous (for example, "We should *not* increase profits"), then the goal can be of little practical value in planning.

Again, many companies' objectives appear to have been conceived more as passive predictions than as goals to be won through planned performance. A genuinely challenging goal will be a much more effective perform-

112

ance motivator than a "most realistic" forecast. Unquestionably, a company can substantially shape its own future by the way it establishes its aims and develops plans to achieve them. This means integrating long-range performance objectives with annual budgets and programs, and with individual performance measures, to bring all the resources of the organization to bear on achieving the long-range goals. Otherwise, the company will simply be carried along on the continuation of past trends.

The notion that accurate profit planning "can't be done" owes much of its prevalence to top management's failure to see what can be accomplished with the powerful new tools that have been made available by today's information and data processing technology. We have only begun to scratch the surface of what can and will be achieved, and many mistakes have been made. But the computer—coupled with the operations research techniques that permit its more effective use—can help bring about impressive results in profit planning.

A company I know was trying to plan its investment and marketing strategy in terms of basic raw material versus converted product, and in terms of product mix. Some 68 alternatives were involved. The company had to assign priorities among some 20 market areas. It had to determine its alternatives for enlarging plant capacity in terms of shift expansion versus plant addition. It had to set plant and facility locations and select among a variety of distribution patterns. In short, it had to consider a wide range of variables.

Traditionally, management would have used its own judgment to weigh these many variables, basing its decisions on conventional accounting information. This would be a difficult job in most circumstances, and well-nigh impossible in this particular situation. The solution was provided by a computer-based linear program model containing over 200 separate equations or constraints. Five different environments were considered in terms of population growth, pricing and the like. This enabled management to evaluate the investment and profit impact that would result from eliminating or changing various constraints, as well as from any possible change in the environment.

The same model has also substantially improved this company's profit planning capabilities by furnishing reliable answers to questions like these:

¶ Which of *several* alternative strategies would result in the greatest return on stockholders' investment?

¶ What would be the profit impact created by any of a host of possible changes in selling price, market share, distribution methods, consumption patterns, and product mix?

¶What will be the potential profit impacts of different operating and marketing policies?

¶ How would profits be affected if the company revised its required

113

inventory practices and changed its inventory levels? What would be the effect if different modes of shipment were adopted?

Such questions challenge every company. But in some situations the answers turn out to be more complex than in others. The new information technology enables management to cope with the uncertainty inherent in any planning problem, and to evaluate possible strategies on an objective, quantitative basis.

Getting line involvement

The common notion that profit planning must be a job for staff experts is the second misconception that prevails in many companies. Consider these actual comments:

¶ "We have a special department that does most of our planning."

¶ "The way I look at it, I'm a line manager. I don't have the time or the resources to do proper long-range planning. Our staff guys do, and it's their job anyway."

¶ And, afterwards, when confronted with staff-made plans, "Well, those are your plans, not mine. I'm the one that has to run this department, remember?"

Staff specialists, of course, often play a vital role in gathering and analyzing the relevant data needed for planning. But profit planning becomes pointless unless line managers can be held responsible for the profit results—and this means that they should play the principal role in the planning. Line managers must not only be involved in the plan's development, but also support the assumptions that underlie it. They must view it as *their* plan, aimed at achieving *their* objectives—not as an ivory-tower staff effort that ignores the operating problems they face every day.

I know one rather large and fairly profitable company that once had a staff planning department of over 100 people involved in every conceivable sort of planning and research. The president had appointed his top staff executive to head this department. For more than three years—as it ground out long-range plans of great elegance, detail, and complexity—this department was one of his most important areas of concern. Then he became disenchanted. He saw that the department had been a complete failure. Its long-range plans, never having been accepted by line managers, had not appreciably affected the performance of the company. The department failed the crucial test—it had not won the participation of the managers who actually ran the business and made the operating decisions. Once he recognized this, the president ordered the entire department dissolved. Primary responsibility for planning was returned to the line managers where it belonged.

But planning is not *entirely* a line job. Line managers need staff help.

114

Often they need it badly. But the kind of information staff can provide will only relate to input; it can never substitute for line-management planning.

The problem of participation

The third misconception about profit planning is that it needn't really concern the fellow down the line. More than once I have heard executives comment in this fashion:

¶ "Basically, profit planning is top management's job. Short-range plans are all the operating people need to worry about."

¶ Or, more bluntly: "They do what they're told. That's the way it is, and that's the way it should be."

Ultimately, of course, responsibility for effective profit planning lies with the top managers who set the corporate goals. Yet managers down the line, with their detailed knowledge of operating conditions, will usually be best qualified to translate these broad objectives into specific planning goals and programs. And, most important, only if they participate in the planning will they be truly committed to achieving these goals.

Top management needs to involve the doers at all levels by translating broad objectives into individual performance targets throughout the organization. These targets should be consistent with the overall strategy; they ought to be challenging and provide a concrete basis for performance evaluations—down to the level of the first-line supervisor and the individual salesman.

No vagueness can be permitted. Goals must be defined with sufficient precision to meet two tests:

1. Does each man know exactly what he is expected to accomplish?

2. Have criteria of outstanding performance for each manager been defined explicitly so that people can be *ranked* on the basis of their performance evaluations?

Unless a company can answer yes to both questions, it almost certainly has not been receiving the kind of performance from everyone down the line that real profit planning can provide.

One large manufacturer was faced with the problem of improving sales effectiveness by changing sales-force behavior patterns. The company had a relatively weak market position, and its salesmen were not working on priority improvement opportunities. They were not pushing the right products or pursuing the right kinds of accounts.

To solve the problem, management designed a new sales reporting system to communicate to the salesmen precisely what was expected from them and how performance would be measured. Based on clearly defined criteria for each sales job, the system measures performance against realistic account potentials. It emphasizes account-by-account performance standards and enforces account-by-account planning by the salesman. Each account's sales potential is established by the joint decision of a team involving salesmen, sales managers, and special management advisers.

Special computer-generated sales reports show sales management (1) which accounts offer the best improvement opportunities each month, (2) how much time each salesman should allocate to each account each month, (3) what each salesman accomplished at each account the previous month, (4) how much each salesman must sell before year-end to make up for below-par performance in preceding months, (5) exactly what each salesman must do at each account the following month to achieve that month's potential, and (6) how each man's performance ranks against that of his peers. The keystone of the system is the regular monthly measurement of individual achievement in terms of clearly defined and weighted performance factors. Six months after introducing this system the company had improved both its sales performance and its market position by several percentage points.

Tying in staff functions

Finally, profit planning in many companies has been crippled by the mistaken notion that certain functions in an organization are immune to profit planning. This belief may be reflected in statements like these:

¶ "You can't relate staff functions directly to long-range profit objectives."

¶ "How do we measure the contribution of functions like advertising or personnel? On the basis of expense budgeting. How else?"

The difficulty of putting a dollar value on the results of some staff activities should not be offered as a reason for abandoning all efforts to establish quantitative objectives for these functions. Besides, advertising, personnel, or any other staff function *can* be directly involved in profit planning, can set specific, measurable individual objectives, and can be evaluated accordingly.

One large consumer goods company had been badly burned by a number of inconsistent and uncertain advertising programs. The results came through as elusive and ill-defined; costs were getting out of bounds and the company was losing market position. Eventually, the company faced up to some basic questions. Management reasoned:

What are we really trying to accomplish with advertising? Does it— or can it—increase our profits? Sales? Market share? No; it can contribute to all three, but we can't measure the contribution. Advertising is a communications medium; it doesn't close the sale. So we have to ask ourselves how well we're communicating with the people we want to reach in this market. What attitudes influence their buying decisions? How can we affect those attitudes by communications? And how, in these terms, can we make our communications effective?

As a first step, management carefully identified the market segments it wanted to reach. Because this couldn't be done on the basis of a demographic breakdown, the company determined what attitudes significantly influenced customers' buying decisions, and to what degree. The market was segmented in terms of these key attitudes. The priority of market segments was determined and the company's present position in each segment carefully analyzed.

Once it had defined its communication problem, the company was able to define its advertising objectives in measurable terms. For example, "Reach and influence housewives in the $10,000+ income group so as to raise from 45 percent to 60 percent in the coming year the proportion of those who identify our product as a convenience food." With agency help, management decided what reach-frequency and intensity of advertising would probably be required to accomplish each objective. Thus this company has established performance standards that reflect advertising's measurable contributions to profitability.

Four basic rules

As an antidote to the misconceptions we have discussed, let me offer four positive principles for more effective profit planning. These may appear simple and obvious, but they have proved surprisingly effective in practice.

1. Prepare and disseminate in written form a comprehensive statement of overall strategy in terms of specific objectives and policy.

2. Develop individual performance criteria for key positions at all levels consistent with that strategy.

3. Insist on written plans at all levels—plans that specify responsibility assignments, expected results, action steps, and deadlines.

4. Test performance against the stated targets.

Without rigorous, consistent, objective performance measurement, profit planning becomes a meaningless academic exercise—if not, indeed, a myth.

11. Rediscovering profits in manufacturing

John M. Updegraph, Jr. and Burton C. Person

The marvels of the computer, space-age R & D, new products, and novel marketing approaches have all but thrust the humdrum realities of plain old manufacturing off the front pages of our business journals. Unhappily, in many corporations they have come close to pushing these same realities off the list of subjects commanding serious top-management attention.

Ironically, in these same companies manufacturing efficiency often makes the difference between a less-than-adequate profit performance and an outstanding one. In industry after industry, differences in manufacturing costs go far toward explaining why such a gap separates the industry leaders from the also-rans. These significant variations from company to company in the same kind of business challenge the complacency of any management content with the proposition that it has been doing as well as it can with its manufacturing operations.

This was demonstrated recently when a well-known industrial equipment company found its return on investment falling far behind that of the competition. The critical factor turned out to be a 14 percent difference in cost of manufacturing, a discrepancy not immediately revealed in conventional accounting data or operating reports. Because the root of the problem had not been readily apparent, this management had spent a good deal of time and effort strengthening its product line and sharpening its marketing effort. Sales volume accelerated, but profit margins continued to sag. Analysis finally disclosed that competing companies had a 25 percent higher ratio of production per employee, 32 percent more production per square foot of plant space, and 66 percent faster inventory turnover.

This explained the difference in profitability. Bringing the cost of manufacturing down to the average of its three major competitors—in this case not an unreasonable or unattainable objective—would, it was revealed, raise the company's return on investment from 7 to 22 percent, about the level of the more successful organizations in the industry. And additional improvements in manufacturing (for example, reduced in-process inventories) would boost earnings by another 11 percent, bringing the company's return on investment to a handsome 33 percent.

Opportunities like this are not unusual in manufacturing. In fact, differences in manufacturing costs explain one poor corporate profit record after another. But the underlying factors frequently remain obscure.

To cite one of many examples, five facilities of a major office equipment manufacturer were recently surveyed. Each reported to the same top management, enjoyed the same staff support, and manufactured the same products. Yet the difference in output per worker between the most and least productive plants was more than 100 percent. A follow-up study of the causes, and a concerted effort to bring the other four plants up to the manufacturing efficiency of the fifth, eventually added over $400,000 a year to this company's earnings.

Too frequently, companies miss important opportunities to improve profits by neglecting to take a new look at manufacturing and related activities. No matter how fast a company grows, in the last analysis the delivered cost of the product dictates the margin of profit on that growth. Imaginative research and hard-hitting marketing can build sales volume, but manufacturing still has by far the greatest impact on how profitable that volume will be. And its contribution does not end here. For many companies—by making possible greater pricing and promotional leeway—manufacturing can strengthen market position.

Not long ago, a leading capital goods manufacturer found that the firm was losing $7 to $8 million a year in sales, about 10 percent of its total volume. Its reputation was still outstanding, its engineering and quality the best in its field, and yet it continued steadily losing this business to competitors. A customer-by-customer analysis showed that regaining this sizable chunk of volume would be possible only if manufacturing could cut 20 per cent off the cost of the product and thus give sales more pricing latitude. A closer study demonstrated that this was in fact possible.

The forces that create such profit improvement opportunities in manufacturing are widespread, and the pressure they exert has been mounting. In view of this, how should companies go about plugging profit leaks in their manufacturing operations? What can they learn from managements that have been successful in doing so?

In outstanding companies, the original impetus for improving manufacturing operations almost invariably comes from the chief executive. This does not mean that he personally goes into the shop and gets the job done. It does mean that he refuses to accept with complacency the notion that manufacturing lies beyond the area of top-management concern given (for good reasons) to other functions of the business—to marketing, to finance, or perhaps to expansion overseas.

Clearly the opportunities will differ from company to company. But

119

experience with a significant sample of manufacturers in a wide range of industries suggests that five courses of action will be likely to help create profit improvements. We may identify these opportunities in the form of five questions:

¶ Are we organized as well as we could be to take full advantage, on a continuing basis, of technological advances that could significantly affect our operations?

¶ Are we putting to practical use new analytical tools and problem-solving approaches that could reduce our costs and increase our manufacturing effectiveness?

¶ Have we recognized important changes in the profit impact of the different functions that make up manufacturing, and have we adapted ourselves—organizationally and otherwise—to deal with these changing impacts and relationships?

¶ Whether or not we market or manufacture overseas, do we plan and execute our manufacturing activities in a way that takes into account current worldwide developments, instead of limiting our search for improvement opportunities to the United States?

¶ Finally and most important, is profit improvement in our company a sometime thing—an activity carried on by fits and starts and intermittent cost-cutting drives—or have we made profit improvement a way of life and instilled a rigorous, continuing profit orientation in all our manufacturing units?

Keeping up with technology

How effectively does the company deal with the cost and profit impact of technological change in manufacturing? We need not ask here whether the company reacts brightly to these changes after they have become generally known. Rather, we would like to know whether the company has been organized *in advance* to systematically explore and evaluate the challenges that will be presented by new processes and new techniques, new materials and new equipment.

A few examples—all reported within a few weeks of each other—show that the profit potential in these new technological developments has hardly reached the point of diminishing returns.

¶ A plastics producer recently installed a new type of automatically controlled equipment, permitting this company to maintain production while cutting its work force by over 80 percent.

¶ A new manufacturing process recently doubled the capacity of one plate glass manufacturer, with a labor force increase of only 15 per cent.

¶ In another plant, a new insulation system uses recently developed materials and an inert gas to produce a home refrigerator having 28 percent more capacity without any increase in external dimensions. This company will begin with a marked competitive advantage in its marketing effort.

¶ One major steel company has reported that its new oxygen steel furnaces pour 491 tons of steel an hour, almost five times the rate of a typical open-hearth shop.

How many companies have been set up to make the most of the opportunities offered by such advances in technology? Our experience with a broad sample of companies and our study of a number of major industries lead us to an unhappy conclusion: all too few. For example, it was discovered several years ago that nearly two-thirds of the machine tools being used in U.S. plants were more than ten years old, having been designed and built before the major technological advances of the previous decade. This age ratio was much higher than in British, French, West German, Italian, or Russian plants. Again, more than 14,000 pieces of metalworking equipment in U.S. plants are now operating under numerical control—one feature of recent technological progress. But, despite exponential growth over the past ten years, this represents only 0.5 percent of the almost 3 million metalworking machine tools in use in the United States.[1] The first oxygen steel furnace in the United States was installed a dozen years after these furnaces began to be used in Europe. Only recently have some of the major U.S. steel companies installed such equipment.

The evidence is clear. A costly lag may be found between our technological progress and the rate at which this progress is being applied in manufacturing operations. Why is this? What prevents companies from taking advantage of technical advances? The answer, in part, must be that the *pace* of change and the many fronts on which change occurs make staying ahead difficult. Even so, staying ahead is management's job, and requires management's unflagging attention.

One company, Corning Glass, has a well-deserved reputation for leadership in glass technology. For years, Corning had an informal staff process engineering group, which about ten years ago was organized into a formal department. This unit was charged with the responsibility for keeping abreast of new technical developments applicable to the operations of its various manufacturing divisions. A process engineering laboratory was then established to increase its capabilities. More recently, the process engineering department and a number of related staff groups have been integrated with the research and development staff to form what Corning now calls its Technical Staff Division. This in turn is broken down into 17 groups of specialists, each assigned to a specific area of materials, process, or equipment research. Another, the engineering technology group, pays close attention to new developments in equipment. Supporting

---

[1] Figures taken from *American Machinist Tenth Inventory*.

the units, a Technical Staff Services Group processes information gathered by the various staffs and transmits it to plant managers throughout the company.

This organization reflects the unqualified commitment of Corning management to staying on top of technological progress in any field that might affect the destiny of the company. While Corning does put a sizable percentage of its earnings into this effort—a percentage much higher than the industry average—the investment has proved more than worthwhile. Technological leadership makes a major contribution to Corning's ability to earn a rate of return on sales and on equity that runs nearly 50 percent above the average of its industry.

For similarly committed managements, five major steps are indicated:

1. Designate a man or a group charged with the continuing responsibility for seeking out, developing, and adapting technological improvements in all areas of company interest.

2. Conduct periodically (at least annually) a formal review of operations to evaluate critically where new materials, equipment, or processes might make a significant contribution.

3. Develop procedures for assessing the use of technological advances by competitors and by related industries.

4. When potential opportunities have been identified and screened, investigate each systematically and determine its cost, payoff, and— particularly important—its effect on all functional areas of the business, in the light of both present and probable future conditions.

5. Develop an ongoing labor relations strategy that will face squarely the problems resulting from automation and other technological advances. More than one company has been paying dearly because its technical planning failed to take account of labor relations. But a few farsighted managements have demonstrated that thoughtful planning can not only avoid these problems but can earn labor's active cooperation in keeping up with technological developments.

New analytical techniques

Closely related to developments in technology, and equally dramatic in their own right, have been recently developed analytical techniques that can significantly affect manufacturing operations. The proficiency with which they are used separates the outstanding performers from those who have difficulty meeting sharpening competition and the continuing pressures on profits.

These techniques range from sampling and probability theory to linear programming and simulation. They include a number of specialized management approaches, such as Critical Path Scheduling with all of its

122

more sophisticated ramifications. Because such methods too often sound abstract and abstruse rather than tangible and practical, some conservative engineers have been reluctant to accept them. Yet, evidence of their potential contribution to upgrading manufacturing operations can no longer be questioned. In particular, they have proven useful in measuring the uncertainties and risks of employing facilities, machines, materials, and manpower—especially when a large number of variables is involved.

Consider, for example, the problems of a large food manufacturer. The company must decide how to assign production of different items to different plants, then stock its warehouses so that the sales force can serve customers most efficiently. Week to week—sometimes day to day—a staggering number of possible combinations present themselves; in this instance, over 700,000. Which would yield the greatest profit? As it turned out, the application of linear programming added over $880,000 a year to profits and opened up the possibility of further substantial savings by reduction in inventory costs. The linear program determined the most practical number and location of distribution points to meet present and future customer demand. No fewer than ten warehouses were eliminated, and delivery areas were reassigned. The result was a substantial reduction in production, warehousing, and transportation costs without any impairment of customer service.

The sheer size of the savings that these techniques may effect sometimes gives rise to the misconception that they can be applied only in giant companies. While the cost of sophisticated applications may sometimes be justified only in large-scale operations, it nonetheless remains true that they may be used in many ways by small companies. A corporation with sales of less than $10 million found that inspection costs had risen much faster than its output. Statistical sampling techniques helped reduce the number of inspectors required on each assembly line from eight to five, thereby cutting manufacturing costs on the company's six production lines by almost $90,000 a year with no loss of quality.

Some of the new analytical approaches are relatively simple to apply, especially in warehousing, physical distribution, and certain types of scheduling. Somewhat more difficult—hence less common, though frequently more profitable—have been applications of these measures to scheduling and control of production operations. Here they promote more efficient use of available raw materials, equipment, space, and manpower, and cut down requirements of both in-process and finished goods inventory.

In a metal processing company, ores of different grades were available from 90 mines scattered over three states. They could be processed in any one of four mills, each with different production cost and processing capabilities. Now that a linear program has replaced judgmental decisions, management can reliably determine on the first of each month what ores should be brought from which mines and to which mill each should be sent—in order to end up with the lowest total cost, including raw materials, processing, and transportation. Estimated overall savings fall between 15 and 20 percent.

One company recently turned impending disaster into a small victory by the application of Critical Path Scheduling to a complex scheduling problem. A heavy equipment manufacturer needed to sharply speed up the market introduction schedule for a certain new product. Under the original schedule, the new product would have reached the market two years behind the competition, with a consequent 14 percent drop in market share and a $10 million loss in potential profits. Management decided to try CPS as a way out of this situation. They found that they could bring the product to market 18 months earlier than had been considered possible, in time to meet the seasonal demand peak. As an important by-product, the cost of doing so was reduced significantly by identifying the relatively few steps that required expediting.

A major industrial equipment manufacturer allocated its production among five plants largely on the basis of transportation costs, which had always been regarded as most critical to efficient use of its facilities. Simulation of this company's manufacturing operations showed that productivity per worker and space utilization varied widely from plant to plant as a result of their differing scales of operations in each facility, as well as the varying effectiveness of their managements. This model made possible the mathematical analysis of a wide range of alternatives. One of the most profitable turned out to be closing down two of the five plants; although this did increase transporation costs, still greater savings were achieved in equipment and manpower. A linear program was then developed that further improved the utilization of facilities. In all, these measures added more than $9 million a year to the company's profits.

The success of analytical techniques raises the question why more companies do not use them. The answer is that the specialists possessing the technical skills required to apply such procedures will usually not be the operating people. And operating management, intimately familiar with the nature of the problems at hand, will be responsible for applying the techniques. A number of surveys have revealed a chasm in many companies between staff technical groups and operating management, and especially manufacturing management. Leaders in the application of these new analytical techniques have successfully bridged this gap.

One company, starting from scratch, has demonstrated that analytical techniques can be quickly introduced throughout a manufacturing operation with a minimum of frustration. The president of this firm, a major producer of construction equipment, sensed that executives of his manufacturing group had not used mathematical decision-making approaches because they thought these techniques theoretical and impractical. Accordingly, he persuaded the head of one division to try a linear-programming approach to scheduling the output of one product line. An operations research expert was hired for the purpose and assigned to the manufacturing vice president, to avoid the gap between the headquarters staff and the line manufacturing executives that would have opened up had he been attached to the headquarters group. All managers with manufacturing responsibility were invited to attend a three-day seminar conducted by an outside consulting organization to acquaint them with some of these new techniques, and to provide workshop experience in their application. Before the seminar was over, more than 40 applications had been identified; within a few months they were being used to make many important manufacturing decisions. They have now been routinely applied in production allocation and scheduling, improved sales forecasting for use in facilities allocation, in new product development and introduction, and even in the preparation of budgets.

A few simple rules of thumb for introducing and gaining acceptance of new decision-making approaches can be derived from this history:

1. The technical know-how required for using these analytical tools should be organizationally positioned close to the operating managers who are expected to use them.

2. Operating management executives must become familiar with the capabilities of these techniques so that they will accept their usefulness and be able to identify opportunities to apply them profitably.

3. General familiarity with the techniques is not enough; manufacturing management needs application-oriented exposure.

4. In applying such measures, operating management must from beginning to end participate actively in identifying the problems with the most promising payout, marshaling the information that provides the input for the analysis, and acting on the information gained so that the analysis will lead to a profitable conclusion.

5. Having seen to it that these steps are taken, top management must keep two more points in mind. First, these approaches will be most productive when subjected to periodic review. This is the only way to assure that the new capabilities are being applied in the areas of greatest profit impact. Second, the application of these techniques tends to cut across established lines of authority and responsibility. This will probably call for top-management involvement. In most companies, it takes a certain amount of top-level intercession to get all of the responsible operating executives accustomed to working together.

Changes in emphasis

Most of the progress in manufacturing in recent years has been made in lowering the cost of routine production activities. But the very technological advances and analytical approaches already discussed have combined with changes in the marketplace to give new importance to other aspects of manufacturing. These are the functions in which concept and system and organizational relationships have now proven to be at least as significant as new techniques or technology—frequently more so. Here the opportunities for improvement reside more in people than in processes. Hence, the paradox: the more sophisticated a production operation *per se* and the more tightly managed, the more important will be the opportunities for improvement in these *other* related manufacturing activities. Let us consider just one of these opportunities: the upgrading of the maintenance function.

With recent advances in mechanization and automation, maintenance is becoming an ever more important factor in overall cost and effectiveness. Even without these advances maintenance costs would make up a larger percentage of total manufacturing costs in today's more efficient fabricating and processing operations. In oil refining, for example, where automation has progressed further than in most industries, it has not been unusual for maintenance to represent from 25 to 30 percent of total refinery costs.

Maintenance has also come to be more important than ever because of its effect on the utilization of costly production equipment. The cost of equipment magnifies the cost penalties of downtime. A paper company, for example, recently found that reducing downtime by one percentage point was worth as much in added profits as a $200,000 a year increase in the value of added production capacity. In a company that can sell all the paper it produces, the impact of maintenance on profitability will obviously be substantial, but even in companies with excess capacity, downtime can cause a sizable increase in costs. Related to this impact, of course, will always be the effects of maintenance on product quality, scrap, and raw materials waste.

Perhaps because they have led in automation, oil refining companies now are among the first to upgrade maintenance. Many years ago one such company, identifying the first signs of this opportunity, embarked on a program of developing management skills in maintenance that continued over ten years. First, one of its most promising engineers, a man with proven executive talent, was made head of maintenance. Management provided him with a staff of highly qualified technicians. These men, too, had previously demonstrated managerial capabilities, which equipped them to take on planning, coordinating, and analytical assignments, and in turn made them useful to line managers in various plants. Additional staff support was provided by specialists in metallurgy, corrosion engineering, and nondestructive testing. The company also revised qualifications for line managerial posts in the maintenance department, and graduate engineers began filling key positions. These specialists were all given additional on-the-job training in economic analysis and project evaluation.

The payout of the long-term program has been dramatic. Over a ten-year period, while production has gone up 70 percent, maintenance forces have been reduced 55 percent. At the same time, the refinery's on-stream record has been significantly improved. The increase in profits directly attributed to this change in maintenance management has been estimated at close to $15 million a year.

Noteworthy advances of the same kind have been made in the process industries, mostly among the larger companies. An impressive number of firms in other industries, including a number of smaller enterprises, have recognized that the craftsman who has risen through the ranks—however skilled and otherwise qualified—may not have the educational background or the managerial qualifications to head the kind of maintenance operation needed.

In a smaller manufacturing company an outstanding executive with an engineering background was recently promoted to chief plant engineer. The man he replaced had started with the company as a mechanic and come up through the ranks. Unhappily, he lacked the high-level qualifications required to administer maintenance. Responsibility for heading the staff was assigned to a talented young engineering college graduate. He, in turn, took charge of a newly created staff department having the responsibility of analyzing the company's maintenance methods and costs and coming up with programs to improve the operation.

Effective management will also take advantage of *improved equipment*, notably new developments in inspection technology. The analytical techniques discussed above have proven applicable here, and both Critical Path Scheduling and linear programming are being applied more and more to the planning and control of maintenance activities.

The experience of companies that have improved their manufacturing capabilities suggests that their success has been created by a number of specific measures:

1. Action taken by *top management* based on an awareness of *true* manufacturing costs. Frequently, these are not disclosed by the conventional reports received from accounting, but must be gleaned from a composite picture. For instance, the true importance of maintenance is disclosed if the final calculation includes the cost of downtime and of quality rejects in addition to labor and material. In physical distribution, management's attention will be flagged only when it becomes aware of the

cost of inventories at all points in the pipeline as well as the various transportation and warehouse operating costs.

2. Selection of the most promising managers to head up the function, and elevation of the reporting relationship to bring new developments quickly to top management's attention.

3. Identification of key activities required for successful administration of the function and provision of adequate support staffs with the required skills.

4. Opening up channels of communication between the heads of the business functions so that there can be an across-the-board awareness of how important a *systems* point of view has come to be.

Increasingly, manufacturing has come to have international aspects and implications. The rapid expansion of the world economy now poses a challenge far greater than that of finding profitable opportunities to market overseas or even of putting up a plant abroad. Industrial progress has been worldwide, and it calls upon the ingenuity and foresight of manufacturers. They must ask themselves questions like these:

Where should I produce? Sometimes the answer may not be as obvious as it seems. At least two major sewing machine manufacturers simply assemble parts manufactured to their specifications in foreign countries, a method that has cut their product costs substantially and enabled them to compete successfully with low-priced foreign imports.

Where should I look for technological improvement? Some years ago a major equipment manufacturer who had decided it would not be profitable to manufacture and market overseas nevertheless maintained a manufacturing staff of 50 in Tokyo. Its responsibility was to search out new processes (as well as new parts-manufacturing arrangements) in the Japanese electrical industry that would cut the company's production costs and enable it to compete more profitably with both domestic and imported products.

Where should I carry on my product development? One packaging equipment producer recently moved product development activities to plants overseas, where the costs of both engineering and skilled labor are much lower. A different approach has solved a problem for a major electrical equipment manufacturer, who, facing the shortage of qualified scientists and engineers, searched overseas and found 175 qualified candidates, of whom 45 were hired.

Most manufacturers have an untapped opportunity to upgrade their operations by taking advantage of worldwide industrial progress. The competitive implications of this challenge will become greater, of course, as trade barriers are lowered over the course of time.

The most profitable approach will differ from company to company. Managements that have been most successful in internationalizing manufacturing operations have approached the problem along the following lines:

1. Top management has insisted that company perspectives no longer be limited to their own country. More specifically, objectives should extend beyond merely looking for investment or marketing opportunities abroad. This point of view calls for looking anywhere in the world for parts, processes, or people.

2. For most companies, the new perspectives have organizational implications. Many are not alert to fresh opportunities because their international operations have been confined to an export department or an international division oriented essentially to sales or marketing. If manufacturing is to benefit from worldwide opportunities, alternative organizational approaches are indicated—approaches that will match the manufacturing requirements of the company.

3. Information procedures must be established to tap new manufacturing developments overseas and relate these to the company's requirements. This involves continual analysis of purchasing and processing costs and the development of comparative information on alternatives abroad.

Profit improvement

Behind the achievements of any outstanding manufacturing operation lies something intangible—a conviction that in manufacturing, efforts to bring about profit improvement must, as a matter of course, be put into practice every working day. This attitude and the discipline that flows from it determine how an opportunity is grasped and how effectively each effort can be translated into an increment of added profit.

Executives involved should be prepared to acknowledge a too-often-unrecognized fact—that all operating managers and supervisory personnel have two closely related but quite distinct responsibilities. One, of course, will be the efficient day-to-day running of the business. The second responsibility, overshadowed by the first, is the obligation constantly to improve the operation by seeking out appropriate changes in policies and practices.

The importance of this attitude toward profit improvement becomes most apparent in companies where it does not exist. One chief executive recently expressed satisfaction that his manufacturing group was doing everything it could to keep down costs and maintain the highest level of effectiveness. Yet each of the supervisors, in defining his responsibilities, always enumerated them in terms of meeting production schedules, controlling quality, reducing rejects, and other similar chores. Not a single supervisor mentioned profit improvement as one of his ongoing responsibilities. Understandably, the record of this company was dotted

129

with isolated, one-shot cost-reduction projects. But management defined no goals, had no plans, demanded no systematic search for opportunities, and had no measurement of achievements.

One inevitable result of this attitude becomes apparent when the net effect of across-the-board cost-cutting drives has been evaluated. What company has not had the experience of launching one of these drives, rejoicing in its immediate impact, and then noting a year or so later that either the same excessive costs have reappeared or that new and equally unnecessary costs have crept into the operation? If profit improvement remains a "here today, gone tomorrow" objective; if it emerges from the chief executive's office from time to time in the form of an edict that orders everyone to cut all costs by 10 percent next Monday; then steady and permanent improvement in profits simply does not take place.

Sometimes these arbitrary cost-cutting drives have actually resulted in the elimination of profitable activities. In one company, the order to reduce costs led to the elimination of a 50-man work group that maintained and repaired certain mechanical equipment. The president had ordered a reduction in the work force, and the plant manager complied by arranging to have this work done on contract. Two years later a close analysis disclosed that the cost of maintenance had almost doubled because of the higher charges paid to the outside contractor. These charges were buried in a cost account separate from that of maintenance labor.

But enough successes have been placed on the record to prove how useful profit improvement efforts can be when they are systematically organized and planned. For example, the president of a medium-sized chemical processing company recognized that his sporadic cost-cutting drives had failed to retard a declining profit trend. He launched an organized effort to infuse a tough-minded view toward profits throughout his company. It was made clear that the responsibility for profit improvement would be a continuing assignment for all levels of management. Steady reduction in costs was made part of the job of every supervisor. Outside assistance was sought to help set specific profit improvement goals. Work teams were formed to plan how the goals would be achieved, and to develop ways of regularly measuring progress. In a short time, 62 projects were identified and programmed to reduce manufacturing expenses. Within the first year, savings of $65,000 were realized in purchasing, $80,000 in quality control, $24,000 in maintenance. Additional thousands of dollars were saved in other manufacturing functions. The total amounted to over $1 million annually—enough to more than offset price erosion and rising wages. This company now boasts an upward profit trend, in contrast to an overall decline in the profit averages of its industry.

One of the nation's largest and most profitable consumer foods manufacturers, widely known for outstanding marketing achievements, merits

130

equal praise for its approach to profit improvement. Facing increasing costs after World War II, this company took all the usual approaches to cost reduction: eliminating unnecessary reports, running cost-cutting contests, and the like. They were only modestly successful. After eight years management took stock and found that new savings averaged less than $2,000 a year per manufacturing manager and supervisor.

The company then did an about-face and began a systematic effort to instill the responsibility for profit improvement into its line management and supervisory group. It was made clear to each line manager that his progress in the company would be directly related to his ability to improve operations and reduce costs. The responsibilities of the staff group were also redefined; from that time on they were charged with providing for the profit improvement efforts of line management. (This in no way qualified the ultimate responsibility of line management for achieving results.)

Having launched this program, top management took every occasion to reward outstanding performance. In five years, the company raised its new savings to an average of well over $10,000 a year for every line and staff member of manufacturing management, and this fivefold improvement has since doubled again.

Instilling profit improvement as a way of life requires some forthright action:

1. The top manufacturing executive, with the active support of the chief executive, should make it clear that efforts to achieve profit improvement will be required of every member of the organization. It must also be stressed that existing policies and methods will no longer be accepted as valid explanations for the failure to reduce costs.

2. Worthy objectives are not enough. Specific assignments should be made down the line. These should include periodic review and updating of programs. In short, the entire profit effort must be built into the corporate planning process.

3. When indicated, special project teams or staff groups can be created to supplement the activity of line management in the profit improvement effort.

4. Techniques for measuring and controlling profit performance have to be developed.

5. Profit-improvement performance must be made an important criterion for personal progress in the company.

This type of profit-oriented management of the manufacturing function characterizes the top profit performers in any industry, and—if sustained—often keeps them ahead even of competitors who have outshone them in research and development or marketing ingenuity.

If gains in manufacturing efficiency appear less spectacular than other improvements, they can also be more durable. Such advances will not be eroded by competition. On the contrary, companies with long histories of solid achievement have found that tightly run manufacturing operations put a firm foundation under risk taking. They provide a steady flow of profits from established products and markets, which can in turn support more speculative sallies into new products and new markets. And when manufacturing procedures are sound, you know that if your new product becomes successful or your new marketing approach catches on, the rewards will be all the greater.

12. Profit improvement as a way of corporate life

Richard F. Neuschel

More than once since World War II, and in more than one national environment, large numbers of companies have found themselves caught between persistent increases in costs, especially labor costs, and public pressures to hold the line on prices. In any such period, two phenomena of real significance may be detected in the broad patterns of corporate performance figures.

First, the profit performance of individual industries is decidedly mixed. Second, some companies are notably more successful than others in the same industry at adapting to and counteracting the effects of the profit-depressing forces. When we put aside the industry averages and look more closely at *differences in profit performance among individual companies* within an industry, the difference between the top performer and the bottom performer at any given time usually turns out to be far greater than the difference between the high and low points on the industry trend line over time. In other words, where your company stands in the profit-making spectrum within your industry will be much more significant than where your industry stands on the profit trend line. More often than not, the real profit squeeze begins at home.

The superior performance of the profit leaders sometimes results from the good fortune of being in the right industry at the right time, with the right products or processes or distribution facilities. Outstanding performance can also be the result of a few brilliant strategic decisions—to expand capacity, to integrate vertically, to merge with or acquire other companies, and so on. Sometimes profit leadership comes because a company has assembled an exceptionally competent management group. And sometimes profits are superior because top management has effectively channeled its company's effort toward substantial, continuing profit improvement.

Of the four factors controlling the profit performance of any company, this last—effective profit improvement—stands out as the only one immediately available to any management willing to make the effort. Moreover, an organized, continuing profit-improvement program can by itself make the difference between mediocre and exceptional profit results. Consider the chart just below, which shows the relative performance of

Industry X: return on equity of five top companies

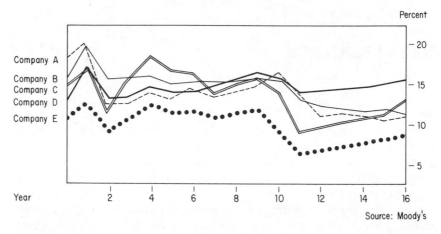

the five largest companies in a major U.S. industry, measured by return on stockholders' equity, over a recent 16-year period. Note that in year 6, after having moved along in a median position for a number of years, Company D—indicated by the heavy black line—began to move upward in relative standing. By year 11 it had become the indisputable profit leader of the industry.

Such performance doesn't just happen. In this instance it came about because this company—in the face of a general downward trend in industry profits—was willing to pay the price to keep its own profits moving upward. For the past ten years, it had been carrying on a well-organized, aggressive profit-improvement program covering every activity and every element of income and expense in the business. The impact of this program on profit results is highlighted by the fact that the company's production volume increased by 60 percent and its profits by 68 percent since year 9, while its total number of employees remained almost un-unchanged.

The story of this company dramatizes what any enterprise can do in spite of downward profit trends and fierce competition in its industry, provided top management is dedicated to the rigorous job of paring off accumulated corporate fat.

Here, then, we find a picture of need and opportunity for a broad spectrum of businesses. In a host of companies, more aggressive and

134

resourceful approaches to profit improvement are needed. And for those who apply these approaches consistently and well, the rewards can range from substantial to spectacular.

But profit improvement will not be achieved simply by recognizing the need for it, nor by once again taking the vow to do better. It will be achieved only through the courage and skill and resourcefulness with which management tackles the job.

The challenge has two main aspects: first, the barriers that stand in the way of effective profit improvement in many companies; second, the essential ingredients of a successful program.

Obstacles to profit improvement

In my experience, four major roadblocks bar the way to an effective profit-improvement program:

1. FAILURE TO APPRECIATE THE SIZE OF THE PROFIT-IMPROVEMENT POTENTIAL. For example, with respect to the overhead activities of a business, most managements would be shocked at the suggestion that reductions of 25 to 30 percent or even more could safely be achieved. As a result, they generally remain content with marginal savings, if any, leaving overhead pretty much alone as long as things seem to be operating smoothly.

During the past seven years, a continuous profit-improvement program in a large consumer durable-goods company has produced savings exceeding the total rise in its direct labor and material costs during that period. And another company, in the face of a 28 per cent rise in its average labor rate over a period of years, managed through an imaginative profit-improvement program to hold the increase in the per-unit labor cost of its product to 2 percent.

2. LACK OF PROFIT CONSCIOUSNESS. As a rule, managers and supervisors of overhead activities do not have to "show a profit" on their operations. This creates a formidable barrier to hard-headed, objective thinking.

Not that the heads of these activities are necessarily poor managers. A given supervisor may be doing a conscientious, highly competent job. Yet like all of us, he tends to concentrate on those parts of his job on which he will be most frequently checked or judged. And because so few cost standards have been established to measure efficiency or optimize performance in indirect or overhead activities, the people who manage them will most frequently be judged by the quality and speed of the service they render.

Not uncommonly, therefore, a department will be overstaffed so that it can handle rush jobs or work peaks as promptly as possible without interrupting the normal routine. The manager usually cannot control these peaks and special demands, so his natural inclination is to be prepared for every contingency. Thus, consciously or unconsciously, he will often resist any effort that might impair his flexibility for rendering this kind of service.

Moreover, managers and supervisors of such activities often lack a well-developed sense of value-cost relationship. The more conscientious they are, the more they tend to become perfectionists and to treat as fundamental the activities that happen to be their own peculiar daily concern. Usually they will be shocked at the suggestion that what they are doing may not need to be quite as thorough and precise as they have tried to make it.

3. LACK OF A STRONG, CONTINUING IMPROVEMENT ORIENTATION. Unfortunately, many of the well-established organizations in all sectors of American business have been geared more to maintaining their operations —i.e., getting the job done, turning out the work, handling problems, and generally keeping the show going—than to *changing*, *upgrading*, or *improving* operations. Most managers think in terms of administering their activities—getting shipments out the door, handling personnel problems, answering mail, and the like. Few really believe that substantially changing and improving their operations can be an equally important part of the job.

4. LACK OF A SOUND APPROACH. Too many companies fail to approach the job of profit improvement in a positive, fundamental way. Instead, they rely on sporadic cost-reduction drives—which all too often turn out to be either superficial and fruitless or arbitrary and harmful.

In some instances, because of management's failure to face up squarely to a difficult job, the entire cost-cutting effort will be concentrated on such peripheral items as the telephone bill, memberships and subscriptions, and company automobiles. Or it may be focused on areas that have been worked over intensively in the past. As an executive friend of mine puts it: "Every time we dust off and start up our periodic cost-reduction drive, we grind the pencils shorter, fly tourist class, and beat on the factory some more."

In still other instances, companies that have resorted to across-the-board percentage cuts by fiat have learned that this sort of unskilled surgery all too often cuts away two pounds of muscle with every pound of corporate fat. Besides, we have a good deal of evidence that reliance on this technique induces even the leanest, best managed departments to acquire a layer of protective fat.

For two reasons, no management can rely on cost-cutting decrees as a permanent solution to the profit-improvement problem. First of all, down-the-line management will be apt to view arbitrary expense reduction as a temporary, short-term measure. Once top management relaxes the pressure, high costs return. Second and more important, arbitrary methods of achieving savings seldom eliminate the basic weakness that brought about high costs to begin with.

Top management's task

To overcome these obstacles and launch an effective, continuing program for improving profits, top management must do four essential things:

¶ Condition itself for major change

¶ Stimulate keener profit consciousness throughout the organization

¶ Develop the conviction among all members of management that the job of profit improvement must be a never-ending one

¶ Make sure that profit improvement is approached in a fresh, skillful, comprehensive way.

ACCEPTING THE NEED FOR CHANGE. The first of these essential ingredients has to do with leadership. Top management must be determined to do something about profits—something substantial and enduring—not merely fire off another one-shot cost-reduction decree. Profit pressures can be licked, but they cannot be licked easily. Management must be willing to pay the price of success. The job requires a long time and a great deal of hard, competent, disciplined work. And the biggest gains will not come cheaply. They require a real willingness to give things up, to take calculated business risks, to accept something less than perfection, and to make courageous, difficult decisions affecting status symbols, present products, and traditional practices.

STIMULATING PROFIT CONSCIOUSNESS. Given this kind of resolute leadership, top management's second key task will essentially be one of communication. Managers must find ways to stimulate a keener profit consciousness in every executive and supervisor throughout the entire organization. As the president of a $2 billion chemical company said to his management team: "We need to learn how to put a dollar sign on everything we propose to do—no matter how difficult it is to measure the payout."

In a recent budget message to the department heads of his company, the chief executive officer of another major international conglomerate spelled out the challenge in these terms:

In the development of budgets and underlying manpower plans, the focus of every department head must continuously be fixed on how he can build the company, not just how he can build his function. This means that all of us must have a proprietary concern about the way in which we spend money. To every proposed expenditure we must apply the tough-minded commercial judgment that forces us to answer such questions as these:

1. In what specific way will this expenditure contribute to the profitability and competitive strength of the company?

2. Is the full amount of this expenditure really necessary, or could we get all or nearly all the anticipated benefits at a lower cost?

By thinking in this way about the business payout or the value-cost relationship of everything we do, we will not only ensure that any proposed budget additions are sound and necessary, but also force ourselves to upgrade the value we are getting from existing activities.

BUILDING A WAY OF LIFE. The third task of top management must be to create an awareness that the job of profit improvement will be a permanent part of the corporate way of life.

Consider the example of a large consumer packaged-goods company, the most profitable in its industry. In this company every executive and supervisor is required to submit his annual operating plans in a form that will supply concrete answers to two questions: (1) In what ways do you expect to improve your operation during the coming year? (2) By what amount do you expect to cut your unit costs?

By making this approach a built-in feature of corporate life, the company has succeeded over the years in producing a breed of manager-entrepreneur strikingly more aggressive and more effective than the "caretaker" types so often found in charge of indirect or overhead activities.

ORGANIZING THE FINAL PROGRAM. The final ingredient of a successful profit-improvement program may be reduced to a matter of approach. For maximum results, the program must be well organized, and it must have both depth and breadth.

To meet the first of these two requirements, one paper manufacturing company ties its profit-improvement effort into its annual planning process. At the start of the budget period, each manager is assigned a dollar profit-improvement target. He is asked, in effect, to seek out ways of reducing his operating expenses by this amount and to submit documented recommendations for projects that will achieve the savings, with an estimated timetable for carrying each project to completion.

As these projects are approved by top management, they become geared to the operating budget; that is, the manager's budget for the next period will be reduced by the expected dollar savings from approved projects that he has committed his department to carrying out. At the same time, top management assigns him a new dollar target of savings to be achieved in the next period.

By this route, the company has achieved profit improvements of more than $1 million each year for the past three years—tangible evidence of the value of a systematic, continuing effort.

A sound approach of this kind must be based on a deeply probing point of view, a willingness to challenge everything and anything. Such an attitude impels people to keep asking: "Why have we been doing it this way? Why are we doing it at all? If we once had to do it, must we still? Is there a better way to accomplish the same thing today? What changes have taken place that might alter our thinking here?"

But the attack must be broad as well as penetrating. Ultimately, it ought to extend to every activity, every element of cost and expense, every product, and every policy of the business.

Consider what happened when a manufacturer of industrial equipment and supplies undertook a fundamental study of its marketing function—more specifically, of the way in which its salesmen were managed. In this company's segment of the market, prices had declined by approximately 10 percent over a four-year period, placing profits under a good deal of pressure. Overall, the company was operating safely above break-even, but the trend of its profits and return on investment gave cause for concern. In this setting, management decided to launch a critical study of operating costs.

It soon became apparent that sales costs had mounted far out of proportion to profit on sales. As one measure of the situation, roughly 150 of the company's customers accounted for nine-tenths of its entire volume—yet the company's total sales force exceeded 300 men.

Basically, the disproportionate growth of the sales force had been allowed to go on because management had failed consistently to check and review its assumptions. For example, a specified increase in sales potential in a given territory was considered—quite correctly, in theory—as sound justification for adding a new salesman. But, having added the new salesman, management never really inquired thereafter whether he actually realized that potential. Nor did anyone check to see whether the other salesmen in that territory were pulling their weight on the same terms. Actually, as the study disclosed, at least 75 of the 300-odd salesmen were not.

Again, product mix was exceedingly important to the company's profitability—since wide variances across the product line in the ratio of fixed to variable costs caused even wider variances in profit margin. Under these circumstances, fairly tight planning and direction of the sales effort might be expected. And, indeed, there was planning, in the sense that product-mix goals were officially established at the corporate level. But in the districts relatively little attention was paid to these goals. Instead, the emphasis was on volume. In consequence, half of the company's sales districts—those more closely attuned to headquarters thinking—were, in effect, bailing out the other half.

This required no ingenious remedy. Once the problem had been clarified, the action required became obvious. And, management resolutely took it —thereby realizing approximately a 12 percent reduction in its total selling costs. The significance of the story lies in the fact that a massive improvement opportunity went undetected until management decided to look for it.

Testing for improvement potential

In evaluating the entire range of improvement opportunities in marketing —only one of several areas in which such opportunities may be undetected—top management may usefully apply such checkpoints as these: LOOK FIRST AT YOUR SALES EXPENSE BUDGET. Does it amount simply to a roundhouse figure based on a fixed percentage of forecasted sales, or has it been developed through really tough-minded analysis of each element involved in selling expenses?

LOOK NEXT AT YOUR SALES OFFICES. Have they actually been treated as profit centers? Have you standards that define *profitable* performance by each of your offices and by each of your salesmen? Have management decisions, including compensation decisions, been based on this profit performance?

LOOK AT YOUR CUSTOMER COVERAGE PATTERNS. Are your salesmen concentrating on the customers with the highest potential and calling on them with the right frequency, so that something tangible can be accomplished on each call?

LOOK AT YOUR DISTRIBUTION NETWORK. Have you reviewed it within the past two years to see where you need stronger representation? What about warehouse and district sales office locations? In aggregate, do they add up to the most effective system possible, at the lowest possible costs? If this question has not been analyzed within the past five years, the answer is very likely no.

LOOK, FINALLY, AT YOUR PAPERWORK COSTS. When did you last carry out a really thorough overhaul of your clerical operations in the marketing area? The chances of an impressive potential here will be very good indeed if you have made no serious attack on these costs within three years.

Similar lists of questions can be developed for other areas of the business—and they can be equally productive for the management willing to face up to the answers and the action they imply.

Nothing radically new, to be sure, may be found in the approach I have outlined. Indeed, very little in the area of basic management principles can be judged really new. A top executive of Procter & Gamble put this point well when he was asked to explain the reasons for his company's outstanding and long-sustained leadership in its industry. He replied: "In the main, our competitors are acquainted with the same fundamental concepts

140

and techniques and approaches that we follow—and are as free to pursue them as we are. More often than not, the difference between the degree of their success and ours lies in the thoroughness and self-discipline with which we and they develop and execute our plans."

Realistically, we must recognize that no secret weapon will ensure industry profit leadership. The magic ingredient that makes the difference is *discipline*—the discipline that enables management to reach for improvement and manage for improvement, year in and year out, steadfastly and well.

PART FOUR

Managing executive manpower

Nowhere have the administrative arts of top management changed more than in the area of managing executive personnel. In recent years, as the following contributions demonstrate, new forces at work in the business environment and the institutional framework of our society have combined to create an unprecedented challenge to all those responsible for the management of managers.

One aspect of this challenge is seen in the rise of superorganizations, public as well as private, and the demands they are certain to make on the coming generation of leaders. To meet these demands, two kinds of manager will be needed: the specialist whose vision extends beyond his specialty, and the generalist who has mastered a full range of complex technical tools. Both, but particularly the latter, declares Gilbert H. Clee in "The New Manager: A Man for All Organizations," will have "a true universality of career opportunity."

Mr. Clee sees " a career pattern emerging, that of the manager-statesman who functions with equal aplomb, and equally clear vision, at the helm of a great corporation, a major foundation, a mega-university or a vast Federal agency." Clearly, managers of this stamp cannot be turned out to order by our universities and schools of business, but these institutions are nevertheless faced with a critical need to serve as seedbeds for leadership of the quality to match tomorrow's task.

Another, even more immediate challenge is posed by the worldwide shortage of trained executive manpower. The potential impact of this shortage in the U.S. prompted Arch Patton to examine, in "The Coming Scramble for Executive Talent," techniques used by successful American companies to secure an adequate supply of these scarce resources and obtain the largest possible returns from their use. As the "raiding" of talent by executive recruiting firms intensifies and companies make off with one another's executives, Patton notes, protective salary increases place a heavy burden on the payroll. Among the means he describes to help secure management's best men are better conceived promotion policies, stronger compensation structures, and measures calculated to strengthen the often-neglected personnel function.

A discussion in depth of "Compensation and the Executive Career Cycle" is contributed by George H. Foote. "An executive's compensation needs reflect his career position," Foote points out. "The ideal compensation package for a senior executive may work real hardship on a young department head, and vice versa." Failure to recognize this fact costs companies millions annually. More important, it costs them the services of able men who move on to competing companies with better designed compensation packages.

Sometimes a managerial art can become so highly structured and rigid in its application that it no longer serves the purpose for which it was originally designed. A case in point, noted by Robert K. Stolz in "Executive Development—New Perspective" is the formal executive development program of yesteryear. The "pomp and ceremony" attending such programs has largely been dropped; but appraisal and development programs themselves, far from being downgraded, have in many instances been strengthened, renamed, and put on a less formal basis, with considerably stronger participation by line management. Classroom training, advanced management courses offered by universities, and special, shorter courses and seminars still figure largely in executive development, but the emphasis has shifted from the academic to the operational—trying the executive out in new assignments, testing his abilities under fire, and developing his capabilities by exposing him to a well-planned sequence of real-life managerial challenges.

Two essays by Arch Patton complete this section. The first, "Motivating Tomorrow's Executives," emphasizes the new set of professional concerns and desires that characteristize the younger managers now taking over positions in the middle and top echelons of industry. Managements that are insensitive to these new motivational patterns may risk frustrating valuable young executives they can ill afford to lose, Patton warns. The new breed of executive has no fearful memories of the Great Depression of the 1930s; for him, the need for financial security is no longer a dominant motivation. More risk-minded than

144

his predecessor, he seeks a congenial environment, "the excitement factor" inherent in challenging work, and the possibilities of fast-track promotion.

In the final selection, "A Demanding Environment: The Role of Compensation," Patton develops the proposition that a challenging work environment is essential to a company's long-range achievement. Without it, organizations tend to become complacent. They lose their spark and the driving force that first brought them to success. Why good executives require a "demanding environment," what it entails, and how management can maintain it are the main themes of Patton's discussion.

13. The new manager: a man for all organizations

Gilbert H. Clee

Proverbially, ours is the age of the giant institution. The great industrial conglomerate, the mega-university, the government agency with a budget of billions—all these have taken up more and more room in our expanding economy and our society as a whole.

Over a recent five-year period, total government employment, measured as a fraction of the U.S. working population, increased by more than 65 percent. Enrollment in our five largest universities rose significantly faster than total enrollment in all our senior colleges. Predictably, the most significant gains are found among the largest industrial corporations. A growth comparison of the *Fortune* "500" with all manufacturing companies for the past decade shows that the giants' growth sharply outstripped the average in both sales volume and employment.

We see a spiral process at work. Growth begets growth. With increasing social complexity and advancing technology, the "critical mass" of institutional resources required to deal effectively with the central needs of our society becomes even greater. And the growth of giant organizations, in turn, fosters greater structural complexity and increases the acceleration of technological progress.

The giant institution has the resources, diversity, and scope to fulfill its mission. Whether it accomplishes that mission will depend largely, first, on the quality of management, and second, on the management processes needed to permit such great companies to operate effectively despite their complexity of structure. Will lasting solutions to the fundamental problems of the urban areas be solved? Will the great universities be able to generate scholarship and develop leadership for the next generation? Can higher social and human values be engendered in our society? Can the industrial corporation contribute in proportion to its size to the wealth and growth needed for a steadily rising standard of living, and produce continuing benefits for its shareholders as well?

The answers here depend not on things but rather on people—specifically, on the effectiveness of the people in leadership roles. Increasingly,

146

many of the developing countries have been coming to the realization that lack of resources is not the real bottleneck to economic development. If the developing country has leaders capable of planning, organizing, and producing instruments of economic value, resources can and will be found.

The leadership of giant institutions presents especially difficult challenges. As the dinosaur skeletons in museums remind us, size has its dangers—the dangers of dulled perceptions, sluggish reflexes, and a fatal loss of rapport with the environment. The great and still growing institutions of our day cannot suppose themselves to be exempt from this possibility.

Whether they will in fact survive in good order will largely depend, it seems to me, on the quality of their leadership—by which I mean both the technical skills of management and the caliber of the men who will be at the controls. The essence of the challenge was foreseen by Brooks Adams over half a century ago. "Modern society, if it is to cohere," he wrote, "must have a high order of generalizing mind—a mind which can grasp a multitude of complex relations—but this is a mind which can, at best, only be produced in small quantity and high cost."[1]

The common denominators

What is the nature of the task facing tomorrow's "generalizing minds," the men at the controls of the great institutions? What will be its human and technical requirements? Let us look at certain characteristics of the great institutions and see if they suggest an answer. Four seem to me especially relevant: (1) the degree to which these institutions are shaped by the forces of technological change, (2) their interrelatedness with one another and with their social environment, (3) the increasingly international character of their interests and commitments, and (4) their evolving managerial requirements.

TECHNOLOGICAL CHANGE. The pace of current technology, its impact on our lives, and its challenge to the leadership of our institutions have become familiar themes. Indeed, we hear so much about these problems that they seem a peculiarly mid-20th century phenomenon, like miniskirts and Mars probes. They are not, of course; but they appear vastly more acute today than in Brooks Adams' day. Technological change, we know, has gathered breathtaking momentum. Time has telescoped: Where we could once measure technological advances in 500-year intervals, today we must tax our imaginations to envision the advances of the next few decades. Even then, as Herman Kahn observes, our expectations may fall absurdly short of future realities: "Thus, a study in 1937 missed not only the computer but atomic energy, antibiotics, radar, and jet propul-

---

[1] Brooks Adams, *Theory of Social Revolutions*, The Macmillan Company, New York, 1913, p. 205.

sion, nearly all of which had been around in principle and waiting for development."[2]

With the aid of more sophisticated technological forecasting techniques, we may hope to do a little better at identifying those keys to tomorrow's world that are at hand in principle today. But the surest thing about even our shrewdest forecasts for the year 2000 must be that they will miss the mark, and the second surest thing, that they will miss on the side of conservatism.

Without question, industry has given technology its most spectacular role as both catalyst and consequence of growth. "More even than machinery," as John Kenneth Galbraith puts it in *The New Industrial State*, "massive and complex business organizations are the tangible manifestation of advanced technology."[3] Industrial R&D budgets, the seed money of technological advance, have more than doubled, decade by decade. Not surprisingly, the lion's share of this growth is claimed by a handful of giant enterprises. Already in 1963, 500 great companies were employing almost nine-tenths of all the scientists and engineers engaged in industrial R&D.

Again, research income constitutes the fastest growing source of financing for our great universities, outstripping the rise of student fees, endowment income, and grants from local government. At the University of Michigan, for example, research volume rose from $35 million to $60 million in a recent four-year period.

Although the seedbeds of new technology may be found in the giant industrial company and the great university, it is hard to imagine how *any* of today's great institutions could survive and function without the fruits of technological discovery. Their organization structure, their objectives, the very thinking and behavior of those who work in them are profoundly, if not always consciously, conditioned by technology. Ours is a technological culture. Nowhere can this be seen more clearly than within the great institutions that technology has helped to build.

INTERRELATEDNESS. As giant institutions in both the public and the private sectors have grown, their spheres of interest have increasingly tended to overlap and their contacts and mutual commitments to multiply. Part of the explanation, of course, lies in the nature and organization of advanced technology. Although most of the research in the United States is done in the laboratories of our great corporations and in university research facilities, two-thirds of the funds to support it have come, since 1945, from the Federal Government.

[2] Herman Kahn and Anthony J. Wiener, *The Year 2000: A Framework for Speculation on the Next 33 Years*, The Macmillan Company, New York, 1967, p. 21.

[3] J. K. Galbraith, *The New Industrial State*, Houghton Mifflin Co., Boston, 1967, p. 16.

But the interlocking interests of great institutions have not been confined to the domain of the so-called knowledge workers in research and technology. By virtue of their sheer size, these institutions have become more and more involved with the public interest, as most of their leaders recognize. The recognition goes far beyond lip service to such well-worn concepts as "corporate citizenship." It transcends a decent respect for community opinion and an enlightened circumspection in taking any action likely to affect one or more of the institution's many "publics." It means active, cooperative effort—often, though not always, between the public and private sectors—to help solve or at least ameliorate some of the most severe social and environmental problems of our day: urban decay, poverty, and inequality of opportunity, environmental pollution, the crisis in mass transportation. These issues have come to threaten the very fabric of our society. They demand responses on a scale no single institution, not even government, is yet organized to provide.

The emerging pattern of interinstitutional collaboration for public purposes takes many forms. It has been characterized by varying blends of altruism and self-interest—or more precisely, perhaps, by varying blends of longer and shorter range self-interest. With the aid of government grants, many firms have helped their communities and themselves by training marginal workers for skilled or semiskilled jobs. To attack the problem of urban blight, a group of major life insurance companies decided not long ago to invest the sum of $1 billion—8 percent of their total investment budget for the next 20 years—in low-cost urban housing. Each participant will invest in its own region, while an industry-wide group, the Life Insurance Committee on Urban Problems, will promote the project and recruit builders and sponsors. (Cooperative action on major public projects is nothing new to the insurance companies. These organizations shared with the Department of Health, Education and Welfare in the task of setting up the Medicare system in the United States.)

At a level of far greater complexity, of course, is the joint endeavor to develop a worldwide communications satellite system. This enterprise fairly compels public-private cooperation. The required resources are so enormous, the expertise so rarefied, and the risks so formidable that neither the Federal Government nor any group of private companies would care, or be well advised, to undertake the development task alone.

Other problems may lend themselves to a similar approach. It has been suggested, for example, that a company patterned after the Communications Satellite Corporation would be a logical vehicle for helping American industry invest—profitably, be it noted—in the solution of the nation's urban problems.

In all these cases we see an emerging pattern of planned cooperative response to the massive environmental challenges of our day, a pattern reflecting a growing awareness of common problems and purposes and a growing belief in the efficacy and, broadly, the profitability of concerted action.

INTERNATIONALISM. A third significant dimension in which today's great institutions operate has been the increasing depth and breadth of their international commitments. Many large U.S. corporations have come to be as truly international in climate and character as the International Labour Organization or UNESCO. Out of 144 large U.S. companies surveyed by the newsletter *Business International*, 13 had more than half their assets invested abroad by 1967, and 20 were earning more than half their total net profits from foreign operations. With respect to corporate outlook, and increasingly with respect to organization structure and functional characteristics, these exemplify the true world enterprise. They assess their markets in the light of global alternatives. In the design of corporate strategy, organization structure, management processes, investment decisions, and personnel policies, they seek to plan and control the enterprise as a worldwide whole, devoting its resources to those endeavors and in those places that promise the greatest long-term growth and profit opportunities.

In itself the multinational corporation, or world enterprise, serves as a great internationalizing force. It becomes a conduit, or rather a network of conduits, through which not only capital and technology but human resources, particularly management resources, can be exchanged and circulated on a global scale. The postwar era, which has seen the emergence of the profession of international civil servant, has witnessed also the birth of the truly international manager. His touch may be observed everywhere at the topmost levels of business enterprise.

This transnational dissemination of skills and resources is reflected at the opposite end of the scale in the International Executive Service Corps, which furnishes small foreign companies with the short-term advisory services of seasoned U.S. executives. By the end of 1967, this so-called "Executive Peace Corps" had almost 500 projects completed or under way in a score of less developed nations. In a sense, the domestic trend toward public–private cooperation finds an international parallel in the proliferating contract arrangements between major companies and the governments of other nations, such as Fiat's contract to produce automobiles in a plant in the Soviet Union, or—even more suggestively—Litton Industries' $10 million assignment for the Greek Government in Crete and the Peloponnesus, where teams of agronomists, biochemists, and engineers are using systems analysis to identify the problems of the area and create a master plan to solve them.

MANAGEMENT DEMANDS. The impact of technology, the growing coordination of approaches, and the increasingly international character of their interests and commitments do not represent the only common dimensions

150

of our great institutions. Perhaps more significant, because more organic, are the links of common structure, technique, and internal function that we see developing among organizations as diverse in external function as a major university, an international agency, and a great industrial conglomerate. More and more, functional disciplines such as long-range planning, systems analysis, marketing, financial management, public affairs, and education and training have become identifiable common elements across the entire spectrum of large enterprises applying organized human effort for the attainment of economic or social objectives. Increasingly, the atomization of specialties on the technical level has been counterpointed by common challenges and by a growing universality of opportunity on the management level.

Here again technology—especially in the form of the computer—has been a moving force. It is safe to say that the computer has accelerated the spread of many associated management techniques on which its effective use depends and to which in turn it lends a power and precision hitherto unattainable. For example, systems analysis, simulation, and the use of management models in general come readily to mind. With its ability to handle fantastic numbers of interrelated computations, without man and without error, the computer has immeasurably increased the application of these disciplines.

But the proliferation of other functional tools and techniques owes little to the impetus of information technology. Formal long-range planning, for example, has been practiced everywhere from the Pentagon to the headquarters of the Salvation Army and the Girl Scouts of America. Industrial personnel management techniques such as job evaluation and performance appraisal are used today by hospitals, religious orders, and civil rights organizations. Under a variety of names, marketing and public relations methods play an increasingly vital part in institutional efforts ranging from university fund-raising to the "packaging" of national political candidates. Management control mechanisms such as the so-called "war room" have spread from military headquarters organizations to industry's executive suites and may soon be added to the management resources of state and urban governments. Already, it is worth noting, 35 out of the 50 states have established departments of administration, in many cases specifically charged with providing staff assistance to the governor in such fields as planning, control, and financial and personnel management.

The increasing commitments to education and training by large organizations outside the universities must not be overlooked. We often hear it said that education has moved out of the classroom to become a lifelong project. In a recently published study tracing the job histories of 100 company presidents, Professor Eugene M. Jennings of Michigan State University found that they had typically spent 600 hours in formal development programs after completing their college educations. A third of them were still, as presidents, attending training programs of one kind or another.[4]

The impetus given to the concept of continuing education by the accelerating obsolescence of knowledge is probably not fully appreciated. It has been estimated that business spends annually on training and development more than twice what it costs to operate all our colleges and universities.

The United States Government, the largest organization in the U.S., duplicates the full spectrum of disciplines and techniques to be found in the great private corporation. Long-range planning, computerized management information systems, and financial planning generally overlap here as they do in the private sector. A notable example of the overlap is the so-called Planning-Programming-Budgeting System introduced by Robert S. McNamara in the Defense Department in 1961 and subsequently made mandatory for other Federal departments and agencies. One key feature of the system: the preparation of five-year plans, updated annually, that incorporate cost-benefit studies based in part on sophisticated mathematical analyses of alternatives.

The United States Government also engages in marketing on a scale of which few people are aware. The Forest Service has become the largest seller of timber stumpage in the country; the General Services Administration carries on a $300 million business annually selling minerals out of the nation's strategic stockpile; the Defense Department is probably the world's largest marketer of weapons and weapons systems.

The Government, moreover, has now become a large consumer and a major dispenser of education and training. Within the past five years the U.S. Civil Service Commission has launched a massive educational effort combining in-house training, the use of schools and universities, and the establishment of a number of special institutes. Other agencies, notably the State Department, the National Security Agency, and the Peace Corps, operate extensive separate training facilities of their own.

One factor that has doubtless aided in the cross-pollination of functional disciplines and management techniques among different types of large institutions has been the rise in recent years of management service organizations. John Gardner, Chairman of the Urban Coalition, suggests a picturesque analogy: "Just as the crocodile has a bird that picks its teeth and parasites in its digestive tract, so the modern large-scale organization is picked over and used as a supportive environment by an incredible variety of outsiders. . . . Within limits top management can put its finger on almost any function within the organization and decree that hence-

---

[4] Eugene M. Jennings, *The Mobile Manager*, University of Michigan Press, 1967, p. 21.

forth that function will be performed by an outside organization or contract. For the organization that wishes to maintain maneuverability . . . this offers priceless opportunities."[5]

Priceless or not, they constitute opportunities that large institutions are busily exploiting on an ever-widening scale. Dozens of service organizations exist chiefly to advise the Department of Defense and its dependent services. Hundreds more serve a mixed clientele. Some are specialists: auditors and tax consultants, computer service organizations, public relations firms, executive recruiters, advertising and market research agencies, public opinion analysts. Others are equipped to help any large organization find the solution to any major management problem it would be likely to encounter.

It would be surprising if the activities of these service organizations had not in some measure served to strengthen the functional and technical common denominators among institutions of vastly different origins and social purposes—for it is precisely these common denominators, known collectively under the name of management, that in one way or another define their charters.

Two dimensions of leadership

What sort of management requirements, then, may be implied by these institutional common denominators of intensive technologies, interrelatedness, internationalism, and similarity of internal functions? What sort of "generalizing minds" will be needed to guide these great institutions, maintain their effectiveness of action, and keep them sensitive and responsive to the challenges of an increasingly complex and stressful environment? What kind of educational experience will be needed to prepare tomorrow's managers for this unprecedented challenge?

The answer, it seems to me, must be twofold. More than ever, we need specialists to run the complex machinery of our institutions. Beyond this, we need generalists to coordinate the growing multiplicity of disciplines and functional efforts that the specialists represent. Both specialist and generalist will find legitimate paths to positions of power and leadership in the institutions of tomorrow, but both will be confronted with new requirements. To function effectively as a leader and manager, the specialist must unlearn his parochialism and learn to see beyond the horizons of his discipline. He must become a generalist by conversion, as it were, secure in his own background of technical competence but at the same time intelligently and consciously committed to broader goals.

We see today an unprecedented dispersion of functional specialists among large institutions of every stripe, and, for the individual specialist,

[5] John W. Gardner, *Self-Renewal*, Harper & Row, New York, 1963, p. 84.

153

an unprecedented freedom of movement among organizations. The growth of the executive recruiting firms testifies to the increasing mobility of functional managers from industry to industry, while the rise of the academic consultant and the greater ease of transition (in both directions) between the executive suite and the business-school classroom provides a further clue. Indeed, we can point to few fields today in which the holder of an advanced degree lacks a broad choice of institutional affiliation.

What seems to be developing is a true universality of career opportunity. We have all seen the ads that ask, in effect, "What's a philosopher (or an historian, or a linguist, or an experimental psychologist) doing at IBM?" and go on to answer the question in matter-of-fact, entirely convincing, detail. They have become a sign of the times: a few years hence, such questions will no longer seem provocative. Universality of opportunity for the educated will no longer be a prospect but a present reality. Unquestionably, it will foster development of that breadth of vision required for positions of leadership within the great institutions of tomorrow.

But a new breed of generalist will be needed too. We can find his prototype at the interfaces between the great institutions—the areas where public and private purposes meet, coexist, and often cooperate. Here we see a career pattern emerging, that of the manager-statesman who functions with equal aplomb, and equally clear vision, at the helm of a great corporation, a major foundation, a mega-university or a vast Federal agency. This species of manager makes the institutional interface his specialty. He spends his peak creative years functioning at the critical juncture between public and private interest. Business theorists have talked for decades about management as an integrating discipline and the manager as a man for all organizations. In the mobile manager-statesmen, the super-generalists of our day, the theory is brilliantly exemplified.

But this kind of interinstitutional mobility will not necessarily be expected of tomorrow's generalist-managers. What is, or will be, indispensable for these managers is a new empathy with the specialist, a new grasp and sophistication in the use of functional tools, a new mastery of technical methodologies. They must be able to talk the language and understand the professional approaches of the diverse corps of specialists whose activities they will direct.

Many of these new generalist-managers must be bred in the graduate schools of business. We have considerable evidence that the schools will be equal to the task. They are good, and getting better. I do not think there can be much doubt that the new MBAs of today are far better equipped than their predecessors to meet the opportunities and challenges that await them—and I do not doubt that the same will be true of succeeding generations of graduates. Yet the new MBA cannot be a finished product. Much of the knowledge he will need to master before the end of his career has yet to be discovered, and much that he has painfully acquired will soon be obsolete or irrelevant. Simply to keep up with his job, he will be involved in some kind of formal education during much of his working lifetime.

The new generation of MBAs will also find that not all obsolescence is technical. The manager who mentally erects a Berlin Wall between the public and private interests, rejects or ignores their increasing mutual involvement, and lacks patience with all values not preceded by a dollar sign will increasingly suffer an erosion of status and influence. The old-style organization man appears to be well along the road to extinction.

The new universalists

In part for the very reason that he cannot be a finished product, the career alternatives open to the new manager have broadened as never before. He may start his career in a large corporation, in hospital or university administration, in a government agency or a management service organization. But at any time his skills will be transferable and his experience will be relevant across most institutional lines. Like the manager-statesmen of today, he too will be a man for all organizations.

Most of the new managers, of course, will pursue career paths in the great corporations. Many may well find themselves assigned, at some point, to positions or projects that lie along the public-private interface. And some, it seems safe to predict, will at some stage of their career take a "tour of duty" in a public agency, with the support and encouragement of their corporate employers. A few MBAs—probably a growing few—will opt for careers outside the private sector. A remark by Donald C. Cook, President of American Electric Power Co., is pertinent: "The requirements for success in government or business don't differ much," he said. "In government you are a civil servant looking after the public interest, and in business you are a corporate executive with an eye on the requirements of the public interest."[6]

Still other management generalists and functional specialists, I believe, will be attracted to consulting careers. They will respond to the lure of the professional climate, the intellectual challenge of top-management problem solving, and the opportunity to function across the full gamut of public and private institutions. Here, universality of opportunity takes on a unique dimension.

Whatever his chosen career path, the challenges faced by the new manager were surely never so great. But his tools and techniques appear potentially equal to meeting them. Until quite recently, far too many talented managers have spent far too much time analyzing the past for clues on how to avoid previous pitfalls and repeat previous successes. The

[6] Quoted in *Fortune*, March 1967, p. 127.

management tools and analytical techniques possessed by today's MBAs make them perhaps the first generation of managers truly equipped to plan the future with confidence and in detail.

The leaders of tomorrow's great institutions have yet to emerge from the throngs of young men and women who find their way each year from the graduate-school classroom into their first full-time jobs as functional specialists or management trainees. But from what I have seen of these young people—their energies, their talents, their abilities, and their values —I am convinced that the managers of tomorrow will equal or surpass the performance of their most distinguished predecessors. I know no chief executive who does not share this conviction.

Over 40 years ago, the philosopher Alfred North Whitehead, contemplating the gathering momentum of technology in his day, wrote: "The prophecy of Francis Bacon has been fulfilled and man, who at times has dreamt of himself as a little lower than the angels, has submitted to become the servant and minister of nature. It still remains to be seen whether the same actor can play both parts."[7]

The question has become more urgent today. The answer remains in doubt. But, looking at the new generation of managers, I believe we have some right to feel reassured.

[7] A. N. Whitehead, *Science and the Modern World*, The Macmillan Company, New York, 1925.

14. The coming scramble for executive talent

Arch Patton

Evidence is accumulating that a "no holds barred" scramble for executive talent—already in short supply—will develop in the next few years. Indeed, the demand for this increasingly rare commodity could reach such boom proportions by 1975 that even the best-managed companies, which have executive talent in considerable depth today, would be unfavorably affected.

Already, a number of highly regarded companies with reputations for doing an outstanding job of recruiting and developing talent are being subjected to persistent "raiding" by recruiters on behalf of their competitors. It could be said that the better a company's reputation as a talent developer, the more aggressive the raids. In effect, the have-nots are looking to the haves for sorely needed top-caliber executive manpower.

To counter this threat to their hard-earned wealth of talent, a number of leading companies have taken steps to protect their manpower position. So far, the principal emphasis has been on improving executive utilization and in this way increasing executive productivity. But now more and more of these companies are making a major effort to understand better what motivates an executive; in addition, they are studying their competitive compensation position with great care.

Underlying this growing talent shortage are a number of factors that seem unlikely to yield to any easy, short-term solution: the low birthrate of the 1930s; the unprecedented expansion in the size of the average corporation in recent years; the increasing complexity of the management process; and the burgeoning demand for executive talents outside industry —notably in government and education.

Other factors not so easy to identify appear certain to aggravate industry's manpower problem. For example, the rise of the professional manager seems to have been accompanied by an erosion in the executive's loyalty to his employer. Sharply increasing turnover at upper management levels clearly labels this loyalty slump as a malaise of major future consequence. Even the best led companies have lost outstanding executives to their competitors in recent years, a rare occurrence prior to World War II.

With the developing shortage, top management's preoccupation with executive personnel problems will surely increase. Already we see signs of what is to come. Said one corporation president recently: "This spring we were one of 300 companies attempting to recruit at a well-regarded business school. The entire graduating class numbered exactly 275. The economic of this situation is ridiculous."

During the past decade of expansion, company after company has reacted to an internal shortage of executive talent by raiding a competitor for this essential ingredient in growth. But this solution to the problem loses its effectiveness as the wolves begin to outnumber the sheep, and already it has become uncomfortably expensive. Because the recruited executive is usually paid well above "the market," a morale problem may arise among the company's present executive group, unless, of course, the entire executive compensation structure has been adjusted to bring the insiders' pay into line. Companies which have recruited a sizable number of executives over several years often find their total compensation levels being repeatedly jacked up in this manner without any corresponding increase in the quality of performance by the executive group. It is beginning to dawn on such companies that the talent squeeze actually threatens to limit their growth potential unless they act now to develop an overall plan of attack on the problem.

Manpower assessment

The logical first step in any such program—and one that remarkably few companies have taken—is to find the full dimensions of the problem they face. Answers are needed to such questions as: What are our qualitative and quantitative manpower needs likely to be in the coming years? Can we develop these talents ourselves, or will trained personnel have to be recruited from outside? Does the way we are organized minimize the need for executives and provide job challenge to our people? Is our growth effort sufficiently dynamic?

Almost without exception, companies setting out to assess their manpower needs in the years ahead find large gaps in the information required to reach sound conclusions on such questions. For example, it is difficult to determine the talents that should be recruited from the colleges and universities in 1970 without a thoughtful assessment of what the company will be like in 1980 when such recruits move up to levels of executive responsibility. It makes little sense to recruit electrical engineers if the business 10 or 15 years hence will require chemists. In other words, some reasonably long-range, broadly based judgments of the future of the business are needed *today*.

The importance of such a long-term assessment of the industrial environment was driven home to one big company by a painful talent squeeze in recent years. Starting from a single product line, by the early 1960s the company had not only developed several new lines in the same industry but had also moved heavily into two new, technologically competitive industries. Plans for this change in company direction and complexity had been known to the directors for nearly a decade. Yet, because the type and quality of the talent the company recruited in the universities ten years ago had never changed to reflect this recognized future need, the company found itself saddled with scores of inadequate middle managers who had to be replaced by a massive outside recruiting effort. With 20–20 hindsight, the top executives of this company now realize that a future-focused recruiting program, starting in the middle 1950s, would have averted much of their present travail.

Many companies carefully project income and expense budgets five years into the future, but develop no plans for the number and kinds of people needed to meet these budgets. Yet invading a new market, building a new plant, and even growth itself require manpower planning as well as a financial program. Recognizing this logic, a few companies have begun to insist that divisional and functional budgets spell out not only the action required to attain the dollar income and expense targets they establish, but also describe the manpower needed to attain these goals.

Thus, if a new plant is expected to come on-stream with a new product three years hence, the planning system calls for a detailed reporting of the number of hourly, clerical, and managerial employees needed to produce and distribute its output. Such a forecast, in turn, provides the basis for what might be termed the company's manpower stewardship. Since this manpower budget constitutes an integral part of the financial planning process, it is possible to forecast the number and kinds of jobs to be filled in the years ahead on a company-wide basis. This provides a practical means of visualizing what future personnel needs can be met by promotion from within versus outside recruiting.

Promotion analysis

Another gap that frequently confronts companies probing upcoming executive talent needs is the scarcity of facts about the promotion process. How many men must be recruited at the lowest supervisory level to provide adequate manpower in the years ahead *at each level* in the organization structure? What attrition rate can be expected as men move up the promotion ladder? Will there be an identifiable career path to the top? Has the promotion rate been faster or slower than that of competitors? Is promotion significantly faster in some functions than in others?

It is widely conceded that promotion is the Number One executive incentive—since it usually involves both money and status. Yet only a few companies have begun to develop hard information on this subject. If Company A has found a way, by organization or by expansion, to promote its executives every three years on the average, while Company B takes six years to do so, the former has a powerful motivational advantage over the latter. If the sales department of a company promotes two-thirds of its people in four years, while accounting promotes only one-third over the same period, an unfortunate talent imbalance soon develops. Recognizing that the one function offers far greater opportunity than the other, the bright young men who are brought in from the colleges soon either transfer to sales or leave the company.

It may not be possible to correct this kind of situation painlessly, but certainly management should be aware that the problem exists—and without job tenure data its existence is liable to be concealed. Such data will be useful in other ways too: they may disclose that the effectiveness of an executive incentive plan has been undermined by too-short executive tenure, which hampers accurate appraisal of performance. For example, when a majority of executives have been on their present jobs less than 18 months, the boss-subordinate relationship is only nine months! How good a "reading" on a man's performance does less than nine months' exposure provide? Or an examination of job data may show that unduly long tenure is debilitating the competitive environment and causing the better men to drift away.

Skills inventory

Another key ingredient often missing in the company's manpower knowledge has been a "skills inventory" of individual qualities for match-up with jobs needs. How many men, by function or by responsibility level, are promotable? And according to what standards? Confidential studies by several large companies I know have demonstrated beyond serious question that a substantial proportion, often as many as one third, of those tagged promotable by their superiors lack the talents required for higher level jobs. This, of course, raises an ominous question about those deemed *not* promotable by their supervisors. We have little check on those passed over for promotion—except turnover! If those supervisors are missing the target by so wide a margin on promotability, perhaps their judgment regarding nonpromotability may be equally poor.

There are two elements involved in the problem of promoting or not promoting an executive: (1) the demonstrated qualities of the individual in question, and (2) the known requirements of the job. Until very recently, these two parts of the puzzle were evaluated by the instinctive "feel" of a senior executive. Experimental efforts by a number of companies have been directed at separating the two components and fitting them together on a more rational basis. In each case the result has been a substantial improvement over the more common seat-of-the pants judgment. For instance, one large company has concluded from its experimental assessment of individual qualities versus job needs over recent years that upwards of half of its promotion choices today are better than they would have been under the old system. This improvement, in the company's view, involves both the selection of executives having greater talent for specific jobs and the avoidance of "square pegs in round holes" promotions.

A number of top managements have taken advantage of the vast memory of the computer to match up company-wide job needs with individual skills and aptitudes. Typically, they set down the skill requirements of positions that make up what might be called a normal executive career path. These are the jobs critical to company success in marketing, manufacturing, engineering, and so on. At the same time, these managements develop a skills inventory of individual executives by searching out the *demonstrated* skills of those who have held jobs in these critical areas. The matching of the two in such a computer program not only provides better men for job openings, but it also offers a big motivational lift to executives by increasing their confidence that their talents will not be overlooked when an opening does occur.

Increasingly, leading companies have recognized the risks of basing the stewardship of their executive manpower on inadequate information during a period of scarcity. While the effort is still limited to a relatively few companies, I believe more information about the recruitment, development, promotion, and compensation of executives has been brought together in the past two or three years than in the whole preceding decade.

While preparations for dealing with the talent scramble of the next ten years are beyond the embryonic stage in a number of companies, most of them recognize present efforts as a start-up phase. Few regard today's activities as a full answer to tomorrow's manpower stewardship problems.

We have three distinct kinds of action a company can institute in order to minimize the impact of the talent scramble. It can (1) take steps to reduce its future need for executives, (2) strive to hold the good executive talent it already possesses, and (3) look for ways to increase its future supply of executives.

Reducing the need

One of the most significant efforts in today's manpower planning has been aimed at reducing the need for executives. This has taken two interrelated forms: (1) reorganizing the business so as to minimize the number of executives required for effective management, and (2) restructuring individual jobs so as to enlarge individual executive responsibilities.

FEWER EXECUTIVES. Companies—and, indeed, whole industries—that have been profitable for long periods tend to prove Parkinson's Law is no spoof. A classic example of this occurred a few years ago when a number of the major oil companies—faced with a profit squeeze for the first time in some years—reorganized literally thousands of executives out of their jobs. Though less spectacularly, many other companies that decentralized a decade or so ago are now in the process of at least partial recentralization in the interests of lower costs and more effective control over expenses and profits. While the computer has been credited with spurring some of this recentralization, management recognition of simple overstaffing seems to have been the stimulus in most cases.

Thus many corporate reorganizations are triggered by the need to reduce costs. The more astute managements recognize another side to this coin: more efficient organization itself reduces the need for executives. When three men do the work of two men, not only does each of them have less than a full-time job, but they also get in one another's way.

Increasingly, therefore, companies are examining the structure of their organizations. The stress is on clearing away the accumulation of non-productive activities, eliminating overlapping responsibilities, clarifying and simplifying line-staff relationships, and the like. Rare indeed is the company unable to trim overhead by reorganizing and restructuring—and, at the same time, strengthening its competitive muscle.

Some unusual organizational problems have resulted from industry's thrust overseas. These are particularly troublesome when the deployment of technical skills having a major bearing on profitability is not organizationally controlled in the interests of the corporation as a whole. Many companies have found, for example, that decentralizing certain functional activities can result in serious personnel—and profit—problems.

For example, a divisionalized mining or petroleum producer seeking to staff a potentially important area abroad with essential specialized skills, may find that its profit center divisions or regions will give up only the dregs of their staffs. Moreover, once repatriated, the specialists who have served abroad frequently find they have lost ground in their career paths or that they are unwanted when the time comes to return home. Even when responsibility for decisions on organizational matters has been centralized, it often turns out that old organizational habits make the implementation of such a changeover an extremely frustrating and expensive exercise.

ENLARGED RESPONSIBILITIES. Too many executives in the average company today—particularly at middle-management levels—do not have enough responsibility to keep fully occupied. As a result, the paperwork flow and

162

committee activities, as so accurately described in *Parkinson's Law*,[1] increase to fill the void left by the lack of real responsibilities.

One important result of reducing the number of jobs by organizational changes, of course, has been to enlarge the responsibilities of the remaining jobs. This frequently has the beneficial side effect of making a really demanding job out of what may have been a relatively soft berth. In turn, the more demanding job fulfills a motivational need that the behavioral scientists associate with job enlargement. The "easy job" apparently atrophies the driving energy that is nurtured by the "hard job."

Often overlooked, too, is another value in this tightening-up process: as more company-wide responsibility shifts to fewer executives, the relative contribution of each comes into clearer focus. It simply becomes easier to judge who does what if fewer people are involved. In addition to any broadening of the responsibility base, this has what might be called a "job enrichment" value.

For years, top-management thinking has been conditioned to consider the importance of the position, rather than the contribution of the person in the position, as a by-product of the job evaluation process involved in salary administration. This has tended to obscure the internal job–value relationships among top jobs that we used to find before the salary surveys and formal administration programs appeared on the scene. Under the old scheme of things, there were only a few key jobs, and their relative importance to the company was crystal clear to all concerned.

Today, a proliferation of staff jobs and a bubbling up into higher management of line jobs in purchasing, traffic, distribution, and the like has blunted top management's appreciation of the *values contributed to the job by the individual*. In many positions—particularly staff jobs—the contribution of the individual varies far more widely than normal salary ranges. But as organizational shifts clarify the real contributions of individuals, the leveling out of executive pay differentials that characterized the job–value syndrome is giving way to a more realistic recognition of the individual in compensation administration.

An interesting commentary on corporate reorganization efforts is contained in a talk given a few years ago by Roy Ash, the president of Litton Industries:

> Our company has to have builders, so we've tried to create for this type of executive an environment that you might call a "free form" approach to management.
>
> To the extent possible, everybody has a line job. We like our executives to stand exposed to their prospective success or failure individually, rather than as an indistinguishable part of a functionalized crowd.

[1] C. Northcote Parkinson, *Parkinson's Law*, Boston, Houghton Mifflin Company, 1957.

As a company grows more functionalized, everybody holds everybody else up, so you can't tell when one fellow is held up entirely by the crowd around him.

We don't have published organization charts or standing committees, for the same reason. We believe that in the growth process the organization structure should not be developed too tightly. As a practical matter, the biggest volume of creative activity in our company would probably take place in the white space between the boxes on the organization chart—if we had one.[2]

Holding good people

With executive talent growing scarcer, one of the obvious efforts of companies must be to hang on to the executives they have. Since the "cost effectiveness" of compensation in almost any form appears likely to decline as the scramble for executive talent grows more intense, a number of companies have been experimenting in other directions. This effort goes well beyond the usual fringe benefits, such as executive dining rooms, rugs on the floor, country clubs, and use of company cars.

Typically, these companies are attempting to learn more about what motivates their executives, and why. To this end, they have been using the talents of behavioral scientists to help identify hypotheses worthy of further study. A typical example of this activity would be the effort to structure jobs to fit the talent and capacity of an executive, rather than fitting the man into a preconceived job. If this can be done, say the behavioral scientists, it would have the effect of increasing individual productivity and morale, as well as reducing the number of executives needed.

As a practical matter, we have considerable evidence that companies will organize around the talents of outstanding executives when they are in trouble, or when they encounter a critical talent shortage. Many companies have done so without being fully conscious of their break with traditional organizational concepts. But if the individual-oriented approach is useful under conditions of stress, it may well be worth trying under other conditions.

Obviously, a well-administered compensation program also helps hold an executive team together. A few years ago, the average company kept a sharp eye on the competitive level of the cash compensation of its executives. Stock options, pensions, profit sharing, insurance, and the other fringe benefits were considered to be necessary "goodies," but somehow separate and apart. More recently, top management has recognized that compensation is a total package, made up of both current and deferred income,

[2] Delivered at McKinsey & Company's Biennial Conference, New York, October 14, 1966.

which must be consistently administered to be fully effective as an incentive.

Top management has also begun to appreciate the fact that, next to promotion and dismissal, compensation serves as the most powerful signal the company can use to tell the individual executive how he is doing. A compensation signal can be given more often, and also in greater variation, than a promotion signal.

In short, I believe that the increasing pressures to manage executive manpower more effectively as a holding mechanism have triggered an important change in emphasis where pay is concerned. The need to attract, develop, and deploy the *right* men has forced management to give far greater attention than it ever did before to the skills required to do these three things well. As a result, the role of compensation administration becomes increasingly dependent on the manpower actions dictated by these recruitment, development, and deployment needs. Fewer and fewer companies now have performance appraisal programs standing on their own—in a vacuum. Most companies with such programs relate them to an executive bonus plan which, in turn, is usually directly responsive to the profitability of the corporation. Furthermore, the guidelines for such an executive appraisal program are typically part of the company's planning and control system.

Increasing the supply

High on the list of questions to which leading companies are seeking answers is why men want to be promoted; and, more importantly, why they sometimes do not. Power, prestige, money, and self-fulfillment are all known to be important to the former, although relatively little is known about the importance of each to the individual. The fact that men "plateau out" and become unpromotable has been common knowledge. Why they should do so is less clear.

Another potentially productive source of added future talent is the otherwise promotable men who reject the promotional opportunity. Recent private studies indicate that this may be a relatively large group at certain levels of management. One such study, for instance, found that nearly one man in three who was promoted to a job with full profit responsibility (division manager), and was believed to have the talent to handle a bigger job, lost his appetite for greater responsibility.

Little is yet known about this phenomenon, but it certainly behooves management to understand why a man rejects responsibility that he has been judged capable of handling. Is it the disproportion between the added after-tax income and the added effort and risk? Or the emotional reaction to being exposed, individually, to his own success or failure? Or the constant pounding from top management to do better?

As noted earlier, other factors helping to increase the supply of executives include recruiting better executive candidates, training them more effectively, and pounding fewer round pegs into square holes. For example, few companies have yet turned to women as potential executive candidates. Yet many executive jobs, particularly in the staff areas, require the imaginative intelligence and perseverance so many women possess. Furthermore, many graduate schools of business have accepted women, and the supply of female MBAs is likely to increase sharply over the next decade.

New approaches to executive training have received a high priority. For instance, a number of companies have developed what one of them calls an "early warning system" for identifying high-potential men early in their careers. In essence, this is a factual follow-up of all college recruits, applying the same work-oriented performance appraisal standards across the company. This "tracking" of the high-potential men attempts to ensure that each man remains under close surveillance in his early, formative years. In the past, too many high-potential men have been lost from sight, and either have left the company or have vegetated in jobs well below their real talent level.

Upgrading personnel organization

There appears to be a growing awareness among top companies that the typical personnel organization today may well be inadequate to cope with tomorrow's manpower problems. This is only due in part to the considerable pressures stemming from the upcoming talent scramble. It also reflects a realization—at long last—that management has rarely provided the personnel function with the muscle it needs to get the job done.

In the old days, the executive who couldn't make it in a line job was frequently transferred to the personnel department. There he continued to make inadequate decisions, further downgrading the function in top management's eyes and causing good men to give personnel a wide berth because it lacked internal status. Today many of these same companies are putting their "comers" into personnel. To replace a weak top personnel executive, such companies have not hesitated to pay whatever it took in money and status to obtain the right man—from the outside if necessary. Further, top management itself is spending an increasing proportion of its own available working hours on personnel problems.

With time, this upgrading of talent in personnel departments, and the accompanying increase in top-level attention, should greatly strengthen the function's ability to influence top management. As more aggressive and resourceful new executives tackle their manifold problems, top management has begun to take notice. The function undoubtedly has a way to go before it becomes fully accepted at the top, but considerable strides are already evident.

CENTRALIZED AUTHORITY. A related weakness now in the process of correction bears on the responsibility of personnel departments. Corporate efforts to deal with manpower resources are often appallingly fragmented. For example, many companies make one executive responsible for the blue-collar workers, while another handles the white-collar employees—with the president as their common boss. This makes the president the personnel officer. Moreover, in many companies responsibility for the various elements in the compensation package is broken up even further, with salary administration divided between these two executives, the pension plan under the treasurer, group insurance under the controller, and stock options under the corporate secretary.

Such fragmented responsibility has resulted in an untold number of poor decisions. I know of several companies whose executives retire with greater post-retirement income than they ever earned while working! In almost every instance, this costly waste can be traced to a division of responsibility, with the pension plan under one executive and responsibilities for the other post-retirement add-ons—whether profit sharing, savings plans, or deferred compensation—assigned elsewhere.

Obviously, if an executive famine is impending, centralized responsibility for the recruitment, training, and motivating of this group is essential. Since many corporate practices relating to executives also involve blue-collar employees, it is logical to put responsibility for all aspects of manpower resources under a single highly competent executive.

In my view, the upgrading of talent assigned to personnel may well prove to be the single most important action a company can take in dealing with the executive shortage. The new breed of personnel executive does not regard his company role as that of a "keeper of the mystique," a withdrawn practitioner who provides management with his expertise on request. Instead, his job includes the whole range of responsibilities dealing with the acquiring, training, organizing, and paying of employees at all levels. He is expected to lead—to *anticipate* problems, to *plan* for the future, to *support* the economic viability of his company—in short, to be a businessman.

ENLARGED MISSION. Instead of being a backwater function—as it all too frequently has been—the personnel activity becomes the means by which management assures itself that (1) its manpower stewardship is geared to meet future needs, (2) the quantity and quality of the input is adequate, (3) the work assignments develop an individual's natural aptitudes and build an adequate backlog of functional skills, and (4) the promotion process furnishes enough leaders in the several functional areas so that every job opening finds a number of qualified individuals competing for the job. In other words, management development becomes part of the normal process of running the business!

All this means that while the personnel department—with the computer's assistance—still has its housekeeping job to do, its main thrust will be aimed at gaining knowledge about much that is now unknown or little known. This involves expanding present research efforts to recruit the right people, structuring jobs so that the effectiveness of individuals is heightened, exploring the career paths by which executives are developed, and understanding more clearly the motivations of executives.

Conclusion

How hard the impending scramble for executive talent will hit a given company depends in some measure on how effectively today's actions by management prepare for tomorrow. A program that makes better use of talent, provides a competitive work environment, offers the individual executive an interesting challenge, and consistently rewards his efforts will certainly limit whatever damage does occur.

One positive result of such a program, inevitably, will be a real transformation of the personnel function. Its role will be more important. Talented, resourceful people will be required to carry out its mission. Only a relatively few companies have accepted this fact, but the number is rapidly expanding as the manpower pressure increases. Within the next few years I believe that most of the larger companies will have bowed to the inevitable. By 1975, indeed, the competition for outstanding personnel executives may prove the most difficult scramble of all.

15. Compensation and the executive career cycle

George H. Foote

A large primary metals producer found that the practice of paying modest salaries and sizable but variable bonuses was largely to blame for the heavy turnover among the company's younger executives. Faced with heavy immediate financial obligations, yet unable to predict their earnings level from year to year, these executives were yielding to the lure of higher salary guarantees elsewhere—even when this often meant settling for lower total compensation.

An old-line textile company balanced traditionally low salary levels with a generous and costly benefit package for its managers. Finally forced to increase the salary scale in order to attract and hold younger management talent, the company ended up with total compensation costs considerably higher than those for the industry.

A chemicals producer decided that stock options would be the least costly means of making the compensation package more attractive. The options, though profitable, posed a dilemma for many executives in their forties and fifties. These men needed cash, not paper profits, yet they felt cashing in would be a sign of disloyalty. Two key executives resolved this problem by selling their stock and leaving the company.

These three experiences illustrate a common truth: An executive's compensation needs reflect his career position. The ideal compensation package for a senior executive, for example, may work real hardship on a young department head, and vice versa. Failure to recognize this fact costs companies millions of dollars annually in wasted executive compensation outlays, not to mention reduced executive incentive, unrealized potential, and the loss of managers who leave for better, though not necessarily bigger, compensation packages.

The career cycle concept

The compensation needs of executives can best be understood in terms of the executive career cycle. With this understanding, management can identify the most practical means of tailoring its compensation program to executive career requirements, and determine which of these best serves the company's own particular situation.

An executive's career cycle generally spans three main phases, corresponding roughly to the age brackets 30–40, 40–55, and 55 and up. The boundaries, of course, are fuzzy, and individual executive situations differ widely in each phase. But there is enough consistency in the pattern to permit some useful generalizations. To illustrate, let us examine the career cycle of a hypothetical executive, Philip Donaldson, employed by a large, diversified manufacturing concern.

THE EARLY YEARS. Midway in his thirties, Philip Donaldson holds a middle-management position as assistant controller of his division. After four years in the job, he is confident of his ability and impatient to move up. Although loyal to his company, he does not necessarily regard his present employment as a career commitment. His age, experience, and mobility make him a natural target for executive recruiters. In fact, several have already approached him, and he has seriously considered one or two offers.

Married and with three young children, Donaldson finds it hard to keep up with his growing family obligations, despite three substantial pay increases in the past four years. He has a sizable mortgage on his house, a year to go on his car payments, and the prospect of more than $2,000 in orthodontal work for two of his children. Though his life insurance program is barely adequate, he complains of being "insurance poor." He now feels the pinch of progressive income tax rates, and the total of his various tax obligations has already become discouraging. Understandably, he cannot make much progress in accumulating capital.

Donaldson's compensation requirements are easily definable. He needs all the current income he can get, and he needs to be able to count on it. He needs to protect his income from the impact of large, unpredictable expenses such as massive medical bills. And he needs to provide his family with a source of continuing income in the event of his death or disability.

THE MIDDLE YEARS. Consider Donaldson's position 12 years later. Now in his late forties, he has become a vice president of his division, and management considers him to have the potential to fill a top corporate post. Because of his reputation as a "comer," he still receives an occasional call from executive recruiters. Though he finds the attention flattering, the bait is less tempting. The chances are that he will stay put.

His financial situation, too, has changed, even though his expenses remain perilously close to his income, now approaching $40,000. With two children in college and the third expecting to enter in a couple of years, he faces an education expense of roughly $7,000 annually for the next few years. He carries a much heavier insurance program. He owns a bigger

170

house with a bigger mortgage. Other visible consequences of his higher executive status include a two-year-old Cadillac, a late model station wagon, membership in one of the better country clubs, and a more elaborate wardrobe for Mrs. Donaldson. In addition, the tax pinch has by this time become really painful.

Not surprisingly, Donaldson still finds it difficult to build capital, though he now follows the financial press closely to prepare for the day when he has more money to invest. In other respects, his financial requirements have changed subtly but significantly. For one thing, he has more control over the timing of his major expenses during the year. He can thus tolerate some fluctuations in his income and no longer needs to receive it all on a regular monthly basis.

Second, while Donaldson's age and tax bracket make death and disability coverage increasingly costly, his insurance outlays now constitute a substantially smaller proportion of his total income. And finally, the problem of building a retirement estate now looms as urgent. Heavy expenses have kept him from doing much in this direction, and he has less and less time left to build his nest egg. At this stage of his career, then, Donaldson needs to start building retirement capital, as well as to maximize his yearly cash income.

THE LATER YEARS. Now consider Donaldson's situation midway in the final phase of his career cycle. At 58, he is an officer of the corporation. His compensation is approaching $60,000 a year. It appears virtually certain that he will stay in his present niche. Although Donaldson has lost none of his managerial effectiveness, he feels occasionally tempted to rest on his laurels during his remaining tenure and finds himself less willing to maintain the same physical pace as in the past. He travels less, takes longer vacations, and is more conscious of the need for "conserving himself."

Donaldson's expenses have declined, but not nearly so much as he had once expected. Continued financial outlays on behalf of his children (a daughter in graduate school and a son beginning medical practice) are still a heavy drain. His earnings peak will inevitably be accompanied by a peak in his tax bracket, further eroding the margin of any income that can be invested. His retirement fund goal is still far out of sight—too far, at his present rate of saving and investment, to leave him much hope of reaching it in the remaining few years of his working career. His most urgent financial need, then, is twofold: to minimize the tax bite on his income and to build up his retirement estate.

Tailoring the compensation package

What implications does the executive career cycle, of which Philip Donaldson's is fairly typical, have for the design of the corporate compensation program? In most companies, at any given time, the executive group includes individuals at every stage of the cycle. How can a company fit the pay package to the varying needs of executives at different stages of the cycle, and at the same time maximize the stockholders' return on the compensation dollar? Considering the range of compensation devices available—salary, bonus, deferrals, stock options, pension, and insurance —which should be applied where and in what forms?

CURRENT CASH COMPENSATION. Salary, or salary plus bonus, usually accounts for the bulk of the executive compensation package. Unlike other forms of compensation, the form of base salary cannot be ingeniously tailored to fit individual needs but a company can decide what part of the cash compensation package will be paid as base salary. This, to executives in the first stage of the career cycle, will be a critically important decision. As we have seen, younger executives typically need all the cash they can get their hands on, and they want it to be coming in regularly. Because their expenses will generally be high and their budgets inflexible, unpredictable fluctuations in their cash income can work a real hardship.

As a result, except for the rare young executive who is high enough in the company to influence profit results significantly and be paid accordingly, most men under 40 must be seen as poor candidates for inclusion in incentive bonus plans. They cannot really afford the risk, inherent in a true incentive plan, of having their income depend in part on company performance. For most executives in this stage of the career cycle, therefore, salary should be the major form, if not the sole form, of direct compensation. The incentive element should be supplied chiefly through merit and promotional increases.

In contrast, where executives in the middle and later stages of their career cycles are concerned, an incentive bonus plan can be advantageous for the man as well as for the company. First, it gives the executive an opportunity to earn unusual rewards as a result of unusual performance. Beyond this, a variable annual bonus award is less likely to be fully absorbed by current living expenses than is the monthly salary check. Incentive pay can thus be a real help to the executive accumulating capital.

DEFERRED COMPENSATION. As companies have tried to tailor compensation to offset rising taxes, deferred pay arrangements have gained in popularity. As a rule, these arrangements aim to reduce the tax bite on executive incomes by postponing some portion of salary or bonus until after retirement when the individual will be in a lower tax bracket.

But the usefulness of such deferred income ought to be seen as sharply limited. For the young executive not yet in a high tax bracket, deferrals are obviously pointless. And even for the executive midway through his career cycle, the advantages often prove illusory. Simple arithmetic demon-

172

strates that the typical middle-aged executive would do better to take all his compensation on a current basis, pay the tax on it, and invest the excess in tax-exempt income or for long-term capital gains than he would to defer a portion of his income for 25, 20, or even 15 years.

For one thing, the 20-year accumulated earnings of the current after-tax income will usually far exceed the anticipated tax savings. For another, those savings may not even materialize if the individual succeeds in building up a substantial retirement estate.

But highly paid executives only a few years from retirement have a real interest in accumulating retirement capital. For these men, deferrals can offer a great deal. Also, when an individual executive stands to benefit from a deferral arrangement, his company can increase his potential gain by putting his deferrals to work for him. Thus, deferrals may be used to pay premiums on a corporate-owned life insurance policy, increasing the benefits in the event of the executive's death or disability. Or the deferred amounts might be invested in company stock or in other equities to permit their value to increase through income and appreciation.

The use of the company's own stock as the vehicle has the added advantage of increasing the individual's incentive to improve company performance and stock values. If deferrals are to be paid out over a period of years in the form of company stock, they may even provide some additional incentive for the executive to develop a top-flight successor who can help to maintain company performance at a high level.

One way of providing deferrals for those who can benefit from them, without creating disadvantages for others, will be to give each participant in an incentive bonus plan the option of deferring part or all of the payout. One company, for example, offers each executive three options: (1) to have future incentive bonus awards paid 100 percent when earned, (2) to take these awards 50 percent when earned and 50 percent after retirement, or (3) to defer the whole amount until after retirement. The deferred amounts are invested in company stock or government bonds at the company's discretion. Over the years, it should be noted, surprisingly few bonus plans have offered such flexible deferred compensation arrangements.

STOCK OPTIONS. For more than a decade, stock options have been the most popular of all specialized executive compensation devices. From management's viewpoint, increased executive stock ownership serves as a strong incentive to improve company performance. Options cost shareholders nothing unless the shares increase in value; even then, the cost will not be reflected in earnings per share but takes the more subtle form of a dilution in equity. And, unlike many other compensation devices, stock options can be selectively applied and easily administered.

To the individual executive, options offer an appealing opportunity to share in company profits without having to share in losses. Equally important, they provide a means of building income via the tax-favored capital gains route.

But stock options can easily be misused. When granted to executives who exert no significant influence on profits (a not unusual practice) they hardly seem justified from the shareholders' standpoint. Where executive income is not yet high enough to give the options real tax appeal, the device becomes little more than a costly and inconvenient status symbol. Most younger executives would much prefer cash, which, being tax deductible to the company, costs the shareholders less and does not permanently dilute equity.

Clearly, the most logical prospects for stock options will be higher ranking executives in the middle and older phases of their career cycles. Normally, such executives directly influence corporate results and stand to benefit most from the tax advantage of options. Even for senior executives, however, the attractiveness of stock options may be clouded by certain aspects of their tax treatment. Thus, the usefulness of stock options cannot be taken for granted, and management will be wise to consider each application carefully.

The retirement program

In nearly every company, the retirement program is one of the costliest, most important, and most closely regulated of fringe benefits. Its meaning to the individual executive changes as he passes through the three phases of his career cycle.

The younger executive obviously worries a good deal more about meeting his family expenses right now than he does about benefit levels 30 years from now. If he is realistic, he recognizes that he may have moved on to another company by then. At the other extreme, the senior executive who expects to stay put and has accumulated too little retirement capital becomes vitally concerned about retirement benefits—often, and quite rightly, even more than about his current income.

Where a pension plan has been established as the basic retirement vehicle, several ways of tailoring the program to meet these divergent executive needs may be worked out. One possibility: to base benefits on average compensation during the final five or ten years of service, rather than the total period of employment. This has special appeal for executives, whose earnings typically rise more steeply with time than those of other employees. Its special advantages for the "late bloomer" are also obvious.

Integrating the pension formula with Social Security may increase executive benefits. Generally this can be done by providing larger benefits on earnings in excess of the maximum earnings base. Alternatively, a separate plan may provide benefits *only* on compensation above a specified minimum. At Sears, Roebuck, for example, a pension plan supplements the basic profit-sharing plan, covering only those employees who earn more than $10,000 (the maximum recognized earnings under the profit-sharing plan). Providing benefits for past service offers another useful way to help older executives meet their retirement needs, especially where the pension plan has been in effect for only a few years.

Where the basic retirement vehicle is a profit-sharing plan, the retirement program cannot so easily be tailored to individual needs. Under such a plan, formula-based benefits, past service credits, and, for all practical purposes, integration of the plan with Social Security are effectively precluded. True, it will be possible to permit limited withdrawals to meet major expenses, such as buying a house or putting a child through college. Also, the plan can be drawn to permit voluntary contributions by the participants, so that they can accumulate additional retirement funds and defer taxes on the income buildup. But these particular possibilities will be more likely to benefit executives in the first and second phases of the career cycle than those nearing retirement.

Whether the basic retirement vehicle is a pension or a profit-sharing plan, the rate of required employee contributions should be set with care. A contribution rate higher than 5 percent of base salary may be too much of a drain on the incomes of most younger and middle-aged executives. It can even be a heavy burden for the older, more highly compensated executive, especially if contributions are calculated on the basis of total earnings. In one leading company, which until recently imposed a 10 percent contribution rate on the total earnings of management employees, executives at the $50,000 level were contributing 17 percent of their after-tax incomes. At the $100,000 level, an executive was obliged to contribute 22 percent of his after-tax income.

A company can tailor its retirement program to the needs of executives at various stages of their career cycle in still another way. A supplementary retirement arrangement provides for postretirement payments based on performance, in addition to the executive's pension benefits. For example, a company's regular incentive plan might make it possible for executives within ten years of retirement to earn, by outstanding performance, additional retirement benefits equal to a specified percentage of their average compensation in the final years of employment. Besides helping the executive better his retirement position, this arrangement provides an incentive for continued high-level performance at the very stage of the career cycle when many executives are inclined to "coast."

THE INSURANCE PROGRAM. Because it has the advantage of group rates and a tax deduction for premiums, a company can provide its executives with life insurance, disability income protection, and major medical coverage far more cheaply than the executives can do it for themselves. Again, care will be called for in the design and application of these benefits.

Executives in the first stage of the career cycle, for example, need proportionately more life insurance protection because of their heavy family obligations and the long period to be protected. Thus, one company's contributory group insurance plan gives employees the option of coverage equal to either one years' salary or two and one-half years' salary. This permits employees to choose the level of protection that best fits their needs. Another company determines the amount of group life coverage by taking into account both the executive's salary and the number of years to his retirement, thus giving the younger executives higher coverage.

The group life program can be tailored in still other ways to the needs of executives in the final stage of the career cycle. But extending group term insurance into retirement becomes an expensive proposition, as some companies have discovered. Since the mortality rate for retirees ultimately reaches 100 percent, the cost of group term insurance for retirees will always end up at 100 percent of the face amount. An effective alternative is to combine paid-up life insurance with term insurance.

One company provides its employees with regular group term insurance until age 45. At that time, the employee's contribution increases from 60 cents to $1.30 a month per $1,000 of coverage, and his entire contribution is applied to the purchase of paid-up insurance. The company, in turn, pays the cost of term insurance to make up the difference between the paid-up life purchased to date and the total coverage guaranteed the employee. When the employee quits or retires, he has a paid-up insurance policy to provide him with continuing protection at a substantially lower overall cost to the company.

The growth of contributory major medical plans and long-term disability income protection for selected employee groups also reflects both the interest of companies in helping employees and the willingness of employees to pay the cost of such protection when provided at low group rates. Undoubtedly, here is an excellent opportunity to improve the compensation plan at little or no cost. For a company can make desirable coverages available to its employees at low group costs, without itself incurring any additional expense beyond the costs of administering the program.

How can a company improve the fit of its compensation plan to the changing requirements of the executive career cycle? How can it decide which compensation techniques will be most applicable to its own executive group and its own environment?

First, the company should analyze the mix of its executive careers. Is the executive group spread fairly evenly over the career cycle or has some one phase become predominant? Will a major shift in the mix be in prospect as the result of wholesale retirements, a planned expansion, or some other move? What is the career mix among promotable middle-management personnel?

Second, it should sort out the key compensation needs of each career-phase group. Do employees require current compensation most urgently, or can deferred compensation and longer term capital accumulation offer advantages? What are their retirement and insurance needs? Most important, how much flexibility can be built into the compensation plan?

Finally, the existing compensation package should be appraised against these key needs. Where can be found the greatest opportunities to improve the plan? Will the company be able to obtain economies without reducing benefits? Will contemplated changes in these areas create problems down the line—and can these problems be resolved?

These questions, considered in relation to the executive career cycle and its meaning for the compensation plan, will point the company toward a compensation program that both gives management more for every compensation dollar and increases morale and productivity in the executive group.

16. Executive development—new perspective

Robert K. Stolz

Of all the current misconceptions about executive development—and there are many—the most prevalent one is that it is dead. Top managers of prominent companies often seem to be driving nails in its coffin by stating that they long ago abandoned their executive development programs. But let no one be misled; the problem is one of semantics. For these companies today devote more time and effort, with far more enthusiasm, to the development of management talent than ever before. True, in many ways their methods and procedures differ fundamentally from what they were attempting ten years ago. But the effort may still be counted as executive development—alive, vigorous, evolving, and contributing to profits.

Today, executive development is sustained not by personnel specialists but by a new breed of developers: line managers and top executives. Companies have abandoned the rigid and highly systematized procedures that were the hallmark of executive development programs in the early 1950s. Instead, executives are doing what comes naturally to help subordinates develop themselves.

The participation of line executives has unquestionably been the strength of the effort, but it has brought problems, too. It has, in particular, tended to diffuse and disguise what executive development really consists of. As a result, the company president seeking to assess the current "state of the art," or to derive a practical program for his own organization from industry's 20-year experience, can easily find himself hopelessly confused. The president of a European company, visiting the United States to study our executive development methods, put it this way: "I came to get the measurements of the American development uniform, but this is like taking a tape measure to a ghost!"

His reaction was not surprising. In recent years executive development activities of leading companies have become exceedingly varied and difficult to identify, define, and study; and this has led to serious misconceptions that confuse and impede the progress of the effort throughout industry.

178

Before identifying and discussing the current misconceptions, let me first point out that the term executive development, as used here, describes the full range of actions that management may take, consciously and intentionally, to speed or improve the development of managers. Included in this definition are on-the-job training, job changes and off-the-job courses. Now let us turn our attention to seven misconceptions—all of them widely held in the business community.

Misconception #1

Most prominent companies gave up on executive development long ago. Generally speaking, only unsophisticated, second-string companies are still trying.

This belief has arisen naturally enough. Leading companies make no bones about having dropped the pomp and ceremony characteristic of their executive development programs in the early 1950s. But they distinguish sharply between (a) the formal *programs* and (b) the organized, managed *approaches* designed to stimulate and help their managers build competence. The latter represent an effort to which prominent companies are firmly committed.

For instance, several times I have been puzzled, and then amused, to hear a General Motors executive state that GM simply does not believe in executive development programs—and in the next breath describe the earnest efforts he is expected to devote to developing the talents of his subordinates.

This leads us to a simple but basic premise: Companies that devote the most attention to developing management talent are those that consistently lead their industries in profit growth, and in some cases have been doing both for 30 to 40 years. In short, the leaders in executive development are the bluest of the blue chips—in chemicals, Du Pont; in the automobile industry, General Motors; in business machines, IBM; in electrical equipment, General Electric; in utilities, A. T. & T.; in soap, Procter & Gamble; in food, General Foods; in retailing, Sears, Roebuck; and so on.

We have no conclusive proof of this premise; and, like most generalizations, it admits exceptions. But we do have strong supporting evidence:

1. Among the specialists "in the trade," the companies I have cited are considered leaders in executive development.

2. Each is the envy of its competitors for having on tap a seemingly endless supply of competent men to fill key jobs.

3. These companies have been the favored hunting grounds of the leading executive recruiters. For example, when a secondary company in the chemical industry wants a competent outside man to fill a top management post, nine times out of ten the recruiter is told, "Get him from Du Pont."

Most of the companies named above as leaders in executive development are giant corporations. But this does not mean that executive development will be practicable only for large companies. True, a formal approach to executive development—as to other management processes—is needed more in larger companies. Yet many small companies have equally urgent manpower problems, and they are just as concerned with developing workable solutions.

Still, size does make a difference. In the small company, executive development problems are usually fairly easy to see; in fact, they will often be painfully obvious. But if diagnosis appears simple, the cure may be difficult. With few executive positions involved, personnel moves to deal with problems may be quite limited. For instance, the second highest ranking executive may by his performance have clearly demonstrated that he is not capable of succeeding the president. Yet he is too valuable to lose. The problem then arises, where to move him? Complicating matters for the small company, relationships among the top people often become so close—even if family kinship is not a factor—that the chief executive finds it excruciatingly difficult to deal with the urgent "people problems" that confront him.

In the large corporation, circumstances are frequently reversed. There will be plenty of alternative solutions to choose from, but the problems are likely to be so diffused among different divisions and locations that diagnosis proves to be extremely difficult. Consider this case:

For years a large company in the consumer goods field had drawn heavily on its regional sales managers, and to a lesser extent on its district sales managers, to fill key positions at corporate and division headquarters.

Gradually, as the executive squeeze grew tighter, the regional and district managers promoted were replaced with second- and third-choice men—supervisors either much older or less competent than their predecessors. This process evolved so gradually that top management—though increasingly concerned with the difficulty of finding qualified men for important openings—failed to recognize what was happening.

Finally, a manpower analysis showed that both regional and district managers no longer offered a reserve. All the regional managers were either close to age 60 or performing at no better than minimum standards. And the situation had become equally critical at the district-manager level.

Once the difficulty was clearly identified, management could act to alleviate it. (Granted, it would not be easy to correct.) But the problem had required an incisive manpower analysis—by no means an exceptional need in large companies.

Misconception #2

In companies that still carry on executive development, the activities are haphazard, unorganized, and have little in common.

This belief likewise is understandable. The development measures these companies take appear so varied and diffuse as to seem haphazard, particularly to the outside observer. Yet in fact most of these development actions are part of carefully thought-out plans, tailored to the needs of individual managers. For example, a development step for the plant production manager—a man not notably cost conscious—may be to make him chairman of the plant cost-reduction task force. Or, similarly, the production manager weak in labor relations may be placed in the industrial relations department to train foremen in more effective day-to-day relationships with the union.

The use of individualized plans for the development of particular men has, in fact, become the most important characteristic of executive development in this country. Basically, the process follows a set pattern:

A man's performance will be periodically appraised by his superiors. Questions are raised—"Is his potential greatest as a manager or as a staff specialist?" "What are his strengths and weaknesses?" "Where can he make his greatest contribution?"

Next, sometimes in consultation with the man himself, tentative decisions will be made on what might be done to advance his development.

Usually the resulting plan is reviewed at a higher echelon of management, where it may be challenged, changed, or added to. But out of the discussion and debate emerges a development plan tailored to the individual's unique needs.

We may identify other common denominators in the approaches of leading companies that are frequently not recognized by the outsider. To comment briefly on three:

First, apart from classroom courses, development action nearly always means a change of job responsibilities. Sometimes development objectives may be met by adding responsibilities to the man's current position. But the most usual and effective action will generally prove to be a complete job change—a promotion to a more demanding responsibility or a lateral transfer into a new functional area to broaden the man or test his versatility.

Second, in the matter of appraisal method, leading companies are no longer particularly preoccupied with techniques. Rather they seem distinctly gimmick-shy. They have long since dropped the highly structured procedures and elaborate rating forms of the early 1950s in favor of simpler approaches relying heavily on the appraiser's judgment and common sense. Line managers in these companies, knowing that their evaluations of subordinates must stand up to searching questions from superiors, have learned to think through their appraisal judgments. Companies recognize the danger of personal bias and guard against it by constantly challenging appraisal conclusions by upper-level executives. And fact-oriented judgments must back up the appraisal rather than off-the-cuff personal opinions.

Third, in leading companies, top executives—and particularly the chief executive—actively take part in executive development decisions. Their example in giving personal time and attention to the development effort speaks volumes to lower levels of management. Obviously, a chief executive cannot make a personal judgment on the development plan of every young executive. Nevertheless, the depth of top management's actual involvement is often surprising.

At Standard Oil of New Jersey, for example, executive committee members meet on Monday afternoons to decide on specific executive development actions and compensation matters. They also review all recommendations on appointments to some 350–400 selected top jobs in Jersey's subsidiary companies. By thus formalizing the involvement of top executives, Jersey has helped to make executive development a way of life in the company.

Misconception #3

The "crown prince" approach is dead.

According to this theory, the crown prince inevitably will be "shot down in flames" by his envious peers as soon as his identity becomes known. A corollary line of thought informs us that only the democratic approach, dedicated to helping every man develop equally, will really be effective.

Now, either there must be enough truth to this or the issue is so emotionally loaded that the crown prince approach *has* been pretty effectively driven underground. But top managements of leading companies, though they may keep quiet about it, do have their crown prince lists. Names are added, and names crossed out. The list may be in the mind rather than in the memo book, but top management persists in keeping it, despite the pleas and protests of the company executive development specialist.

To most managements this appears as a matter of elementary economics. The more able the individual is judged to be, the more time and effort management will put into his development. According to this approach, the process of planned development is *inherently selective*.

Granted, the crown prince tendencies may be pretty well hidden, for usually every manager from supervisor to vice president is appraised annually. But development effort soon concentrates on the most promising individuals, on those whose age and performance indicate they are approaching a career milestone, and on those whose lack of progress places obstacles in the paths of others. The process will be selective; but if a promising man has been missed one year, he is given a fresh look the next.

Selectivity has been the salvation of more than one executive development effort. Thus:

An important capital goods company, which had been drawing up individual development plans for every man above a certain salary level, found after several years that well over 90 percent of these plans had never been carried out. Indeed, middle management had tagged the effort the "executive no-development program."

In reevaluating its effort, the company concluded it simply did not have the time, training resources, or available openings to develop everyone. Nor was everyone anxious to be developed. Moving to a more selective approach enabled the company to concentrate the effort within manageable bounds and start doing first things first.

Misconception #4

Executive development means spending money now for an uncertain return in the far distant future.

Almost the opposite is true. Many companies that put vigorous and imaginative effort into executive development are making more money *now* because they have been using their best management talent more fully. For example, the president of an ethical drug firm recently told me:

"It sounds hardboiled, but I really think what we are doing in executive development is learning how to make more money on people. We have always believed that the key to success is having good people, and for years we kidded ourselves that we were operating on that principle. Lately, though, we've been playing for keeps. Having good people can't be just a slogan; you have to work at it. We do nothing radically different from what we did before, but there are three areas where we're a lot more effective. We're getting better information on who our best performers are, we give more thought to how to use them, and we're more willing to move the mediocre performer to a spot where he can't hurt us—and this frees up his old job for one of our 'comers'."

The experience of leading companies suggests that an important key to a quicker return from executive development is a more compatible marriage of business planning and personnel planning. Increasingly, companies prepare and review more comprehensive business plans to cover the activities of each principal division for the coming year—reviewing then with upper levels of management against the backdrop of longer range strategic plans. Many leading companies now simply tie discussions and decisions on personnel assignments into these business planning sessions.

Standard Oil of New Jersey, in its well-known business reviews of subsidiary companies, has been doing this for many years. IBM, GE, Lever Brothers, Du Pont, and many others now regard decisions on important personnel moves as an integral part of their business planning process. A top-ranking executive may be reluctant to change a key man's job assignment for development reasons alone, usually on the basis that he is needed right where he is. But he may quickly approve the job change when it is part of a plan to solve an important business problem.

By pointing to near-term benefits, I do not imply that a company can avoid occasionally risking operating efficiency to provide a development opportunity for a promising man. Some personnel shifts or training programs will increase expenses in a given year, just as advertising, product engineering, or raw materials development frequently do. Nor will leading companies pursue executive development mainly for the sake of its near-term benefits. But they find that putting their most capable men *now* in the most demanding jobs both develops and tests these men faster and makes more money for the company. Sound executive development carries itself. Even though some of the moves may be geared to the long run, current expenses can be offset by immediate benefits.

Misconception #5

The prime purpose of a man's development plan is to broaden him or add to his store of knowledge or experience.

Rather, the primary purpose of development action is to *test* the man under fire. The broadening and experience values are often secondary. To illustrate:

A food processing company moved a promising young plant manager from the modern, efficient plant he had "grown up in" to the company's most trouble-ridden and inefficient plant. His instructions: "Turn the plant upside down if necessary, but get costs back into line."

The president explained the move this way: "We thought first about moving one of our older, more experienced managers into this spot. But we decided instead to take a chance on Don. We knew he was good, but we had to find out how good. We figured we would never know if we left him in a plant that he knew like the back of his hand. We gave him a tough job and he did it well. Before long we're going to give him a tougher one."

One might conclude from this and other examples that top management seems less concerned with the development of decision-making ability than with finding out who its best decision makers are. There is truth in this.

184

Few top managements can be sure of their ability to teach decision making, but most believe that they know how to select real decision makers *if* they can observe them in a variety of demanding assignments.

The new president of one of America's most prominent corporations brings this point out in describing his role in management development:

> I'm 53, and I'm the third consecutive chief executive of this company to be appointed under the age of 55. If the directors have any choice, I know the next president will go in at about my age. That means that if I stay ten years, the man who will succeed me is now probably between the ages of 40 and 45.
>
> One of my most important jobs as president is to identify the 20 to 30 best managers in the company in that age range and put each of them through an obstacle course. We have to find out who the real decision makers are. Once we've separated the men from the boys, we'll know where each man can make his greatest contribution. And at the same time, I hope to find the next president.

Of course, testing a man also develops him. The man who has run a profitable division and finds himself suddenly placed in charge of one in the red is not merely being tested. He will also be learning for the first time to deal with some hard economic realities.

Clearly, then, the values of "testing by fire" and of added experience may both be considered inherent in most development moves. But in my observation, top managers who regard executive development as a means to prove out their judgments on people tend to involve themselves more deeply in the development effort than those who see it simply as a way of providing additional experience.

Misconception #6

Executive development courses are passé. Sophisticated managers have learned that you cannot teach a man executive skills in a classroom.

True, management today has become a great deal more realistic about what can and cannot be accomplished through classroom training. But the importance of formal management education has not by any means declined since the early 1950s. Despite their belief in job experience as the most potent tester and developer of management talent, top executives are now better educated and more education-conscious than ever before. Moreover, technological advances in computer applications and in other fields, together with changes in the business environment, may well trigger an explosive proliferation of management courses designed to retool executives to meet new job demands.

Still, some changes have been taking place in both the nature and the application of formal management education programs. Three of these trends may be judged particularly significant.

First, though there has been no lessening of interest in the 4- to 13-week advanced management programs offered by universities, companies are now more selective in deciding who should attend and which program seems best fitted to the individual. Programs differ in a number of ways— average age of participants, organizational levels represented, content and teaching method, and even living facilities. Every one of these factors enters into the selection. Also, the man himself frequently participates in the decision.

This greater selectivity, along with obvious improvements in the caliber of courses, has given leading companies confidence that they are receiving more value from such programs. The courses offer not only education in general management, but exposure to managers from other industries and time away from job pressures to reflect on the individual's own management ideas.

Second, shorter, special-purpose programs, which probe a single facet of management in considerable depth for a one- or two-week period, have rapidly gained ground. Several of these courses, designed and run by outside professionals for presentation within the company, offer rigorously tested educational material. The company may arrange for a course to be offered to selected executives, say, twice a year.

The strength of the special-purpose program has been its unique adaptability to individual development plans. A program in problem and decision analysis may benefit the man who has a tendency to be careless with his facts and an inclination to shoot from the hip. A course in group dynamics will be likely to help the individual who ruffles the feathers of his associates. Special study in the fundamentals of finance may meet the need of a new man in the planning department who has been handicapped by the lack of a financial background.

Obviously, not all the special-purpose programs will be of equal value. Several leading companies have found that only a limited number offer subject matter and instruction of the caliber suited to experienced managers. As with university programs, careful investigation and selectivity are necessary.

Third, most educational programs, particularly special-purpose courses, are increasingly offered in an atmosphere of tension, pressure, and competition. This is in marked contrast to ten years ago. Statements by men recently attending such programs bring out this point:

¶ *About a seminar on group dynamics:* "I can't quite explain what I got out of it; I think every person would have to experience it for himself. But I would say that I was shocked when I began getting the signals on how

186

other people reacted to me. It wasn't funny; and, believe me, it certainly isn't for everyone."

¶ *About a course on decision making:* "I think we all felt the same when the course was over—just like we had been put through the wringer. Right now I don't see how I could ever make a careless decision again. That thing is a killer from start to finish."

¶ *About a program in economic analysis:* "You won't believe this, but I went there with the idea that I was going to improve my golf game. Instead, the program floored me. I learned that I'm just a babe in the woods when it comes to applying even the elementary tools of economics to a business problem."

Several factors contribute to this new atmosphere. For one thing, there will be obvious pressure to learn. The participant is expected to assimilate a body of knowledge. He has homework to do, and may be given tests. He must apply himself and show results. Also, competition develops among the participants. Acknowledged or not, it exists—intensified by the fact that each student executive has little time to prove himself.

Another important factor is that the individual's performance in the course may be evaluated by the faculty, with significant implications for his future advancement. This may not be done openly, but sometimes it is. For example, IBM, in much of its training at Sands Point, Long Island, makes no bones about the fact that the participant's performance will be evaluated and reported to top management when and if the man is considered for advancement. Many professional educators oppose such evaluation in view of the obvious hazard that too much weight will be given to behavior in the artificial course situation and not enough to performance on the job. Good or bad, it is being done, and it adds to the pressure.

Misconception #7

Executive development deals mainly in abstractions and it also involves an array of special activities.

This is another legacy from the old program days, when the glossy brochures on executive development implied that this was a new art involving a complex of new activities. In actual fact, even then most of these "new" processes were actually extensions of practices already common among many progressive companies, such as defining individual executive responsibilities or drawing organization charts to clarify working relationships.

Today, most executive development has become concrete. It consists of the same activities that virtually every company carries on in order to recruit and advance men to executive positions. Formal executive development simply puts these activities on a more organized and fact-founded basis and supports them with consistent top-management policies.

One catches a sense of all this from comments by line managers on their companies' executive development efforts:

¶ "Today we have good information on our people. Not perfect—but good."

¶ "It's a lot harder now for a good man to get stuck in a dead-end position."

¶ "We had to face up to moving aside some men who were good specialists but poor managers. Frankly, we found we had waited much too long. The men themselves were happier after being moved, and I know it was better for the company."

¶ "You have to know whether a salesman or an engineer has management ability well before he reaches age 40. We've learned to start testing these men in supervisory positions in their early thirties."

¶ "For a long time we moved men around willy-nilly. But then we found that a lot of this wasted the most valuable time in a man's career. Now we have pretty good bench marks on what kinds of assignments in each function contribute most to an individual's development."

¶ "It used to be taken for granted that a division would hoard its best people, even if it meant holding them back. I don't believe a division manager would dare do that today. His own reputation as an executive is at stake."

The tangibility of modern executive development can perhaps best be appreciated by seeing it as a decision-making process. The statements of top executives in three different companies bring this point into focus:

¶ "When you get down to bedrock, our executive development effort is simply an organized way of making important decisions on people. When I first came into business, the thing that really floored me was the careless, haphazard way management reached such decisions. I don't mean little decisions. I mean big ones that can make or break a man's career. We've struggled a long time with executive development, and our program certainly isn't perfect, but it gives us an organized way to approach these important decisions. Now we get the facts, and we are deliberate."

¶ "This is my third company. In all three a man's chances for advancement have depended on what part of the company he came from and whom he knew. Sometimes it was just luck—a question of who happened to be under the nose of the executive who had an important job to fill. Executive development has changed all this. Now when we fill an important vacancy, we treat it like any other important decision—we get the facts. We canvass the entire company and come up with a factual decision on who is the best qualified of all the well-qualified men."

¶ "For years our college recruiters said that advancement opportunities

188

were company-wide, not limited to the division or department a man would start in. In all honesty, this wasn't quite true. Now our executive development procedures require us to survey the entire company when we fill important vacancies. And that's only part of the story. Actually, we do much more. For one thing, we start evaluating the qualifications of our men early enough so that we really get to know them and know what we are doing in our development moves."

Executive development as a means of making sounder decisions on people bears an analogy to long-range planning. As generally recognized, long-range strategic planning amounts simply to a more highly organized approach to making decisions on the future course of the business. In the same way, executive development can be recognized as simply a means of giving a company better information and a more organized approach to the management and advancement of its executive personnel.

Conclusion

The most significant characteristics of executive development activities in leading companies have been well camouflaged by a diversity of method, emphasis, and philosophy. But a closer look inevitably brings out common denominators.

In companies where executive development proves most successful, line executives have assumed responsibility for developing their immediate subordinates and for seeing that these subordinates, in turn, recognize their responsibility to develop their men.

Under the approach widely used in the United States, each individual's development plan will be unique—based on study of his own needs by his superiors.

The nub of the problem remains that of appraisal. Now appraisal becomes a continuous, cumulative process. As promising younger men are tested in increasingly difficult job assignments, management constantly adds to its knowledge of individual capabilities and of the company's total manpower resources.

Though many of the awkward and superficial procedures of the old executive development programs have been dropped, the need for sound procedures will continue. In particular, management must review the manpower situation in each division, anticipate future needs, and initiate development action to meet them. Work so proceduralized gets done. When a company relies on completely informal approaches, without procedures or schedules, the work will too often be left for tomorrow.

Off-the-job education continues to play a crucial supporting role, but companies now appear more realistic, for example, in what they expect from the broad general management courses offered by universities.

Management has also become more skillful in selecting the men most apt to profit from attendance and in matching each man with the appropriate program. Finally, in management education today there may be found an atmosphere of pressure to learn; competition has become the rule among participants. This may not be an unmixed blessing, but even so constitutes a refreshing change in the industrial training field.

Despite increasing involvement of line executives in this area, most companies still need the advice and support of an executive development specialist. But his role has undergone a fundamental change, and his traditional title of Executive Development Director is giving way to a variety of new labels. Not only have his responsibilities and functions been altered, but so has his perspective. No longer does he try to do the whole job himself or force company-wide executive development efforts into a rigid, detailed mold devised by him or borrowed from other companies. Typically, his staff is smaller but of higher quality than before. Among his key responsibilities are these:

¶ Using factual information on the background of men in the company, plus appraisal information supplied by line managers, to point up current and future manpower strengths and weaknesses in each function, in each division, and in the company as a whole.

¶ Seeing to it that top line executives also understand the problems that must be met, and constantly "needling" them to take the appropriate action. This process calls for nice judgment. The executive development man must not be too patient; yet many argue that he will do well to avoid the reputation of being ten years ahead of his time.

¶ Advising line managers on specific development actions to meet the needs of individual men.

¶ Keeping abreast of developments in management education and outside training courses, and advising executives on the use of these programs. In this responsibility he serves less as a teacher or a writer of training material and more as a consultant on how training needs can be met.

¶ Providing facilities for screening executive candidates within the company to find those best qualified for specific vacancies—regardless of their current assignments—and advising line managers on setting criteria for selection decisions.

Like most sensitive staff positions, the job of an executive development specialist is not easy. It calls for a man of considerable personal stature, strong analytical competence, confidence in himself, and ability to win the confidence of key executives.

Top managers of leading companies did not consign their old executive development programs to the ash heap without pain and embarrassment. But despite frustrations they never flagged in their belief that building depth in management competence was vitally linked to the profit growth of their

190

companies. They see the trap in the old laissez-faire philosophy: "Do nothing and the cream will rise to the top." They recognize that the complexities of business too frequently prevent the cream from rising fast enough. They understand that the job of identifying, testing and developing management talent is one that has to be managed, and they remain committed to doing just that.

17. Motivating tomorrow's executives

Arch Patton

About five years ago, a highly successful large company began losing valued middle managers. Year after year, to top management's perplexity, the exodus increased. As the president remarked at the time, "It almost seems as though the policies and practices that were so successful for us in the past no longer work." Investigation confirmed the accuracy of his diagnosis. Since World War II, the age mix of the middle-management group had shifted markedly toward youth, yet the company had still clung to obsolete motivational approaches on the grounds that "you don't argue with success."

This company is not an isolated example. Increasingly, top managements in some of the best run companies are beginning to note that the old motivational tools are losing their edge. Yet only a few suspect the reason: Slowly and subtly, as a new generation of talent takes over at middle- and top-management levels, a new motivational value system is evolving among executives. In fact, the pattern of motivational priorities is being reshuffled.

Underlying the change is the difference in outlook between the aggressive generation of managers in their thirties and forties and their more conservative seniors. This difference is largely attributable to three background factors:

1. Executives over 55 today were subjected to the Great Depression trauma, while those now under 50 have grown up in an ever-expanding economy. Having experienced few major setbacks, the younger managers tend to have far greater confidence in their own abilities.

2. The technological explosion since World War II, and the changes that followed in its wake, have meant opportunity to the younger executive. To his Depression-haunted older colleague, in contrast, change tends to take on the aspect of a threat.

3. Because he has had more formal intellectual training, the young executive tends to be less patient with the "rituals of the system" than his older counterpart.

Predictably, the older executives, who set the motivational pattern today, are influenced by their own past experience. For example, the Depression-scarred senior executive frequently acts as though money were a motivation in itself. But although the younger executive expects his pay to increase steadily, he views money more as a scoring device—a measure of his peer-value relationships both inside and outside the company—than as an incentive. Again, an older executive's attempt to motivate by the inferential threat of dismissal may simply prompt the young executive to seek out an executive recruiter and look for greener pastures.

Indeed, industry's motivational fences do seem to be in a state of disrepair. Even recruiting high-talent university graduates is becoming increasingly difficult. More and more of these bright young men are taking jobs with government agencies, universities, and service organizations.

Sensing these changes, a few companies are beginning to develop a new set of motivational approaches. Notable among them have been the so-called growth companies, typically characterized by the comparative youth of the executive group. In the two fastest growing companies in a representative sample of large companies recently studied by McKinsey & Company, nearly 30 percent of the executives were under 40, while in the two slowest growing companies barely 3 percent were in this age bracket.

Early glimmerings found in a relatively limited number of well-run, fast-growing companies today may cast some light on what will be the most important of tomorrow's motivational approaches. None of these approaches is wholly new, but experience indicates the priorities are. They foreshadow, I believe, significant changes in our present management processes.

The importance of environment

The environmental factor will, I believe, play an increasingly important role in executive motivation. A company president I know, whose firm recently moved into new headquarters, told me not long ago, "You'll laugh, but I believe this move was the most important single decision I've made as chief executive, from the standpoint of benefit to our stockholders. It seems to have cleansed us of our old habit of looking backward, for the old building was a constant bridge to the past. People are taking more pride in their work, and productivity has substantially improved. Our new look has even been transmitted outside, for several potential sources of the major lines we sell, who used to ignore us, have been seeking to become suppliers."

The point here is that environment, both psychological and physical, can be critical to the success of an enterprise—and to individuals within that enterprise. Its importance as an element in executive motivation may easily be overlooked because it is obscured by the history of events affecting the company, the character of the industry itself, the accident of top-management succession, the management myopia that results from

193

organizational inbreeding, and so on. Environment may be described as the sum total of all the factors that make up an organization's way of life. But it often becomes hard to recognize the environmental forest because it is made up of so many administrative trees.

Real environmental change, moreover, is not easily achieved. It takes a willingness to uproot comfortable habit patterns. When Harold Geneen became chief executive of International Telephone and Telegraph Corporation, his first annual report told stockholders that he expected to double the company's business in five years. This put company executives on notice that the past growth record was unacceptable, and that the new chief executive looked to them to inject new dynamism into the growth process. Obviously, without the will to bring about that change, the forecast would have been little more than wishful thinking. But ITT sales did, in fact, double in five years. There can be little question that the biggest problem Mr. Geneen tackled was changing the company's environment; and there can be little question that he succeeded, though considerable blood, sweat, and tears were doubtless expended in the process.

Environment in the average company reflects the cumulative influence over the years of its chief executive's leadership characteristics. Rarely has corporate environment been so consciously developed to meet a need as at ITT. But as companies see their executive motivational requirements more clearly, I believe more and more organizations will increasingly strive to develop the subtle strengths inherent in a competitive, performance-oriented environment.

Job excitement

The second key component in tomorrow's managerial motivation approaches might be called the excitement factor.

When Roger Lewis assumed the presidency of General Dynamics Corporation in 1961, it had just sustained the largest loss ever reported by a publicly owned company—a $168 million deficit. Five years later, the company earned a $58 million profit.

About the same time, Eastern Air Lines, Inc., was experiencing an equally dramatic corporate turnaround. When Floyd D. Hall became chief executive in 1962, Eastern had just achieved the dubious distinction of having lost more money—$38 million—in the previous 12 months than any other airline in history. Yet at the close of 1965, Eastern reported a $29.7 million profit.

Both new chief executives revitalized their ailing companies with the powerful assistance of a little-understood executive motivation: *the excitement generated by the purposeful pursuit of a demanding goal.* Recognizing that the desperate conditions of the moment demanded corrective action, both set crystal-clear objectives that stretched the talents and energies of everyone. The resulting excitement generated a unified sense of mission and breathed new life into their organizations.

But excitement as a leadership instrument is by no means limited to companies on the brink of disaster. No one who has been exposed to the management in such growth companies as IBM, Xerox, Polaroid, or Texas Instruments could fail to notice the pervasive feeling of pressure to get things done. Decisions in such companies tend to be made against tighter deadlines, often without the benefit of fully completed staff work, and individual failure is less tolerable than in the average company. Yet executives in these companies give little indication of consciously responding to pressure from above. Instead, they appear to be engaged in a kind of self-generated speedup, exhilarated by a challenging management environment.

In these growth companies, of course, this excitement will in part be attributable to the constant pressures of technological change. New processes, new materials, new end uses, and new products all have their effects on the responsibilities of the individual executive. No heart palpitations result in such companies when a packet of responsibilities is taken from one executive and given to another; such reshuffling happens too often to be unusual. Change becomes an acceptable way of life because the need for change is so evident.

Excitement within an executive group, we have seen, cannot be generated solely by pressure from the top. But the critical spark that generates the excitement factor in a growth company must be provided by a leadership that sets demanding goals and somehow secures a common belief in them. The chief executive of one growth company in the electronics industry insists that sales *and* profits grow at a minimum of 15 percent annually. At every opportunity he pounds home the thesis that this talent-stretching objective will be achieved—or else. It has proved to be a powerful stimulant to profitable, change-producing actions.

The chief executive, of course, must personally spearhead the drive toward such demanding goals, for lower echelons of management pay more attention to what he does than what he says.

Obviously, excitement is easier to generate in some businesses than in others. An airline, for instance, has an almost limitless number of ways in which to assess its own performance: the "on time" record, baggage handling, passenger complaints, oversold seats, equipment breakdowns, and so on. But unless top management *uses* these measures effectively, there will be no excitement, hence no motivation to improve. The old management of Eastern Air Lines had all these yardsticks available, but the new management *used* them.

But this tool is by no means available only to growth companies. A competitive, resourceful leader can inject excitement even into a regulated business. For example, one utility president developed a competitive internal environment by a series of organizational moves. First, he divided the company into four regions and pitted them in competition with each other in such areas as growth rate, maintenance costs and system extension costs. Next, he established annual goals for the company's 40-odd districts within these four regions and evolved a means of assessing their relative performance. Finally, he consistently rewarded, by promotion and merit increases, those executives who performed outstandingly in terms of these yardsticks.

Internal competition, based on taking advantage of change, often contributes to the excitement factor. This, of course, requires a company environment hospitable to change and encourages constructive, team-spirited competition in pursuit of change. Admiral Ben Moreell's Seabees during World War II were well aware of this motivational opportunity; they pitted one base-building crew against another in a race to complete their respective construction jobs.

High promotion rate

A high promotion rate, often characteristic of a company that ranks high in the excitement factor, will be a third means of motivating tomorrow's managers. Considering the potency of promotion as an executive incentive, the company that provides more of this kind of motivation inevitably has an edge on its competitors, other things being equal.

A study of promotions among the highest executives (that is, the highest paid one-half of 1 percent of all employees) in 23 representative large companies is revealing. During a seven-year span roughly one-third of the top executives were promoted more than once, another third received one promotion, and the rest received no promotions at all. The range of promotion frequencies among companies was surprisingly wide. What was not surprising was that the fastest growing companies reported the highest promotion rate.

Growth, whether internally generated or the result of acquisition and merger, creates increased promotion opportunities. Indeed, a high promotion rate over the long run is inescapably linked to growth. This is why a company that wants to encourage the strongest possible executive motivation had better establish growth as a top-priority corporate goal—and see that it comes about.

Another way of providing promotional opportunity is through organizational change. This need not involve the creation of new positions or new levels of management—although such changes do add to the promotion potential of a company by making more top jobs available. Rather, the realignment of executive responsibilities carries with it one of the big motivational values in a job change: the challenge of doing something new. A number of growth-minded companies continually reorganize their activities, moving individual executives from job to job. The new job may not be in a higher grade or compensation level, but a salary increase goes with the move, and the executive group regards it as a promotion. This gives it value in the eyes of the reassigned executive and makes it a real motivational force.

Continual organization change of this sort generates the same kind of internal excitement as growth. Like growth, it says to the executive group, "Things are happening here." And competitive people like to be where the action is.

Lateral promotions are a different matter, but they have motivational impacts of their own—impacts that I believe will be more widely recognized in the future. First, lateral moves, if they are part of the company's way of life, have some of the built-in excitement value noted in organization shifts. The man has a new job to master, which is exciting in itself.

But the lateral promotion has a second important motivational value. As the current shortage of executive talent becomes more acute, companies increasingly realize the importance of *consciously* managing the careers of their best employees by matching the functional requirements of the job to the individual's demonstrated aptitudes and interests. Lateral promotions can provide experience without which an otherwise outstanding man might be unable to advance to greater responsibility.

Despite the importance of promotion as a factor in executive motivation, few top managements have taken the trouble to analyze their companies' promotion rates or given much thought to the career paths they are providing for their top executives of tomorrow. As they become aware of the great untapped motivational opportunity in promotion, greater emphasis on this potent incentive will be sure to follow.

The other side of the coin, demotion, also is likely to receive greater attention in the years ahead. The few companies that have had the courage to make deliberate use of demotion find it a practical way of salvaging executives who are "in over their heads" without putting them on a high-priced, but frustrating, shelf. In a company where frequent reorganization of functional activities is a way of life, demotion need not bring heartbreak. And the advantage of management's having a second guess in the promotion process argues for more widespread use of this neglected tool.

More effective performance appraisal

Better use of performance appraisals has become a fourth key factor in executive motivation. Men who are strongly achievement-oriented need to

197

have a feedback on their own performance. Behavioral science studies have repeatedly indicated that substantial performance improvement can be expected from the individual who: (1) knows the strengths and weaknesses in his performance, (2) knows what he can do to improve it, (3) has the power to make this change himself, and (4) has the incentive to do so.

These four points provide the keys to effective performance appraisal. If any one of them is missing, the usefulness of the appraisal process will be seriously compromised. Yet too many performance appraisal systems in the past have failed either to pinpoint the individual's weaknesses and show him how to build on his strengths, or to provide the means or the incentive for him to change.

Behavioral scientists have long maintained that individual performance appraisal has often been disastrously weakened by management's natural tendency to tie it to discussions of compensation. What happens, of course, is that the emphasis on pay-for-performance in the appraisal interview sidetracks the principal objective of performance appraisal: performance *improvement*. Constructive criticism aimed at improving performance can be accepted and acted on rationally, but criticism tied directly to pay action touches a defensive nerve and often triggers strong emotional resistance.

Companies have found that individual goal-setting can greatly improve the chances of upgrading performance. When the individual and his superior discuss his goals for the coming year, an "improvement factor" designed to offset agreed-upon weaknesses and take advantage of basic strengths can quite naturally be worked into the plan. This enables performance appraisal and pay administration to be kept, as they should be, on separate tracks.

Yet an executive's compensation *should* reflect his performance; there must in fact be a direct relationship between performance and pay. Three important requirements for such a relationship have been noted. First, the superior must understand that the purpose of appraisal is to speed up the subordinate's learning rate. Interviews should be *improvement*-oriented, not *blame*-oriented. They should be fact-based ("Here are the goals we agreed upon, and these are the results"), and they should be focused on improvement ("Here is how you can do better").

Second, the factors on which a man's performance is assessed should be under his control. If they can be quantified, so much the better. But in the final analysis, the superior must make his own balanced judgment of the individual's success in attaining agreed-upon goals, using both objective and subjective yardsticks, and also weighing in factors bearing on the difficulty of accomplishment, such as competitive windfalls or the lack thereof.

The third key factor in tying individual performance to pay is careful planning and execution of performance interviews. The average executive feels so uncomfortable in such an interview that he tends to bumble through a series of bland generalities that never "reach" the subordinate. Far more often than most managers appreciate, the subordinate may emerge from the discussion without realizing a performance appraisal interview has taken place at all!

A number of forces now at work will probably compel industry to improve its performance appraisal techniques. One of these forces is the growing shortage of executives. As the supply of available talent dwindles, the need for correctly judging the quality of this talent obviously increases. A second force for better performance appraisal is the so-called career-path approach to manpower management that has been developing in recent years. This approach, which seeks to build up a "talent bank" for future years, becomes a useless exercise without sound early performance judgments to ensure that talent actually available five or ten years hence will be adequate to do the job required at that time.

But the newest and potentially most explosive pressure to improve performance appraisal is the extraordinary increase in compensation being proffered, year after year, to the young men emerging from technical and graduate schools. This upward thrust is having a profound, if little understood, influence on industry's compensation practices. Most important, it has made a few companies recognize that the normal pattern of promotion and merit increase will no longer suffice for the high-potential performers. For these men a "fast-track" compensation structure is needed.

Though fragmentary, the evidence already available to support this thesis has proven highly suggestive. For example, the average starting salaries of law, technical, and business school graduates have risen at a rate between 6 and 9 percent a year for a decade or more, and the upswing appears to have accelerated in the past few years. Moreover, in the first ten years or so of their business careers, the compensation of these well-educated young men has been increasing at a rate of 10 to 15 percent *compounded*. At 15 percent, their pay doubles every five years. Thus a graduate of one of the well-known business schools starting at $8,000 in 1960 would be making $32,000 in 1970 at the age of 34!

Compare these figures with the normal upward movement of the typical executive compensation structure. In the average well-run company, the increase in the *structure*, as distinct from individual pay, reflects: (1) the inflationary updrift and (2), for the top executive jobs, increase in company size. The latter often accounts for half to two-thirds of the increase. Over the past decade, for example, many companies have doubled in size, and typically this adds between 20 and 30 percent to the value of executive positions having company-wide responsibility. In any case, taking both sources of increase into account, most such pay *structures* have been advancing not much faster than 3–1/2 percent a year, compounded, over the past ten years.

How have individuals fared within this structural framework? On this point we have less evidence. Executive compensation surveys tend to focus on organizational level and responsibility rather than age. But a recent survey by McKinsey & Company provides some suggestive insights. This study was designed to determine the compensation (salary and bonus) of executives (defined at the highest paid 1 percent of all employees) at the various age levels in a limited number of large companies. The study showed that executives in the 90th percentile group (the top-paid 10 percent) who are presumably the top performers, had received a compensation increase for each added year of experience of only 2.3 percent compounded between age 32 and age 65. Surely this raises some very fundamental questions about compensation administration at the executive level.

What seems to be happening is that companies are becoming uneasily aware of the growing pressure exerted on the entire pay structure by the rising tide of highly paid, potentially fast-track men being recruited lower down in their organizations. They are beginning to realize that they cannot afford to balloon the entire pay structure out of shape to accommodate this high-talent group.

If a fast track for high-talent people is to be fitted on top of a normal compensation structure, an effective means of judging the performance of those on this track becomes a necessity. And, because the potential cost of a fast track cluttered with has-beens would be prohibitive, management must have some means of getting the individual off the fast track when his performance no longer warrants his being there. Only a sound performance appraisal program can do the job.

The fact that many companies spend as much as 40 percent of their sales dollar on compensation suggests the urgency of the need to obtain better performance for these outlays. This need, in turn, guarantees a greater future effort on management's part to set demanding individual goals, to devise sound executive job performance standards as a basis for appraising the effectiveness of the individual in attaining these goals, and to adequately reward the outstanding performers.

Three-track pay system

The compensation factor will undoubtedly play a crucial role in future approaches to the problem of motivating managers.

Some new administrative approaches are almost certain to be tried. One such approach, it is logical to expect, will be to sort executive into fast-, middle-, and slow-compensation tracks early in their careers. The density of the traffic on the three tracks would probably vary substantially from industry to industry. A rapidly growing company requiring sophisticated management talent would certainly need relatively more fast-track talent than a stable, slow-moving business. Similarly, because of the difficulty of accurately identifying potentially outstanding performers early in their careers, the density of younger managers on the fast track would be considerably higher than that of their elders.

Some companies are already considering use of the three-track idea to demonstrate career earnings potentials that might result from various levels of performance. Suppose, for illustrative purposes, that fast-track compensation were to increase 12 percent annually over a career, while the middle and slow tracks advanced at 6 percent and 4 percent respectively. On this basis, if three college graduates joined a very large company in 1966 at $7,500 each, the fast-track man would earn $8.1 million over a 42-year career, with the middle- and slow-track men receiving $1.4 million and $825,000 respectively over the same time span.

When the newly hired college graduate thinks of his career opportunity in these terms, the advantage of extra effort on his part comes into rather sharp focus. What he gains by exerting himself to attain the fast track is not just a few thousand dollars a year, but as much as a sixfold increase in career earnings. Indeed, an MBA starting at $11,500 two years later than these college graduates could earn $1.8 million more over a 40-year career for his two extra years in school if he achieved the fast track, thanks to compound interest and his higher starting rate. And his chances of getting on the fast track to begin with would probably be greater as a graduate school man.

In real life, of course, the compensation prospects of the individual are reduced by the sharp shrinkage in the number of higher paying jobs as he nears the top of the corporate pyramid. There is also the natural leveling-off process as individual executives run out of steam in their climb up the corporate ladder. However, the impact of compound interest on career earnings is far greater than most of us realize—and so is its potential motivational value.

In the early growth years, up to about 40, an individual's compensation can rise at 12 percent a year without coming up against many barriers imposed by company size or industry practice. (Indeed, some U.S. graduate schools report that the *median* pay level of their graduates rises at nearly 15 percent compounded for most of this period.) In these years, moreover, a man can change jobs with little risk.

After age 40 some important constraints begin to affect an executive's compensation progress. If he works for a small company, the government, or certain low-paying industries, he may hit a built-in ceiling. At this point, too, promotions and the big compensation gains that go with them become less likely, because there are fewer jobs at the top of the corporate structure. Finally, the individual who finds his progress blocked has less and less opportunity as he grows older to switch jobs with safety.

Hence, the number of executives on the fast track will decline rapidly after age 40.

We should note the obvious risk that the three-track compensation approach may develop crown princes who will have to be uncrowned at a later date. But more and more companies are facing up to the need for demoting executives who cannot perform effectively after promotion. And, as the scramble for profits intensifies, it will become increasingly necessary to take early action on selection mistakes.

The three-track compensation approach would not eliminate the need for some consistent internal structure of position levels or grades for valuing individual positions, nor would it do away with the necessity to check prices in the job market. But it would keep the individual's potential constantly in management's mind when candidates are being considered for promotion. If a fast-track man were proposed for a job priced below the individual's track position a year or two ahead, his candidacy would naturally be scrubbed.

Monitoring an employee's progress in terms of his age fosters some disciplines frequently overlooked in personnel administration today. For example, a number of studies have shown that one of the best clues to an individual's future potential is his current position relative to his peers. The man who outshines his contemporaries at 35 is also likely to be outstanding at 45 and 55. Thus an administrative system that starts comparing current performance among peers at an early age makes possible a sounder selection of tomorrow's top management.

Obviously, the three-track approach can complicate an already complex compensation apparatus that includes stock options, bonuses, and a wide range of supplemental benefits. But it should give management more courage in paying the better performers what they deserve, and it should provide a more effective vehicle for monitoring individual compensation progress.

Need for discipline

The final key factor likely to shape tomorrow's motivational approaches is job satisfaction.

Perhaps because they are disenchanted with money as a motivator, behavioral scientists have laid much stress on job satisfaction in their studies of executive motivation. Few executives, for that matter, would question its motivational power. A job that is both a man's vocation and his avocation is one he likes and will do well. But it seems to me that behavioral scientists have paid too little attention to another extremely important ingredient in the work situation: discipline. As a result, it has been easy to oversimplify their findings. Indeed, some evangelists of "human relations" seem to have concluded from their research that if you turn a man free from the constraints established by an autocratic boss, his job satisfaction will soar and he will immediately begin to contribute more productively to company goals.

This is nonsense. In the first place, it can hardly be assumed that corporate goals are crystal clear to all concerned. In the second place, we have no reason to suppose that everyone will do his best to attain these goals if only he is free to do so in his own way. The realities argue otherwise.

In my view, it is possible to provide the high motivational value of job satisfaction in industry without giving each individual complete freedom to do things as he pleases. Most of us, after all, feel more comfortable if we have an agreed-upon "game plan" that aims our efforts toward predetermined goals. Indeed, evidence indicates that few of us want to work for an overly permissive boss. A study of foremen's effectiveness in one large American industrial company suggests that employees actually prefer to work for foremen who are strict in their insistence on approved methods.

In short, I suspect that much of today's discussion about job satisfaction may be a bit unrealistic. Without the backbone of discipline to strengthen the direction and degree of effort, organized activities— corporations, armies, churches and, indeed, civilizations—tend to come a cropper.

Any thoughtful assessment of current trends in industry will be likely to lead to the conclusion that change is occurring faster than our ability to assimilate its meaning. But the phenomenal expansion of conglomerate companies, the obviously high morale and spirit of executive derring-do found in the companies whose major objective is profitable growth, the need for more effective motivation as professional management proliferates, and the difficulty companies are having in attracting and keeping good executives, all indicate strongly that tomorrow's management incentives will be a lot different from yesterday's.

To my mind, the key to tomorrow's executive motivation can be found in the drive that the competitive player in almost any sport brings to a game: the will to win. But it also involves an environment in which constructive team effort works toward a corporate goal, and it requires a sound assessment of the individual's contribution to the team. Indeed, sharpened value judgments of the individual's contribution—that is, performance appraisal—may well prove to be the most important single motivational advance that top management will make in the years ahead.

At any rate, the younger companies, in terms of executive age, will be in the forefront of the changes occurring in motivational patterns today. And this is logical. Younger people are not only more open to change than their elders, but also more eager to compete and more confident of their own ability to pass the test of performance.

18. A demanding environment: the role of compensation

Arch Patton

Arnold Toynbee's monumental work *A Study of History*, which reviews the rise and fall of the 23 civilizations known to man, reaches some conclusions that come as no surprise to the top executive. For example, his researches indicate that civilizations develop "in response to a challenge of special difficulty which rouses man to make an unprecedented effort," and that a successful response to such a challenge is more likely to occur in a "hard" than an "easy" environment.

Toynbee's study of mankind's behavior leads him to conclude that the growth of a civilization originates with creative individuals or small minorities, which first achieve their inspiration or discovery and then convert their particular society to this new way of life. Interestingly enough, Toynbee found that a group which responds successfully to one such challenge tends to be less effective in dealing with the next and finally fails because its members grow complacent and "rest on their oars." In addition, he indicates that the success of a particular group in the first stages of some new technique, such as the invention of the paddle steamer, makes that group slower than others to adopt a later and more efficient development such as the screw propeller.

All except one of the 23 civilizations examined by Toynbee—our own— is either dead or in the death throes. In his judgment, their demise involves one common weakness: a drying up of the creative effort of leadership. Presumably, this failure of the leaders in these civilizations resulted from a weakening in their will to meet increasingly difficult challenges. Or they attempted to solve current problems with solutions that worked yesterday but did not meet current needs.

If we change the word "civilization" to read "corporation," and "challenge" to read "competition," Toynbee's remarks fit the history of corporate enterprise remarkably well. For a corporation is a small society, a civilization in miniature. It develops around the central core of objectives established by the entrepreneur and matures as aggressive leadership attains these goals.

Like a mature civilization, the successful company seems to carry the seeds of its own destruction. The momentum of success makes it possible for the comparatively young company to fend off competitors with relative ease. But these early victories tend to delude executives into believing that their product or service is indispensable. As competitive forays grow more massive, momentum offers less and less protection, and the responses of company leadership to these challenges become increasingly important. If the entrepreneurs who built the business have been replaced by lesser men or if the old management has grown tired, responses of the executive group to competitive attack tend to grow successively weaker.

There is scarcely a business that was not at one time a "growth" industry, whose product or service replaced that of yet an earlier "growth" industry. In mass transportation, for instance, the stagecoach gave way to the railroad, which gave way to the bus, which, in turn, gave way to the airplane. Each was a "growth" industry that appeared indispensable in its day.

Just as civilizations become soft and eventually succumb to their internal weaknesses, so the corporate society may permit years of affluence to undermine its ability to meet the challenge of a hungry competitor. In both instances, the softening-up process frequently occurs during a period of great material prosperity. The civilization or the company with its fortunes at flood tide can choose to ignore a challenge to its dominance and still maintain outward signs of strength.

Each time a challenge is avoided or compromised, however, the *will* to respond to a future competitive challenge deteriorates a little. Having accepted weakness in one situation, leaders apparently find it increasingly difficult to demand the old high standard of performance when the next challenge comes along. In other words, when a dominant society—either nation or corporation—shrugs off challenges to its position, the future internal environment demands less of the individual members. And the "little failures" in meeting competitive challenges may then become acceptable in a society that once found any weakness intolerable.

A growth industry, then, is simply a new product or service that an established industry has ignored, usually because of its vested interest in old ways of doing things. In other words, a growth industry represents the failure of another industry to recognize an opportunity, to maintain a sufficiently demanding internal environment to protect its dominant position.

But what constitutes a demanding environment? And how is this environment maintained? Like so many other intangibles, the definition of a demanding environment is subject to highly personal interpretation, for the intensity of the demands on executives does vary from industry to industry, depending on competition. Yet it seems to me that the key elements in a demanding environment can be reasonably identified despite variances that occur from company to company. The two major groupings might be characterized as centering around the work environment, on the one hand, and the more complex factors making for company success on the other.

The work environment

One company which can boast of the highest return on investment and the outstanding record in a low-margin industry has some unique work habits for a billion-dollar business today:

¶ The headquarters is located in a reconditioned warehouse in the "wrong" part of a big city. It is not air-conditioned. But occupancy cost comes to less than one-sixth of that paid by many of the company's competitors.

¶ Members of top management, from the chairman down, follow the practice of turning lights off when they go to lunch. Also, all executives take the bus rather than a taxi to the airport—and after the 5:00 p.m. closing time.

¶ Since the field organization starts working at 8:00 a.m., the headquarters group follows the same practice. Furthermore, the physical demands on the field staff are such that retirement is mandatory at 60—and top management lives by this same rule.

¶ Being thrifty in the conduct of business, management expects employees to be equally thrifty in their personal lives. One evidence is a pension plan to which all employees contribute 8 percent of their compensation.

¶ With profits hard to come by in their low-margin business, salaries are low. But compensation is high by industry standards because a profit-based incentive plan amply rewards executives for the unusually high return on investment they achieve.

Here is a work environment that demands a profit-and-cost-centered performance from its employees. By present industry standards, it may be considered Spartan in those areas that are nonproductive. But there is no stinting where facilities, research expenditures, or compensation for demonstrated performance are concerned.

Approximately the reverse of this situation occurred early in World War II when the newly elected president of a large airplane manufacturer arrived one morning to take up his duties. He noticed a large crate in the reception room and asked the receptionist what it contained. "I don't know," she said. "But it's been sitting there for weeks." Inquiry disclosed that the crate contained parts for lack of which a major production line had been shut down for nearly a month.

Before leaving the reception room, the new chief executive asked to see the list of executive office personnel who had arrived before him. This revealed that, although it was 8:15 a.m. and the starting time was 8:00 a.m., only 6 out of 37 executives were on hand. A subsequent review of the attendance record for several previous weeks showed that the usual arrival time for top executives was 9:30 or later, with lower echelons arriving 15 to 30 minutes earlier than their bosses.

These two incidents provided the president with unmistakable evidence of a relaxed environment—and, among other derelictions, the reason why the company was delivering only one airplane a week against a budget of eight.

Lack of dedication and discipline, i.e., a demanding environment, among the leadership group had become the major factor in this internal deterioration.

Clearly, habits thus developed often mean the difference between outstanding and poor profit performance. The company in the low-margin business discussed in previous paragraphs does not have a higher profit margin than its competitors because of a low headquarters occupancy cost or as a result of turning out lights. But the frugal habits developed by consistently following Ben Franklin's admonition that "a penny saved is a penny earned" makes cost control in this company virtually habitual.

Actually, these relatively simple elements in the work environment greatly influence what "demanding" means to individual executives. More than one company during the postwar period of executive hoarding reduced the responsibilities of executives to the point where two individuals were doing one man's job. It is a little difficult to maintain a demanding environment when top executives set easy goals for themselves and expect equally little of their subordinates.

The most demanding work environments of my experience were established by men who conducted their business like a war to be won. The hard work, self-discipline, and profit-mindedness of the environment they created were simply part of the training process to condition subordinates for the rigors of this competitive war. These men set high standards for themselves and insisted that the survival of the individual subordinates depended on how effectively they met these standards.

Factors making for success

A work environment should "demand" those attributes essential to the success of a particular business. What may be a necessary element in one company's environment may have little bearing in another.

Avon Products, for example, had the highest return on investment—a whopping 37.3 percent—in a recent *Fortune* survey of the 500 largest companies. No useful purpose is served by insisting on an environment of Spartan frugality in such a case, for low rent, turning out lights, and the like contribute little to this company's phenomenal profit record. Profits resulting from reduced costs are minuscule compared with those resulting from Avon's successful new products and the company's aggressive sales effort. Therefore, the key "demand" in Avon's environment has been for a commercially oriented creativity that produces a steady flow of new ideas in products, advertising, promotion, and selling.

The company that sells parts to the automobile manufacturers operates in a different economic climate; it must be a low-cost producer to survive. The internal environment in such a firm should demand constant reductions in product costs by the introduction of new materials, manufacturing process, and equipment. In the chemical or ethical drug industry, on the other hand, a five-year-old product has probably seen its best profit days. Therefore, the creativity of the research function—its ability to develop marketable new products—becomes the key to success.

Few will question that success in most enterprises—whether it be professional football or selling soap—depends on people. This being the case, it would seem almost self-evident that management would do whatever was necessary to recruit the quality of manpower to produce the greatest possible profits. Yet retailing—one of the most competitive of industries— has complacently permitted the six-day week and low starting salaries to erode the quality of manpower being attracted and trained as the top management of the future. One of the leading business schools reports that, whereas 20 years ago retailing was the largest recruiter of their students, it is near the bottom today.

To be sure, the retail environment must demand hard work and tight control over expenses, for the business involves an enormous amount of detail that directly affects profits—and has one of the lowest profit margins in industry. But many retailers have not recognized the need for making their necessarily demanding environment attractive enough to those entering it to recruit and keep the kind of personnel needed to assure future profits. One large retail chain, for example, loses over two-thirds of its new recruits within two years—and probably loses the best of them.

The point is not that the demands of the environment be relaxed but that the industry accommodate its thinking to the realities—higher starting salaries and the five-day week—of their manpower needs.

One of the outstanding characteristics of highly successful companies is a demanding environment. The top management of such organizations sets ever-increasing standards of performance for the company and sees to it that subordinates make an all-out effort to meet them. Competitive challenges are seen as inevitable, and management expects company personnel to feel comfortable with this way of life.

At the other extreme we have the companies that, like the older civilizations, have accommodated themselves to a more relaxed environment. For the most part, performance standards deteriorate because management can not bring itself to meet competitive challenges. Several of the old "corner-grocery" chains for instance, have disappeared because their executives ignored the rise of the supermarket.

Obviously, the quality of leadership determines the environment in a specific company. But it has been my experience that a demanding corporate environment and a performance-oriented administration of executive compensation go hand in hand. I suspect that the reason the two are so closely identified is that compensation administration simplifies the problem of maintaining such a competitive environment.

The reason, I think, is clear. A soundly conceived and administered compensation program becomes an instrument that unifies the various needs of the business. It is not as money that compensation makes its major contribution, but as a sort of "all-purpose" motivation that has widely varying shades of incentive value to different people.

For example, the purchasing power of money will be critical to the younger executive with voracious family needs, while the status implication of money becomes more important to the older man. Small variations between bonus payments will be highly significant to top-level peer-group executives whose compensation is a matter of public record, whereas substantially larger differences in bonus checks are required to accomplish the same motivational objective in another environment.

On the other hand, compensation—money—is the only motivation that can be measured in reasonably precise terms from person to person. Therefore, it is easier to assess the motivational impact of money than, for example, leadership, or job security, or responsibility. In other words, compensation is the most flexible of motivations, hence the most useful to a skillful management.

And compensation can be many-faceted. If entrepreneurial incentives are needed, stock options may be available to prod the profit-making instincts of top executives. If the competition is rugged and profit-influencing decisions are traceable to individuals, incentive compensation can be used to reward profit-mindedness.

But the key motivating force exerted by compensation lies in its power to reward and penalize. Promotions, merit increases, and bonuses should be administered to the same end: more effective individual performance.

Top management frequently applies reward and penalty with great trepidation, fearful that a strong dosage of penalty will hurt morale. In my judgment, such timidity undermines the basic objectives of the entire reward-and-penalty concept. A large, divisionalized company recently had an experience that bears significantly on this point. Its executive incentive plan routinely paid what was regarded as a normal bonus. But a year came when profits tumbled. Several divisions received substantially

210

reduced bonus payments, but none had their bonuses eliminated entirely.

The profit decline continued the next year at an accelerated rate. The company ended with a bonus fund 60 percent below the "normal" paid out two years before. Several divisions had done very poorly—considerably worse than their competition. But three divisions had done an outstanding job of cutting costs and maintaining their competitive profit leadership.

If reasonable incentive payments were to be paid executives of the three top-performing divisions, no bonuses could be paid the poorly performing divisions. The chief executive decided to be consistent with the philosophy of the company's incentive plan—despite a certain amount of hand wringing among top staff executives—and paid only a few "special-situation" bonuses in the substandard divisions. The three top divisions received normal awards.

This action shocked executives of the weak divisions. Even so, there was surprisingly little grumbling. And, more important, without any prodding from headquarters the laggard divisions immediately started cost-reduction programs that have greatly improved their profit position.

The key to the resounding success of this chief executive's decision lay in the demonstrable superiority of performance in one group and demonstrable weakness in the other. In addition, the company's history of demanding outstanding results from its executives undoubtedly was a contributing factor.

Thus, compensation administration provides the instrument that permits top management to recognize the variances in the demands placed on the executive group, and to reward or penalize in accordance with the importance of each to company profits. It enables management to channel executive efforts into activities likely to be most productive, by rewarding the most important activities with higher salaries, larger bonuses, and faster promotions. And when compensation of executives is above the industry average, above-average demands can be made of the executive group. (Top management shies away from asking much of executives who are paid below the industry average—which is one thing that makes below-average compensation so expensive.)

If compensation administration is to be done well, the experience of a good many companies indicates the need for two supporting efforts on the part of management: (1) a clear-cut understanding of who is responsible for what and how important each activity is to the company, and (2) the development of a sound basis for appraising how well each man accomplishes what is expected of him. This latter presupposes sound market and economic information, as well as a superior personnel staff.

It is this need to integrate the various elements in the management process that has made compensation administration such a potent competitive weapon. In effect, when compensation is administered effectively, top executives are virtually *forced* to do a superior job of clarifying individual responsibilities, developing yardsticks of individual performance, and discriminating between the performance of individual executives. This, in turn, is reflected in an administrative process that develops better executives by ensuring that merit increases, bonuses, and promotions are related to individual performance.

The secret of the demanding environment, in my judgment, lies in making competition a way of life for a company, rather than the kiss of death. And compensation administration is one of leadership's most important instruments of maintaining such an environment.

PART FIVE

Market and distribution strategy

It is already a truism that every product has its allotted life span. Sooner or later all, from cake mixes to computers, must pass through the stages of growth, maturity, and obsolescence. Here there is scope for the practice of one of management's newest and subtlest arts, described by Donald K. Clifford, Jr., in "Managing the Product Life Cycle." Of late, Clifford notes, the thinking of creative marketing executives has been changed by the realization that the life cycles of individual products do not move at a fixed rate but can, to a significant extent, be reshaped and controlled. As a corollary, the author shows, long-term profitability can be increased by improving the overall mix of life cycles in a company's product line.

Other present-day trends in marketing proceed from the same general assumption: that conditions in the marketplace can be anticipated, redirected, even created by skillful, detailed, and imaginative product planning. Yet as B. Charles Ames reminds us in "Keys to Better Product Planning," this recognition is only the beginning of the battle. The follow-through, in terms of effectively organizing the corporate marketing effort has proven both difficult and confusing for many managements.

For many, the product manager system has seemed to offer great promise. This approach has worked for some, but for others it has failed miserably, largely because top management failed to give its newly appointed product managers the support they needed. The working of miracles has no place in the arts of management, and Ames leaves no doubt that a product manager on his own, with a minimum of support and guidance from his superiors, will have to be nothing less than a miracle-worker to come through with positive results.

213

A second contribution by Ames, "Marketing Planning for Industrial Products," explores the reasons why formal planning has proven so much more useful for consumer goods companies than for those in the industrial field. Basing his discussion in part on research findings, he pins the blame for many failures on lack of proper direction from the top. A striking example of the managerial art is cited in this essay. One company found that, year after year, its marketing plans had amounted to nothing more than extrapolation from past thinking. Countering this, management called upon its planners to come up with alternative strategies. The result: a painful but exceedingly instructive and ultimately profitable reexamination of past marketing policies.

A recurrent theme in this anthology, the reader will have noted, is an insistence that management must remain rigorously pragmatic, basing its decisions on factual evidence, undisturbed by emotional or personal considerations. The touchstone of decision, in the words of one McKinsey author,* must be "what is right, not who is right." This approach, sound as it may be, is not always easy to follow. In "Shaping Distribution Channels to Your Needs," A. L. McDonald, Jr. calls attention to the difficulties that may ensue when a marketing manager confronts the need to make changes in the distribution of his company's products. "Distribution channels are, after all, outside the company and beyond management's direct control," he points out. The task of evaluating distributors' performance can be a thankless one, where longstanding personal relationships are involved and feelings may be easily hurt. Here the arts of negotiation and conciliation are called into play—for the marketing manager must be prepared to put through changes unwelcome both to distributors and the company's own salesmen.

Physical distribution lies in a kind of no-man's-land between marketing and manufacturing. For that reason, suggests Robert P. Neuschel in "Physical Distribution—Forgotten Profit Frontier," it has seldom been very well managed. Citing a McKinsey survey on the economics of distribution, he identifies this as a profit opportunity "of major dimensions in many companies"—often, it appears, because of simple unawareness on management's part of the sheer magnitude of the costs involved.

Neuschel's essay serves as a reminder that the arts of management in many instances have nothing to do with arriving at brilliant, farsighted decisions. Often they consist of whittling away at costs: for example, aggressively negotiating lower rates with carriers, obtaining

* Marvin Bower, "Organization: The Harness to Help People Pull Together," page 61.

214

better freight servicing and warehousing, making the best possible use of company equipment, ceaselessly reviewing customer selection policies, relocating plants and warehouses, and in general bringing to light previously hidden disorganization and waste. All this may not qualify as a spectacular art, but—as Neuschel demonstrates in detail—it is an indispensable one in the truly competitive company.

19. Managing the product life cycle

Donald K. Clifford, Jr.

Not long ago, a leading marketer of consumer packaged goods was building a brand of toilet soap. Growth had been fair but not spectacular. Market tests suggested that an increase in spot TV advertising, backed by a change in copy, could enable the new brand to reach the "escape velocity" it needed to become a sales leader. But marketing management, feeling the funds would be better spent in launching a new detergent, vetoed the proposal. The detergent was a moderate success, but the promising soap brand went into a gradual sales decline from which it never recovered. Management had pulled out the props at a critical point in the product's growth period.

A supplier of light industrial equipment felt that his major product was not receiving the sales support it deserved. Unconvinced by the salesmen's claims that it was hard to sell, he developed new presentations and sales kits and persuaded sales management to run special campaigns. At year-end, volume had shown no improvement. In fact, the product had long since passed the zenith of its potential sales and profits, and no amount of additional sales support could have profitably extended its growth. Yet in order to give extra sales support to this problem case, management had cut into the marketing budgets of several highly promising products that were still in their "young" growth phase. In short, management had failed to consider each product's position in its life cycle.

As these two cases suggest, the concept of the product life cycle—familiar as it may be to most business executives—seems too frequently forgotten in marketing planning. Yet there appears to be conclusive evidence that companies can make far more effective marketing decisions if they take the time to: (1) find out where each of their products stands in its life cycle; (2) determine the overall mix or balance of life cycles in their product line; and (3) analyze the trends in their life-cycle mix and the long-term profit impact of these trends. Without this information, some products will receive neither their rightful *share* of marketing attention, nor the right *kind* of attention. With it, marketing management has a twofold opportunity:

¶ To reshape and control the life cycles of individual products.

¶ To raise long-term corporate profitability by improving the overall mix of life cycles in the company's product line.

The size and profitability of any business depend on the product life cycles that make it up. But while companies may continue to grow in sales and profits, no product escapes eventual maturity and decline. Allocating resources so as to reconcile corporate aims and ambitions with the life cycles of the company's products is the objective of life-cycle management. My purpose here is to show how the classic life-cycle concept can be turned into an active profit-making tool, and to describe an approach to life-cycle analysis that has helped some companies make more profitable marketing decisions.

The life-cycle concept

The product life-cycle concept derives from the fact that a product's sales volume follows a typical pattern that can readily be charted as a four-phase cycle (see the next page). Following its birth, the product passes through a low-volume introduction phase. During the subsequent growth period, volume and profit both rise. Volume stabilizes during maturity, though unit profits typically start to fall off. Eventually, in the stage of obsolescence, sales volume declines.

The length of the life cycle, the duration of each phase, and the shape of the curve vary widely for different products. But in every instance, obsolescence eventually occurs for one of three reasons.

First, the need may disappear. This is what happened to the orange juice squeezer when frozen juice caught on.

Second, a better, cheaper, or more convenient product may be developed to suit the same need. Oil-based paint lost its position in the home to water-based paint; plastics have replaced wood, metal, and paper in product categories ranging from dry-cleaning bags to aircraft parts.

Third, a competitive product may, through superior marketing strategy, suddenly gain a decisive advantage. This happened to competing products when Arthur Godfrey's personal charm got behind Lipton Tea, and again when Procter & Gamble secured the American Dental Association's endorsement of its decay-prevention claims for Crest toothpaste.

As the chart on page 218 shows, a product's profit cycle is shaped quite differently from its sales cycle. During introduction, a product may not earn any profit at all because of high initial advertising and promotion costs.

In the growth period, before competition catches up, unit profits typically attain their peak. Then they start declining, though total profits may continue to rise for a time on rising sales volume. In the chemical industry, for example, rapid volume increases often more than offset the effect of price reductions early in the growth phase.

During late growth and early maturity, increasing competition cuts deeply into profit margins and ultimately into total profits. For instance, as a result of drastic price cutting, general-purpose semiconductors, once highly profitable, now return so little unit profit that major companies such as CBS and Clevite left the business some time ago.

Finally, in the period of obsolescence, declining volume eventually pushes costs up to a level that eliminates profits entirely.

The product life cycle concept

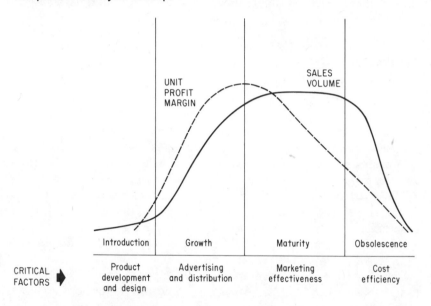

In recent years, as most marketing men are aware, products have been maturing more rapidly and life cycles growing shorter. Indeed, this trend has been responsible for some of the major problems facing marketers today.

Where consumer goods are concerned, the proliferation of new products has contributed to more rapid maturity. Consider, for example, the great variety of cookies and dry cereals that have appeared on the supermarket shelf in recent years. Extending this trend to the store as a whole helps explain why the average supermarket grew from 2,800 items in the mid-1940s to more than 7,000 two decades later. Since the average purchase in a supermarket did not even double during this period, the average product was receiving a smaller and smaller share of the shopper's food dollar. Obviously, this tends to reduce any item's ultimate volume and hasten the time of maturation.

218

Razor blades may be seen as another classic example of accelerated maturity. For decades, with Blue Blades and thin blades, Gillette dominated the market and enjoyed steady growth. Ten years ago, Super Blue Blades arrived—a new product with greatly improved shaving qualities, which could normally have looked forward to a growth period of many years, if not decades. But in less than three years, the stainless steel blade was re-introduced into this country, and the Super Blue Blade started on its way to obsolescence, suddenly shifting from growth to maturity.

The trend to more rapid maturity can be observed in industrial products as well. In chemicals, the competitive advantage afforded by a new product such as nylon once ensured growing sales for a decade or more. But in recent years, the tempo of product innovation and substitution has quickened to the point where some companies, rather than risk heavy research investments on products that may mature within two or three years, now concentrate on exploiting present products and on rapidly copying the products introduced by market leaders.

Not only do products mature more rapidly, but product life cycles generally appear to be growing shorter. For more than 15 years—to cite one conspicuous example—the DC–3 held its place as the leading commercial airliner. But the DC–7, and later the turbo-prop Electra, were rendered obsolete in less than five years by the pure jet DC–8, the 707, and others like them. Today's complex military weapons systems, unlike the weapons of World War II, become obsolete almost before they leave the drawing board. Even the lifespan of the humble cracker has typically shortened to a few years or even months.

Failure to manage the life-cycle

Faced with the challenge of earlier maturity and shortening life cycles, few leading companies have seen the opportunity in life-cycle management, and fewer still have capitalized on it. Most have either (1) failed to recognize that their products have a life cycle, or (2) failed to apply the concept by analyzing the life cycles of their product lines in order to shape marketing strategy.

The railroads of the United States stand out as a classic example of the first kind of failure, which I call the commodity illusion. For decades they viewed their service as a commodity, a changeless product that would forever meet a changeless transportation need. Only recently have the railroads begun to realize how much ground they have lost—and how much they are still losing—to air, water, and, particularly, over-the-road transportation.

A similar commodity illusion misled the many textile companies that failed to adapt their wool and cotton equipment and marketing capabilities to synthetic fibers in the decade following World War II. In product after product, market after market, companies that had regarded their traditional products as commodities went out of business or were absorbed by more wide-awake competitors.

The second cause of inadequate life-cycle management—neglecting to apply the life-cycle concept—may be illustrated by an electronics company whose products typically have life cycles of two years or less. Too much concerned with present problems, not enough with future opportunities and needs, this company had failed to assess the life-cycle mix of its product line.

As a result, it suddenly found itself with two products late in the growth phase, nine in the maturity or obsolescence phases—and none in introduction or early growth. New and improved products, the lifeblood of any organization in this industry, had simply been allowed to dry up. Had it failed to recognize its predicament in time, the company might well have been out of business in another two years. Fortunately, rapid development and acquisition programs were carried out in time to provide the new products it needed for survival.

Again, a chemical corporation I know is still pouring money into product improvement on a plastic that was made obsolete soon after its introduction by a competitor's new and superior product. Mesmerized by the supposed potential of its own "growth product," the company refused to face the facts. Because of management's failure to apply life-cycle analysis, this lost cause is still draining off money and talent that might profitably be devoted to growth products with a far greater potential.

Such failures by management to fully understand or act on the changing requirements of the company's products and product mix are all too common. And as life cycles grow shorter and products mature more rapidly, the problem for many can only become more acute.

The classic life-cycle concept holds that marketing decisions should be largely determined by a product's position in its cycle, since—as the chart indicates—the critical factors affecting its profitability change with the four phases of its growth and decline.

In the introduction phase, product development and design are considered critical. For industrial goods, where customers have been slow to change from a proven product, technical superiority or demonstrable cost savings will often be needed to open the door. For consumer products, willingness to invest in future volume through heavy initial marketing expenditures may be critical.

During the growth period, consistent, reliable product performance must be regarded as essential to success for most industrial products—and for technically complex consumer products as well. A reputation for quality, backed by adequate production capability, can win a manu-

220

facturer the leading market position, as it did for Zenith in black-and-white TV. In contrast, for consumer packaged goods and other non-technical products, effective distribution and advertising have traditionally been the key factors.

The key requirements during maturity, though harder to define, usually come under the heading of "overall marketing effectiveness." Marketing skill may pay off in a variety of ways—for instance, generating incremental profits by reducing price so as to reach additional consumers; finding and promoting new uses for the product; or upgrading distribution channels to reach prime markets more efficiently.

During obsolescence, cost control becomes the key to generating profits. The product of the low-cost producer and distributor often enjoys a profitable "old age" long after its rivals have disappeared from the scene.

Though valid within their limits, the traditional generalizations about management decisions and the product life cycle do not really go far enough. They fail to take into account the all-important fact that *life cycles can be managed.*

The dimension of control

Life-cycle management has two basic aspects:

¶ Controlling the mix of life cycles in the product line by: (1) planned new-product effort and product-line pruning, and (2) planned allocation of money and manpower among existing products and product groups according to the profit opportunity reflected by their respective life-cycle positions.

¶ Controlling individual product life cycles to generate added profits.

Experience indicates that there may be opportunities at any stage, except for the very end of the line, for marketing management to profitably alter the shape and duration of an individual product's life cycle. The introduction period, for example, can often be shortened by increasing marketing expenditures or securing national distribution more quickly. In the next phase, growth can be speeded and sales and profits ultimately pushed to higher levels by exploiting additional markets, by pricing the product to encourage wider usage, or by more vigorous advertising or sales efforts—in short, by more effectively planned and implemented marketing strategy.

The maturity stage usually offers marketing management the greatest opportunity to change the shape and duration of product life cycles. Has the product really approached obsolescence because of a superior substitute or a fundamental change in consumer needs? Or does obsolescence merely seem near because marketing management has failed to identify and reach the right consumer needs, or because a competitor has done a better marketing job? The question will be crucial, since often the supposed condition of "maturity" is misleading. The challenge may be rather to extend the product's youth by repackaging, physical modifications, repricing, appealing to new users, adding new distribution channels, or some combination of marketing strategy changes. Frequently, as subsequent examples will show, a successfully revitalized product offers a higher return on management time and funds invested than does a new product.

Of course, this will not always be possible. Maturity is forced upon some products by a basic change in consumer habits or the introduction of a greatly superior competitive item. In this event, determining when to cut back the investment of management time and money—and give higher priority to new or more active products—becomes the key marketing decision.

Finally, in obsolescence, marketing effectiveness becomes almost entirely a matter of knowing when to cut short the life of a product which has been demanding more than the small share of management attention that its profit contribution deserves.

Controlling the life cycle

The tremendous impact of effective life-cycle management may be demonstrated by the success of several leading companies in directing the progress of both individual product cycles and the overall life-cycle mix. Consider these examples:

¶ Spurred by rapid technological change and by the trend toward packaging everything—a consequence of our self-service way of life—packaging has been a growth industry for well over a decade. One of the industry leaders has been E. I. du Pont de Nemours & Co. Du Pont has been strongest in cellophane, a product so well known it has become almost a synonym for transparent packaging.

With the end of World War II, flexible packaging, and cellophane in particular, entered a period of accelerated growth, but in the 1950s new products—notably polyethylene—began to meet certain packaging needs more effectively. Polyethylene film, for example, was less easily ruptured in cold weather—and in time, it also became lower in price. Consequently, cellophane began losing its share of the flexible packaging market. It became clear that sales volume would soon begin falling off unless strong corrective action was taken.

Faced with the immediate threat of obsolescence in a highly profitable product, Du Pont—followed by the two other cellophane manufacturers—introduced a series of modifications designed to maintain cellophane's growth and prolong its maturity. These included special coatings to reduce winter breakage and increase protective qualities, new types of cellophane designed for the needs of different products, and lighter grades at prices more competitive with the newer packaging materials. In all, the customers' choice of cellophane types grew from a handful to well over 100.

The cumulative effect of these improvements had an impressive impact on cellophane sales. Contrary to widespread predictions of dramatic decline, cellophane maintained the bulk of its sales volume—of which the traditional grades now represent a relatively small fraction.[1] With more than half of a $300 million market, Du Pont has been the primary beneficiary of this reversal of fortunes.

Further testimony to Du Pont's effectiveness in life-cycle management can be found in its control over the life-cycle *mix* of its flexible packaging products. Recognizing the maturity of cellophane, Du Pont developed a strong position in polyethylene and in other new packaging materials. While *maintaining* its leadership in flexible packaging by reshaping the life cycle of cellophane, the company also provided for *growth* by adding new products to strengthen its product mix.

¶ During the mid-1950s, Procter & Gamble's Gleem had attained a strong position in the toothpaste market. But the total market was growing at a slow rate, and P&G wanted to grow faster. Having introduced Crest as the first decay-preventive dentifrice, P&G found the way to explosive growth by obtaining endorsement of the new toothpaste by the American Dental Association—an achievement that had evaded other manufacturers for years. P&G thus reshaped the life cycle of the new dentifrice. Crest's share of the toothpaste market *quadrupled* between 1958 and 1963, while the sales curves of other brands of toothpaste showed strong signs of obsolescence, declining on the average more than 15 percent.

¶ Another success in changing the life cycle of a product was scored by the same company in the cake mix market. Here, P&G introduced a large number of new cake types. This built sales in three ways:

First, by broadening its line, P&G appealed to a wider market.
Second, by increasing the variety of cakes a homemaker could serve, it persuaded women to make cakes more often.
Third, by vastly increasing the number of cake mix types to be stocked in supermarkets, P&G achieved a billboard of cake mixes on the shelf, which inevitably attracted the shopper's eye and drew additional sales from competing products.

In brief, Procter & Gamble effectively increased the demand for cake mix and then filled the added demand through the strength of its distribution.

¶ Decades after the introduction of Jell-O, General Foods succeeded in

---

[1] Author's note: While cellophane volume has declined significantly since this article was written in 1965, it is still one of the largest selling packaging materials, and Du Pont continues to reap the benefits of effective life-cycle management.

converting it from a mature to a growth product by a revamping of marketing strategy. GF changed the Jell-O formula, repackaged the product and repriced it, found a host of new uses for Jell-O, and publicized them to the housewife through stepped-up advertising. Today, Jell-O remains one of GF's biggest selling and most profitable products.

¶ Some years ago, a small candy company drastically changed its life-cycle mix by eliminating all but four of the 800 items in its product line. By eliminating a host of problem children, putting its muscle behind a single strong growth brand, and maintaining only three other products to offset swings in production, this company shifted its life-cycle balance from early obsolescence to growth. From a marginal producer, it has become one of the most profitable small companies in the confectionery business.

¶ Aggressive life-cycle management was also demonstrated when International Business Machines introduced its "Series 360" computers early in 1964. By the early 1960s, competition in this field had rapidly become severe. IBM controlled three-quarters of the computer business, but intensified competition was shortening the life cycles of its computer line. Management foresaw that the rapid growth it had enjoyed in the 1950s would soon slow down unless the company undertook a major shift in product and marketing strategy.

The solution adopted by IBM was to rapidly obsolete its own equipment—much of which had been on the market for less than four years. At the same time, the company moved to secure its entrenched position in computers by providing an expandable system that would make it uneconomic or inefficient for customers to switch to competing systems as their computer needs grew.

While there is no substitute for solid marketing judgment, these examples serve to suggest that the odds on making good decisions will be increased if management knows where its products stand—individually and collectively—in their respective life cycles.

Life-cycle analysis

One proven means of positioning a company's products in their life cycles —a way that has proven effective for some forward-looking companies—is life-cycle analysis. This may be described as a disciplined, periodic review resulting in (a) a formal audit that pinpoints each product's position in its life cycle, and (b) a profile of the life-cycle mix of the product line as a whole.

Although the steps followed by marketing management in carrying out the first part of a life-cycle analysis may vary among companies, the following are typical:

1. Develop historical trend information for a period of three to five years (longer for some products). Data included will be unit and dollar sales, profit margins, total profit contribution, return on invested capital, market share, and prices.

2. Check recent trends in the number and nature of competitors; number and market-share rankings of competing products, and their quality and performance advantages; shifts in distribution channels; and relative advantages enjoyed by competitive products in each channel.

3. Analyze developments in short-term competitive tactics, such as competitors' recent announcements of new products or plans for expanding production capacity.

4. Obtain (or update) historical information on the life cycles of similar or related products.

5. Project sales for the product over the next three to five years, based on all the information gathered, and estimate an incremental profit ratio for the product during each of these years (the ratio of total direct costs—manufacturing, advertising, product development, sales, distribution, etc. —to pretax profits). Expressed as a ratio—e.g., 4.8 to 1 or 6.3 to 1—this measures the number of dollars required to generate each additional dollar of profit. The ratio typically improves (becomes lower) as the product enters its growth period; begins to deteriorate (rise) as the product approaches maturity; and climbs more sharply as it reaches obsolescence.

6. Estimate the number of profitable years remaining in the product's life cycle, and—based on all the information at hand—fix the product's position on its life-cycle curve: (a) introduction, (b) early or late growth, (c) early or late maturity, or (d) early or late obsolescence.

Developing the life-cycle profile

Once the life-cycle positions of all the company's major products have been determined, marketing management proceeds to develop a life-cycle profile of the company's entire line. Again, this involves a series of steps:

1. Determine what percentages of the company's sales and profits fall within each phase of the product life cycle. These percentage figures indicate the present life-cycle (sales) profile and the present profit profile of the company's current line.

2. Calculate changes in the life-cycle and profit profiles over the past five years, and project these profiles over the next five years.

3. Develop a target life-cycle profile for the company, and measure the company's present life-cycle profile against it. The target profile, established by marketing management, specifies the desirable share of company sales that should fall within each phase of the product life cycle. It can be determined by industry obsolescence trends, the pace of new pro-

duct introduction in the field, the average length of product life cycles in the company's line, and top management's objectives for growth and profitability. As a rule, the target profile for growth-minded companies whose life cycles tend to be short will call for a high proportion of sales in the introductory and growth phases.

With these steps completed, management can assign priorities to such functions as new-product development, acquisition, and product-line pruning, based on the discrepancies between the company's target profile and its present life-cycle profile. Once corporate effort has been broadly allocated in this way among products at various stages of their life cycles, marketing plans can be detailed for individual product lines.

Both the depth of life-cycle analysis and the factors it takes into consideration vary almost as widely as do company needs, objectives, and product lines. Hence, there can be no overall formula for weighting the various elements that combine to determine a product's life-cycle position. But this flexibility should not be seen as a drawback. Rather it emphasizes the versatility that makes life-cycle analysis a useful and widely applicable management tool.

20. Keys to better product planning

B. Charles Ames

Imaginative marketing planning, as more and more companies realize, has become increasingly vital to gaining or holding a competitive edge in the marketplace. As product lines proliferate under the stress of competition, demands on the marketing planner have multiplied rapidly. Today, in a great many businesses, product lines have grown so large and diversified that detailed planning for the entire family of products has simply come to be too big a job for one man.

More frequently than ever, companies failing to recognize this fact and strengthen their organizations accordingly have found their product-market strategies in trouble. New products fail because marketing executives, already overloaded with current product responsibilities, lack time to plan for introducing the new entries. When minor products do not realize their full potential, marketing managers often have been too busy trying to meet their major goals.

Hence, more and more businesses have turned to the product manager concept. The results in many instances have been impressive:

¶ Better definition of each product's market, future direction, and needs, and a more precise idea of the company's relative competitive position and opportunities.

¶ Clearer understanding of the economic consequences and market impact that will derive from alternative decisions and strategies for each product.

¶ More explicit and better integrated product goals (for example, volume, profit, market share, and so forth) and sounder programs for their achievement.

¶ For key line executives, a greater understanding of these goals and strategies, and of the efforts required to bring them in line with one another.

¶ More effective implementation and follow-up of agreed-upon plans, and more timely adjustments when needed to strengthen product positions and profits.

Consider the recent experience of a leading electronics manufacturer. For years, this company had dabbled with little success in the nuclear instrumentation field. Its sales growth had lagged behind competition, and profits were too slim to support the development efforts needed to keep pace with the field. Understandably, management had its doubts about what to do, but problems in other product areas always seemed more important. For some time, the instrumentation business was allowed to drift.

Eventually, under pressure, the company decided to reorganize its marketing department along product management lines. One manager was assigned full-time to the company's nuclear instrumentation program. His charter: to devise a strategy for moving this line, or a plan to withdraw from the business.

Within three months, the product manager became convinced that the nuclear instrumentation potential alone was too limited to justify the manufacturer's continued interest. But he had also identified a challenging opportunity to expand into the much broader and more attractive controls field. Pursuing the new conception, he submitted a plan that called for adding technical staff and acquiring a small foreign manufacturer. In this way, he pointed out, the company would be able to obtain the broader base of products needed to compete in the controls area. His plan was adopted, and today this new product line has become the fastest growing and most promising segment of the company's entire business.

Such successes, unhappily, are far from universal. In fact, a great many companies adopting the product management concept have been sorely disappointed. To cite two recent examples:

¶ A marketing vice president in the basic metals field complained: "We moved to a product management setup because we thought we could improve our profits. The idea was to have managers with full-time responsibility for planning to improve the mix of products moving through our plants. Now it's beginning to look like we were kidding ourselves. Our product management group costs us $150,000 a year, but I can't honestly say our product mix is any better today than it was in the beginning. Our product managers have put all kinds of plans together, but not one has really done the job we wanted."

¶ The president of an automotive parts manufacturing firm said: "My engineers and plant people have always done a good job of running their operations according to plan. When we run into scheduling or delivery problems, sloppy marketing planning usually turns out to be at fault. We thought we could lick these slip-ups by assigning managers to plan for each of our product lines. Well, we've tried it for three years now. We still have as many missed deliveries as ever, and our engineers have no better idea of future product design requirements than they ever did. Our product managers are busy as beavers, but they certainly haven't helped us do any better at planning in areas that really count."

Why should corporate experience with product management be so mixed? How is it that managers have markedly improved product planning in some companies—and have failed so abysmally in others?

My work with a number of different companies suggests that the blame for bad planning, usually pinned on the hapless product manager, should more often be laid at top management's door. Too often, companies adopt the product management concept and then proceed to make it impossible for the responsible men to do their jobs. Too often, management fails to define the product manager's planning responsibilities or to provide him with the direction and support he needs to plan effectively.

From its early start in consumer goods companies, the product management concept has rapidly spread into other industries. Today, product manager assignments have become as common for electronic gear and heavy machinery as for toothpaste or baby food.

Within such a broad spectrum of products and marketing requirements, such assignments understandably show important differences in focus and structure. A product manager for toothpaste will primarily be concerned with advertising, promotion, and packaging—the keys to his product's success. In contrast, his counterpart in the heavy equipment field will be likely to spend most of his time on individual account analysis, production costs, and product specifications. And the efforts of a product manager for textile fibers will probably be devoted to coordinating sales with production to ensure efficient capacity utilization and the best possible marketing mix.

Despite such differences, all product manager jobs have an identical core. Whatever his product assignment, the product manager's basic responsibility will entail *effective planning and coordination of the activities vital to his product's success.*

Keys to sound planning

In my experience, successful product management groups may be distinguished by four basic approaches to planning.

First, over 70 percent of the managers interviewed in a recent survey prepare a written plan for their product lines, incorporating in some form the five basic elements illustrated on the next page. Despite many variations in content and format, the function of this plan will always be explicitly to define product needs and opportunities and to indicate what can be done to meet them.

No magic results can be accomplished by a written product plan, but it does reduce the chances of planning gaps as well as the occurrence of outright errors. It also provides a far better basis for top-management evaluation. If well done, the written presentation shows everyone

Five components of the product plan

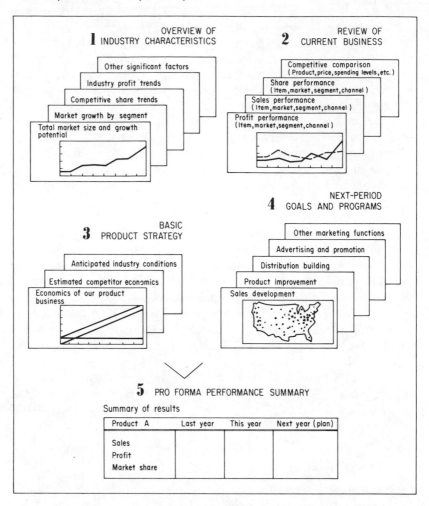

that the product manager has really thought through his program and knows better than anyone else its requirements for success. Without such a plan he has virtually no chance of providing the basic direction and obtaining the necessary line support to improve his product's business.

Second, the planning emphasis should be focused on relatively few areas —those that can make or break the product. As noted earlier, these "key" activities vary from product to product. Often, even for the same product, they will vary over the course of time. For example, one manager in charge of a consumer package item, who had limited his detailed planning to

230

advertising and promotion, found himself obliged to shift much of his effort to product and package improvement when his two major competitors began gaining a larger share of the market through advances in these areas.

Third, in planning, product managers range across company lines, concentrating on the activities crucial to product success wherever they may be located on the organization charts. Often, this involves working into areas that would normally be considered remote from their sphere of influence, such as production or design engineering. To do so without running into organization conflicts, they must have both personal stature and the necessary top-management support.

One product manager for small electric motors found his costs nearly 25 percent out of line and his market position slipping rapidly. Though assigned to the marketing department, he took the lead in pushing through a cost-reduction project that significantly changed both the engineering and the manufacturing of his product, enabling it once again to meet market and competitive requirements. Without actually drawing up the cost-reduction plans himself, he initiated and coordinated the entire program. No organizational repercussions followed, since everyone recognized that the changes had been essential to regaining a strong market position—and that the product manager knew more than anyone else about what had to be done.

Fourth, product planning should be viewed as a continuous process, not a one-shot effort. Of course, the product manager's planning efforts may peak at certain times—for instance, when he is required to draw up an overall plan for his business. But he will constantly be following up on results, initiating new plans and modifying old ones to make certain that his product's volume and profit goals can be achieved. In effect, he serves as a nerve center for all the activities relating to his product. He keeps in touch with developments inside and outside the company, communicates and defines the need for program changes to all functional departments, and sees to it that everything necessary has been done to ensure his product's success in the marketplace.

Companies that have profited most from product management consistently follow certain ground rules:

1. Start with the proper raw material.
2. Spell out the product manager's planning responsibilities in detail, and communicate them clearly throughout the organization.
3. Structure the product manager's job so that he has time to plan.
4. Provide guidance and direction so that he doesn't have to plan in a vacuum.

These rules appear so elementary it would seem hard to believe that they could ever be overlooked. Yet, simply because management has neglected such fundamentals, surprisingly few product managers succeed in doing the planning job that is expected of them.

The proper raw material

Charting the course his company should follow to ensure his product's continued growth and profitability, the manager must analyze the economics of his product's business, identify the market opportunities, determine what his company must do to capitalize on them, and calculate the likely payoff for success. All of these considerations go into his plan. If it is soundly conceived, his product's business should receive the management commitments required for its success. If not, his chances for management support will be limited.

When the consequences of his planning assignment have been reduced to this equation, it becomes clear that outstanding abilities will be essential in his position. And the companies that benefit from sound planning initiated by their product managers do not settle for less.

In one packaged goods company, in which solid planning by product managers has made a strong contribution to the growth and profitability of several product lines, management scrupulously follows a policy of appointing no one to the position who has not been rated as a potential candidate for a top marketing job. Further, once assigned to a product group, he must prove his right to this rating. If some aspect of his performance turns out to be disappointing, he may be transferred out of the product group and another high-potential man will be brought in. Although such measures have increased turnover in the product group, management remains convinced it is the only way to maintain the level of capability required to meet the company's planning needs.

But this approach can hardly be viewed as typical. Although most executives will agree that it takes good men to plan effectively, far too many companies appoint men without the proper background or capabilities to fill product manager positions. Until management makes sure their product groups have been staffed with well-qualified men, they are bound to be disappointed with the planning job that results.

Well-defined responsibilities

Many well-qualified product managers never really do the job they should because they (or others in the company) do not fully understand what is involved. "Planning" is such a vague term that confusion of this kind almost inevitably ensues unless the scope of the assignment and the expected results have been clearly and carefully defined.

Within the marketing area, these responsibilities are fairly easy to specify: The manager recommends goals and programs for advertising, promotion, distribution development, and so forth, as they relate to his product area. He seldom has trouble obtaining approval of these plans, since the men responsible for executing them will generally be in his own functional area. But, as we have seen, his planning responsibilities extend beyond marketing, and outside its boundaries the possibilities of misunderstanding and conflict become much greater.

Consider the predicament of one company whose product managers' planning assignments were not carefully defined:

Product Manager A became so involved in trying to plan everything that he never left his office. Soon he was out of contact with line managers as well as with the market. Consequently, his plans—though impressively detailed and comprehensive—were simply not responsive to the product's needs.

By pushing his planning too far in areas outside the marketing group, Product Manager B became involved in serious conflict with certain line managers who thought he was trespassing on their areas of responsibility. Their refusal to cooperate made it impossible for him to do an effective planning job.

Precisely to avoid such conflict, Product Manager C confined his planning to the sales forecasting area and spent most of his time expediting orders, fielding customer inquiries, and other sales support activities. In effect, he abdicated the planning role that management had expected him to fill.

Since these three product managers were among the most capable men in the entire organization, management tended to blame the product manager concept itself for the planning fiasco. Actually, of course, these men never had a chance to plan effectively, since neither they nor those with whom they had to work had ever been told what management expected them to do.

The implications of this example are clear. Just as it must be the product manager's primary responsibility to plan, it is management's responsibility to provide him with a well-defined charter and a clear sense of direction to guide his planning. It will be management's responsibility, too, to see that the product manager and the rest of the organization have a clear common understanding of how his planning responsibilities are going to be carried out.

Time to plan

If planning may be defined as the core of the product manager's job, then it should clearly receive top priority. Yet I know many product managers who have been so bogged down with other responsibilities that they can find no time to carry out the planning expected of them. Sometimes their jobs were improperly structured at the start; in other instances the men themselves have settled into bad working patterns. Either way the result is the same.

In one company, inadequate planning had made the entire product management group the target of top-management dissatisfaction. The product managers found they were averaging more than 50 hours a week on the job, but that barely a tenth of this time was devoted to planning.

Obviously, their activities represented more than a full platter. In fact, their jobs had been overloaded with sales administrative activities from the start, and—as management belatedly agreed—something had to give before they could spend more time on planning.

Compare this with the situation of a packaged goods company I know. A major effort had been made to structure the product managers' jobs around their planning responsibilities. This company's product managers are expected to prepare, during the third quarter of each year, a written plan for their product covering the year ahead. Beyond this peak planning period they have various administrative and control responsibilities. But all these activities have been defined in relation to the job of preparing the annual product plan.

For example, the stated purpose of the product managers' field checks has been to "evaluate the results of existing programs for your products and size up the need for new ones." This enables them to strengthen their product plans as well as to avoid slipping into the role of supersalesmen, to the detriment of their planning effectiveness.

Guidance and direction

Unless product plans have been tied both to overall company objectives and to other functional planning, they can stray so far out of line with management's intent—or with the capabilities of other departments—as to be unworkable.

The disappointing experience of a large plastics converter shows what can happen when product planning has been done in a vacuum. The president of this company was convinced that operations could be made more profitable by targeting the marketing effort at the right market segments and gearing all functional activities (sales, product development, and production, for example) to support it. Accordingly, three product managers were added to the sales manager's staff to spearhead the planning job. But no further effort was made to establish overall company planning. The product managers were on their own, with virtually no counseling from top management and no planning system to tie into.

Understandably, their efforts to develop useful plans for their product areas could not help but be futile. In some instances, product plans were never even developed; in others, they emerged in unrealistic form or were completely unrelated to overall company goals. After two years, with the company no closer to operating by plan than it had been at the start, the product management concept was abandoned. It was impossible, the president concluded, to plan in such a complex and volatile business.

Admittedly, any plastics converter operates in a fast moving, highly competitive environment. But the fact that the manager must contend with a host of variables ought to be seen as an argument for good planning, not against it. Proof can be seen in the experience of another company in exactly the same field.

Top management had decided its planning could be substantially improved by appointing product managers, each of whom would be responsible for drawing together all the plans for a given product area. These assignments, it was recognized, would have to be fitted into the company's marketing design; the new product managers would need extensive coaching. Accordingly, the marketing vice president worked closely with the product managers, making sure that the information at his disposal and his knowledge of overall company objectives were made available to the newly appointed planners.

Within this company, in contrast to its competitor, the importance and effectiveness of the planning effort have never been doubted. Nor has the product managers' contribution to the overall planning process been questioned. The difference stems from the simple fact that one company gave its product managers guidance and direction in their planning assignment, while the other did not.

Lessons for management

Several points now become clear. First, the product manager's reason for being is to improve the planning for his assigned product line.

Second, many multiproduct companies have achieved significant improvement in their planning and ultimately in their profit results by employing the product manager concept.

Finally, there appear to be definite common denominators in the planning approaches of successful product managers.

¶ They commit their plans to writing.

¶ They concentrate their fire on a few make-or-break areas instead of scattering their shots across the board.

¶ They learn how to respect all the functional groups and cut across organization lines diplomatically but effectively in order to get the job done.

¶ After the completion of the annual product plan, they gear their efforts to vigorous follow-through, evaluation, and replanning to move their product's business ahead.

In summary, a product manager's ability to carry out his planning assignment depends largely on whether top management creates the proper environment. What this requires above all is attention to fundamentals: starting with the right men, carefully defining their planning responsibilities, structuring their jobs properly, and providing the necessary guidance and direction. Far too many companies neglect or stumble over these requirements, obvious as they may seem. And, in doing so, they have needlessly cut themselves off from the important benefits they might have received from effective product management.

21. Marketing planning for industrial products

B. Charles Ames

Corporate life would be a lot easier if management could forget or wish away the whole idea of formal marketing planning. For no one yet has been able to figure out how to put marketing plans into written form without a great deal of hard work. But, if anything, this process is likely to become a more important management tool in the future as companies continue their scramble to add new products and markets to their base.

Consumer goods companies have relied increasingly on a formal marketing planning approach to coordinate product strategies, and to map the tactics for sales and profit growth. Going through this discipline helps avoid the mistakes that are bound to occur when one tries to ad lib his way to the marketplace with a complex product line.

Not surprisingly, many industrial companies have tried to follow suit. If marketing planning can sell more products to housewives, it ought to sell more tractors, more chemicals, or more electronic components to industrial customers. So reasoning, makers of industrial goods have set up sophisticated planning systems designed to gear their business more closely to the requirements of the marketplace.

Yet many—and perhaps even most—of these companies have found that this approach, which works so well for consumer goods makers, somehow loses its magic in the industrial marketing context. Too often, their top executives have been sadly disappointed in the results of costly and time-consuming planning efforts. The comment of one vice president is typical:

> We knock ourselves out every year with a major time commitment and massive paper flow to put together a plan for the business that's heavily based on marketing input. But we can't really trace any substantive benefits from all the extra effort. As I see it, our marketing group has not done the planning job it should. If it had, we'd have a lot stronger edge in the marketplace. At this point I am not sure whether it is something important that we ought to do better or just a fad that we ought to get rid of.

Why should his reaction be the rule rather than the exception? Why should the concepts that work so well in consumer goods companies be so difficult to apply successfully in the industrial field? Is it really fair to blame marketing when results fall short of expectations? Most important, what lessons can be learned from the experience of those few industrial companies which can point to concrete results from their marketing planning activities?

These are the questions that a McKinsey project team recently set out to answer through a study of the planning practices in 50 industrial companies. The names of these companies cannot be disclosed, but since they are all large multidivision businesses listed in *Fortune's* "500," they may be presumed to have all the necessary skills and sophistication to manage an effective planning job. In carrying out this project, our team worked directly with general managers and marketing executives of each participating company to obtain a comprehensive picture of their marketing plans and procedures.

Practitioners' pitfalls

Ignorance of planning theory or mechanics does not appear to be the cause of the disappointments so many companies are experiencing. Most executives we talked to—in both line and staff positions—were well aware that effective planning (a) depends on market and economic facts, (b) focuses on points of leverage, and (c) results in operating programs, not just budgets. Few seemed at all mystified by formal planning concepts. (These concepts have of course received their share of emphasis in business literature and the academic world over the past few years, and apparently most executives have learned their lessons well.)

Yet major problems crop up when companies set about putting the concepts into practice. Our study findings strongly suggest that the reasons for disappointing results fall into three categories:

¶ Failure to fit the concept to the industrial context
¶ Overemphasis on the system at the expense of content
¶ Nonrecognition of alternative strategies.

FAILURE TO FIT CONCEPT. To a large extent, the industrial companies' lack of success reflects their failure to realize that the concept of marketing planning cannot be borrowed intact from consumer goods companies and applied successfully to their particular situation. Large industrial corporations have two distinguishing characteristics that dictate the need for a different planning approach.

First, each of the many markets and channels in which they operate will require a discrete marketing strategy. A consumer goods company typically markets its several brands through one or two channels, but a multi-product industrial manufacturer will be likely to sell in a wide range of different markets through a variety of channels. For example, one electrical equipment company participating in our study sold one of its major product lines in 30 distinct markets through several different channels. The company had been trying to cover this complex network of markets and channels with a single marketing plan. Actually needed were 30 separate marketing plans.

But an industrial marketing department must do more than juggle a multitude of markets and channels. It must also plan around the constraints imposed by other functions, since marketing simply does not control the forces that make or break performance in the marketplace. In the *industrial* world, marketing success depends largely on the activities of other functions, such as engineering, manufacturing, and technical service. This means, in turn, that changes in marketing strategy are likely to be based on product design, cost, or service innovations. For a *consumer goods* company, advertising, promotion, and merchandising will generally be the key elements of the marketing plan.

Given these circumstances, it seems unrealistic to expect product managers, market managers, or even the head of marketing to handle the job without the full participation of corporate and operating managers at every stage of the process.

The role of the marketing planner in an industrial company will be *significantly* different from that of his counterpart in consumer goods. Rather than developing self-contained marketing plans, he analyzes and interprets market requirements so that top and operating management can decide how best to respond.

Obvious as this point might seem, it has frequently been overlooked by the management of industrial companies. Having embraced formal marketing planning, many executives try to implement the concept by turning the entire job over to marketing. After two or three years of frustration, they are ready to write off marketing planning as a monumental waste of time. Unhappily, the real cause of their disappointment lies not in the concept but in the way it has been applied.

For example, one major chemical company added a group of six industry planning managers to its marketing organization. Once on board, each was given a format to follow and was told to develop a written plan for achieving a stronger and more profitable position in his assigned markets. All six men, eager to earn their spurs, embarked on a massive fact-gathering and writing effort. After several months, hundreds of pages of plans and supporting documentation had been written, but no one in top management was much impressed. The president of the company put it this way:

I'm being generous when I say the end products are only slightly better than useless. Admittedly, we have some better market facts now, but the plans are based on a lot of ideas for product and market development that just aren't in line with my idea of the direction this business should take. On top of that, they've left out a lot of technical and capital considerations that really count. I've concluded that our industry managers are simply too far out of the mainstream of the business to do an intelligent job of planning for us.

Not surprisingly, the industry managers felt that they too had good cause for complaint. As one of them put it:

The first month of effort was worthwhile. We were putting a fact base together that is essential for intelligent planning. But after that we were flying blind. We never had any idea from top management on the kind of business the company wanted or didn't want, the minimal return it expected, or the kind of support it would be willing to throw into various markets. Worse still, we had no cooperation from the development group or the plants, where decisions are made that really control the business. The planning we did was bound to be a bust.

Unfortunately, this kind of situation has occurred in a great many otherwise well-managed companies. Marketing planning has not been built solidly into the management process. Instead it has been carried on as a parallel activity that receives more than enough lip service but little real attention from the decision makers.

OVEREMPHASIS ON SYSTEM. During the past several years, makers of industrial goods have placed more and more emphasis on committing plans to paper for their various product/market businesses. Many have developed comprehensive systems that lay out formats and procedures in great detail. Although some of this formal blueprinting is necessary, we can cite a number of instances in which the system became so detailed and highly structured that it acted as a hindrance rather than a help to the planning process. In effect, the system served as the end product rather than the means to an end.

Of all the problems described to us, this one drew the most vehement reactions from executives. They recognize that sound planning must be put together by hard work and cannot be done without a certain amount of pencil pushing. But they bitterly resent demands for excessive writing that serves no practical business purpose. A product manager for an electronic equipment manufacturer voiced this complaint:

As part of my planning responsibility, I have to follow a format prescribed by the corporate planning group that calls for a point-by-point discussion of history and a laundry list of problems and opportunities. I'm "gigged" if I don't cover every point in the format, and there's no way to do it in less than ten pages of text. That takes a lot of time—mostly wasted time. All the product managers are sore about it. Much of what we have to write is a rehash of the same old things year after year. In effect, we're being discouraged from concentrating on the aspects of the business that are really critical. What they want to see, apparently, is a nice, neat set of plans that all look alike. It just doesn't make sense.

The study team encountered a great number of similar situations and comments. As a rule, someone or some group had designed an over-structured and overdetailed planning system out of phase with the realities of the business. Typically, the resulting paper work chewed up great blocks of precious time without producing anything more than a codification of what would have been done anyway.

NONRECOGNITION OF ALTERNATIVES. In company after company, when we compared the plans developed for a particular product or market over several years, we were surprised to see how few planners showed any breadth of vision in thinking about how the business should be run. Many plans were hardly more than straight-line extrapolations of the events of the past.

This tendency to base current plans on past programs was forced into the open in one company when each planner was asked by top management to outline alternative strategies for developing his assigned market area and to summarize the commitments (e.g., financial, manpower, facilities) required and the payoff expected (sales, profits, ROI). The request drew a complete blank. The planners were so locked into their accustomed way of thinking about their markets that they could not conceive of a different approach that made any commercial sense at all.

Insufficient or less-than-candid analysis is a prime cause of unimaginative planning. Many planners either misjudge or fail to understand the underlying economics of the business or the changes going on in the marketplace (e.g., competitive moves, shifts in usage or demand patterns) that call for alternative strategies. Many planners also appear reluctant to face up to unpleasant truths about their competitive situation—such as high price, low product quality, or poor service—that place the company in an untenable marketing position. Without a thorough, candid appraisal of the business climate, the need for fresh ways of running the business goes unrecognized. Thus, instead of weighing a set of alternatives, top management has to be content with a single recommendation, usually calling for the continuation of stale or imitative strategies.

Imaginative insights

If the true purpose of formal planning is to conceive more imaginative ways of developing the business, the picture presented by these companies could hardly be more dismal. Yet the experience of the participating companies that have successfully applied marketing planning in the industrial context provides some encouragement and some useful insights. Without exception, these organizations have taken the necessary steps to avoid the pitfalls just described. On the positive side, they concentrate on making the development of market-oriented plans an integral part of their basic management processes. Our study indicates that they have reached this level of sophistication primarily through:

¶ Better definition and direction from the top

¶ Development of fact-founded product/market strategies

¶ Superior programming for strategy implementation.

BETTER DEFINITION AND DIRECTION. Marketing planning produces results in the leader companies because it recognizes the multiplicity of products, markets, and channels, and the need for a technical, rather than a sales or merchandising, orientation. As one president in our survey commented:

> It took me three years to realize that our marketing people couldn't come up with the kind of plans I wanted for our products and markets unless I worked closely with them. They have always been able to develop a picture of where our markets are heading, identify opportunities, and interpret what we have to do to build the business. But so many considerations and options require a general management perspective. Marketing can't be expected to come up with recommendations that make sense from my point of view. Unless I set the basic direction for our business, specify who is to plan what, see to it that engineering and manufacturing really work with marketing, and then challenge and contribute any ideas I can on how our business ought to be developed, the whole planning effort is nothing more than a paperwork exercise.

This comment underscores the four ways in which top management must participate in marketing planning to make it pay off.

1. SPECIFY CORPORATE OBJECTIVES: Throughout our study, inadequate direction from the top was a common complaint from planners. "If only top management would tell me what they want!" I am sure we heard a hundred variations on this theme. A few of these men no doubt would like top management to spell everything out for them in detail; they may well be using its failure to do so as an excuse for their own inability to do the planning job.

Even so, top-management guidelines that spell out the rules of the game are unquestionably needed by anyone who holds a marketing planning responsibility. At a minimum, these guidelines should include definite long-range growth objectives or a statement of corporate goals declaring in specific terms how fast top management wants the business to grow, what products and markets should be emphasized, what kinds of businesses should be avoided, and what profit returns will be acceptable. These guidelines need not be expressed with precision, and they are certainly not immutable. But without some definition of this kind, product/market planners will be working in a vacuum—and the marketing plans they come up with will almost inevitably be out of phase with top management's interests and objectives.

2. DETERMINE ORGANIZATION ARRANGEMENTS: Clear-cut organization arrangements are vital for any company but particularly so in a large-scale industrial complex with its numerous product/market businesses. Since marketing planning requirements vary so widely from business to business, no single organization structure can be valid for all companies. Nor will the organization structure that is right for a given company at a given point in its history necessarily be valid for all time.

For example, the marketing organization in a capital goods company had traditionally been structured around products. The product managers were responsible for planning the growth and profits of each major product line. Obliged to sell to three distinct markets, the managers found their responsibilities spread so thin that they could not do a thorough job of planning for any one of them. Also, since each manager's focus remained fixed on his product lines, he failed to perceive the broader needs of the individual markets.

Management soon recognized in the organization arrangement serious obstacles to planning for development of the total market. To provide the needed market orientation, the company restructured its organization around the market managers, who became responsible for identifying all the needs of their assigned markets and planning to meet them.

This is not to suggest that market managers will do a better job of planning than product managers. But the example does demonstrate how important it can be for top management to think through the planning objectives and requirements for each business, and only then to design the appropriate organization structure.

3. PROVIDE INTERFUNCTIONAL COORDINATION: Even the most carefully conceived structure will fail unless the marketing planners (a) work effectively with the other functions that influence the performance of a business in the marketplace and (b) command the respect of their functional counterparts. And all concerned must have a clear understanding of how they will be expected to work together. This is especially important in

industrial companies, for without interfunctional coordination the planners hardly stand a chance.

A manufacturer in the building products field set up a group in its marketing organization to spearhead the marketing planning for each product area. During the first two years of the group's existence, the plans fell far short of everyone's expectations, and there was much friction between the planning group and other functions.

One of the product planning managers put his finger on the problem. He pointed out the many functions other than marketing and sales he had to work with in order to do a good planning job. Much of his difficulty came about, he said, because so few functional managers understood how the marketing planning job was to be carried out. Even the product planning managers themselves, he added, appeared unsure of their responsibilities.

Recognizing the need to put the product planning group on a more sound footing for dealing with other functions, the marketing vice president took three steps. He decided first to replace four sales-oriented product planning managers with men possessing stronger technical backgrounds and a better grasp of the business as a whole. He then eliminated the position of group product planning manager—thus putting the product planning managers on an organizational par with their opposite numbers in other functional areas. Since they had a broader understanding of the business, they were able to communicate more effectively. Even more important, they now reported directly to the head of marketing and, therefore, could keep in close touch with top management's thinking.

Finally, the marketing head persuaded the president of the company to hold a meeting with the executives of all major functions. At this meeting the president explained what the product planning managers were trying to accomplish and how the different departments should work with them. He made it clear that these managers would be expected to develop plans geared to the characteristics and requirements of the marketplace:

> We are going to bank everything on their interpretation of where the market is heading and what we must do internally to respond to market needs. I expect all functions to cooperate with our marketing planners and follow their lead completely. If we don't operate along these lines, all of our talk about being a market-oriented company is just a lot of hot air.

This no-nonsense statement on the role of marketing cleared away the misconceptions previously blocking effective interaction between the product planning managers and other functions.

4. CONTRIBUTE TO MARKETING PLANS: If top management truly wants to find ways of improving profits and encouraging growth, it must actively participate in the development of marketing plans, first, by challenging

their underlying assumptions and, second, by contributing alternative ideas on strategy and programs. To be sure, most top executives try to do this; but the way they do it often stifles rather than encourages new ideas. They should take pains to avoid any atmosphere of an inquisition and, instead, must stimulate open exchange of ideas and opinions.

In such an environment one idea leads to another, and the management team soon finds itself exploring new and imaginative ways of developing the business. An interfunctional give-and-take discussion like this led a heavy machinery manufacturer to adopt a new market strategy that gave its parts operation a chance for survival. Consider:

In this company, as in many others, parts sales had traditionally been a major source of profits. Now management was concerned because "parts pirates" (local parts producers) were cutting sharply into their business. Asked to develop a marketing strategy that would reverse the trend, the parts manager first came up with a plan that called for adding three salesmen and cutting prices on a large number of parts to be more competitive. As he acknowledged, his plan was essentially no more than a holding action.

During the planning review session at which all functions were present, the company president encouraged everyone to take an entrepreneurial look at the parts business and to try to think of ways to preserve or even enlarge it. Predictably, fresh ideas were hard to come by in a business that had been run the same way for years. But eventually three embryonic ideas emerged: (1) build a service organization and sell contracts for maintenance service instead of only parts, (2) decentralize the parts business and set up local parts and repair shops to compete head to head with local "pirates," and (3) start to buy and sell parts for other manufacturers' equipment in order to spread overhead costs.

The parts manager was naturally somewhat reluctant to do any of these things, since they would revolutionize his end of the business. But with top-management backing and encouragement, he carried out the required analytical work and came back with alternative strategies, based on the first two ideas, that offered a much more attractive outlook.

Of course, it would be foolhardy to assume that this process always leads to a more viable product/market strategy. It will not always be possible to overcome the scarcity of fresh ideas in a business which has been run the same way for years. Nor will alternative strategies always be available. But the more successful companies insist that their planners seek out alternative strategies to avoid being locked into a self-defeating "business as usual" pattern of thinking.

This kind of give-and-take among marketing, top management, and other functions is really the heart of the planning process. During these discussions marketing presents the requirements of the marketplace. The other functions then become responsible for working out feasible ways to answer them. With all the opportunities and constraints out in the open, top management can allocate corporate resources more wisely. Once the best combination of ideas has been agreed on, the various functions will be in a position to make commitments on the timing and costs of the alternative actions that underlie the marketing plan.

FACT-FOUNDED STRATEGIES. The marketing planning carried out by leader companies is aimed at the development of strategies realistically tied to market and economic facts. Once developed, these strategies point the way for each business, serve as underpinning for overall corporate long-range planning, and provide direction for programming key activities and projects in all functional areas.

Strategy development is an art few companies have mastered. Those that have this expertise stress the need for studying the economics of the business and the trends of the market. More specifically, this means that planners must become well grounded in the economics of their competitors as well as of their own businesses. It means knowing where value is added, how costs behave with changes in volume, where assets are committed, and so on. To complete their understanding, planners must also become familiar with the way the market is structured and be in a position to determine what forces will be likely to affect the company's market position and outlook.

With this understanding, planners can recognize points of leverage, as well as areas where the company might be vulnerable to competitive thrusts.

One outstanding company built a marketing strategy for its major product line on just this sort of understanding. The planners in this organization which I shall call Company A, recognized that they were operating in a slow-growth business, offering a commodity product for which demand was routinely predictable. They therefore concluded that (a) it would not make sense to sacrifice short-term profits in order to build a larger share position, since the value of a share point would not increase enough to pay off such an investment, and (b) although price was an important consideration in market share, it would not influence total demand.

This market analysis brought a further important trend to light: Company A was losing market position to its strong second-place competitor, Company B. As no other important shifts in market share had occurred, Company A concluded that its marketing strategy should be aimed first and foremost at reversing its losses to Company B.

Next, the planners at Company A compared their own profit structure with that of Company B to pinpoint the weaknesses and strengths of the two companies. Their analysis produced the information shown in the table below. (Admittedly, information of this sort about competitors is not easily obtained. No one will hand it to you, and it will seldom be available in published material. But bits of data on competitor sales and capacity levels can be pieced together from annual reports, newspaper articles, and trade and government publications. By combining such data with one's own experience, conservative assumptions can be made about competitor costs and efficiency to fill out the picture.)

By the time the planners in Company A had completed this comparative analysis, they were in a position to predict what Company B's strategy was likely to be. Assuming that the rival organization knew its own market and economic position, it would:

¶ Cut prices on the products competitive with Company A's highest volume products to upset price stability and to force Company A to retaliate or give up volume.

¶ Add new industrial distributors by giving larger discounts, and go after Company A's distributors in prime markets.

¶ Emphasize development of lower cost products, thereby gaining more flexibility to compete on a price basis.

Comparative analysis of two competitive companies

(Dollar figures in millions)

Economic indicators	Companies		Conclusions
	A	B	
Current dollar sales	$403	$146	A's sales volume is roughly twice B's
Breakeven point	$217	$121	B's breakeven point is lower, but B is operating much closer to breakeven than A
Contribution margin rate (sales dollars less variable costs)	48%	45%	Contribution margin rates are about the same
Contribution loss from 5 percentage point drop in unit margin	$20	$7.3	However, because of differences in dollar volume, Company A stands to lose far more marginal income than B by lowering unit margin
Volume gain to offset 5 percentage drop point in unit margin	$46.5	$18.2	Thus, the volume needed to offset a 5 percentage point drop in unit margin would be much greater for Company A
Equivalent share point gain	7.0 pts.	2.8 pts.	

Starting from these assumptions, Company A planners proceeded to develop a counterstrategy. These were its key points:

¶ Avoid going for volume on a price basis or by adding to unit costs.

¶ Hold a firm price line with distributors—even at the risk of losing share in the most price-sensitive markets.

¶ Build the marketing program around the changes in costs which are nonvariable with volume—e.g., upgrading and enlarging the sales force, strengthening distributor programs, and improving the physical distribution and warehousing network.

A superficial review of the situation would have suggested a quite different strategy. For, in view of the high contribution rate and apparent profit leverage on volume, the most obvious strategy would have been to cut price to counteract any aggressive pricing actions of Company B. Instead, Company A's planners decided to avoid price concessions or any actions that would raise unit costs. They recommended concentrating on marketing programs where costs could be amortized over their much larger unit volume and on other programs that would reduce their cost base. Management agreed, reasoning that this strategy would enable the company to lead from strength rather than play into the hands of its major competitor.

The details of Company A's strategy may be open to dispute. The example does, however, illustrate how a penetrating analysis of market and economic facts can provide a reasoned basis for strategy development. By this process sophisticated planners are gaining three significant advantages. They can:

1. Center management's attention on fact-founded actions that will really count in the marketplace.

2. Adopt an aggressive posture instead of having to rely on retaliation or defensive maneuvers.

3. Minimize the impact of surprise competitive moves by developing alternative contingency plans.

SUPERIOR PROGRAMMING. Everybody goes through the motions of programming, but leader companies follow three ground rules that enable them to do a superior job of strategy implementation.

First, management will approve no major program or project unless it is inextricably linked to a product/market strategy. This approach may sound a trifle stuffy, but it makes good sense, for there can be no other way to evaluate a program's usefulness. Moreover, the linkage keeps the functional areas of a business working together for a common purpose and prevents them from being sidetracked on interesting activities that lack commercial relevance.

Second, management makes some sort of organization provision for follow-through on major programs, particularly those that cut across

248

functional lines. In some instances, companies have enlarged the role of their product managers. In others, they have set up a task force with responsibility for following a program through to completion.

Consider, for example, the industrial controls producer we surveyed. When it became clear that the company's product line had slipped behind those of its competitors, management saw that holding market position would require a complete redesign of the product line, both to improve performance and to take out cost.

Even though the bulk of the actual work had to be done by engineering and manufacturing, the president pulled the responsible product manager out of the marketing department, placed him directly under his wing, and made him fully accountable for coordinating and pushing the program through to completion. As the president told us:

> This program can make or break us in the marketplace. It's so vital to us I'd watch over it myself if I could let some other things slip. Since I can't, I want someone to do it for me, and the product manager is the logical one to do it. I know I'm stretching his role somewhat in giving him this assignment, and I know some noses are going to be out of joint in engineering and manufacturing, but the job is too important not to have a full-time program manager.

This is one way of shepherding a crucial program. There are others; but the objective will always be to ensure interfunctional coordination for all major programs.

Third, leader companies see to it that the detailed steps of major programs are mapped out in such a way that performance can be measured against them. A few industrial goods makers are already applying network scheduling techniques (e.g., PERT, RAMPS) to ensure interfunctional coordination on a wide variety of programs that affect market performance.

In one company, the program for introducing a new line of flow meters was broken down into 25 steps over an 18-month span. The first step was a kick-off meeting between R & D, engineering, manufacturing, and marketing to define performance and cost requirements. Subsequent steps tracked the new product idea through development, manufacture, and market launching. Each week management received a report showing whether scheduled steps had been completed and, if not, where the bottleneck was. This feedback made it much easier to trace problems to their source for corrective action. Said the president: "The program is too important to us to rely for control on typical accounting reports. They simply tell us after the fact whether we won or lost. They're no help when it comes to making sure the program doesn't collapse."

It would be absurd to structure every program in so much detail. But detailed planning has proved essential for effective control over major programs that involve many functions and require tight scheduling—as well as careful adherence—in order to achieve profit and market objectives.

In summary

Formal marketing planning can undoubtedly make a strong contribution to the performance of any industrial company, just as it has in consumer goods companies. But if marketing planning is to have a powerful impact on the industrial side, it will have to be adapted much more closely to the particular requirements of the business. This demands much less emphasis on the system—that is, format, sophisticated techniques, and lengthy writing assignments. Instead, the whole focus must be on achieving substantive improvements in thought and action by means of tough-minded analysis, continual interchange between marketing and technical executives, and more explicit top-management involvement.

22. Shaping distribution channels to your needs

A. L. McDonald, Jr.

It was late Friday afternoon in the office of Lester Wadsworth, an elderly Kansas City farm equipment dealer. Larry Richardson, the new regional manager of Benson Tractor Company, had just broken the news that his company was adding a distributor in the Kansas City area. According to his figures, Wadsworth's sales would not suffer. But Wadsworth, who had enjoyed an exclusive franchise for many years, was not taking the decision with good grace.

"Twenty-seven years I've been selling Benson tractors," he was saying. "It's the better part of your lifetime, Larry. Bart Benson and I have come a long way together. We've done a lot of business, and we've shot a lot of duck up at Bart's place in Michigan. I know Bart pretty well, Larry. He doesn't have any use for a salesman who isn't out to break every record in the book. But basically Bart's a pretty sound, conservative guy. Sure, he's for growth. But somehow the Benson Tractor Company has stuck with Les Wadsworth for 27 years, while the bright young fellows with the big ideas about expanding distribution have come and gone. It's worth thinking over."

Richardson took a week to think it over and then phoned Wadsworth to tell him that the decision stood. Within a month the new distributorship became a reality, and a year later Benson tractor sales in the Kansas City region had risen by 40 percent. Wadsworth's sales had not suffered by the loss, but he was still bitter.

Few sales executives are eager to walk into a disagreeable situation like this. Even on the top-management level, taking action on a distribution problem is apt to be hard, uncomfortable work. For that reason, many companies avoid it until their distribution channels have turned into profit drains.

It would be hard to find a businessman today who is unaware of the vast changes taking place in distribution patterns or who would deny the key importance of distribution to his company's marketing success. But in practice operating executives are strongly tempted to stand pat, often despite recognized soft spots in the distribution structure. Understandably, the executive whose experience and knowledge have been limited to traditional channels is apt to be especially reluctant to take the personal risk involved in disrupting long-standing distributor relationships. For the greater the potential benefits of a change, the greater the penalties of a mistake are likely to be.

Quite apart from this, the very idea of actively *managing* distribution channels is foreign to the great majority of companies. This is understandable enough. Distribution channels are, after all, outside the company and beyond management's direct control. Distribution policies cannot be administered like other management policies; working with and through independent middlemen becomes a job of negotiation rather than supervision. It cannot be done by issuing directives.

In addition, organizational factors tend to perpetuate the status quo. In most companies no one has been responsible, in any real sense, for distribution development. In theory, the top marketing or sales executive bears this responsibility, but in practice it will often be fragmented and neglected. Sales managers straining to meet the current quota are unlikely to make distribution changes that might hurt the current quarter's sales. Marketing executives have more exciting and seemingly more profitable projects to think about—new-product development, advertising budgets, and sales promotion campaigns. Not having time or staff to spare, they will seldom be inclined to invest the necessary effort in improving distribution.

Costly passivity

Naturally enough, then, management comes to regard its distribution structure as a framework within which the company will be obliged to work. "That's the way it is in the trade. We've got to go along," is the answer generally given the outsider who questions some aspect of distribution policy. Yet trade conditions, after all, amount to nothing more than the sum of the activities of a multitude of individual enterprises, whose only common purpose is profit. There can be nothing immutable about "the way it is in the trade." In fact, experience suggests that a company making a disciplined, carefully planned effort to manage its distribution channels can often come very close to writing its own ticket in the marketplace.

For evidence, consider a relatively small maker of TV sets who entered the market along with many others following World War II. Sizing up his distribution prospects, he saw he could not hope to match the breadth and penetration of his major competitors, whose products were sold through a broad base of electrical appliance outlets and service dealerships. So, instead of attempting to cope with "the way things are in the trade," he decided to create his own strategy. He selected a few key retailers in major cities—mostly major department stores—who either controlled or could build high volume in TV sales.

In the electrical appliance industry, marketing strategy has always been built on breadth of distribution. Hence, this decision was unusual. It gave this manufacturer only a tenth as many retail outlets as his major competition. But by selling directly to these stores, he could make his line more profitable for them, thus securing a major sales advantage at the retail level. The success of this strategy has been spectacular. In a period when small manufacturers of TV sets were going out of business left and right, this smaller company outstripped many of its larger competitors in sales and far outdistanced all of them in profitability. Largely because of a single bold distribution decision, its return on investment, after taxes, rose to above 20 percent, compared with an average of roughly 12 percent for the industry at the same time.

Ordinarily, of course, a company with long-established distribution channels and commitments has no such freedom to strike out with a fresh strategy. For such a company, successful major distribution change frequently turns into a complex, time-consuming, and delicate process. But management's determination to shape distribution channels to the company's needs, rather than passively acquiescing in the distribution status quo, has proven to be the secret of more than one outstanding marketing success story.

Recent studies of major consumer and industrial marketing problems by McKinsey & Company suggest that the quickening tempo of market change has been creating an ever-increasing variety of unexploited distribution opportunities. But to take advantage of such opportunities, a company must first recognize them. And it is unlikely to do so without an intensive reexamination of present distribution strategy in relation to the dynamics of its market. Such an analysis may uncover profit opportunities that can be realized by a minor modification in the existing dealer structure —or it may dictate a completely revised marketing program, calling for a fresh approach in the entire sales promotion, advertising, and selling effort.

Because no two companies have identical distribution practices and problems, the pattern of improvement opportunities uncovered by an evaluation of channels will always be unique. Geographical area, class of customer, prevailing trade practices, and company warehouse locations are only a few of the considerations that may affect the right distribution mix. Intimately linked to other aspects of the overall marketing program, distribution strategy often influences or even determines advertising, promotion, pricing policies, product warranties, or sales strategy. Therefore, in this area of marketing, perhaps more than in any other, easy answers can be dangerous.

For all the difficulty of generalizing about distribution problems, we still can distinguish five broad types of opportunity that may be disclosed by a basic evaluation of channels and methods. These are (1) filling in distribution "holes," (2) revitalizing the distribution network, (3) developing a multichannel system, (4) switching strategy, and (5) creating a new channel.

Filling in holes

No distribution network stays intact for long. In the normal course of market change, distributors add new lines, drop others, and sometimes alter their businesses entirely to take advantage of new opportunities. Thus, gaps in coverage develop. Among companies operating in fairly stable markets, whose distributor relationships have settled into comfortable routine, these gaps will be especially likely to go undetected.

Most manufacturers, of course, keep "current" distribution maps on file, showing complete coverage of all their important markets. For three years one such company, a maker of automobile accessories and supplies with a loyal and long-established dealer network of automotive accessories stores, had been suffering a steady loss of market position in this growth business. Its regional manager in upstate New York decided that an informal audit of competitive activities in his area might throw some light on the problem. Accordingly, he had his salesmen survey every retail outlet in his region. The survey showed that the rapid growth of service stations selling competitors' lines had cut deeper into his dealers' market share than he had ever thought possible.

The regional manager took his evidence to headquarters and convinced top management of the need for a nationwide distribution survey. Its findings were conclusive: the company's market share had shriveled because it had seriously underestimated the rapid growth, in several key areas, of service stations selling competitive lines.

Why had no one discovered the situation earlier? The reason was plausible enough: Most of the company's local sales managers valued the good relations they had with their dealers too much to be interested in making changes—so they tended to play down the growing importance of service stations. In consequence, the distribution network so neatly plotted on the map at corporate headquarters was full of holes.

The lesson this particular manufacturer learned the hard way applies to almost any company selling through independent distributors: Over a three- to five-year period, the distribution network will be almost certain to develop serious flaws unless a program exists for keeping it in good repair.

This job belongs primarily to sales management. If salesmen are really interested in building and sustaining distributor relationships, serious gaps will not go undetected for long. But merely writing the responsibility into salesmen's job descriptions will never be enough. To most salesmen, the pressures of meeting the current quota and earning bigger commissions or bonuses seem far more urgent than the tedious assignment of keeping tabs on distributors. Unless this duty becomes a meaningful part of their job performance, it will almost surely be neglected.

Sizing up distributors

Given the right strategy, how can a company effectively keep tabs on the people distributing its products? Here is a sound approach used by one company which periodically reviews the performance of each distributor:

STAGE 1: HEADQUARTERS ASSESSMENT. Management reviews its figures on the sales growth achieved by the distributor. It compares his share of market in the assigned territory against the national average. His growth in market share is compared with the national norm. Finally, the district sales manager is asked to rank distributors as excellent, good, fair, or poor, taking account of attention given to the products, the quality of coverage in the assigned area, and capacity to grow. Putting the headquarters data and the district managers' judgments together, management can quickly identify its better distributors and mark the doubtful ones for further evaluation.

STAGE 2: FIELD EVALUATION. Armed with a detailed headquarters assessment of each "problem" distributor, the person responsible for the field evaluation studies the distributor's operation in order to rank him on ten key criteria:

¶ Adequacy of business experience, as reflected in quality of customer service

¶ Coverage of assigned area and time available to seek added business

¶ Distributor's competence in managing his own business (sales management, financial control, record keeping, warehousing, and inventory control)

¶ Historical trend of volume, as measured against performance requirements established by the company's district sales manager

¶ Share of market in assigned area

¶ Demonstrated willingness to carry a full line of products to service all customer needs

¶ Condition of equipment

¶ Efficiency of warehouse facilities

¶ Financial position (accounts receivable, cash position, outstanding obligations, inventories, fixed assets, and payment record)

¶ Ability to grow in the assigned area.

255

STAGE 3: HEADQUARTERS CLASSIFICATION. Having rated the distributor on each count (10 for excellent, 8 for good, 5 for fair, and 0 for poor), management next calculates his overall score as a basis for positive action. A score of 86 to 100 identifies a prime growth candidate; 76 to 85 calls for a plan to strengthen the distributor's weak areas; 61 to 75 automatically puts the distributor on six months' probation; and 60 or below signals the need for prompt replacement.

The troubles that beset a distribution network will usually be insidious, but once uncovered not difficult to correct. Moreover, the review of performance usually offers management an opportunity to add fresh strength to the distribution network rather than merely plugging the gaps. Attacking this problem, many manufacturers have significantly stepped up the effectiveness of other marketing activities, particularly advertising, by gaining a broader base of market exposure.

Revitalizing the network

Effective management of a distribution network means much more than simply keeping the holes plugged. It demands an awareness of each distributor's economics, based on his discount structure and selling costs. It also requires constant alertness to the relative performance of individual distributors.

Often a manufacturer will be confronted by the problem of getting more effort out of his effective distributors and replacing those who will not do an adequate job. To accomplish this successfully, management must be able to grade the performance and potential of its distributors and concentrate its support programs on those who show the strongest potential for growth. It becomes just as important to face up to the task of replacing the losers, even when their volume has been substantial.

Over a three-year period, the southeastern area sales manager for a large maker of commercial electrical equipment had watched his total sales decline from third to fifth place among the company's six sales regions. He decided to take a hard look at his distribution network. After talking with each of his 30 distributors and analyzing their sales performance over recent years, he sorted them into three categories:

Satisfactory. Twelve distributors whose market shares of his brand stood at or above the national average

Growth candidates. Fifteen distributors short of the national average but capable of reaching it

Replacement situations. Three distributors for whom the national average seemed hopelessly out of reach.

Next, this sales executive set up a vigorous program of sales support for the growth group. Most of them, he found, had not been assigning enough sales manpower to the line because they were satisfied with their present volume and doubted that added efforts would bring them substantial added profits. Poor deployment of salesmen and failure to analyze accounts effectively further weakened their sales effort.

To induce them to build volume, the sales manager assigned five business management specialists to work full time with these 15 distributors for a six-month period. He also arranged to subsidize the cost of six months' base salary for an additional man on each growth distributor's sales force. Finally, he sought out three strong replacements for the low-potential distributors, providing each with a full-time missionary salesman and a direct subsidy for the first year. To avoid retaliation for loss of the franchise from the replaced distributors, he negotiated payments to compensate them for most of the profit each stood to lose during the next year.

The program was difficult and time-consuming, but ultimately it paid off. Sales dropped at first, largely because of the three replacements. Six months later the lost ground had been regained. In a little more than two years the sales total had climbed by almost 35 percent, bringing the area from fifth to second place in the nation.

The program was a radical departure for this company, which had never before replaced a distributor. But its success so impressed top management that the organization has embarked on a national program to increase its market share by upgrading and strengthening distribution.

Improving the performance of distributors can be approached in many ways. All tie in directly to the other aspects of a complete corporate marketing plan, frequently depending on other parts of the program for their success. Sometimes, for example, financial aid—in the form of inventory, equipment, or accounts receivable financing—will provide the means for the smaller distributor to expand his volume. Sometimes a new cooperative advertising plan will tip the scales to gain better distribution support. And in certain instances, specialized sales support to assist in dealing with big customers will greatly strengthen a distributor's performance.

The natural instability of distribution networks has been more than matched by changes in the marketing environment. The so-called distribution revolution of recent years and shifts in consumer buying habits have immensely complicated the distribution patterns of many manufacturers. To take a simple example, screwdrivers used to be sold through hardware wholesalers to retail hardware stores and a few other retailers. Today they can be bought in discount houses, department stores, variety stores, automotive accessory stores, and even in some drug marts and supermarkets. Examples like these have become so familiar that many manufacturers regard them as history, forgetting that similar changes—less spectacular but no less pervasive—may be taking place in their own businesses today.

Developing a multichannel system

Manufacturers who have traditionally relied on general-line distributors often appear especially slow to read the message of market change. The decision to supplement a network of general distributors with other channels—for example, brokers and direct sales in the food business—will admittedly complicate the life of marketing management. But, as the examples of General Foods and Campbell's Soup show, this decision can be profitable. Both companies have begun to use independent food brokers to supplement the activities of their large company-operated sales forces on certain product lines.

Failure to recognize that established distribution channels may no longer be able to serve the changing market often proves costly. For many years a small manufacturer of hypodermic syringes and needles had been selling through hospital supply houses and drug wholesalers. A steady decline in market share finally made management realize that its important hospital business had been undermined by competing lines that were being sold direct.

Instead of reacting to the implications of this situation, the company merely brought more pressure on its supply houses to step up their sales efforts to these giant customers. Predictably, these efforts had little success. With their great purchasing power, the large-volume customers were able to extract price concessions that left the supply houses no room for an operating profit. The syringe maker's market share of hospital sales continued to shrink. At the same time, the company became aware that its sales to physicians in private practice were lagging behind the growth in the physician population.

With sales being squeezed from both sides, this manufacturer finally decided to take a long-overdue look at its entire distribution setup. The ensuing study led to the design of a five-channel distribution system. A selected group of hospital supply houses were retained to handle sales to smaller hospitals and nursing homes. But, in addition, the company hired several technically qualified representatives to handle direct sales to large hospitals. (Management overcame old-line distributors' objections by pointing out that more widespread professional acceptance of the brand would also benefit their sales.) To strengthen sales among private physicians, the company negotiated franchise arrangements with physician supply houses in certain key areas. Further, it was decided to begin selling direct to key drug chains and independents, while continuing to serve smaller retail outlets through drug wholesalers. To accommodate its five categories of distributors, the company updated its price structure.

Ultimately, this manufacturer surpassed his original market share. But

258

top management estimates the cost of this distribution lesson at nearly $200,000 in lost profits. And the company acknowledges that its market share would be much smaller today had it not acted to strengthen the distribution network.

Often the task of designing a multichannel distribution system will be thrust upon a manufacturer when he brings out a new product that cannot be profitably marketed through traditional channels. Adding a new distribution channel frequently affects relationships with the old distributors and may even call for a redesign of the entire marketing program.

Again, overnight a company may find itself with a multichannel distribution system on its hands following an acquisition. When the acquired company manufactures a product closely related in some way to that of the acquirer, management must be sure to look twice before concluding that its own distribution setup can handle the new line. If the patterns of retail coverage for the two lines differ significantly, or if the move would divert selling effort from the company's established products, ways may have to be found to mold the two networks into a workable multichannel system. But whatever the reason for redesign, the need to base it on a clear and realistic understanding of the distributors' profit economics can hardly be overemphasized.

Switching distribution strategy

Management seldom realizes the need for a basic shift in distribution strategy until it faces an acute marketing problem—shrinking market share, declining profitability, or unexplained failure to attain realistic growth objectives. Such a shift can take many forms—e.g., replacing brokers with direct salesmen, eliminating distributors and selling direct to key retailers, or replacing direct salesmen with distributors in markets that cannot economically support direct sales coverage. In any event, a shift in strategy will most often be stimulated by changes in retail patterns.

A well-known manufacturer of household products had brought out an improved version of its main product line in the early 1950s. It won a strong position in hardware stores, then the established channel for products of its type. For a time, the company's sales curve rose steadily. Then a new change occurred: food stores taking on houseware items began to cut deep into the hardware store sales. Like its competitors, this company saw what was happening. Unlike them, it feared that adding food brokers to its distribution network would alienate its hardware distributors. Management's reluctance to change cost the company dearly. Within ten years, 75 percent of all sales for its type of product had moved into food stores where its retail coverage depended on spotty missionary selling by hardware distributors. Moreover, hardware retailers made no effective efforts to give the company's line special support. As a result, its market share had dwindled alarmingly.

The solution to this manufacturer's problem was simple enough, at least in principle: sell to the food chains through food brokers. Once the details had been worked out, management did not have to wait long for the effect on sales. Today this company is selling more through both food stores and hardware outlets. It has more than regained its earlier market share. But the company will never regain the profits lost by delaying the decision to reshape distribution policy until its survival was at stake.

A classic example of a planned shift in distribution channels is furnished by a well-known maker of pharmaceuticals that brought out an important new dietary product a few years ago. At the start, the product was introduced through its traditional drug channels. Then, after the product's image had been established in the consumer's mind and the market build-up was well under way, management shifted the bigger share of the distribution to food stores in time to meet competitive imitations and answer popular demand. Largely because of this carefully timed shift, the product's success was tremendous. And the company has since succeeded in maintaining the two channels—drug wholesalers and food brokers—side by side with very little friction.

Creating a new channel

The creation of a new distribution channel is apt to be the result rather then the cause of a major new marketing strategy. It reflects management's decision to meet a market demand, present or potential, that cannot be economically satisfied through existing channels. Often this becomes a formidable task. And because distributor relationships take time to build, the profit payoff may be slow in coming.

A necessary first step for management, before a new channel has even been designed, is to analyze the entire sequence of selling operations. The aim here will be to determine the most economic division of sales functions between manufacturer and middleman. This means analyzing the economics of the proposed distributors' operations, for a new channel cannot possibly be effective and developed into a marketing force unless profit incentives have been provided at every stage of the selling operation.

Some years ago, a large food manufacturer saw the opportunity to build a new business by marketing a key product to institutions—hotels, restaurants, cafeteria chains, and the like. Management knew that the food brokers who handled the company's sales to supermarkets and grocery chains were not equipped to sell to institutions. In fact, no ready-made distribution channel existed to suit the company's needs. Another answer had to be found: the company set about creating a network of wagon delivery distributorships, each designed to service from scores to hundreds of local eating places.

Through want ads and other recruiting methods, management screened nearly a thousand candidates and came up with some two hundred individuals with suitable backgrounds and capital to invest in an exclusive franchise. The company provided ample assistance in financing trucks and setting up the franchisees' books. It held training seminars for the new distributors. Its salesmen spent a great deal of time helping them get under way.

Three years later, sales of the product to institutions had almost tripled. At this point, the sales growth leveled off. Investigation showed that a number of wagon distributors, having achieved their personal income goals, had lost interest in further growth. Others had taken on different lines and were devoting less effort to this manufacturer's product. Still others were losing ground because they had not kept pace with the increased sophistication of the food service managers in the institutions they served. In short, the supervision exercised by the sales force at the start had faded to the point of ineffectiveness.

Obviously, the remedy was to recognize that the salesman's key functions had now become the training, motivation, and guidance of the distributors. To this end, the company began reorienting its sales force, setting new selection standards, and adjusting sales objectives to meet the new requirements. Within a year, its institutional sales were again climbing at an acceptable rate.

The first steps

Before a company can begin to estimate what it might gain by a thorough overhaul of distribution channels, it must assemble and evaluate information going beyond distribution and extending into areas so basic that the answers may have long been taken for granted. Because objectivity and sound critical judgment are needed to explore these questions, responsibility for the project should be assigned to someone who combines the best marketing judgment with the least personal stake in the distribution status quo. Facts—not the opinions of headquarters executives—must be the only basis for a sound evaluation. And facts, however difficult to face, should not be obscured by defensive explanations.

Such an examination of distribution channels ought to provide a firm factual base for a recommended improvement program. As in most marketing situations, there are likely to be alternative routes to improvement, and management should insist on a reasonable choice among them.

Before selecting an alternative, management should carefully price each one according to (1) cost of implementing the recommended change, (2) cost of providing sales and marketing support to the new distribution network, as against that of the old, and (3) sales and profit results that can realistically be expected. It should also discuss the feasibility of these alternatives with the distributors concerned, both present and prospective.

Having made the decision, management should not look for immediate results to justify it. It may be months before the corporate sales curve shows a positive response. Almost invariably, a thorough evaluation of distribution channels requires a substantial investment of top-management confidence. Soundly conceived and executed, however, such an investment is likely to pay off handsomely in long-term marketing effectiveness.

23. Physical distribution: forgotten profit frontier

Robert P. Neuschel

If the half dozen major functions vital to the operation of any industrial business were to be ranked in order of the time and attention they receive from top management, it is safe to say that physical distribution would come somewhere near the bottom of the list.

Yet, if the same functions were ranked in terms of their dollar costs, in a good percentage of industrial companies physical distribution would come out near the top. In primary metals, chemicals, and petroleum, for example, these costs come to about 25 percent of the sales dollar; in the food manufacturing industry, they reach 30 percent or more.

This paradox points the way to an untapped (or only partially tapped) profit-improvement opportunity of major dimensions in many companies. And it becomes all the more striking in view of the energies these same companies have so willingly expended on shaving costs of production, selling, and administration—often for a fraction of the profit improvement that might be realized from comparable efforts in the physical distribution area.

To be sure, some evidence of progress can be seen in the decline of distribution costs as a percentage of gross national product over the past decade—due at least in part to the better tools provided by computers and computer-related disciplines. Yet, because so few managements have learned to make the most of such new tools, this progress has been slow and sporadic. With the aid of operations research techniques and new high-capacity computers, a few companies have been able to achieve something close to the optimum-cost distribution system. But others have flailed away for years at the same problem with little success, and many more have succeeded in automating only segments of a system.

Computers aside, physical distribution rarely has been managed with the same effectiveness and efficiency as, say, manufacturing and marketing. Lying as it does in a no-man's-land between these two functions, physical distribution performance is difficult to measure and control. It will be especially vulnerable to the impact of many kinds of marketing decisions:

small changes in customer service policy may greatly increase distribution costs; selling incentives that result in sales peaking may lead to costly excessive staffing in distribution; and decisions to increase sales dollar volume may require uneconomic levels of inventory and service, again driving up distribution costs. In recent years, as hotter competition has stepped up demands for distribution service, longer product lines have complicated distribution cost and control problems.

Survey findings

In the face of these developments, what have the best managed companies been doing to exercise more effective control over this function and reduce its cost? To find out, McKinsey & Company studied the management and the economics of distribution in 26 large and profitable companies. These organizations represent a wide range of industries, including food processing, chemicals, petroleum, building materials, and metal fabricating. Each company was ranked *good*, *average*, or *poor* in four basic elements of physical distribution management: (1) generation and use of meaningful and timely control information, (2) aggressiveness and overall competence of distribution personnel, (3) concern with distribution economics displayed by top management, and (4) capacity to deal with the overall distribution problem.

The results of this study reveal a surprisingly wide-ranging quality of management performance. They also point up the high degree of interdependence among the rating factors. Of the 26 companies studied, 16 emerged with identical marks on all four rating factors: five were ranked *good* on all four counts, six *average*, and five *poor*. Among the remaining 10 companies, moreover, those doing well in one area tended to do well in others; those doing poorly in one tended to rank low on one or more of the other counts. No company with a *good* rating in one area of physical distribution earned less than an *average* score on any other. A symmetrically contrasting pattern occurs among the poor performers. Most significant, only one company that failed to rank *good* on the first count—control information—scored higher than *average* in *any* of the other three areas.

The five companies qualifying as *good* on all four of the rating factors were also, significantly, among the best in return-on-investment performance. Among the 26, in return on investment two ranked first and second, two more were in the top quartile, and one fell in the upper half. While these companies' high return on investment cannot be attributed entirely to their solid performance in distribution, this must have been a contributing factor. A top executive heading one of these five companies—his ranked second in return on investment—emphasized that the excellence of its distribution system had played a key part in his organization's competitive success.

The common denominators to be found in the practices of the higher ranking companies in the sample suggest some useful guidelines for other managements.

Control information

Is cost information complete? How accurate and timely are the company's basic cost figures relating to the principal segments of its distribution operations? Does management use the data to control costs, measure results, and improve policies in such areas as inventory planning, plant sourcing, transportation methods, production planning?

Executives in seven of the surveyed companies admit to a concern that top management may well be inadequately informed on distribution costs, either by segment or in the aggregate. As a result, these executives feel frustrated in their own efforts to pinpoint the areas of operation in which significant savings can be realized. More typically, sheer unawareness of costs will be responsible for high distribution expenses. One major food processor with sales above the $1.5 billion mark offers an extreme example.

In this company, as in the industry generally, distribution represented a large part of the cost of doing business. Yet management had only fragmentary information on its costs. When asked about the company's total dollar outlay for transportation, key executives could only give off-the-cuff estimates ranging from $65 million to $120 million. Deeper probing revealed that effective control over this high-cost operation really stopped at the level of the traffic department, which simply secured the best rate and route for each shipment—a graphic illustration of the piecemeal attack on distribution not uncommon even among profitable companies.

By contrast, a few companies in the sample show considerable sophistication in generating distribution information. For example:

A building materials company with sales over $300 million has been doing a particularly thorough and competent job of breaking down its distribution costs in terms of major product categories—i.e., modes of transportation (rail, common carrier trucks, and company-owned fleets), warehouse operating expenses, and general administrative costs. To help top management measure effectiveness from period to period, a quarterly report comparing current costs to the previous year's figures is prepared for the president. This enables him to take timely action whenever costs in any segment show signs of getting out of line. In the past five years, largely because the up-to-date cost data have been available, management has been able to reduce its distribution costs as a percentage of sales by more than one-sixth.

Almost without exception, the companies that appear to be most successful in controlling costs do identify and regularly report the penalty costs incurred. As a rule, the better performers also keep a close eye on penalty costs of not shipping by the cheapest mode of transportation.

¶ Whenever such a premium is incurred, one container manufacturer requires its transportation department to indicate on an internal copy of the bill of lading which department has requested the shipment and why. Regular reports of this type have helped management to reduce its total shipping costs by a significant percentage.

¶ Again, a large chemicals manufacturer has established, and recorded in its computer system, lowest cost standards for shipments to thousands of different destinations. Costs of each shipment are compared to these standards, both for operational purposes and for after-the-fact review by management.

Even among the companies rated *good*, there has been considerable variation in the type and amount of distribution data collected. Predictably, the companies generating the most meaningful and timely data do the best job of controlling and reducing costs. Such information will be useful to them in at least four ways: (1) it brings cost problems into sharp focus, stimulating top management to come to grips with them, (2) it pinpoints the areas where cost action can most profitably be taken, (3) it provides a gauge of progress, and (4) by enabling management to keep tabs on the quality of service, it puts isolated customer complaints in proper perspective and ensures against the precipitous and unnecessary corrective actions to which so many companies are prone.

Personnel competence

Important to successful distribution are the imagination and skill that can be brought to bear on cutting costs and improving service—for example, in negotiating rates with carriers, instituting a guaranteed delivery program, or pressuring carriers to provide maximum service.

Quite apart from top-management policy decisions, transportation and other operating personnel have achieved significant savings on their own initiative in several of the surveyed companies. Aggressive and alert transportation personnel can help to educate other executives in the need for a "total look" at distribution. The best performers cite four sources of operational cost reduction as the most fruitful: negotiating with carriers, selecting economical transport methods, making the best possible use of equipment, and using proprietary trucking.

NEGOTIATING WITH CARRIERS. By aggressively negotiating lower rates and obtaining better service from its freight carriers and public warehouses throughout the country, one company has reduced its distribution costs by

$2.5 million over the past five years. Surprisingly, it has accomplished this in the face of a sizable sales increase.

Few companies in the sample have actively and effectively sought rate reductions. Many, judging by the statements of their executives, have tended to accept freight and warehouse charges as being in the nature of fixed costs. Yet, in fact, they are not fixed. Sharp negotiation over both local and long-distance rates can achieve substantial cost advantages. For example:

A company in the building materials industry, whose freight business is worth some $20 million a year to outside carriers, has its transportation people continually whittle away at this transportation bill in a variety of ways—such as negotiating lower rail freight rates for higher-weight loaded cars, using barge or water rates to secure a lower rate for certain routes, and obtaining large, special equipment to lower unit costs.

Although for-hire truckers have rapidly become more sophisticated in their costing, many contract carriers still have only approximate knowledge of their own costs. Hence the alert user may often be able to point out how specific routes can be covered at a lower rate. Consider:

One of the sharpest negotiators in this area is a company that makes use of several different approaches—pitting one form of transportation against another, suggesting that it will substitute its own trucks for outside carriers, and using its knowledge of trucking operating costs to pressure carriers for rate adjustments. In this fashion, the company has been able to reduce its dollar cost of distribution by 6 percent over the past several years, despite a 16 percent increase in sales volume.

SELECTING TRANSPORT METHODS. Due to the complexity of published tariffs, an element of mystery has always hung over this function of the traffic department. The experience of better performers in the survey sample demonstrates that behind the veil of mystery lies a worthwhile savings potential. To illustrate:

Growing alarm over the sheer size of its transportation bill has led one company with annual sales in excess of $500 million to analyze its bills of lading for a three-month period to (a) gather data on the mode of transportation for each shipment, (b) obtain the cost premium (if any) over the cheapest method of shipment, and (c) find the reason (when available) for selecting a higher cost method, as occasioned by a change in schedule or an order requiring faster shipment. By projecting its findings, management estimates that total shipping costs can be reduced 10 percent merely through more effective control over the mode of transport used.

There will, of course, be times when—for service or other reasons—the lowest cost form of transportation is not the best, and when higher cost transportation may contribute to lowering total distribution costs. But the evidence of the survey underlines the point that where selection of a transportation method receives only nominal control, costs become unnecessarily high.

MAKING THE BEST POSSIBLE USE OF EQUIPMENT. A third area where companies with a better record of performance have found significant savings is the selection, sizing, and utilization of equipment. For example:

¶ One company has persuaded its carrier to provide 40- and 48-foot trailers for all its over-the-road shipments, thus adding over 20 percent more load capacity.

¶ Another firm, which for several years had shipped on a 20,000 pound truck rate, discovered that a large percentage of its recent shipments were moving with a load of 28,000 pounds or more. Armed with this information, the company has been able to negotiate a truck rate for 30,000 pounds, securing a rate saving of 8 percent whenever it ships to the heavier weight.

Three common-sense guidelines for gaining cost advantages in selection and use of equipment emerge from the experience of the surveyed companies: (1) establish rate structures based on varying weight of loading—and always ship at the maximum practical weight rate, (2) minimize less-than-carload or less-than-truckload shipments, and (3) whether shipping by common carrier, contract carrier, or company-operated trucks, make sure the equipment will be of the size and type that provides the best service at the most economical rate.

USING PROPRIETARY TRUCKING. Over 70 percent of the companies in the sample operate their own truck fleets (owned or leased). Some do so to give their customers better service, but most are motivated by cost considerations. Proprietary trucking can help to reduce operating costs, as may be seen in these two illustrations:

¶ A manufacturer of canned goods employs a fleet of leased trucks to distribute his products throughout the Midwest. Recently, by comparing his 1968 costs with the published tariffs of for-hire transportation, the manufacturer discovered that he was getting the same service for 20 percent less.

¶ Another company in the container business ships most of its products by common and outside carriers, but also operates a small over-the-road fleet of its own on which it maintains excellent cost records. Armed with these cost data, the transportation people have succeeded in paring down the rates paid to their outside carriers to the tune of 15 percent to 20 percent savings on the company's overall trucking costs.

Distribution economics

Because the economics of distribution are significantly affected by policies and decisions made in other areas of the business, management's alertness to these relationships will play a decisive role in the cost and effectiveness of distribution.

This has been underlined again and again by the experience of the companies in the sample. Several executives cited small changes in customer service policies, such as faster delivery, that substantially increased the cost of transportation. In one firm, the design of a new salesman's compensation plan caused a monthly peaking of sales which added sharply to shipping problems and costs. In a consumer goods company, many products must be included in a single shipment. Often poor manufacturing planning and scheduling has wrought havoc with distribution costs and service.

Unfortunately, management all too often lays the sole blame for mounting distribution costs at the door of the traffic department. For example:

The president of an Ohio-based, $350 million business, on finding that his company's distribution bill had reached a new high of $35.8 million, or $8 million more than the company's profit, called his director of traffic severely to task. A little historical analysis showed, however, that the sharpest increase in total distribution costs had followed a series of top-management policy decisions in which the traffic man had had no part. During the previous four years, management had authorized product line additions that nearly doubled the number of items. And only six months before calling the traffic manager to task, the president had announced that all orders to Mountain States customers would be serviced within 48 hours of receipt—a decision that necessitated shifting, at substantial added expense, from rail to truck.

The experience of the survey sample indicates that three basic policy and strategy issues—quality and kind of customer service, selection of customers, and size and location of plants and warehouses—have the greatest impact on distribution costs and service. Recognizing the complex interrelationships of these and related factors will clearly be a critical step in any organized approach to improving the cost/effectiveness of distribution. Lacking such a perspective, management can hardly hope to make the right cost-versus-advantage trade-offs to arrive at the best solutions.

KINDS OF SERVICE. Few of the companies in the sample take a really tough-minded approach to determining customer service needs and their cost implications. Only four companies of the 26 systematically analyze the economics of providing different levels or types of service. The majority simply try to give the best and fastest service possible, without much consideration of trade-offs. Here are two representative examples:

¶ Pressured by field sales personnel, who were convinced they could substantially increase sales in the Midwest by offering faster deliveries, an East Coast company decided to cut its order-filling cycle in a large Midwestern market to 48 hours. To do so, it had to set up a warehouse in Cleveland and maintain substantial inventories there. The sales increase proved disappointing, and the added income barely covered the added expenses—which had not been thoroughly costed out to begin with.

¶ Again, a medium-sized food manufacturer—none of whose many plants make all its products—considered setting up a number of product distribution centers, each warehousing the full line. The company's object was to "mix-ship"—that is, to include a full range of items on a single truck or railcar—as do many other companies in the grocery trade. Before making the decision, management analyzed the economics of several alternative ways to mix-ship. This meant examining each important cost element involved: transportation, warehousing, materials handling, and possible revenue reductions resulting from loss of the premium price which had been charged to customers for small-quantity shipments.

Having pinpointed the probable cost of setting up the proposed redistribution warehouses, management could make a hard-headed assessment of the extra service's competitive values. The examination of alternatives clearly indicated the most economic pattern of warehouse locations should the company decide to go ahead—as it ultimately did.

CUSTOMER SELECTION. The practices employed by the surveyed companies in this area tend to bear out the opinion of an executive who remarked: "I'm afraid there's no customer selection worthy of the name in our company. Management has just plain abdicated the responsibility." The reason, it seems, comes down to nothing more mysterious than an obsession with volume, rationalized by the assumption that higher sales mean higher profits. Consider these examples:

¶ One company, with volume growing but profits sliding off, decided to take a close look at its customer selection practices. Analysis disclosed that it was not covering costs on some 27 percent of its customers, representing some $31 million worth of the company's $300 million business. Reason for the loss? Nothing but the high cost of servicing and shipping small orders.

¶ In another company the president commented that he was becoming increasingly concerned over customer selection policies because of growing competition and pressure on profit margins. "Traditionally," he said, "we've made these decisions on the basis of marketing considerations alone. Now I'm trying to get my people to consider *all* the important costs. And that emphatically includes physical distribution."

¶ A food processing company makes store-door deliveries to grocers and various other retail outlets. Delivery operations constitute one of the few opportunities for improving the organization's cost economics, yet its salesmen—paid a straight commission based on dollar volume—have been going after distant customers regardless of the size of the order. Lacking control over customer selection, this company has paid a heavy cost penalty trucking small orders to out-of-the-way customers.

Adequate consideration of the customer's distance from the supplying plant, his volume requirements, his ordering practices, and the amount of inventory required to service him are basic to economic customer selection. Yet interviews with executives of the surveyed companies only occasionally disclosed any substantive management attention to the profit impact of such considerations.

LOCATION OF FACILITIES. In the surveyed companies as a whole, the cost of transportation typically constitutes nearly one-half (44 percent) of the cost of physical distribution, followed by warehousing and handling (20 percent), inventory carrying cost (18 per cent), shipping room (11 percent), and administrative costs (7 percent).

In the calculation of transportation costs, distance will be the largest single determinant. So plant and warehouse location decisions heavily influence the ultimate cost of distributing the product. Several companies in the survey, burdened with marginally located plants, have begun to find that the cost of transporting into some major markets eats away at their margins and diminishes their ability to price competitively. For other companies, the product mix turned out by individual plants has been so limited that excessive rehandling and warehousing of items at common points is required to fill a complete customer order on a single shipment. These two stories illustrate the importance of strategic plant and warehouse location:

¶ For one $400 million company in a process industry, distribution costs average 20 percent and net income 8 percent of sales. Top management has been assessing the long-term economics of dispersing production in its five present plants to ten or more smaller plants, strategically located near important markets. Until recently, the technology of this industry favored massive plants. Little concern was given to the high cost of shipping the product to distant markets. Yet centralized production is no longer a technological necessity, and raw materials for the product have become available everywhere. Estimates indicate, accordingly, that the proposed change will result in eventual savings on the order of $5 million annually, or a 16 percent addition to the company's after-tax profits.

¶ A medium-sized company, manufacturing and distributing canned food products, had 128 warehouse facilities, mostly consisting of leased space in public warehouses. Management knew it was much more costly to maintain such a warehouse configuration than to ship directly from the plants. Even so, it was felt that the better service justified the additional expense. Unfortunately, all the extra costs, such as the added inventory investment—no inconsiderable sum when inventories at all 128 locations, individually modest, were taken together—had not been calculated. Nor had the significant added costs of transferring between warehouses when slow-moving stocks created inventory imbalances. Hidden even deeper were the costs of trying to maintain control over widely scattered inventories.

Since locating a plant or warehouse determines an important part of the ultimate cost of distribution, the need to factor transportation costs into the facilities decision can hardly be overstressed. Often, to be sure, uneconomic location decisions can subsequently be corrected. But the cost will generally be high.

The overall problem

How effectively is management balancing distribution cost and service in order to deliver the product to the customer at the greatest advantage to the company? The 26 surveyed companies vary enormously in their ability to grasp and cope with the myriad decisions and conditions involved in this problem.

Their efforts fall into three distinct approaches:

1. The narrowest of these may appropriately be labeled the *traffic department* concept. Here, the principal role of distribution is to secure the most advantageous rates and routes, usually with a strong bias toward a single mode of transportation.

2. Less narrow is the *transportation* concept, which concentrates on minimizing transportation and warehousing costs. Companies governed by this distribution philosophy often show considerable skill and imagination in ferreting out the lowest cost ways to transport their products.

3. The most sophisticated of the three approaches may be termed the *total logistics* concept. This technique thoughtfully balances the economics of transportation against other key factors such as customer service, manufacturing, and warehousing. Companies committed to the logistics approach are able to get markedly more from their distribution dollars than the others in the sample.

TRAFFIC DEPARTMENT CONCEPT. About a third of the companies under study traditionally confine themselves to a single means of transportation. Their competence, accordingly, has largely been limited to selecting routes and identifying the appropriate rate. Performance is measured in terms of cost per ton mile, freight bill audits, and periodic reports on rate reductions obtained by the traffic department. Thus:

A large container company, with a corporate traffic department dominated by personnel with long railroad experience, did a superior job of negotiating rail rates. But no one gave much thought to identifying and costing out other transportation alternatives, much less to analyzing the economics of redistribution points or achieving the best possible product mix at each manufacturing location. At the time of the survey, top management had become aware of some of these missed opportunities, and was beginning to move out of its traditional narrow mold toward more aggressive handling of its distribution function. This corrective action was

272

taken by assigning to each product operating division direct responsibility for the most effective distribution of its product line.

TRANSPORTATION CONCEPT. About half of the organizations examined have some competence in working with more than one mode of transport and are accustomed to comparing and selecting transportation alternatives. Most of these companies keep an accurate record of shipping and warehousing costs, and take an aggressive approach to rate negotiations. Further, their personnel are highly skilled in the "tricks" of transport operations. For example:

One company, with sales in the $300 million bracket, has been particularly successful in working with truckers and railroads to shave costs by securing equipment tailored to its operations and by negotiating lower volume rates. This company uses its own truck fleet not only to handle certain shipments more economically, but also as a lever in rate negotiations. Yet for all its aggressiveness in the transportation area, many of the company's marketing and service policies go unchallenged by top management. No one is really concerned with analyzing the functional interfaces or making imaginative cost-versus-value appraisals.

TOTAL LOGISTICS CONCEPT. Of the 26 companies studied, five stand head and shoulders above the rest by virtue of both their sophistication and their success in managing the distribution function. The common feature of their approach—consistent regard for the total economics of shipping products to the customer—has been manifested in three principal ways.

First, the executives heading up major functions in each of these five companies have clearly been both willing and able to deal with distribution activities from a corporate rather than a functional viewpoint—even when it means giving up service or product features, or incurring extra costs, for the sake of greater benefits elsewhere in the company.

Second, each of these companies boasts a nucleus of transportation personnel free from the parochialism found in many of the traffic departments studied. To be sure, these people are highly skilled in the techniques of their trade—that is, within the limits of their own operations they know how to cut costs from transportation, warehousing, and related activities. But they also show a keen awareness of the impacts their activities can have on marketing and manufacturing costs, and on operations—and vice versa.

Third, these companies stress adequate and timely cost information. With the help of such data, they have been able to identify and price out alternatives as a basis for making trade-offs (e.g., an increase in transportation cost for an improvement in competitive service or a reduction in warehousing expense). They have also been doing a superior job of planning product distribution in individual markets, establishing effective cost control over these operations, and measuring overall distribution cost

273

effectiveness. Thanks in part to superior cost data, one multiplant company with national distribution has developed a complex linear programming model to (a) balance manufacturing, warehousing and shipping costs, plant capacity, service, and other factors; (b) allocate orders automatically to the right plant; and (c) prepare monthly production schedules.

Useful lessons

What can other managements learn from the experience of these 26 companies? In brief, four principal guidelines emerge.

1. KNOW YOUR COSTS. Little progress will be possible without accurate information on the cost of each important segment of the distribution system. With such information management can see problems in perspective, set the right priorities, identify potential savings, and take appropriate action to upgrade performance.

2. RECOGNIZE AND UNDERSTAND YOUR DISTRIBUTION PROFIT ECONOMICS. Just as basic cost information must be important, so will sophisticated use of this data be significant in managing transportation and supply. Not only top management, but functional executives as well, need to know their profit economics of distribution and the multiple impacts of alternative distribution configurations and strategies.

Unless top management understands how a decision made in one area will affect overall cost and performance, it cannot sensibly trade off one cost against another to obtain a lower-cost, competitive total system.

3. APPLY THE RIGHT TECHNIQUES. Excellence in handling distribution will demand techniques expressly selected and designed to fit the system requiring control. Many of the companies observed were preoccupied with techniques and computers, but lacked a clear understanding of the distribution task and its profit economics. In contrast, the leaders in distribution performance *combined* enthusiasm for new techniques with a thorough knowledge of their own distribution systems; they realized that a technique would be useful to them only if it answered the specific requirement at hand.

4. UPGRADE DISTRIBUTION SKILLS AND CAPACITY. The talents and expertise needed to manage distribution cannot be legislated into existence by changing titles and shuffling organizational relationships—an approach that has actually been tried by several of the surveyed companies. At one time or another, all five of the top performing companies have gone outside the department, or even outside the business, to bring different skills or broader management perspective to bear on distribution activities. The total logistics concept calls for a level of skills and management competence that many top managements are not accustomed to regard as necessary to the distribution function. Quite simply, it takes men of un-

274

usual caliber to deal successfully with the complex of factors and techniques integral to successful management of distribution.

It should be pointed out that the companies in our survey sample display a nearly universal determination to upgrade management of the distribution function. True, the majority of them still have a long way to go. But this fact should hold little solace for their competitors, since almost all are actively striving toward better, tighter, and more sophisticated distribution management.

PART SIX

Harnessing the technological explosion

The single most critical test for many managements in the years ahead will be to secure the greatest possible return from their investments in technology. Never before have research and development strategies so decisively determined corporate fortunes. Year by year, in petro-chemicals, pharmaceuticals, electronics, and other high-technology fields, the task of maintaining innovative momentum becomes more crucial and more costly.

Today, points out Alcon C. Copisarow in his essay "The Future Impact of Technology on Management," executive choices of action can be outdated almost as soon as they are made. The decision-making process comes under especially heavy strain when the allocation of R&D resources is being considered: "The penalties for ineffective technological strategies escalate just as rapidly as the rewards for successful breakthroughs." Probably the most painful dilemma con-fronts management when it suspects that R&D expenditures have begun to show signs of diminishing returns. The question is simple enough: How can progress in research and development be evaluated? The answer is not easy—but it can be arrived at, Copisarow suggests, with the help of a set of well-thought-out performance criteria.

The problem of how to dovetail R&D programs with a company's overall plans and capabilities comes under study in "Strategies for a Technology-Based Business" by H. Igor Ansoff and John M. Stewart. Chief executives no longer accept R&D on faith, the authors note.

Again we encounter management's need to find ways of measuring R&D results: "to sort out and make sense of the multitudinous symptoms, causes, facts, and opinions bearing on the technological dimension of corporate strategy." To this end, Ansoff and Stewart examine the key variables of the corporate research effort: the research vs. development mix, the degree of downstream coupling, the shape of the product life cycle, the R&D investment/expense ratio, and proximity to the "state of the art".

"The Successful Innovators" by David B. Hertz forcefully reminds us that the power to create and innovate is no longer merely a desirable competitive advantage. Rather, it must be recognized as a condition of survival. Among the subtlest of all the managerial arts, fostering innovation is profoundly conditioned by the degree of top management's commitment to research goals, and by the ability of corporate researchers to identify with management objectives.

Hertz points to two assumptions which, research suggests, may stifle much potential innovation in industry: first, the notion that little or nothing can be done about resistance to change within a business organization; second, the belief that the communications barrier between scientist and management is so basic as to be, in effect, insurmountable. Both assumptions, he insists, are false. Change can be brought about and the two sides can work together, provided that "management of a high order" does not hesitate to take vigorous charge of the research program and manage it in accordance with the company's overall objectives, the economics of the business, and the talents available.

"R&D as a Partner in World Enterprise," another contribution by Dr. Hertz, furnishes some guidelines to help the management of multinational corporations to avoid missteps in decentralizing their research and development facilities. Despite the promise of lower costs, an enlarged pool of talent not usually available in a single country, improved technological intelligence on the international scene (a "window on research") and other sound reasons for establishing international research centers, such arrangements often fail to work out according to plan.

A McKinsey study reported in this chapter suggests that many companies have not really thought through the risks and limitations of their approaches to international technology. Some of the unfortunate results are summarized here. Ostensibly lower costs in Europe may be cancelled out by the heavy expense of supervising a research program from a distance. Selected locales have proven to be wrong for certain development programs. Scientists of different cultural backgrounds have not always worked well together; communications channels between management and researchers have too often been unclear; and consistent performance standards and control mechanisms have not always been established.

This chapter provides ample evidence that the management of technology—a complex enough assignment in one country—presents a formidable array of difficulties when businessmen and scientists of several nations must work together. There can be no guarantee of harmony, the author suggests; but, if its objectives are carefully enough defined and communicated, a multinational research and development undertaking will have every prospect of success.

Project management is basic in aerospace and construction companies, but too few managers outside these industries have recognized its value and learned how to realize its potential. Those who have "are bringing new products to market faster than their competitors, completing major expansions on schedule, and meeting crucial commitments more reliably than ever before." This is the thesis set forth by John M. Stewart in "The Promise of Project Management." Mr. Stewart discusses the main difficulty encountered by project managers: the inability or unwillingness of top management to define their working relationships with line management and to provide overall guidance once the project is under way. He explores project management in depth, pointing out its pitfalls as well as its tremendous potential.

24. The future impact of technology on management

Alcon C. Copisarow

Twenty years ago hardly a scientist or technologist confidently expected that by 1969 man would be walking on the moon, that computers would be squeezing the work of years into seconds, or that chemists would be wresting the secrets of heredity from nucleic acid and proving that even a woman's beauty could be merely a matter of chemistry, pure and applied. Nor did many businessmen or politicians then appreciate that the demand for automobiles would multiply at such a rate that choices would sometimes have to be made among complete redesign of city centers, a major limitation of road traffic, or inevitable self-imposed chaos.

Earlier predictions would almost certainly have been confounded by events because almost no one guessed that science and technology would soon be supported on the scale we have come to accept as normal today. In most industrial countries over this period, overall investment has been growing by less than 3 percent and investment in general education by less than 6 percent, but investment in research and development has been mounting at a rate of 6 to 15 percent a year compounded. Britain's annual expenditure on R&D in the decade 1957–1966 grew by 250 percent, to $2 billion a year, while in the United States it multiplied three times, to the $20 billion a year mark.

Because of the time lag effect, the impact of much of this expenditure has still to be felt. Even so, the new large science-based industrial organizations that have sprung up during the past 20 years have brought about substantial changes in long-range planning philosophies. Of the 150 largest U.S. manufacturing concerns at the end of World War II, only 20 had vice presidents in charge of research. Two decades later the number had nearly quintupled, and the number of chief executives with backgrounds in technology is now mounting as well.

And the task of managing technology seems to become more difficult day by day—with the threat from worldwide competition mounting and technology growing ever more complex as the number, range, depth, and interdependence of scientific disciplines steadily increase.

Importance of innovation

A company's size alone does not ensure its survival. Technological innovation is also required. An early study of this subject by the Brookings Institution showed that over a 40-year period, only 36 of 100 large corporations remained in the same business category. An up-to-date survey would indicate a lower proportion still. The modern history of industry is dotted with examples of firms, such as the telegraph and locomotive companies, that lay snug in their technological complacency until they had forfeited both their status and their security.

The age of computers, jet engines, solid-state devices, and other major breakthroughs has seen the birth or burgeoning of some businesses and the decline or death of others. As the time scale for technological achievement continues to grow shorter, more and more companies and industries will be threatened in this way. In the field of energy alone, the fuel cell, MHD generators, solar cells, atomic batteries, thermionic converters, and thermoelectric devices have among them the potential of rendering present power technology as obsolete as making fire by rubbing sticks.

The most profitable opportunities as well as the most serious threats will often arise from advances in other fields. We have already seen natural textiles and rubber supplanted by the products of basic chemistry. We have seen structural packaging and metals profoundly affected by polymer research, machinery by numerical controls, and communications by solid-state devices.

Whatever the sector, speed and flexibility in approach and response have now become of paramount importance. Management decisions are more quickly outdated than ever before. The penalties for ineffective technological strategies escalate just as rapidly as the rewards for successful breakthroughs.

If we compare the cost of innovation in the use, say, of microwave communication with that of the earlier telephone cable, or that of jet engines with that of piston engines, the rise has been astronomical. Were this the sole problem for management the solution would simply be to provide still greater R&D resources. Unfortunately, in an ever-increasing number of high-technology fields such as petrochemicals, pharmaceuticals, aircraft, and electronics—industries that owe their very existence to research and development—R&D expenditures have begun to show signs of diminishing returns and are leveling off. Spending on R&D in the United States and Western Europe may still grow a further 50 percent within the next decade, but it seems clear that economic benefits in the future will accrue more and more to those who make the most effective use of available technological resources.

Crucial issues for management

Now I would submit that management faces no more critical test than its ability to obtain a maximum return on its investment in technology. In order to do this, I would suggest, it must face at least five crucial issues: (1) establishing the objectives and strategy for technology, (2) defining the role of R & D, (3) setting the scale of R & D activity, (4) evaluating the results of R & D, and (5) coupling science with management.

1. OBJECTIVES AND STRATEGY OF THE COMPANY. The first requirement will be, quite naturally, to arrive at an explicit definition of overall corporate objectives and strategy, based upon a thorough analysis and forecast of markets, and a realistic assessment of the company's technological resources. Management must make sure the research department knows the intended rate and direction of company growth, and the relative importance placed on improving operations, improving and diversifying products, or altering the industrial base. It should also make clear, for example, whether product improvements are sought primarily in the area of quality, performance, or price. Again, R & D executives must know whether their efforts are to be geared to hold-the-line strategies, modest-gain strategies, or breakthrough strategies.

Interestingly, those companies with the best developed and most successful strategies seem, generally, best able to recognize their own peculiar strengths and weaknesses in this area. A remarkable example can be seen in the story of Texas Instruments. In 1949 this was a good small company with sales of nearly $6 million and a net profit of $250,000. Then management decided that Texas Instruments was going to become a good big company, doing approximately $200 million worth of business and earning $10 million a year net. Patrick Haggerty and his colleagues felt confident that the future of electronics would be profoundly influenced by knowledge already available on materials at the structure-of-matter level. But it was late in the day. Bell Telephone Laboratories had already invented the transistor in 1948. Texas Instruments' strategy, therefore, was to enter into the development, manufacture, and marketing of semiconductor devices. The procedure would be to seek a patent license from the Western Electric Company, set up a project engineering group, and later establish appropriate research laboratories. This was done in 1953.

It was quickly decided:

¶ That semiconductor devices would find widespread application in military equipment, but that temperature limitations on germanium would restrict their use

¶ That mass production would ultimately be necessary, and an application would have to be found demanding large quantities of high-quality devices at economic prices

¶ A dramatic achievement by the company would be needed to awaken potential users to the fact that these devices could be supplied immediately.

This was the strategy. Tactical R & D programs were designed to contribute to its fulfillment. First, a small signal transistor was developed to military requirements, and the technology immediately transferred to the semiconductor products division. Second, because a pocket transistor radio was considered both technically and economically feasible, a commercial model was completed in collaboration with the I.D.E.A. Corporation of Indianapolis. These two successful programs, carried through manufacturing and marketing, produced exactly the kind of dramatic impact needed.

From 1952 to 1955, a period when its total net profits were running less than $1 million a year, Texas Instruments spent $1.25 million *net* on R & D, and invested another $3 million in plant and tools. By 1960 the company had attained its $200 million per year sales volume objective.

Thoughts had also turned by then to the possibilities of creating whole electronic circuits in a wafer of semiconductor material—the concept of the integrated circuit—with the prospect of realizing immense savings.

Patrick Haggerty has made two interesting remarks about the firm's success: first, that Texas Instruments did not fully recognize until about 1960 that strategic and tactical programs had to become its prime management concern; second, that although the company's technical and commercial leadership enabled it to grow more than 150-fold in 19 years, its technical impact could have been far more effective. Despite Texas Instruments' 64 different specific objectives, its 333 tactical programs currently under way, and its $350 million sales level, it is believed that not enough breakthrough strategies were evolved, that the company's objectives were often badly communicated and in some instances ill-conceived, and that the R & D programs it established frequently turned out to be inadequate.

The inference is clear that in cases such as these it becomes essential to determine key strategies utilizing all of the firm's technological resources.

2. THE ROLE OF RESEARCH. Broadly, there will be three possible roles for research, depending on company strategies and objectives: (1) fundamental or basic research to acquire knowledge; (2) applied R & D to increase the prospect of successful innovation within an existing business; and (3) R & D leading to the establishment of new businesses.

In each of these roles, alternative tactics can be followed and the correct choice is of great importance. The tactics may be aggressive, as with Texas Instruments; or they may be defensive—paying an insurance premium, as it were, to guard against competition.

Again, the tactics may be those of a pioneer and leader; or, alternatively, the tactics of purchasing know-how; or the tactics of diversification or of interfirm collaboration. A company may aim to be first in the field; if so, it must recognize that this usually calls for special research resources, both in quantity and quality, and aggressive management. Or the firm may aim at being second in the field, applying its own knowledge to the pioneer work of others. Or again, given immense resources, it may seek to diversify and, without fully assessing all the technical and economic aspects of every project, aim to turn out more than enough winners to pay for the losers. Or, where the resources needed are beyond the reach of the parties individually, collaborative R&D becomes a further tactical alternative.

Undoubtedly, special prestige rewards the successful pioneer, but pioneering will by no means always be a prerequisite to success. Elliott Automation in the United Kingdom was largely founded upon the development of know-how purchased cheaply in the United States. Du Pont provides an excellent example of a company whose large and talented staff have done well in both directions: they have created 100 winners themselves, but have probably been even more successful, in my opinion, in identifying the potential winners that they could purchase.

Once its overall objectives have been established, research management must then determine its future role, tactics, and program in the light of technological threats as well as opportunities. Even for a company with massive R&D resources there may be many more promising opportunities worthy of support at any given time, if the personnel are competent and in the forefront of their fields. Priorities will have to be determined by management in collaboration with the research department. The research staff will search for the best research portfolio, but management must participate even at this stage if it is to play its full part in establishing priorities for development later on, when expenditures begin to assume greater proportions. Frequently, mistakes made at this early stage pass unnoticed until much later, when the company has already been committed to huge production or marketing expenditures.

3. HOW MUCH R&D? Management must face a third general problem: How great should be its total investment in R&D? In the science-intensive industries, where a high degree of ingenuity is built into the product, the R&D investment will inevitably be high—in some years averaging 28 percent of sales for U.S. aircraft and missile makers, for example. By contrast, the producers of bulky construction materials need not spend more than a fraction of 1 percent on R&D. Technology in this latter industry, and others like it, will generally be characterized by a succession of small improvements rather than by breakthroughs. Major innovation, when it does occur, usually results from cross-fertilizing traditional materials and processes with some advanced technology.

In the case of Texas Instruments, it should be noted, no decision was made as to what proportion of the company's total resources should be devoted to R & D. A modest, fairly constant amount of quite basic research (perhaps 1 percent) will be appropriate to a company such as this—and the level of applied work should relate to specific needs and opportunities.

At the same time, management must consider the threshold level of technical effort, varying from one company and industry to another, below which R & D effectiveness falls off rapidly. In electronics, for example, a company must keep abreast of technical changes in components, introduce a flow of improvements, and launch completely new models when forced to do so by the competition. This becomes the threshold level of effort— an absolute level of resources, not a ratio of sales. This may be derived by dividing the estimated R & D costs of new products by their typical lead times—defining lead time as the time required to take a new idea from the initial decision through R & D and design to first regular production.

To develop a high-quality oscilloscope, let us say, a team of about 20 qualified scientists, engineers, and designers may be required full-time for about three years. The annual cost in the United Kingdom would, therefore, be some $500,000. For small and large computers, the corresponding R & D costs might be $2 million a year and $15 million a year, respectively. A communications satellite with a five-year lead time would require some $30 million a year. In each instance, a manufacturer aiming to shorten the lead time sufficiently to become the leader in the field might well have to double the indicated annual expenditure.

If a firm with a small market share merely matches the ratio of R & D to sales of a larger and more successful competitor, its research expenditure may fall below the "threshold" level. Management may be caught in a vicious circle. Because its effort continues below the threshold, lead times will be too long, and the company's market share will decline further. Its ratio of R & D expenditure to sales will rise, diminishing profitability and reducing the cash flow needed for future development and investment. Many companies both in the United States and in Europe found themselves in this situation.

If the R & D threshold in a particular field has been judged too high for a particular company, the only alternative to abandoning this product line may be to join with another company which has resources sufficient to exceed the threshold for a period long enough to retrieve the positions.

4. EVALUATING R & D. The next questions for management are: Do research investments, growing as they are, appear worthwhile at all? Do the returns compare with those of alternative investment opportunities? Is the scientific effort proceeding with maximum effectiveness? How, in other words, can we judge the success of our research effort? Clearly, we must have a pretty tough-minded system of evaluation.

Research can be regarded as a business in itself: the processing of raw materials (ideas) in a factory (the laboratory) to give usable products (marketing). To ensure that research continues to be productive, therefore, these three functions must all be properly carried out.

Calculating precise returns has never been an easy matter. What is the equivalent of money in the research balance sheet? Certainly men constitute the most valuable by-product of the R & D effort. In many companies a man may leave and reenter research more than once during his career. Such a policy ensures the best possible collaboration between departments. In industries undergoing rapid change, valuable experience is less likely to be built by long tenure than by executives moving easily between research, development, production, and marketing. In addition, the encouragement of lateral mobility opens the way to top-management positions for men with a thorough understanding of science, technology, and change.

In any event the human product cannot be subjected to quantitative evaluation. Nor can many of the other benefits that flow from R & D—greater policy flexibility and the spreading of risks which it may allow; the acquisition of technical intelligence; the creative drive that can inspire other departments; the technical services made available to other departments; and all the indirect contributions to morale, company prestige, and so on. Though relevant, these can only be imponderables in any rate-of-return calculations. Unsupported, they cut little ice with top managers who are constantly being asked to approve the allocation of even greater resources for R & D.

Quantitative tools for evaluating R & D do exist, but they differ among companies. In basic chemicals, food processing, mining, and electronics, for example, they are quite different.

The first requirement for evaluation is clearly defined targets or objectives to serve as criteria of success. A company with a highly competent and successful R & D effort might show poor profit performance because of the inadequacy of other departments. Conversely, poor R & D might not noticeably hurt the profits of a company with a sound current technical position, if other departments were outstandingly good.

The main quantifiable achievements fall into nine categories: (1) new and improved products and processes (improvements may be measured in quality, reduced material costs, reduced capital outlay, or other operational savings); (2) new uses for old products; (3) product replacement to make use of existing manufacturing and distribution facilities; (4) patents, which give a competitive advantage as well as royalties; (5) other licenses of know-how; (6) net income from contract research; (7) upgrading of raw materials; (8) profitable disposal of by-products; and (9) information valuable for the promotion of the product and its use. In many cases, the majority of these benefits are quantifiable. Whatever evaluation criteria may be most appropriate in a particular case, their application calls for thoughtful judgment—not least in apportioning the credit fairly between the R&D department and all the others contributing to success.

Companies can derive most valuable information from such reviews. Britain's Imperial Chemical Industries has determined its record of research success and failure in efforts to improve existing processes and products, in specific new products and processes, and in exploratory research investigations. A few years ago, Sir Ronald Holroyd showed in a published report that of ICI's successful programs, less than 5 percent had stemmed from the company's own research staff. Over 80 percent had been based on ideas from other sources inside the company, and about 15 percent on ideas from external sources. It is noteworthy that a far larger share of Du Pont's achievements, covering much the same product range, appears to have come from outside. Successful programs based on external leads are normally more costly to pursue, and whether the pursuit is warranted in any particular instance will be, in part, calculated from the ratio of R&D to prospective sales. ICI's management at that time believed that every $1 million it had spent on R&D had produced a yield of $200,000 a year for perhaps ten years.

Evidence that R&D spending appears worthwhile, overall, does not come down to proof that it is as efficient as it could be. (We could go some distance in this direction given a careful and objective assessment of both the input and output factors of R&D, better records, and adequate information feedback.) Probably the most commonly observed single reason for failure in the planning of new products and processes, in industry generally, is top management's failure to understand what the research staff has been doing.

5. COUPLING SCIENCE WITH MANAGEMENT. The fifth, and in my view the most important, means of achieving the greatest possible return from a company's investment in technology will be the effective coupling of the scientist and manager. Research serves as the company's liaison with the future. Basic research personnel, therefore, must have the freedom to wander over uncharted fields and even to go off on tangents in the process of creative inquiry.

Top management must recognize the aims and aspirations of the individual scientist, who seeks principally the approval and accolade of an audience of his co-professionals. How can these intensely personal ambitions be reconciled with those of the organization? How can a research scientist in the chemical industry, who would delight in obtaining the maximum yield of the end product, or the quickest reaction, be persuaded to bow willingly to overriding company requirements such as simplifying manual operations or minimizing capital costs?

The answers will vary across the research and development spectrum.

287

At one end, the basic research effort in a large organization will by definition take place at the frontiers of science. The practitioners must be judged by their professional peers and not found wanting. They must be insulated from the day-to-day problems of the enterprise yet not isolated from its overall objectives. At the other end of the spectrum the development personnel mainly concern themselves with quite specific corporate aims. It is their responsibility to make certain that the company never falls behind. Their minds must be on the end product and the marketplace. Between these two "beginning and end" positions lies a critical area that should be staffed by able people with a dual allegiance. They have to understand basic science and appreciate what it does for technology and for the organization. At the same time, they must ever be sensitive to the way product goals and profit objectives can be influenced by deploying scientific and technical resources.

Now, the need for coupling the R & D, manufacturing, and marketing functions varies greatly from industry to industry. In construction equipment firms, for example, the technical know-how built into the product design will often be important only to the R & D people. But in most mechanical, chemical, and electrical engineering firms a considerable measure of technical sophistication is required of the production people as well. And in companies manufacturing materials such as plastics, the marketing department as well as the manufacturing department must have full technological awareness.

In science-intensive firms, where coupling is high, the technological impact affects virtually every company executive. Technically qualified people must be shared among all departments in a properly balanced fashion, and all must be involved in the assessment of innovation. Without careful monitoring and control of quality or performance at the boundaries of a problem, there will always be a dangerous tendency to shift responsibility and blame from one management function to another. Because many problems cut directly across two or more company operations, hybrid or interfunctional assignments will be required.

Hence, in organizations where coupling is high, technological awareness becomes intrinsic to every part of the business. In those companies for which technology is changing most rapidly and exerts the greatest leverage on marketing, a flexible management structure with a fast information feedback system will be most essential.

The nature of coupling varies widely. Where the introductory phase of the product life cycle is short, it may be necessary in the interests of speed to strike a compromise between technical and marketing aims. When the life cycle is longer, the technology may be planned in a more orderly fashion, with a view to economy rather than speed. When the technological effort has been great but the commercial life is likely to be short and the

288

return uncertain, it becomes important to apply the technological cutoff at the point when returns begin to diminish, rather than wait for technological perfection.

When companies diversify into products with different life cycles, problems may arise for the managers who cannot learn to change their methods to meet these changing requirements. When the nature of the business undergoes a real metamorphosis, such as the change from manufacture of data processing equipment to that of making computers with a far shorter life cycle, some organizations go to the wall altogether. Certain companies eventually succeed, because their sales forces understand the market changes, their engineering staffs remain strong and alert enough to meet new requirements, and the coupling between them is close and vital.

The challenge ahead

Inevitably, the direction and control of technology will continue moving up the management ladder. Significant dialogues already take place between scientists and administrators at the highest levels of government. In industry the process has been slower, mainly because chief executives have not always clearly perceived their own critical roles. But this is changing. Top management has begun to recognize the true dimensions of the problems raised by the inexorable advance of technology. And recognize them it must, for companies that do not prepare to face up resolutely and effectively to newly emerging technological problems—and opportunities—are sowing the seeds of their own future weakness and vulnerability.

25. Strategies for a technology-based business

H. Igor Ansoff and John M. Stewart

With the unprecedented impact of technology on business and the growing prominence of research and development in the spectrum of corporate activities, more and more attention has been directed to the special problems of R&D: its organization, planning and control, budgeting, and especially the stimulation and management of the creative process.

A breakdown of traditional management approaches in R&D has been conspicuous, and it has caused profound concern in many industries. Indeed, a substantial literature already exists for the guidance of executives responsible for R&D leadership.

Yet in technology-based industries, a subtler but no less significant complex of problems has escaped the recognition of many managers. This is the challenge of dovetailing R&D with a company's overall plans and capabilities. Consider two examples:

¶ A few years ago a profitable small manufacturer of high-quality electronic components was acquired by one of its major customers, a top-ranking aerospace corporation. Within months it had been "helped to death" by its acquirer, much to the latter's puzzlement. The subcontracts which it had accepted from the parent, apparently at a fair price, presented formidable technical problems. What had not been apparent was that a small development and manufacturing organization could hardly be expected to turn itself overnight into a research-oriented aerospace hybrid.

¶ A large international industrial products company was plagued with cost and schedule overruns after stepping up its new-product introductions. Costs were continually being underestimated, and the output of other product lines was repeatedly disrupted. As it later turned out, management had failed to "shift gears" in its schedule, cost, and inventory controls to fit the advanced rate of product introduction. Cost of the lesson—more than $2 million.

Such problems as these have lately become a source of increasing top-management concern. Not that this should be surprising, since R&D

290

activities have grown until today in many industries they rank among the two or three heaviest consumers of company funds.

Chief executives, who once accepted R&D on faith, are no longer willing to keep "hands off" and let the technological tail go on wagging the corporate dog. Many have begun to look for ways to measure results, which they rightly suspect are not always what they should be. And they continue to grope for better ways to sort out and make sense of the multitudinous symptoms, causes, facts, and opinions bearing on the technological dimension of corporate strategy.

But analyses carried out in recent years across a wide range of industries reveal that the management processes of every technology-based company appear particularly sensitive to certain key variables, and that companies acting on recognition of these variables seem more likely to excel in competitive performance.

Management issues

As yet no foolproof formula for obtaining the best possible results from R&D has been developed—nor is one likely to be, since each company's requirements are in some sense unique. Here are key questions that appear practically universal:

BUSINESS STRATEGY. Is our R&D investment consistent with our corporate strategy? Should we invest in the same technologies as our competitors, or in different ones? How can we identify the threats and/or profit opportunities from the technology of competitors within our own industry and those in other industries?

ORGANIZATION. How can we give the greatest possible flexibility to our organization structure in the face of rapid technological change? How should this structure and company work assignments be changed as products mature through their life cycles? How can technology best be transferred from R&D to manufacturing and marketing?

PLANNING AND CONTROL. How ought we to formulate research objectives? Should we control research differently from development? How can project planning and control be integrated with periodic functional reporting?

MARKETING. What kind of product/market strategy ought we to follow? What technical advantages in our products, at what cost or investment level, will be needed to secure a real competitive advantage?

Our object will not be specifically to answer these questions but to suggest a conceptual framework which will help top management in its efforts to define and resolve them. Such a framework, applied to a hypothetical company, is illustrated on page 292.

The technological parameters we shall examine are the research vs.

development mix, the degree of downstream coupling, the shape of the product life cycle, the R&D investment/expense ratio, and the proximity to the "state of the art."

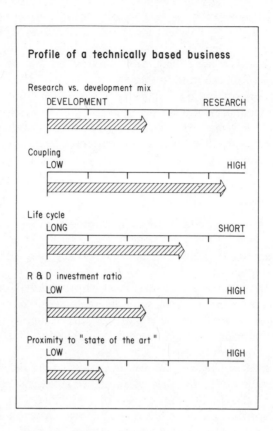

Profile of a technically based business

Research vs. development mix
DEVELOPMENT — RESEARCH

Coupling
LOW — HIGH

Life cycle
LONG — SHORT

R & D investment ratio
LOW — HIGH

Proximity to "state of the art"
LOW — HIGH

Research vs. development

The two concepts of "research" and "development" have become so closely linked in management thinking by the expression *R&D* that important differences between them are often ignored in executive decision making. This becomes particularly apparent when companies attempt to apply the lessons of their research experience to problems in development, or vice versa.

Rather than attempt to formulate a generally acceptable definition of the two concepts, we will simply use the terms "R-intensive" to denote commitment to the basic and experimental and "D-intensive" to describe a tendency toward commercial product design on the other. Most companies, of course, fall somewhere in between, but they can best be described in terms of the two extremes.

R-intensive organizations in general display six characteristics:

1. They work with indefinite design specifications. Since management can usually identify the problem but cannot specify the desired solution, the task of the R-intensive organization will be to discover and evaluate *alternative* solutions, rather than to implement a single solution.

2. They tend to "broadcast" objectives and market data among technical people, rather than channel specific kinds of information to individuals. Being unable to present specific requirements to research, they use broadcast communications to stimulate generation of alternatives that will be consistent with top management's objectives and strategy.

3. They are nondirective in work assignments. Since design specifications in R-intensive companies will generally be less definite, and technical insight and potential contribution are individual rather than group attributes, managers must permit freedom for individual initiative and progress rather than assign individuals to develop specific parts of a well-defined solution.

4. They maintain a continuing project evaluation and selection process. Research is constantly turning up alternative solutions of varying worth, and these supersede previous solutions. Moves by a competitor, or results achieved on another project, may render obsolete a piece of research or change its priority. This demands continuing revision of the project portfolio to permit changes in the slate of projects, even within the normal routine planning period.

5. They stress the perception of significant results. Where a research problem has not been tightly structured, the solutions—even if found—are not always obvious. An essential skill of the technical manager has always been his ability to recognize technically or commercially significant results. The history of invention is replete with instances, like Carruther's discovery of nylon, where a flash of insight into the possibilities of wholly unanticipated experimental results led to great discoveries that might otherwise have been missed.

6. They value innovation over efficiency. Economy in performing research will be less important than achieving a markedly better solution with clear market or profit advantages. Innovation is thereby prized, even at the cost of some efficiency in organization structure, planning, or control.

In contrast, D-intensive organizations can usually be recognized by four characteristics:

1. Well-defined design specifications. With research essentially complete, the development objective becomes reasonably clear, and performance tests can be specified early during design. The task is not to create new solutions but to reduce available alternatives to a single solution.

2. *Highly directive supervision.* The work to be done is highly inter-related from the beginning of design to successful testing. Managers tend to specify objectives, give orders, and carefully measure performance. The relatively large numbers of people in the D-intensive organization—designers, test engineers, draftsmen, production engineers—also call for a more structured management approach than that required for the R-intensive company.

3. *Sequential arrangement of tasks.* Unlike the R-intensive organization in which many people can work together in parallel projects or on different aspects of the same problem, the D-intensive organization requires a disciplined sequencing of tasks, with sophisticated controls to ensure that technical objectives are achieved within planned time and cost limits. Scheduling tends to be thorough and precise, as in manufacturing. When faced with tradeoff decisions between efficiency and innovation, managers will usually opt for efficiency and higher output.

4. *Vulnerability to disruption by change.* Given its relatively high man-power commitment, its sequencing of tasks, and its relative proximity to actual production in the new product development process, the D-intensive organization can be severely affected by managerial or administrative changes ordered in midstream. Studies by McKinsey & Company indicate that management or program changes contribute more heavily to cost and to schedule overruns, as a rule, than do engineering or technical changes—a point that often escapes the managers involved.

Given these differing characteristics, the hazards of managing a D-intensive organization with concepts and controls suited to the R-intensive company, or vice versa, should be apparent. Consider this example:

The president of a technically based electronics company was convinced that a strong research department would be the key to innovative products and high profits. The department generated plenty of ideas but few marketable products—a situation to which the president reacted by further increasing the research staff. The company's marketing, manufacturing, and financial managers began resigning in disgust. Profits dropped; so did the company's stock. Not long thereafter, the president was replaced by a new man from the outside.

President No. 2 began by strengthening the functions that had atrophied during the research binge and hangover. Then he began to trim the research staff, which by some estimates was three times what the company could support. In the seven years since he became chief executive the company has successfully marketed a series of technically innovative products against strong competition. Its development, manufacturing, marketing, and financial functions have now become equal to those of its most formidable competition. The quality and management of research, despite a substantial staff reduction, have suffered no serious decline, but the management processes to support that research have been drastically altered.

Downstream coupling

A second important characteristic of high-technology businesses may be described as the degree of *downstream coupling*. This is the extent to which the success of the company's product introduction depends on communication and cooperation between R&D, manufacturing, and marketing—all further "downstream" toward the customer. Clearly, industries differ in their downstream coupling requirements. Some need a great deal of information and interaction with as little filtering as possible; others require little or none. Being aware of the coupling requirement and managing it properly not only can avert the frictions occurring so frequently at the marketing-engineering interface, but also can channel the familiar conflicts between manufacturing and engineering toward more productive ends.

We may distinguish three degrees of coupling—high, moderate, and low. High coupling requires close interaction among the technical, manufacturing, and marketing functions of the business. Accurate and detailed market information is essential to adequate product-line planning. The selection of R&D projects will be influenced heavily by manufacturing costs, availability of raw materials, abilities of the marketing organization, and countermoves by competition. Minimizing the disruptive effect of new product introductions on manufacturing is critical. Tight control of product quality will be essential to successful customer applications and minimum service engineering effort. Finally, time pressure is usually acute.

Many technically based industries require exceptionally high coupling. In specialty plastics, for example, the functions of product and process development, production, and field technical service must be closely linked by a tightly knit communication, decision, and control process. Management has often vainly tried to achieve this by shifting the technical service group from marketing to development, or to production, or independently to the chief executive.

Again, in present-day electronics, integrated circuit producers find that they must work more closely with equipment designers, field service men, and marketing planners than component suppliers ever did. Significant increases in the product coupling have made necessary corresponding increases in the management coupling of R&D with the departments downstream.

In a highly coupled organization, management will usually be concerned about the downstream effect of new-product introductions and about the marketing and production impact of R&D actions. The coupling-conscious management of one chemical company, wary of a proposed $3 million investment in a new chemical process developed by a recent acquisition, kept pressing for more information. The facts confirmed management's misgivings: more than $20 million of additional investment would be required before the parent company's target rate of return could be achieved. The $3 million "down payment" was not approved.

In such companies, management should maintain a constant balance of influence among development, production, and technical service to the customer. If development becomes too strong, uneconomic products or processes are rammed into manufacturing, and current customer complaints must defer to future development work. If technical service grows too powerful, future development is downgraded in the interest of extinguishing the fire-of-the-minute. Occasionally, manufacturing projects its self-interest strongly enough to reject desirable product changes in order to maintain high efficiencies. Or it may schedule output for maximum machine utilization rather than to meet customer commitments. In a highly coupled organization, correct balance among these three technically competent functions may be seen as dynamic, never static.

But functional dividing lines may create serious problems. Since objectives on either side of the marketing-engineering interface can and often do drift apart, some kind of results-oriented interfunctional control will be needed to keep pulling them back together. Sending two men—one from each function—on customer complaint calls is one way. Organizing functionally, with cross-functional responsibilities for project completion, is another. Giving senior executives corollary duties that straddle functional lines (a tricky business) can also help to reduce the problem. This can take the form of making the vice president for R & D responsible for training technical service men, or of giving a marketing staffer the job of coordinating all functions to complete an application project.

Although interfunctional responsibility may narrow the gaps between, say, marketing and R & D, it cannot eliminate interfunctional boundaries or the impacts that occur across them. Care must be taken to assess potential collisions in advance. Too often an executive gives the order to release a design to manufacturing without realizing that subsequent engineering changes will produce unanticipated results. This seems to be particularly true in moderately coupled companies: manufacturing and engineering often become bitter adversaries because neither really identifies or explains what is happening.

Still another "problem" interface, especially in moderately coupled companies that lack the formal controls characteristic of highly coupled organizations, may occur when joint product planning is assigned to marketing and engineering. In one company, technically competent engineers in marketing found themselves hopelessly at odds with R & D engineers working on market research and development. Each side was working without discipline or clear executive direction; their positions were based on inadequate data, organizational prejudice, and a minimum of analysis. Senior executives can do much to avert such waste of talent by insisting on a logical process for new-product planning.

Finally, since coupling constitutes an interfunctional problem, no single functional vice president can manage it successfully. A general manager, whether a president or a division head, must be the one to provide the necessary direction and arbitration.

Product life cycle

Life cycles may vary in length from a few months (e.g., the hula hoop) to years or even to decades (e.g., the wooden pencil). In technology-intensive businesses, the length of the cycle may have initial strategic implications, particularly in planning and control.

Characteristic of short-cycle companies will be a need for speedy management action and response, high concurrency of activities in product introduction, and approximation rather than precision in pursuing technical objectives. Here business success requires intelligence for early appraisal of competitive moves. As a matter of strategy, an alert company should plan to be among the first to bring out a new product or break into a new market, since competition thereafter will generally force prices down fast, depressing profit margins and return on investment.

Organizationally, the short cycle puts a premium on quick response. To observers in slower moving industries, the short-cycle company appears to be in perpetual chaos. It will tend to favor short-circuit devices—such as product managers, project managers, or interfunctional committees—which speed up the transfer of information from one department to another. Faced with the choice of structuring the organization for economy or for rapid response, management will usually pick fast response, even at high cost. Many short-cycle companies, for example, maintain separate engineering-change organizations; these are nonexistent in companies characterized by long product life cycles.

Functional planning in a short-cycle business is usually overlapping or simultaneous. Manufacturing may begin to frame its plan, and marketing may set target dates for product introduction, before R & D planning has been completed. This, in turn, means that the input to technical plans from marketing and manufacturing is much higher than in the long-cycle company. Engineering approaches must often be changed for manufacturing or marketing reasons, and much prior planning tends to be discarded in the process. Plans are often remade in the short-cycle company; the result being a series of increasingly accurate approximations of introduction dates, product specifications, and detailed plans for market introduction.

Short-cycle companies need close coupling between product marketing specialists and technical staff. Marketing managers tend to be familiar with technology, and they often contribute substantially to product definition and development.

In long-cycle businesses the converse is generally true. With adequate time to learn about competitive market developments and to plan countermoves, there is less need for unusual market sensitivity. In the long-cycle company emphasis concentrates on established procedure and routine. Organization will usually be functional. Managerial decisions usually favor economy and efficiency at the expense of rapid response. (In the eyes of managers in short-cycle companies, such organizations appear rather ponderous.)

Moreover, planning is usually sequential. Detailed R & D will be completed before the manufacturing and marketing planning has begun. Manufacturing and marketing seldom become deeply involved in technical planning. In fact, the technical staff may include market research specialists to help with the long-range R & D planning.

Again, in long-cycle companies, marketing people often will be unfamiliar with technical problems or objectives, since a new technical problem is rare and coupling between marketing and technical people low.

Occasionally, companies and industries undergo a shift in product life-cycle characteristics. In the 1940s and 1950s, for example, as computers replaced punched-card data processing equipment, the cycle shortened noticeably. One painful consequence of this shift was that many managers who had been highly successful in the era of punched cards proved unable to adjust to the planning and control, organizational structure, and strategy implications of the shorter life cycle.

The same adjustment problem may arise when companies diversify. Managers in the oil industry often have trouble adjusting to the shorter cycle and more rapid product obsolescence characteristic of the petrochemical business. The problem becomes still more acute for petrochemical managers whose companies integrate downstream—say, entering the plastics business, where some product introduction often takes place under near-crash conditions because life cycles are so short. To take a manager trained in the oil business, move him within a few years to a petrochemical subsidiary, and then to a plastics operation is to subject his personal adaptability and the flexibility of his management methods and outlook to the severest possible test.

The life-cycle conditioning that a manager receives is an asset to him in his present business, but might be a liability in a different business. When recruiting a key executive, presidents of nontechnically intensive companies too often go after a manager from the technically glamorous industries. Such a man, even though an outstanding performer in his old environment, may flounder for months or years in new and different surroundings.

Investment ratios

How much ought to be spent on research and development? How should the investment be apportioned between basic and applied research projects?

As yet, we have seen there can be no generally accepted measure of R&D investment (taking "investment" to mean total dollar resources committed, without regard to the accounting treatment). Of late, the familiar practice of expressing R&D investment as a percentage of sales has been falling into disrepute—and rightly so. The results of R&D, after all, cannot be realized immediately and, in fact, affect sales instead of being affected by them. Measures that begin, but only begin, to do justice to R&D's mission of protecting corporate assets from technical obsolescence treat the R&D investment as a percentage of total investment or of profits or cash flow.

However measured, the ratio of R&D investment/expense will be important. High ratios, we may note, are characteristic of technically intensive industries such as pharmaceuticals, chemicals, and electronics; low ratios of nonintensive industries such as food, lumber, and cement. Most industries fall between the extremes—for example, farm equipment and petroleum may be found near the middle of the range.

In our view, high investment ratios have four significant implications for management:

1. *They require a serious and continuous evaluation of technology procurement alternatives:*

¶ Whether to buy technology through licensing or through hiring consultants

¶ Whether to buy a company in order to acquire the latest technology in an unfamiliar field

¶ Whether to hire top people with the specific technical competence desired

¶ Whether to develop additional technical competence by internal training in order to stay competitive.

Where R&D investment ratio is low, it may be possible to develop technology inside the company with relatively low risk of being outpaced by competition. Higher ratios characteristically allow less lead time and make the acquisition of technology a more attractive alternative. In any case, they call for constant review of the alternatives by a corporate-level group aware of the pace of development inside and outside the company and also sensitive to competitive moves in the field.

2. *They usually accelerate product and process change.* This, in turn, requires an adaptive organization, which can quickly shift to new levels of efficiency and effectiveness as technology changes the work to be done. The source of the change in a high-ratio company can be either external or internal. Externally, competitors investing in the same technology may render obsolete a market, a plant, or an investment—compelling the organization to respond swiftly. Internally, research and development results can produce similar pressures for change. In a company with a high R&D investment ratio, a major criterion of organization will therefore be the ability to adapt to new technology without sacrificing market share or efficiency.

3. *They usually mean a dynamic product market.* Such markets—in which products readily substitute for one another and emphasis rapidly shifts from new-product development to low unit cost and vice versa—impose three special requirements.

The first is clear visibility of resources, permitting management to cut off a development project quickly or to switch resources into a new technology. If it cannot foresee the implications of such decisions in terms of total corporate resources over the entire product life cycle, the company may become more deeply committed than management intended.

The second requirement is explicit strategy formulation. In a rapidly changing market, executives can lose perspective and make unwise or conflicting technical or product decisions. An explicit strategic framework permits clear definition of project alternatives and enables managers to choose more wisely among them.

The third special need is a well-developed planning system permitting the company to redirect its resources promptly and effectively. The system must be explicit, providing for control of technical resources consistent with strategy by tying R&D closely to corporate planning and control.

4. *They require closer supervision of technical efforts.* Since the company is highly dependent on technology for competitive survival and therefore commits proportionately more resources to the effort, the senior managers need to know more about technical problems and performance. They should be aware of the long-term corporate effects of lower level decisions and maintain a good grasp of the time and cost implications of particular technological developments. This is important because technology in high-ratio companies usually has a substantial effect on other functions. Thus any executive making a substantial investment in technology will need assurance that these effects are consistent with his overall objective.

300

In general, the effects of low R & D investment/expense ratios will be the converse of those described above. Technology can be developed internally within competitive lead times—or, in some industries, purchased with the capital equipment into which technology has been incorporated by the manufacturer. It is unnecessary for organization structure to be highly adaptive. Since technical developments are evolutionary, only occasional changes in functional structure will be needed. Resources do not have to be specially identified because historical accounting data on expense and investment adequately reflect the impact of product or process replacements. Finally, marketing need not be closely coupled with the technological functions, since marketing requirements can be communicated via top management or through formal planning and control mechanisms.

Our evidence does not support the common assumption that the effects of R & D investment vary directly with the investment ratio as the latter ranges from zero to some high percentage. It appears, on the contrary, that R & D efforts are almost entirely ineffective below a certain critical level.

This level is not easy to pinpoint, but it may be located in a general way by examining the technical results of competitors. Has a given company developed successful commercial products? How long did it lag behind the industry leader in developing competitive technology? What is its record of innovation? How old is its current product line?

When possible, arraying the competitive results of a series of companies against the amount of technical effort expended by each should suggest the approximate level of resources below which little or no results can be expected.

The question of critical mass is complicated by the factor of quality. Since high-quality research personnel can generate a return out of all proportion to their number, quality as well as quantity affects the critical mass. For want of any real yardsticks of quality, such an analysis must be highly judgmental.

Another complicating factor is the mix of disciplines found in the technical staff. Managers working with interdisciplinary groups have repeatedly noted that even in technical efforts of similar quantity and quality one mix of disciplines will result in higher innovation and output than another.

Although few yardsticks to measure technical effort exist, an understanding of these implications can help the manager of a business which has become technically intensive to structure his effort more effectively. Hopefully, too, such understanding will enable him to avoid certain costly mistakes.

One company maintained a staff of 16 highly qualified PhDs in a remote laboratory for several years before the president decided to find out why they had produced no significant results. The problem, as he eventually learned, was threefold: the staff lacked direction, it was too research-oriented, and it was too small. Noting that his chief competitor had a development effort strongly directed at visible, emerging market needs and staffed by no less than 150 development engineers, only a sprinkling of whom were PhDs, the president belatedly remodeled his own company's department to match.

State of the art

For most managers, the term "state of the art" denotes the frontier of a technology. Inside this boundary, but not beyond it, reliable and tested technical solutions will be available.

But state of the art has different implications in research and in development. For research, it denotes the frontier at which investigators seek to discover new phenomena or to devise a solution to a known problem. For development, it refers to a less rarefied zone where the validity of a theory or solution has already been proved, but a successful commercial application remains to be achieved. For development, in other words, the state of the art depends on economics as well as on technology.

How close a company's technology comes to the state of the art has important implications for management planning and decision making. These implications may be considered under three headings: (1) stability, (2) predictability, and (3) precedent.

Stability is closely related to distance from the R&D frontier. A firm working near the state-of-the-art boundary must keep trying for rapid advances like those through which it achieved its current position. At the same time, it will be alert to possible breakthroughs by competitors, perhaps by dramatically improving a product or significantly reducing costs. The market position of such a company remains perpetually in jeopardy from all competitors working in the same technical area.

Top managers in firms of this kind should be keenly aware of their dependence on a well-developed technological intelligence system. Surveillance of literature, attention to competitive developments, and attendance and participation in scientific societies should all be developed and encouraged. In addition, top managers should make a continuing effort to understand and keep abreast of the state of the art.

For companies well back from the boundary, radical breakthroughs will be unlikely. Technical progress is evolutionary, with relatively little innovation. Breakthroughs by competitors are no immediate threat; rather the danger is that breakthroughs in other industries and other technologies may obsolete the entire mature technology.

Predictability is low for companies near the state-of-the-art boundary.

Since their researchers work in areas of partial knowledge, the nature and, even more, the timing of results will be difficult to foresee. Unless the implications of low predictability are understood and allowed for, company plans can be hardly more than guesses, subject to all the vicissitudes of technical investigation.

Conversely, far from the boundary of the state of the art, where breakthroughs are unlikely, predictability remains high. Small improvements in products or processes can be foretold with confidence and timed with a high degree of accuracy; their achievement depends on the resources invested rather than on technical innovation.

Precedent, which underlies so much management activity, is sparse near the state-of-the-art boundary. Past experience supplies little guidance to help managers judge whether people are doing a good job, whether capital should be committed to a particular project, whether the product has a commercial life—whether, in fact, the entire effort will be profitable. In view of the uncertainty and lack of precedent, senior executives cannot afford to demand infallibility in middle managers' decisions. Their task, it must be recognized, differs greatly from that of their counterparts in companies far from the state of the art, who can rely on established management doctrine that prescribes the scope of managerial discretion and assures the manager that he is well within his responsibility—and even may guide many of his individual decisions.

The implications of stability, predictability, and precedent are substantial in the areas of planning and control. Near the state of the art, a company must settle for more approximation and less precision in goals and standards. Thus planning and control systems must be tailored accordingly. In such a company, judgment is critical, and precision often specious.

Failure to take account of these implications may be exceedingly costly. In one diversified company, an electronics division devoted to the development and marketing of highly sophisticated microwave equipment was expected to plan as far ahead and in as much detail as the industrial products divisions did. When the division manager continued to protest that the requirement was unrealistic, he was replaced by an accountant. Within 15 months, half of the technical people had left, and all momentum was gone from the R&D program.

Besides the company's distance from the boundary, the rate of advance in the state of the art itself must be considered. Since this is largely a function of industry-wide investment, heavier R&D expenditures (and a higher critical mass) become the rule when the boundary is moving rapidly. But in view of the differences between research and development, total resources invested may not be an adequate clue to the effectiveness of a company's investment. Development budgets normally tend to be much larger than those for research; but a large development input, unless balanced by an equally strong research component, turns out to be of little use when the boundary is fluid.

Rapid change in the state of the art means rapid obsolescence of managerial decisions. Planning assumptions are more quickly superseded by events. Since even the most carefully projected capital investment decisions may turn out badly, rapid payback of investment or flexibility in capital facilities, or both, become crucial. In this situation, executives who take their one- and two-year plans very seriously may with some justification treat five-year planning as a paper exercise.

Swift obsolescence of some managers who do not keep up with new developments is another consequence of rapid change in the state of the art. The engineering director of an electronics company estimated that in 12 years four generations of managers had either relearned their technology or become obsolete. The point is one to be kept in mind during budget discussions. Resources for keeping abreast of technological development too often tend to be trimmed as "superfluous," resulting in the slow erosion of technical awareness and competence.

Rapid change in the state of the art creates more opportunities but also more blind alleys for technical management. It puts a premium on the ability to cut off projects before their proliferation saps the main effort. Moreover, it requires some degree of management sophistication in all the main aspects of the technology. Technological progress is seldom monolithic. Rather, it evolves as the result of many advances by researchers, located in different laboratories and employing slightly different approaches to the same basic technology. These specialists are continually forging ahead in different aspects of research. Management should have some knowledge of the directions being pursued by important competitors, including smaller companies with highly competent research teams which sometimes outperform even the large laboratories.

Sensitivity to potentially profitable ventures will always be a valuable managerial asset, and an executive who possesses it may well be forgiven for otherwise unforgivable administrative weaknesses.

The need for flexible organizational response extends beyond the R & D function to selling, production, and distribution. In a highly coupled technical company, for example, all the sales engineering and application people may have to undergo frequent retraining. Production departments may have to adapt to new processes, new tooling, and even new kinds of operating equipment.

During a rapid development period, manufacturing efficiency becomes far less important than it is for a maturing product. In the early days of solid-state electronics, transistor yields on the order of 10 percent of the total material committed to the process were more than adequate for substantial profits. A little later on, crystal manufacturers had to achieve 80 percent to 90 percent yields. But when the next technical advance occurred, production management again had to be content with 10 percent yields until the product line matured. When the cycle of product technology moves as rapidly as this, all management systems are severely strained.

What does all this mean to the manager? At a minimum, it calls upon him to use great care and judgment in borrowing other companies' techniques. Also, it suggests that the type, accuracy, detail, and frequency of planning in a technically intensive division of a conglomerate company ought to be quite different from that of a mature technology division. And for a company whose technology is maturing, it may suggest the desirability of substituting a more formal, precise system of management for the stimulating but inefficient turmoil of infant technology.

Marketing strategy

We have examined the parameters of technically intensive businesses and their impact on strategic, administrative, and operating problems of top managers. By way of summary, let us consider the impact of these characteristics on a strategic issue: the timing of the technologically intensive firm's entry into an emerging industry. The alternatives may usefully be grouped into four major marketing strategies, recognizing that most companies will—or should—adopt a blend of these according to the requirements of their different markets or product lines:

First to market—based on a strong R & D program, technical leadership, and risk-taking.

Follow the leader—based on strong development resources and an ability to react quickly as the market starts its growth phase.

Application engineering—based on product modifications to fit the needs of particular customers in a mature market.

"*Me too*"—based on superior manufacturing efficiency and cost control.

Each of these strategies has different strengths and weaknesses in varying competitive situations. Intelligent selection and execution of the appropriate strategy normally will strengthen the company's posture *vis-à-vis* its competitors.

FIRST TO MARKET. This risky but potentially rewarding strategy is characterized by: (a) a research intensive effort, supported by major development resources; (b) close downstream coupling in product planning, and moderately close coupling thereafter; (c) high proximity to the state of the art; (d) high R & D investment ratio; and (e) a high risk of failure for individual products. The company must recruit and retain outstanding technical personnel who can win leadership in the industry. It must keep these technical people in close and useful communication with marketing planners to identify potentially profitable markets. It must often risk large investments of time and money in technical and market development without any immediate return. It should be able to absorb mistakes, withdraw, and recoup without losing its position in other product lines. As the nature of the market becomes clear, initial plans must quickly be modified and approximation refined into precision.

Perhaps most important, top management must be able to make important judgments that relate to proper timing—whether, for example, it will be best to delay entry into the market in order to come out with a better product, thereby running the risk that someone else may get there first with a competing product. Such a company must have more than its share of long-range thinkers capable of assessing market and competitive trends in their earliest stages.

FOLLOW THE LEADER. This marketing strategy implies: (a) D-intensive technical effort, (b) moderate competence across the spectrum of relevant technologies, (c) exceptionally rapid response time in product development and marketing on the basis of finished research, (d) high downstream coupling of R & D with marketing and manufacturing, and (e) superior competitive intelligence.

The company that follows this strategy is—or should be—an organization that gets things done. It uses many interfunctional techniques, responds rapidly to change, and often seems to be in a perpetual fire drill. It has few scientists on its payroll, but some of the best development engineers available. Senior executives are at all times concerned with maintaining the right balance of strengths among the technical, marketing, and manufacturing functions so that the company can respond effectively to the leader's moves in any of these three areas.

APPLICATION ENGINEERING. This strategy requires: (a) substantial product design and engineering resources but no research and little real development, (b) ready access to product users within customer companies, (c) technically perceptive salesmen and sales engineers who work closely with product designers, (d) good product-line control to prevent costly proliferation, (e) considerable cost consciousness in deciding what applications to develop, (f) an efficiency-oriented manufacturing organization, and (g) a flair for minimizing development and manufacturing cost by using the same parts or elements in many different applications.

The applications-engineering strategy tends to avoid innovative efforts in the interest of economy. Planning is precise, assignments are clear, and new technology is introduced cautiously, well behind the economic state of the art. Return-on-investment and cash-flow calculations will be standard practice, and the entire management is profit-oriented.

"ME TOO." This strategy, which has flourished in the past decade as never before, is distinguished by: (a) no research or development; (b) strong manufacturing function, dominating product design; (c) strong price and delivery performance; and (d) ability to copy new designs quickly, modifying them only to reduce production costs.

Competing on price, taking a low margin but avoiding all development expense, a company that has adopted this approach can wreak havoc with competitors following the first-to-market or follow-the-leader strategies. The "me-too" strategy, effectively pursued, shortens the profitable period after market introduction when the leaders' margins are most substantial. The "me-too" strategy requires a "low-overhead" approach to manufacturing and administration, and a direct hard sell on price and delivery to the customer. It does not require any technical enthusiasm, nor does it aim to generate any.

Technology is here to stay. Managing it well takes no more effort than managing it poorly, and the results will be a great deal more profitable. The best way to achieve such results, we suggest, is to formulate a technological strategy based on a systematic analysis of the company's technological profile.

26. The successful innovators

David B. Hertz

Industry no longer looks upon innovation as merely desirable. Increasingly, the power to create and develop new methods and products has been recognized as a condition of survival. That innovation—whether in process, product, or means of distribution—can spur corporate profits has long been understood. That a company's position in the present competitive environment can be threatened without it has become the newer realization.

Thus, broad segments of industry strive for innovation. Companies hire scientists, increase their research budgets, and wait expectantly for exploitable discoveries to pour forth. More often than not, they are disappointed. It soon becomes apparent that simply turning loose a competent scientific team to explore new areas does not invariably produce creative action.

To discover what does give rise to such action, McKinsey & Company recently undertook an inquiry into the key elements of innovative effectiveness. To keep this study within defined limits, we examined companies that have successfully explored new conceptions through technical R & D.

The elements of successful innovation did emerge from our study, and we were also struck by two basic assumptions that *inhibit* innovation in industry. The first of these is that nothing can be done about resistance to change within organizations; the second, that the communications barrier between scientist and management must forever be unbreakable.

Historically, of course, managements and the researchers have experienced difficulties in both areas. Organizations are naturally conservative and do in fact resist change. The businessman and the scientist or engineer do often have trouble understanding each other. The differences between the two were nicely caricatured by Harvey Sherman, president of the American Society for Public Administration:

> By and large, the scientist sees the manager as a bureaucrat, paper shuffler, and parasite; an uncreative and unoriginal hack who serves as an obstacle in the way of creative people trying to do a job, and a person more interested in dollars and power than in knowledge and innovation.

The manager sees the scientist as a temperamental individualist with no skill in interpersonal relations, a narrow specialist with no interest in efficiency and economy or in the overall objectives of the enterprise, a person who looks for the right answer even in fields of human affairs where there is no single solution, who purposely makes his work mysterious and objects to all types of control, who is more interested in impressing other members of his profession than in the success of the enterprise for which he works.

Companies that manage profitably to exploit new conceptions and methods have not ignored these inherent difficulties. The difference between successful innovators and those that have not done so well in commercializing their R&D efforts may be summed up in a phrase: the former regard these difficulties as a beginning; the latter, as an end.

Managements conducting effective R&D operations seem to feel that poor communication between scientist and businessman need not be an unalterable fact of life. When such a barrier blocks the way, they insist that a path can be hacked through between laboratory and the front office. Some even seem to feel that the tension between the two may actually contribute something positive to the creative process.

Holding these beliefs, the successful innovators have experience on their side. The record proves that the spirit of science is by no means incompatible with that of business enterprise. They can point to such companies as Du Pont, IBM, Corning Glass and 3M Company, among others, where science and management working together have produced some of the most significant breakthroughs of our time. Thus, today's successful innovators recognize both the essential importance and the feasibility of drawing together and maintaining contact between the two functions—management and research—in order to make industrial innovation a continuing reality.

Once they overcame the idea that such barriers are immovable, we found that managements proved eminently capable of pushing ahead towards the breakthroughs they needed to enhance the profits and ensure the continuity of their businesses. They were then free to analyze and devise effective approaches to releasing the company's creative energies. From their successful experiences we extracted five criteria for successful innovation: (1) commitment of top management to research goals, (2) involvement of research scientists with management goals, (3) balanced selection of programs for research, (4) effective organization of manpower resources, and (5) energetic application of results obtained.

Top-management commitment

Where R&D has successfully achieved creative results, the chief executive and other top managers form an integral part of the research process.

Thus, George H. Lesch, as chief executive of Colgate-Palmolive, declared, "The research and development function is one requiring the highest priority among all my responsibilities."

Where chief executives hesitated to "interfere" with the direction the company's research scientists took, they in effect abdicated their responsibility for the future and sometimes seriously jeopardized the survival of their firms. At least one of the reasons for General Dynamics' financial disaster some years ago was the reluctance of top management to become actively and personally involved in the progress of research at one of its major divisions.

Our analysis indicates that close to half the productive research ideas developed by innovative leaders in the chemical, petroleum, and aerospace electronics industries were originally suggested by top executives rather than by researchers! It appears that managers may be better at spotting research opportunities for their own companies than they sometimes realize.

Yet this should not be surprising. Management, after all, is in the best position to see the entire picture of company operations. It also has the authority to suggest any course of action. The company scientist often feels restricted to problems that have a suitable theoretical base. In fact, if he were in the academic world his choice would be extremely narrow, centering on problems in his field clearly delineated for him by his peers and by traditional limits of inquiry. Thus, the professional scholar rarely has the orientation that would lead him to originate the kinds of tasks so frequently required for innovation in industry. Finally, only top management can keep academic means in alignment with commercial ends at each stage of the innovative process.

The task is never easy. Management of a high order will be required to identify a creative program that is at the same time a good fit to the market, the economics of the business, and the talents available, as well as to the state of the technical and scientific arts involved. Two keys to success turned up in survey interviews. First, the successful innovators have a tendency to resist negative evidence and to push on with new approaches to the problem. They refuse to take no for an answer. A few years ago, for example, the first commercial plant for the continuous casting of steel went into operation. Those responsible for this breakthrough in steelmaking did not become discouraged by the fact that engineers had been trying and failing for decades to bring the process under control.

Top-management commitment, the survey findings suggest, often entails financial commitment beyond what appear to be affordable levels. Companies that have not been successful in achieving innovation seem often overly hampered by conservatism. Scientists prefer to tackle well-defined, finite problems that appear to be solvable with the methods and evidence

310

available. Managements prefer to tackle problems that have some guarantee of payoff. These two conservative thrusts tend to restrict the innovative value of much research and development in industry. Indeed, the preference for the "safe" R&D undertaking may be one of the greatest obstacles to really significant innovation.

But when the scientist is willing to tackle problems that lack the precise definition of those in a university research laboratory, when management has proven ready to accept the significant risks that go with uncertainties in the economic-scientific world, and when both make the required commitments, the results may well exceed all expectations.

Involvement of scientists

While a company's creative drive requires management involvement, the willingness of R&D people to think in terms of the business itself also becomes crucial to success. The more business-oriented the scientist, and the more he identifies his efforts with management's objectives, the better the chances for practical progress through R&D for the company as a whole. When such identity of purpose can be shared by management and the scientific staff, technical progress and development of the business become simply two aspects of the same management process. The benefits of creating and maintaining this sense of common purpose linking laboratory and front office have been particularly evident in the aerospace industry, where top management and scientists talk each other's language as a matter of course.

In our survey we found the channels of communication between manager and scientist often clogged with irrelevancies. Where, for example, committees were set up to bring R&D people together with marketing people, they tended to talk about minor technical and procedural problems instead of focusing on business opportunities. In contrast, our survey indicates that the kind of exchange that leads to successful innovation deals with long-range objectives formulated in terms of socio-economic trends as well as technological developments.

The problem of poor communication leads directly to another of our findings: Committees restrict top-management involvement, since their members tend usually to be staff people rather than those with ultimate responsibility. Thus, by delegating innovation to a committee, management removes itself still further from the process. It runs the risk of failing to make personal commitments and maintain direct relationships with the research people involved.

Selection of programs

Innovative companies have a knack of picking the right projects for research. These are likely to be the most broadly based projects. Before settling on a research program, the innovators take into account the entire economic environment in which their companies operate. Rather than dissipate resources on short-term product modifications and improvements, they concentrate their energies on broadly conceived and forward-looking projects where the chances for significant results and real payoff seem to be the greatest. Often, the research and development programs will be tied directly to long-range planning for the business as a whole.

Most companies with a history of success in R & D judge proposed research projects in the light of three questions:

1. What technological obstacles stand in the way?

2. What economic factors in the environment will influence the profitability of successful results?

3. How soon must the problem be solved to make the project either technologically or economically practical?

These questions tend to be discussed in down-to-earth terms. There is a trend away from such older generalities as "fundamental vs. applied" or "long-term vs. short-term" research. The feeling has grown in the more advanced companies that it will be much more important to define the purpose and objective of a given project than to put it in a category. Thus, the statement of objectives has been given the highest priority in the selection of R & D projects. One electronics company, for example, distinguishes between specific and general R & D objectives in these terms:

General: to stay actively in touch with technological changes and to keep up with the pressures of technological competition.

Specific: to select specific areas in which to be a leader, recognizing that (1) in some areas a company cannot do anything, (2) there is a threshold of effort below which research would be inefficient and too slow to match competition on a specific problem, and (3) it will be better to hit specific targets hard with enough of the top people in the research organization deeply involved than to amble along at half speed across a wide spectrum.

But pinpointing objectives and keeping them up to date is only one aspect of project selection. Our survey of the successful innovators shows that along with these efforts to rationalize R & D went a robust acceptance of the risk element. As one research director puts it: "Research is a gambling game. If we play skillfully and often enough, we're bound to win a few games. And a few is all we need to win." A research group must not be afraid to take risks on ambitious goals. That this kind of boldness pays off in the long run Du Pont proved years ago with nylon and more recently with Corfam. On the other hand, if R&D has been directed only at relatively sure things, it will rarely produce a big winner.

Organizing manpower resources

With top-management support and well-selected projects, many forms of organization structure can produce adequate results. However, certain changes have taken place in the organizational aspects of research management.

Organization along functional lines is giving way, especially in the aerospace industry, to a combination of project and functional organization—often called "matrix" management. In the matrix approach, assignments are made from various functional groups to teams that consider all aspects of given technological innovation, including manufacturing and sales. This means that the business can respond quickly to research results, with the new product moving quickly to the field. Researchers can see their contributions put into practice; the research organization itself then becomes more responsive to business needs.

Thus, one aerospace company has a number of technical departments organized by discipline, such as mechanical design, propulsion systems, guidance and control, tracking and telemetry, each staffed and equipped to work in depth in each of these areas. As projects are launched, specialists can be drawn from each of the disciplines as required, and in this way a project team is brought together. Team members can work closely in the project and still draw on the resources of the various technical departments.

Matrix management both develops specialists and makes generalists out of specialists by broadening the individuals. Also, specialists can work on several projects at one time. Despite the fact that a man ends up having several bosses, the resulting flexibility seems to pay off handsomely.

In this same vein, a trend has developed toward "flatter" research organizations, using fewer titles and levels. For example, one successful chemical industry laboratory has only two titles: "Member of the Research Staff" and "Associate Member of the Research Staff." The title "Project Leader" is disappearing from the hierarchy of permanent ranks, continuing in use only as an administrative device. That is, leaders are selected for projects from various ranks in the organization, but not permanently assigned to the leadership role.

There is a subtle interaction between the ability to utilize research personnel effectively and freedom in selecting projects. As already noted, management can—with its scientists—work on whatever line of research it chooses. But, as with the alchemists of old, the problem may easily turn out to be a mismatch for the talents and abilities available. And this, our

313

interviews suggested, has too often been the case. When problems are too difficult, too specialized, or too broad, no solutions will be found. When the selected research project is discovered to be too simple, the result will usually be waste and frustration. Thus, successful innovators consistently try to keep R&D goals and personnel resources in balance.

Our study also shows a marked effort by the more advanced companies to achieve flexibility and mobility in the assignment of R&D personnel. At least one company attempts to change its project and departmental teams as often as practical. As the research director puts it: "If a team has existed for four years, it is probably stale. We find that after 18 months it's about time for change."

Finally, it has become increasingly obvious that a key to innovative success is constant evaluation of research personnel. Researchers not making a substantial contribution to the effort must either be trained to higher effectiveness or dropped from the team. The best researchers will sooner or later be reassigned to higher responsibilities. Ranking scientific personnel not only seems to keep the staff strong but provides management with a guide in making assignments. In terms of this guide, researchers can be assigned technical challenges that will be within their scope and at the same time profitable to the enterprise.

Where projects have been well chosen but little progress is evident, a number of companies give up on the team before giving up on the project. Thus, rather than terminate a significant project, the team will be reassigned and a new group formed to tackle the problem. But most companies agree that an important part of successful research is knowing when to terminate projects and then having the courage to do so.

Application of results

Successful innovation requires that the results of the R&D effort be put to use. Today, more of an effort is being made to apply results, techniques, and findings not only in one but in many projects, so that each laboratory effort may make the greatest possible contribution to the overall research effort. Several companies do their best to apply the findings and techniques developed in each project to other projects. Thus, the results of an apparently unsuccessful effort may contribute to another project's success. The more industries in which a company participates, of course, the greater the chance that such an effort will be profitable.

But the success of a research project is not concluded in the laboratory. It results from having someone push the innovation through to production and sales. And often a real push is needed since most projects have more opponents than proponents, particularly after the outcome of research begins to emerge. The problem is to persuade people in marketing and manufacturing actually to make the innovation. One company facilitates this process by having its R & D people give regular progress briefings and an outline of future requirements to marketing and manufacturing personnel. This avoids the need for long reports, and at the same time conditions key personnel to begin accepting results early.

Some companies have also established commercial development departments within research organizations for two purposes: first, to facilitate transfer of research findings from the laboratory to managers responsible for commercializing these findings; and second, to develop new businesses unrelated to current operating divisions. These departments are staffed with people from all functional areas—marketing, engineering, research, manufacturing, finance, planning, etc. Their essential goal is to develop *new* sales dollars rather than replacement sales dollars.

Several approaches have been devised to facilitate transfer of research findings to practical application. To avoid manufacturing delays, some companies have provided for a manufacturing development budget, separate from the manufacturing and technical budgets. These funds are used to finance or "buy" plant time and facilities. This also lessens the tendency for manufacturing to want to be in charge of the trials. Other companies bring into the project in its early stages a "continuation engineer" responsible for manufacturing methods (usually a manufacturing or methods engineer) who reports to the project leader while the special undertaking lasts.

A particularly effective approach has been employed by a diversified electronics company: As soon as possible after a new phenomenon is discovered or a theory developed in exploratory research, product and process development engineers are brought in from other parts of the organization. In this way, practical application begins at an early stage.

Another approach to transfer of results utilizes researchers in operations. For example, at a refinery or in a chemical company, the researcher who worked on the pilot plan is assigned to work full time with the operating people until the unit goes on-stream. When field trials are carried out, the researcher is temporarily assigned to manufacturing or marketing.

One company has laboratory management send monthly reports to operating people—including the company president—giving only the highlights of the research. Here the idea is to file short reports rather than highly technical and detailed reports—which few if any will read. (The details, of course, are made available to anyone interested.) With this system, the company has found, working papers can be kept on file and few long reports are necessary. Significant savings of time and money result.

Double exposure needed

In summary, our analysis of successful R & D programs indicates that innovators should be judged as important on the exploitation and development side of the picture as on the research side. The successful way of achieving this kind of inventiveness has been to expose researchers to other company activities and to expose marketing and manufacturing people to research.

There are signs, moreover, of inventiveness in means as well as ends. The more advanced companies constantly assess the R & D apparatus itself, searching for better ways to organize and staff it, to relate its functions and its goals to the economic as well as the technological context within which the industry operates.

Our overall impression of successful industrial innovators is that they are whole men. While they recognize that specialization must be considered inescapable in the current state of technological development, they insist that the head innovator in a business must be the head of the business. If, in today's competitive environment, corporate survival depends on innovative capability, this capability hinges on the willingness of top management to provide impetus, direction, coordination and control to research. Without this leadership, R & D tends to become diffuse and ineffectual; with it, new products and processes and whole new markets have been and can be created over the years, almost as a matter of routine.

27. R&D as a partner in world enterprise

David B. Hertz

Conspicuous among the problems facing today's world enterprise has been the task of managing international technology—achieving centralized co-ordination and control over a decentralized multinational network of research laboratories.

Not long ago, most companies carried on all their real research in one place, and technology could be effectively and profitably transferred from country to country by such devices as simple cross-licensing. But with the growth of world enterprises, business has discovered that the demands of the new and increasingly competitive worldwide markets cannot be met by confining research and development and commercialization to one country and then simply exporting the results. More and more companies have stopped merely exporting the products of their own research and buying foreign technologies. Instead, they have begun to produce and market simultaneously in countries around the world, adapting their operations and product lines to local raw materials and markets.

American corporations have perhaps led the way in establishing multi-national R&D, but effective results have also been attained by other companies in Europe and Japan. Industries in the Netherlands and Belgium, for example, have been developing in an international direction for some time—partly of necessity, since they had no research facilities of their own at the end of World War II. More and more, companies in Germany and England have opted to become worldwide enterprisers. Swiss and Italian firms are joining the parade in growing numbers. Among the world enterprises committed to international technology (including the establishment of laboratories in the United States) are Shell, Phillips, Unilever, Geigy, CIBA, Hoffman La Roche, Hitachi, and Volkswagen. These international enterprises view full participation in a country's economy—which means, among other things, the encouragement of local decision making in marketing, manufacturing, and technology—as their fundamental long-run objective. Through their efforts the way is being paved for genuine international progress in developing products and processes suited to local requirements.

Nevertheless, international technology remains in a state of flux. Some companies have avoided developing a truly international technology because they do not want to become involved in the tricky task of managing multinational laboratories. Others have limited themselves to buying technological assistance in selected fields abroad to complement their domestic laboratory work. Still others have relied simply on keeping in touch with developments in important universities and industrial laboratories overseas.

Why international R&D?

To understand why some companies have moved into the forefront of international R&D, while others have decided to limit international research activities and hope for the best, one must consider the motives of the companies now engaged in this effort. It will also be useful to review the obstacles that must be surmounted if they—and others who follow in their footsteps—are to benefit fully from their efforts.

Among those companies already engaged in such activities (or planning to establish them) five reasons are most frequently cited for developing an international R&D capability:

1. To take advantage of skills and talents not available in a single country. There has been a growing awareness in business around the world that no country has a monopoly on new scientific and engineering developments. In the aftermath of World War II, with the European scientific community in disarray and many research installations destroyed, the promise of interesting work and the large-scale facilities available across the Atlantic resulted in a significant migration of European scientists and a consequent upsurge of basic research in the United States. Today, the flow has greatly abated. Despite the so-called technology gap, Europe has once again become the equal of the United States in most areas of basic science.

Nearly every country boasts research scientists in some field at least the equal of their counterparts in other countries. England has superlative neurophysiologists and biochemists; Germany leads in certain areas of chemical synthesis; France is perhaps unsurpassed in the field of pharmacology; and Italy and Austria are making valuable contributions in the mechanical sciences. And for the European companies branching out as world enterprises, the United States offers some unique talent in electronics, aeronautics, and applied petrochemical engineering.

2. To establish "listening posts" and benefit from differences in research philosophy and approaches. If important work has, in fact, been going on in almost every country, it follows that a company may have much to gain from strengthening its "technological intelligence" network. This does not mean the use of cloak-and-dagger espionage techniques. It means establishing national R & D centers staffed by nationals to keep up with the innovations being developed by local competitors and with commercial intelligence in general.

Smith, Kline & French was especially interested in doing this when it decided to go to Europe for some research work. In addition to its research institute in Britain, which management regards as a "window on research," this company maintains a team of "finders" who keep searching for promising research results in noncompeting pharmaceutical companies. As a result, Smith, Kline & French has made significant formal agreements to trade findings and information with companies such as Rhone-Poulenc. Among the fruits of these exchanges has been the development of thorazine, the precursor of the tranquilizing drugs used in severe mental disorders.

Du Pont, despite its decision not to establish foreign research facilities, has found other ways to maintain listening posts and benefit from varied research philosophies and approaches. For example, it regularly brings visiting professors from European and Japanese universities to its own laboratories. Du Pont also provides unencumbered grants to various scientists outside the United States.

Other companies, too, are convinced that they can significantly boost the quality of their research efforts by promoting the exchange not only of information, but of research philosophies and approaches. U.S. research has often been indicted for undue preoccupation with commercially useful results, to the detriment of fundamental research, while many European scientists and engineers have been vulnerable to the opposite charge. Although one may take issue with these generalizations, few would deny that attitudes toward research do differ among countries, or that corporate research efforts can be strengthened by mating these complementary approaches.

3. *To take advantage of lower costs.* Lower costs may not be the primary motive for engaging in research in more than one country, but they have often been cited by U.S. companies as the reason for establishing R & D facilities in Europe. On the average, it has been estimated that it costs a company between $50,000 and $60,000 a year to maintain and equip one scientist in the United States today, as against perhaps $30,000 to $40,000 in Europe, where research salaries are lower and laboratory equipment and space less expensive.

Apart from realizing direct savings in salaries and overhead, U.S. companies in some countries are permitted to conserve their profits by using the foreign R & D establishment as a profit repository. And the U.S. tax laws make ownership of patents and know-how rights by foreign subsidiaries of U.S. companies extremely useful.

4. *To support overseas manufacturing and sales operations.* As companies grow from mere exporters into multinational enterprises with foreign markets that equal or even surpass their domestic markets, they find it increasingly important, even essential, to build up coordinated research programs that will help them adapt to local raw materials and to develop new products for particular markets. This is why several major international corporations have established design and technical service facilities, and in some instances entire R & D organizations, in their major plants abroad.

The Ford Motor Company found it could not successfully handle the technical requirements of its Dagenham plant from Detroit. The American approach to automobile design had proved inappropriate in England, and the excellent design ideas of British engineers and scientists were being lost in the transfer from England to Detroit and back to England. Ford resolved these problems by establishing a sizable research center in Birmingham, England.

5. *To promote the development of local economies.* Multinational R & D makes a unique contribution to the political, competitive, and social environment of the countries in which it has been established. First, it provides stimulating projects and the opportunity to visit, work in, and exchange information with the company's other laboratories. Second, a multinational R & D establishment can often motivate important scientists to stay in their own countries, provide the incentive for additional training, and generally enhance the prestige and importance of local scientific communities.

Obstacles to results

All these may be good reasons for establishing an international R & D capability—yet not all the corporations that have moved into international R & D have succeeded in persuading a large multinational network of scientists to work closely and effectively together. Disappointment with results, in fact, has led some of these companies to reduce the scope of their research efforts outside the parent country.

To explore the reasons why, McKinsey & Company interviewed senior research executives and top corporate officers in a number of these companies. In composite, their difficulties seemed to stem from three principal failings, each capable of fatally undermining a company's efforts to coordinate a group of international laboratories.

The first critical weakness that came to light in our interviews was insufficient consideration of the real reasons why the enterprise needed international technology, and what form that technology should take. As we have seen, many companies have established laboratories in other countries because they were dazzled by the promises of lower costs, untapped talent, and exciting new techniques. But some have not really thought through the risks and limitations of their approaches to international technology.

For example, many companies take it for granted that research costs will be lower in Europe. Yet we found no company willing to put a dollar value on the savings. Indeed, some research executives believed that such savings are largely cancelled out by the costs of running a research program from a distance. Others noted that lower equipment costs in some cases simply mean less sophisticated equipment.

Again, the wisdom of locating R & D facilities in a particular country because of its depth of scientific talent in one field or another cannot always be taken for granted. Yet even large companies with broad international interests of long standing too easily accept certain generalizations concerning science and scientists in other countries. For instance, it has been argued that Americans, for all their tremendous ability to develop and exploit ideas, lack the genius for basic scientific discovery. The Nobel physicist I. I. Rabi has asserted that "behind almost every major innovation, one can find a Frenchman if one digs far enough." And as we all know, the Soviets insist that behind most innovations we can find a Russian—even without digging very far. Such generalizations make a poor basis for decisions on the location of R & D facilities, for the truth is that ideas can be generated anywhere in the world as long as conditions remain favorable and the likelihood of acceptance fairly high.

Picking a locale for development

To be sure, scientific and technological circumstances may make one country the most appropriate place for a given innovation at a particular time, but this does not mean it will necessarily be the best place for the innovation's development. For widespread commercialization, research and development may have to be done in different countries simultaneously. Undoubtedly, some corporations that have sponsored laboratories in a new country primarily to gain access to the talent there have subsequently found these laboratories unproductive—perhaps because the environment was uncongenial to innovation or development. The experience of several companies suggests that, in selecting the place for a new laboratory, marketing and production considerations, rather than the presence of a reputedly superior scientific pool of talent, may be the key to the best decision.

Failure to define and assess its reasons for establishing an international

R&D organization often leads a company to establish a technological network that does not really meet its needs. Many of the companies that have set up R&D organizations abroad without sufficient regard to the conditions of the marketplace have ended up with mere product-testing and technical service organizations. For instance, one major petroleum company, which does all its basic research in a single country, has a large technical service laboratory attached to each of its sizable foreign affiliates in Germany, England, France, and Italy, and a smaller laboratory in Japan, yet it uses them only to support the simplest of its local operations— testing alternative formulations of lubricants and fuel. These laboratories may not even be good listening posts, since the company has established a special European office solely to keep abreast of current scientific developments there.

In contrast, a number of companies have been able to take advantage of international technical capabilities by clarifying in detail the sort of technological network that would serve their best interests. Several years ago, for example, the Imperial Smelting Corporation (the U.K. subsidiary of the RTZ group) scored a major breakthrough in the manufacture of zinc by replacing the vertical retort with a blast furnace. Rather than sell the process outright or build overseas plants of its own, it elected to license the process throughout the world. Its licensing agreement, based on tons of zinc produced, contains a carefully worded "exchange of know-how" clause. Thus, the company has on record every ton of zinc produced by means of its new process throughout the world. In addition, Imperial Smelting receives complete data on operating variables, raw material, and composition. At an annual seminar the company holds for all its licensees, technical people from all over the world present papers describing developments and improvements made during the previous year.

Obviously, one of a company's most critical difficulties in developing a sound management policy for international technology will be that of defining objectives. This entails (1) clearly defining the desired end products and the projects to be carried out, (2) realistically facing up to the problems and limitations likely to be encountered, and (3) carefully assessing the place utility and functional utility of the projects and the laboratory network. Finally, definition must be followed by action: a readiness to commit the money and manpower resources required to establish and maintain the network.

Blindness to national differences

The second critical weakness we discovered in exploring the history of companies disappointed with the results of international R&D was a failure to recognize and adapt to important national differences in cultural

322

and scientific background. Much has been said in recent years about the importance of recognizing national differences in habits, temperaments, and cultural backgrounds when working with people in other countries. This would seem obvious enough. Yet in many instances such differences have been ignored by management.

The language barrier presents one difficulty of this sort—though hardly the most serious. True, it can hamper the communication of research results, but there are ways to cope with this problem. For instance, the German scientists in one American company's German laboratory helped prepare English-language definitions of certain basic terms from scientific German. Then they translated these English definitions into German. The German definitions were revised to express the ideas more accurately and completely, and were then retranslated into English. The resulting English definitions provided the basis for clear-cut communications on a technical plane.

More important that the language barrier, cultural differences come up in problem-solving approaches. For example, output-oriented American managements often find it hard to tolerate the apparently academic outlook of European scientists, while the latter may regard the American enthusiasm for deadlines, standards, multiple testing, and detailed tabulations of experimental data as a waste of time and talent.

Less easily defined, but exceedingly important to a successful understanding of international scientific productivity, will be national variations in attitudes toward scientists and differences in the working atmospheres of American and European laboratories. The easygoing spirit of an American researcher is often disconcerting to the scientist who has been brought up in the German or Swiss laboratory tradition. And the caginess of a French researcher who learned as a student to build walls around himself in order to protect new findings from his own professor may well irritate his outgoing American colleagues.

Different approaches to disseminating information can create serious misunderstanding among members of a multinational research group. The readiness with which many American research organizations open their doors to visitors would be unthinkable in the typical European laboratory, where research is kept strictly confidential until results are ready for publication. In fact, the European scientist may often be reluctant to release information for distribution within the corporate structure itself, and U.S. companies frequently complain that their own foreign subsidiaries lower a curtain of secrecy against their inquiries.

Developing common standards for measuring performance will be one of the most difficult tasks facing the management of an international technological establishment, since performance standards differ from country to country. The language of science makes a chemist's results the same in

Texas as in Rotterdam, but the language of culture creates marked differences in determining the way in which those results are developed, accepted, and coordinated.

Managing an international research technology requires sensitivity in dealing with all these cultural variations. A good deal of effort must be expended on matters ranging from the format of business cards and titles to employment and pension policy. Still, with care and thought, these differences can be resolved.

Deficient management systems

The third reason for many of the disappointments suffered by companies with international technological establishments may be found, our interviews suggest, in lack of an adequate system for managing the R & D network. Experience with more successful companies indicates that three elements will be essential to an effective management and control system:

Centralized decision making. To keep research and development projects in line with corporate objectives and to avoid wasteful duplication of effort, someone must make coordinated decisions governing the programs to be undertaken, how they should be distributed, and how resources are to be allocated for the best results.

Clear channels of communication. Management must maintain effective communication with researchers in the field to provide better guidance on program development and to assure corporation-wide understanding of research and development needs.

Consistent performance standards and control mechanisms. R & D management needs common standards to measure performance accurately throughout the organization and to make program changes where they are needed. Results must also be communicated in a consistent form so that management can put together an accurate picture of how research is progressing and quickly pinpoint problems and opportunities.

Incorporating these elements into an integrated management and control system for a multinational R & D network can never be easy. In centralizing the power of decision making, top management runs the risk of imposing too much control on the individual laboratories. Communications problems arising from national differences may be compounded by distance. Much time and patience will be required to develop common performance standards acceptable to scientists with divergent cultural backgrounds and training.

Developing a coordinated management and control system will not in itself, of course, ensure success in international R & D. Management systems do not guarantee effective control; they only provide the tools. Once management has recognized the need for these tools and committed the resources to obtain them, it must follow through by incorporating them into its everyday administrative and decision-making processes. Managers at every level must see to it that each laboratory is adequately staffed by a number of talented, properly trained people who—whatever their differences—understand, accept, and actively support the objectives of the corporate program.

Once all these requirements have been met, international technology will be on its way to becoming a full-fledged partner in international enterprise.

28. The promise of project management

John M. Stewart

Several years ago, with a good deal of fanfare, a leading food producer opened a new plant in a small Midwestern town. For the community it was a festive day. For top management the celebration was somewhat dampened by the fact that the plant had missed its original target date by six months and had overrun estimated costs by a cool $5 million.

A material-handling equipment maker's latest automatic lift truck was an immediate market success. But its introduction cost—$2.6 million, compared to planned expenses of $1.2 million—cut the company's profits by fully 10 percent last year.

A new press installed by a leading Eastern printing concern has enabled a major consumer magazine to increase the number of its color pages and offer advertisers unprecedented schedule convenience. But developing and installing the press took twice as long and cost nearly three times as much as the printer had expected. It will be years before his investment shows a profit.

Fiascoes such as these are as old as business itself—as old, indeed, as organized human effort. The unfortunate Egyptian overseer who had to tell King Cheops that construction work on the Great Pyramid at Giza had fallen a year behind schedule had much in common with the vice president who winces as he and the chief executive discover that it will be September before their new plant can deliver the production contracted for in June. The common thread: poor management of a large, complex, one-time undertaking.

Unlike the Egyptian overseer, today's businessman has available to him a set of new and powerful management tools with the demonstrated capacity to avert time and cost overruns on massive, complex projects. These tools, developed only recently, are not yet in common use outside the construction and aerospace industries, where such projects are a way of life. But we already have solid evidence that they can be successfully applied to a host of important, nonroutine business undertakings ranging from a new-product introduction or the launching of a national advertising

326

campaign to the installation of an EDP system or a merger of two major corporations.

Project management organization

Commercial project management is usually a compromise between two basic forms of organization—pure project management and the more standard functional alignment. Most construction companies, as well as divisions of aerospace manufacturers, give a single manager full responsibility for the project and full control over the resources needed for its accomplishment. During the lifespan of the undertaking, he may head up an organization comparable in scale and structure to a regular division—and relatively independent of any other division or staff group.

In contrast, *outside* the aerospace and construction industries, the project manager is usually not assigned complete responsibility for resources. Instead, he must share them with the rest of the organization. He may have a project organization consisting of a handful of men on temporary assignment from the regular functional organization. But the functional managers retain their direct line authority, monitor their staffs' contributions to the project, and continue to make all major personnel decisions.

New tools and techniques seldom win acceptance overnight, and those of project management have been no exception. Indeed, few business executives outside the aerospace and construction industries yet appreciate their value and versatility. Fewer still have been able to recognize the need for project management in specific situations, or to apply the powerful control techniques it offers. Meanwhile, the few companies that have learned to apply the new management concepts now enjoy an extraordinary, if perhaps temporary, advantage. They are bringing new products to market faster than their competitors, completing major expansions on schedule, and meeting crucial commitments more reliably than ever before.

When is a project a project? Where, in the broad spectrum of undertakings between a minor procedural modification and a major organizational upheaval, should the line be drawn? At what point do a multitude of minor departures from routine add up to the "critical mass" that makes project management operationally and economically desirable?

Although we have no simple rules of thumb, management usually can determine whether a given undertaking possesses this critical mass by applying four yardsticks: scope, unfamiliarity, complexity, and stake.

SCOPE. Project management can be profitably applied, as a rule, to a one-time undertaking (1) definable in terms of a single, specific end result, and (2) greater in size and complexity than any other that the organization has previously undertaken successfully. A project must, by definition, have a terminus: the date the new plant achieves full production, the date th parent company takes over operating management of the new acquisition, or the date the new product goes on sale in supermarkets across the nation.

The question of size is less easily pinned down. But where substantially more people, more dollars, more organizational units, and more time will be involved than in any other infrequent undertaking in the organization's experience, the test result is clearly positive. Such an undertaking, even though its component parts may be familiar, can easily baffle a divisional or corporate management. Project management enforces a logical approach to the new challenge, speeds decision-making, and cuts management's job to a reasonable level. For example, a large service company with years of experience in renovating district offices established a project organization to renovate its 400 district offices over a two-year period. Even though each task was relatively simple, the total undertaking would have swamped the administrative organization had it been managed routinely.

In terms of the number of people and the organizational effort it involves, a project could typically be charted over time as a wave-like curve, rising gradually to a crest and dropping off abruptly with the accomplishment of the end result. Consider, for example, the introduction of a new consumer product. The project begins with a few people studying the desirability of adding a product to the line. After some early decisions to proceed, perhaps a few dozen engineers will be employed to design the product. Their work passes to scores of process planners, tool makers, and other manufacturing engineers, and finally involves entire manufacturing plants or divisions as the first month's production gains momentum. This momentum carries into the field as salesmen increase their effort to introduce the product successfully. Finally, the project effort ebbs as the new product becomes integrated into routine production and marketing operation.

Again, a merger typically shows a similar "growth and decay" project pattern. Initially, a few senior executives from each company may be involved in discussing the merger possibility. As interest grows, financial and legal advisors are engaged by both sides. Key inside executives will be added to the task force to assist in planning. Then, as the deal moves toward completion, widening circles of executives, technical people, and analysts become engaged in identifying the changes required after merger. Once the merger has been approved by the directors and stockholders of the two companies, the process of meshing the philosophies, structures, policies, and procedures of the two organizations must begin, possibly requiring the active participation of hundreds or even thousands of people. Eventually, as most of the changes are accomplished, employees return to their normal duties, and the corporation resumes its orderly march toward the end of the fiscal year. The merger project has come to an end.

UNFAMILIARITY. Outside the aerospace and construction industries, a project will by definition be a unique or infrequent effort by the existing management group. Lack of familiarity or lack of precedent usually leads to disagreement or uncertainty as to how the undertaking should be managed. Senior executives become more worried than usual about the realism of initial cost estimates and time commitments, and people at lower management levels need to be told more precisely what to do.

Thus, though a single engineering change in one part of a product would not qualify for project management, the complete redesign and market reintroduction of a product line that had been basically unchanged for a decade almost certainly would.

COMPLEXITY. Frequently, the decisive criterion defining a project comes down to the degree of interdependence among tasks. If a given task depends on the completion of other assignments in other functional areas, and if it will, in turn, affect the cost or timing of subsequent tasks, project management will probably be called for.

Consider the introduction of a new product such as a farm tractor. Sales promotion plans cannot be completed until introduction dates are known; introduction dates depend upon product availability; and availability depends on tooling, which depends, say, on the outcome of a disagreement between engineering and product planning over performance specification. Beyond this, many conflicting opinions may be voiced concerning interdependent approaches to marketing, engineering, manufacturing, and finance. If, as seems likely, no one person can produce a properly detailed plan on which all concerned can agree; if estimates repeatedly fail to withstand scrutiny; or if plans submitted by different departments prove difficult to reconcile or coordinate, the critical mass requiring a special project has probably been reached.

STAKE. A final criterion that may tip the scales in favor of project management will be the organization's stake in the outcome. Would failure to complete the job on schedule or within the budget entail serious penalties for the company? If so, the case for project management is strong.

The corporate stake will, of course, generally be financial; for example, the failure of a $50,000 engineering project might jeopardize $12 million in annual sales. But costs of a different kind may also be involved: for example, failure to meet a well-publicized project schedule can damage a company's reputation. Again, failure to meet time and cost objectives may seriously disrupt corporate plans. Not long ago, one manufacturer was obliged to abandon a promising new product line when a poorly managed merger soaked up earnings that had been earmarked for R & D on the new line. In all such instances, the powerful controls of project management offer a much firmer prospect of meeting the time, cost, and quality objectives of the major one-time undertaking.

The nature of project management

Project management provides, above all, the concentrated attention that a complex and unfamiliar undertaking is likely to demand. At very small cost, it greatly improves the chances of on-time, on-budget completion, and it permits the rest of the organization to proceed normally with routine business while the project is under way. But these benefits can be realized only if top management clearly understands the unique features of project management and the steps required to make it work.

This means, first of all, appointing one man, the project manager, with full responsibility for the detailed planning, coordination, and ultimate outcome of the undertaking. Usually drawn from the middle-management ranks, the project manager will be supplied with a team, often numbering no more than half a dozen men for a $10 million project.

Team members, drawn from the various functional departments involved in the project, report directly to this newly assigned executive. For the duration of the project, he has the authority to insist on thorough planning, the freedom to challenge functional departments' assumptions and targets, and the responsibility for monitoring every effort bearing on the project.

Within the framework of the project, his responsibility and authority will be interfunctional, like that of top management for the company as a whole. Hence, the project must be his full-time job. This function *cannot* safely be superimposed on a top executive's regular work load. Every division manager I have known who has been assigned operating responsibility for the management of a complex project has found himself swamped in a tidal wave of detail. Projects call for more and faster decisions than does routine work, and clear precedents are usually lacking. Thus, a general manager who tries to run one of his own projects seldom has any guidelines for making reliable cost and time estimates, establishing cost control at commitment points, or setting adequately detailed targets for each department. Lacking precedents, he is obliged to invent them. This procedure may drain off far more of his time and energy than the division can afford, without really providing the project with the concentrated attention it needs. He may well find that he is spending better than half his working time trying to manage a project representing less than a tenth of his division's annual budget, while divisional performance as a whole slips alarmingly. For these reasons, few substantial projects have ever been successfully managed on a part-time basis.

By its very nature, project management cuts across the established

330

organization structure, demanding contributions from personnel at various levels in many functions of the business. Because a project usually requires decisions and actions from a number of functional areas at once, the main interdependencies and the main flow of information in a project come to be not vertical but lateral. Up-and-down information flow will be relatively light in a well-run project. Indeed, any attempt consistently to send needed information from one functional area up to a common authority and down to another area through conventional channels will be apt to cripple the project and wreck the time schedule. In most organizations, the normal information flow will simply be too slow to meet project management needs.

Interfunctional teamwork

Projects are also characterized by exceptionally strong lateral working relationships, requiring close coordination among many individuals in different functional departments. During a major product development program, a design engineer will work more closely with the process engineering manager and the product manager from marketing than with the senior members of his own department. He will need common sense and tolerance to succeed in the scramble for available resources, such as test-cell time or the help of metallurgical specialists, without hurting relationships of considerable importance to him in his future career.

Necessarily, though, a project will have a vertical as well as a horizontal dimension. At various stages, those involved in it—particularly in making the technical decisions that determine costs—must often go to their superiors for guidance. Frequent project changes also underline the necessity of keeping senior executives informed of the project's current status.

Special sources of trouble

Understandably, project managers face some unusual challenges in trying to direct and harmonize the diverse forces under their direction. Their main difficulties arise from three sources: organizational uncertainties, unusual decision pressures, and vulnerability to mistakes at the top.

ORGANIZATIONAL UNCERTAINTIES. Many newly appointed project managers find that their working relationships with functional department heads have not been clearly defined by management. Who assigns work to the financial analyst? Who decides when to order critical material before the project design is firm? Who decides to hold back design release in order to reduce unit cost? Who determines the quantity and priority of spares? All these decisions vitally concern the project manager, and he must often create his own guidelines for dealing with them. Unless he does so skillfully, the questions are apt to be resolved in the interest of individual departments, at the expense of the project as a whole.

Because of the number of decisions or approvals that almost inevitably arise in the course of a large project—and the number of departments that have an interest in each—the possibility of inderdepartmental conflicts will always be present. At issue may be such matters as priority of spare parts, urgency of design release, new product features, or the need to make engineering changes after field testing. Besides coping with these conflicts, the project manager must juggle the internal schedules of each department with the project schedule, avoid political problems that could create bottlenecks, expedite the work of one department to compensate for another's failure to meet its schedule, and hold the project within a predetermined cost. He must do all this single-handedly, with little or none of the experienced top-management guidance that the line manager enjoys.

UNUSUAL DECISION PRESSURES. The severe penalties incurred by delay often compel the project manager to base his decisions on relatively scant data, analyzed in haste. On a large project, a day's delay may cost $10,000 in salaries alone. The manager can hardly hold everything up for a week to perform an analysis that could save the company $5,000. He must move fast, even if this means going ahead with an intuitive decision that might expose him to charges of rashness and irresponsibility. Decisions to sacrifice time for cost, cost for quality, or quality for time are common in most projects, and the project manager must be able to make them without panicking. Clearly, therefore, he has a special need for support from higher management.

VULNERABILITY TO TOP-MANAGEMENT MISTAKES. Senior executives can easily jeopardize the project's success by lack of awareness, ill-advised intervention, or personal whim. Consider this example: A project manager, battling to meet a schedule that had been rendered nearly impossible by the general manager's initial delay in approving the proposal, found it more and more difficult to obtain the cooperation he needed from the functional executives. He later learned that two of these executives whom he had pressured to expedite contributions to the project from their departments had privately complained to the general manager. Receiving a sympathetic reaction, they sensed that the project manager lacked top-level support—an impression which soon became general. The manager, meanwhile, had been too busy getting the job done to protect himself in the corporate in-fighting. As a result, performance was seriously hampered. The great diversity of projects and the lack of common terminology for the

The great diversity of projects and the lack of common terminology for the relatively new techniques of project management make a detailed general prescription for success hard to formulate. Still, from the experience of the aerospace and construction industries as well as a handful of companies in other industries, three general guidelines emerge.

Guideline 1: define the objective

Performing unfamiliar activities at a rapid pace, those involved in the project can easily get off the right track or fall short of meeting their commitments. If this happens, many steps of the project may have to be retraced. To minimize the risk, management must clarify the objective of the project well in advance by (1) defining the reasons for undertaking it; (2) outlining its scope by identifying the departments, companies, functions, and staffs involved, and the approximate degree of their involvement; and (3) describing the desired end result and its permanent effects, if any, on the company or division.

DEFINING MANAGEMENT'S INTENT. What are the business considerations governing the project?

A clear answer is essential—for three reasons. First, it enables the manager to capitalize on opportunities to improve on the results of the project. To take a random example, knowing top management's rationale for building the new plant, he will be able to weigh the one-time cost of plant start-up against the continuing advantage of lower production costs, or the competitive edge that might be gained by an earlier product introduction.

Second, a clear definition of intent helps avert damaging oversights that would otherwise appear unimportant to lower level managers and might not be obvious to the senior executive. One company failed to secure any repeat orders for a unique product because the project team, unaware of the president's intent, worried only about meeting its schedule and cost commitments and paid little attention to the customer's future needs.

Third, clarifying the intent of the project helps to avoid misdirected efforts at the middle-management level, such as pushing desperately to meet a schedule but missing cost-reduction opportunities on the way.

OUTLINING THE SCOPE OF THE PROJECT. Which organizational units of the company will be involved in the undertaking, and to what degree? Which sensitive customer relationships, private or governmental, should the project manager cautiously skirt? By crystallizing the answers and communicating them to the organization, the responsible senior executive will make it far easier for the project manager to work with the functional departments and to obtain the information he needs.

DESCRIBING THE END RESULT. Top managers who have spent hours discussing a proposed project may easily forget that the middle managers charged with its execution lack their breadth of perspective. An explicit description of how a new plant will operate when it goes into full production, how a sales reorganization will actually change customer relationships, or how major staff activities will be coordinated after a merger gives middle managers a much clearer view of what the project will involve and what is expected of them.

Guideline 2: organize the project

For a functionally organized company, successful project management means establishing a workable compromise between two quite different organizational concepts. This involves (1) appointing one experienced manager to direct the project full-time, (2) organizing the project management function in terms of responsibilities, (3) assigning a limited number of men to the project team, and (4) maintaining a balance of power between the functional heads and the project manager.

ASSIGNING AN EXPERIENCED MANAGER. Though the project manager's previous experience may have been confined to a single functional area of the business, he should be capable of operating as a kind of general manager in miniature. He must not only keep track of what is happening, but also play the crucial role of advocate for the project. Even for a seasoned manager, this task is not likely to be easy. Hence, it becomes important to assign an individual whose administrative ability and skill in working with people have been tested under fire.

ORGANIZING THE PROJECT MANAGER'S RESPONSIBILITIES. While some organizational change will be necessary, management should try to preserve, wherever possible, the established relationships that facilitate rapid progress under pressure. Experience indicates the wisdom of senior management delegating to the project manager some of its responsibilities for planning the project, for resolving disagreements among functional departments, for providing assistance to functional heads, and for monitoring progress. But the general manager should not delegate authority to monitor milestone accomplishments, resolve project-related disputes between senior managers, or evaluate the project performance of functional department managers—a responsibility that strikes too close to the careers of those concerned to be delegated to one of their peers.

The project manager should also hold some responsibilities normally borne by functional department heads. These include reviewing progress against schedule; organizing for, formulating, and approving a project plan; monitoring project cost performance; and, in place of the department heads normally involved, trading off time and cost. Also, the senior executive must encourage the project manager to direct the day-to-day activities of all functional personnel who are involved full-time in the project. Functional department heads, meanwhile, should retain responsibility for the quality of their subordinates' technical performance, as well as for matters affecting their careers.

LIMITING THE PROJECT TEAM. Functional department heads may view the project manager as a possible competitor for their jobs, or at least as a threat to their stature. By limiting the number of men on the project team,

334

this difficulty can be alleviated and the project manager's involvement in intrafunctional matters reduced.

MAINTAINING THE BALANCE OF POWER. Because the project manager must concern himself with change, while the department head continues as before to manage routine procedures, the two will often be in active conflict. Though they should be encouraged to resolve these disputes without constant appeals to higher authority, their common superior will occasionally act as mediator. Otherwise, resentments and frustrations will impair the project's advancement and leave behind a legacy of bitterness. Short-term conflicts can often be resolved in favor of the project manager and long-term conflicts in favor of the functional managers. This compromise helps get the job done with a minimum of friction.

Guideline 3: install project controls

Though they make use of the same raw data as routine reports, special project controls over time, cost, and quality differ greatly in their accuracy, timing, and use. Normally they will be superimposed upon the existing report structure for the duration of the project and then discontinued.

The crucial relationship between project time control and cost control is illustrated in the graph on page 336. This project, to build a new assembly plant and start production, had to be completed in 20 months instead of the $20\frac{1}{2}$ months scheduled by a preliminary calculation. The project manager, under strict initial manpower limitations, calculated the cost of the two weeks' acceleration at various stages and won top-management approval of his request for early acceleration. The undertaking was completed two working days before its 20-month deadline, at a cost only $6,000 over the original estimate. "Crashing" the project during its last month, as the graph shows, would cost nearly $170,000.

TIME CONTROL. Almost invariably, some form of network scheduling such as critical path method or PERT provides the best time control of a project. But whether or not a network is used, the time required by different elements of the project should be pinned down explicitly at the start. To begin with, each department manager involved in the project will be asked to draw up a list of all the tasks it will require of his department. He should then discuss each of these lists in detail with the respective departmental supervisors in order to establish the sequence in the project as it affects all company units. Next, each manager and supervisor should specify the information he will need from other departments, indicating which data, if any, are habitually late. This listing not only gives the project manager a clue to the thoroughness of planning in the other departments, but also affords him a means of uncovering and forestalling most of the inconsistencies, missed activities, or inadequate planning that might otherwise occur.

Next, having planned its own role, each department should commit itself to an estimate of the time needed for each of its project activities, assuming the required information is supplied on time. After this, an overall schedule can be set up.

Once the project is under way, weekly or fortnightly review meetings

The rising cost of project time

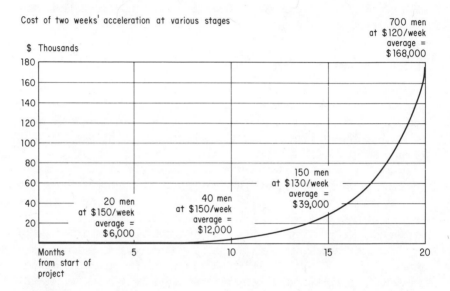

Cost of two weeks' acceleration at various stages

will serve to check progress against schedule. Control must be rigorous. Since the tone of the entire project is set at the start, the very first missed commitments call for immediate corrective action.

COST CONTROL. In applying project cost control techniques, four rules should be observed: (1) break the comprehensive cost summary into small budget units or work packages; (2) devise commitment reports for decision makers—the design engineer, the product planner, the process engineer, the spare-parts planner, etc.; (3) act on early, approximate report data; and (4) concentrate talent on major problems and opportunities.

The direction of a fast moving $15 million project can be difficult for even the most experienced manager. For a first-line supervisor, the job of running a $500,000 project can be equally difficult. Neither manager can make sound decisions unless the cost dimensions of the job are broken down into pieces of comprehensible size. Major cost categories can be successively subdivided into understandable and controllable work packages, each assignable to a first-line manager.

Cost commitments on a project are made when engineering, manufacturing, marketing, or other functional personnel arrive at technical decisions to take some kind of action. In new-product development, for example, costs are committed or created in many ways: when marketing decides to add a new feature to the product, when engineering wants to insert a new part, when a process engineer adds an extra operation to a routing, when physical distribution managers choose to increase inventory, and so on. Conventional accounting reports do not show the cost effects of these decisions until it is too late to reconsider. In order to judge when costs are getting out of control and take timely action to correct the situation, the project manager must be able to assess the approximate cost effect of each technical decision. In other words, he must have cost commitment reports at every decision stage.

Almost without exception, experience shows, 20 percent of the project efforts account for at least 80 percent of the cost to which the company is committed. With the aid of a detailed cost breakdown, the project manager will be able, even after the project is under way, to withdraw people from less important activities in order to concentrate more effort where it will do the most good in reducing costs. In this way, one electro-mechanical company cut its product introduction costs by over $1 million between the dates when the first print was released and the first machine assembled.

QUALITY CONTROL. Experience with a wide variety of projects—new-product introductions, mergers, plant constructions, introduction of organizational changes, to name a few—indicates that effective quality control of results will be crucial to a project's success. This implies defining performance criteria, expressing the project objective in terms of quality standards, and monitoring progress toward these standards.

Quality criteria can be defined rather easily in terms of senior executives' expectations. Yet, although the need to define performance criteria seems universally acknowledged, it all too frequently seems to be ignored in practice. In many cases, such expectations are not explicitly stated until a project fails. But top managers should—and easily can, if they take the trouble—set forth their expectations at the start in terms project members will understand: unit cost targets, share-of-market goals, order-processing time, and the like. If possible, these expectations ought to be expressed quantitatively. For example, the senior executive might expect the project to reduce emergency transportation expenses from 15 percent to 5 percent of total shipping costs. Or he might expect a 30 percent reduction in inventory costs following installation of a mechanized control system.

Since achievement of these quality goals must be a gradual process, the project manager should review progress toward them with the general manager monthly or quarterly, depending upon the length of the project.

Managing the human equation

The executive in his first project management assignment will probably find adjustment to the new role painful, confusing, and at the start even demoralizing. Lacking real line authority, he must constantly lead, push, or badger his peers and superiors through a trying period of change.

Too often in the difficult early weeks he receives little support from senior management. Instead, he may well be criticized for not moving faster and producing more visible results. He may be blamed for flaws in a plan that had to be rushed to completion in a few days because of earlier top-management procrastination. Senior managers need to recognize that needling the project manager can hardly be conducive to getting the job done. By providing him with support at the start, giving him freedom in the details of the doing, the senior executive can greatly enhance the project's chances of success.

Another critical point comes at the conclusion of the project. Results are turned over to the regular organization and the project manager and his team return to their permanent assignments. By virtue of the interfunctional experience gained under pressure, the project manager often matures in the course of a project, becoming a more valuable executive. But he may have trouble slowing down to a normal organizational pace. His routine job is likely to seem less attractive in terms of scope, authority, and opportunity to contribute to the business.

Even the best project manager will be unlikely to have accomplished his project objectives without antagonizing some members of management, quite possibly the very executives who will decide his future. In one instance, a manager who had brought a major project from the brink of chaos to unqualified success was let go at the end of the project because, in accomplishing the feat, he had been unable to avoid antagonizing one division head. Such difficulties and dissatisfactions often lead a retired project manager to look for a better job at this time, in or out of the company.

To retain and profit from the superior management material developed on the project training ground, senior executives ought to be aware of these human problems. By recognizing the nature of the experience that the project manager has gone through, helping him readjust to the slower pace of the normal organization, and finding ways to put his added experience and matured judgment to good use, the company can reap a significant side benefit from every successfully managed project.

PART SEVEN

Management sciences
and the computer

Among the most significant facets of the much-touted "computer revolution" has been the extraordinary impact of the new information technology on the arts of management. Like all revolutions, this one has its intimidating aspects and these are not forgotten in the four chapters that follow. Each deals with some aspect of the effective use of computers by management. Each implicitly or directly counsels company managers to face up to the computer's challenge, and specifically to retain direction of the corporate computer effort.

What happens when company executives do not meet this responsibility is shown in "Unlocking the Computer's Profit Potential," condensed from a McKinsey research report published under the same title. The study found that the range of economically promising computer applications now open to many companies "has become circumscribed by the limited background of computer personnel and the limited initiative of managers." To make better use of computers in the future, industry will need to "expand the horizons of computer professionals and bring managers to a fuller awareness of the computer's vast potential." A principal conclusion of the study might well serve as the theme of this section: "Only managers can manage the computer in the best interests of the business."

"Risk Analysis in Capital Investment," by David B. Hertz, presents the first full-dress description of a computer-based simulation technique (now in wide use) for incorporating the vital dimension of probability distribution into the assessment of investment risks and returns. The crux of the problem, he writes, "is not . . . projecting return on investment under any given set of assumptions. Rather the difficulty lies in

339

arriving at the right assumptions and gauging their probable impact."
Ways and means of doing just that are examined here in detail.

Logistics, according to Alan H. Gepfert, may be defined as "the functional bridge that provides for the physical movement of goods from raw materials sources to plants, from plants to warehouses, and from warehouses to customers." In "Business Logistics for Better Profit Performance," Gepfert reports a number of cases where significant competitive advantages were achieved by managements willing to take an integrative view of the logistics function and apply computer-based management science techniques to the solution of broadly defined logistics problems. Gepfert here stresses, once again, the importance of continuing and vigorous top-management leadership. "No top management," the author writes, "has yet reaped the benefits of effective logistics applications simply by granting a broad charter to the operations research staff in the logistics area and then stepping back to await results."

Perhaps because they have all studied computer technology in some depth, the contributors to this section do not present a monolithic view of the computer's possibilities. C. Ridley Rhind, for example, sets forth some reservations. Management, he maintains, is often seduced by the fervor of computer professionals into believing in the imminent availability of "total management information systems" that will automatically supply all the data needed for any management decision. Properly used, he declares, the computer can provide a quantum improvement in data for decision making. But every company needs multiple information systems, and, Rhind argues, managers will always need to know a lot of things which, even in principle, no computer will ever be able to tell them.

29. Unlocking the computer's profit potential*

In terms of technical achievement, the computer revolution in U.S. business has been outrunning expectations. In terms of economic payoff on new applications, it has rapidly lost momentum. Such is the evidence from a recent study by McKinsey & Company of computer systems management in 36 major companies.

In the course of this study, we interviewed staff and line executives, up to and frequently including the chief executive officer, in 36 large U.S. and European companies from 13 industries, representing all levels of achievement and experience with computers. Because the computer practices and achievements of these companies are so diverse, there can be little point in trying to formulate quantitative performance measures. Success with the computer shows no consistent correlation with level of computer expenditures. Some companies spend heavily for a dubious payoff; others with less ambitious programs reap major rewards.

In view of the many variables involved, any absolute standard of computer success must necessarily be arbitrary. In this study, therefore, we decided to let "success" be defined by the range of performance observed in the survey sample itself. Accordingly, the 36 companies were ranked judgmentally on their overall achievement with the computer, taking into account such factors as measurable return on the computer investment over time, range of meaningful functional applications, and chief executive satisfaction with the computer effort to date.

From a profit standpoint, our findings indicate, computer efforts in all but a few exceptional companies appear to be in real, if often unacknowledged, trouble. Faster, costlier, more sophisticated hardware; larger and increasingly costly computer staffs; increasingly complex and ingenious applications: these may be found everywhere. Less and less in evidence, as new applications proliferate, have been profitable results.

Most large companies have successfully mechanized the bulk of their routine clerical and accounting procedures; and many have moved out into

* Condensed from a *Research Report to Management* first published in 1968.

operating applications. Yet with few exceptions their mounting computer expenditures are no longer matched by rising economic returns.

How to account for the dwindling economic payoff on so many computer systems? What has gone wrong? The answer, our findings suggest, lies in a failure to adapt to new conditions. The rules of the game have been changing, but management's strategies have not. A look at current computer development efforts shows that the prime objective of many continues to be the reduction of general and administrative expenses. Yet for most companies this has now turned into an area of diminishing returns. Many senior executives have begun to recognize that the time has come for a change of course in the computer development effort. "How can I keep on justifying major computer expenditures when I can't show a dollar saved to date from our last three applications?" asks the president of a large consumer goods company.

The hard-to-justify outlays remain insignificant compared to the opportunity costs. While transforming the administrative and accounting operations of U.S. business, the computer has had surprisingly little impact on most companies' key operating and management problems, where its real profit potential lies. Meanwhile, the gap between technical capability and practical achievement continues to widen, the stakes keep on rising, and costs mount ever higher.

The stakes and the problem

Because payroll typically accounts for well over half the cost of the corporate computer effort, and since computer staff organization, personnel classifications, and accounting conventions differ so widely from company to company, attempts to formulate "yardsticks" for corporate computer outlays (e.g., as a percentage of assets, capital expenditures, administrative expenses, or sales volume) are apt to be misleading. What a particular company "ought" to be spending on computers will not be discovered by studying industry averages or the outlays of competitors. In the last analysis this can only be determined in the light of the company's own situation, strategy, and resources, including the depth and sophistication of its computer experience.

Nevertheless, the distribution of costs which go to make up total computer expenditures turns out to be fairly consistent among the companies in our study. About $35,000 out of every $100,000 in total computer outlays goes for hardware; $30,000 for computer operations staff payroll; $15,000 for maintenance programming (i.e., keeping current systems updated), and the remaining $20,000 for development programming and other staff time devoted to new applications.

These development dollars—the only computer outlays subject to significant short-term management control—generally amount to a smaller fraction of the total than the company's annual bill for hardware rentals. Yet their leverage on future costs and benefits is enormous; in fact, they hold the key to the long-range success or failure of the company's computer effort. For unless management segregates these costs and understands the nature of the resources they buy, the direction of future computer developments will be in doubt and the entire activity will be vulnerable to hasty and perhaps emotional review.

In short, the computer management problem as it confronts corporate executives today becomes a matter of future direction rather than current effectiveness. The key question ought not to be "How are we doing?" but "Where are we heading, and why?"

Five years ago this was a less critical issue at the top-management level. As long as computer developments were largely confined to accounting departments there seemed less reason for corporate executives to concern themselves with direction-setting. If the controller carried out his function and kept his costs in line, no one outside his department worried very much about *how* he did it. The situation has taken a very different turn today. Now that the conversion of accounting work to computer processing has virtually been completed—by 30 of the 36 companies in our study— the question "What next?" becomes urgent. Many of the alternatives currently being proposed appear complex and costly enough to require executive approval, but their justification remains obscure at best. When top management looks for a realistic promise of profit, or asks for evidence that the proposals submitted for review represent the best available computer opportunities, it typically finds that no convincing answers are available.

Top management has a right—indeed a responsibility—to raise hard questions about any computer development proposal. The issue such questions address is basically that of *feasibility*—a concept often misunderstood and misapplied, but crucial to soundly based computer development efforts.

The three tests of feasibility

Recently the president of a German chemical company turned down a proposal for a management information system that would have provided him with a desk-side cathode-ray tube inquiry terminal capable of displaying on demand almost any kind of operating data he might care to request. He explained his decision very simply: "I care more about what will happen five years from now than what happened yesterday. And I already get all the routine data I can handle. What would I do with more?"

This reaction typifies a trend. Computer technology has made great strides even in the past several years. Fewer and fewer applications are excluded from consideration because of limits on computer file capacity, internal speed, or input/output ability. More and more technically exciting projects are being proposed for management approval. Yet technical virtuosity does not guarantee problem-solving potential. And with technical feasibility no longer an important stumbling block for the great majority of business applications, it hardly makes much sense to delegate to computer professionals the key decisions regarding uses of the computer, as many companies still do today.

The concept of feasibility really takes in three separate questions. The test of *technical feasibility* asks: "Is this application possible within the limits of available technology and our own resources?" There follows the test of *economic feasibility*: "Will this application return more dollar value in benefits than it will cost to develop?" And finally the test of *operational feasibility* asks: "Once the system has been successfully developed, will it be successfully used? Will managers adapt to the system, or will they resist or ignore it?"

Particularly where complex and ambitious computer development projects are concerned, these key questions will seldom be answered once and for all at the time the project is proposed. Continuous reassessment of the technical and economic risks and payoff probabilities may be vital to keeping such a project on the right track. But a careful initial assessment can go far to avert costly misapplication of scarce computer resources.

Unfortunately, it is dangerously easy to avoid confronting the full implications of feasibility until a project has been under way for some time. Far too often operational feasibility may be neglected until the new application is actually tried out and perhaps found wanting—the costliest kind of feasibility test. And economic feasibility—the measure of how much expected dollar returns will exceed expected costs—is frequently assessed rather casually on grounds that the important benefits are intangible, and intangible benefits can't really be evaluated.

Actually, of course, the very difficulty of measuring intangible payoffs is the best argument for imposing on managers the discipline of explicit evaluation. Computer personnel can provide the needed input on costs, but benefits can be realistically assessed only by executives who fully understand the activities affected and the policies that govern them.

To achieve its economic potential, a computer project may also call for substantial operational changes—new corporate policies, staff reorganization, construction of new facilities and phasing out of the old. It will certainly require the support of operating managers and their staffs, and may also depend on the cooperation of dealers, suppliers, and even customers. Corporate computer staffs cannot really judge the need for such changes, much less implement them. At most, they can advise the operating managers who must make the final assessment of operational feasibility.

Past successes and present problems

Ironically, the basic problems currently besetting the management of the computer effort stem from the successes of the past. In 30 of the 36 companies, conversions of routine administrative and accounting operations to computer systems are already complete or nearly so. Some of the people who accomplished these conversions now constitute the nucleus of a corporate computer staff, often reporting directly to top management.

For obvious reasons, these computer staffs will come under pressure to show results in the form of new computer systems. In terms of purely technical competence, we may expect them to be well equipped to do so. But no matter how distinguished their technical skills, computer specialists will seldom be strategically placed (or sufficiently trained as managers) to assess the economics of a system fully or to judge operational feasibility. And our findings reveal that these limitations have been raising ever more serious obstacles to the success of new corporate computer efforts.

Another obstacle to future success, also stemming from past experience, is line management's lack of exposure to the feasibility problem. Back in the days when corporate computer efforts centered on the conversion of accounting and administrative systems, management seldom had to concern itself with the issue of feasibility. With a relatively orderly manual system, the feasibility question centered on the technical problems of programming the computer. Economic feasibility could be assessed with relative ease once a company had learned how to estimate conversion costs realistically, since the benefits could be measured in terms of clerical payroll deductions. And operational feasibility would be assured when, as was usually the case, a single executive such as the controller had charge of both the development and operating phases of the new system.

Today the situation is very different. Applications have become more complex and their impact on different operating departments more far-reaching. The feasibility issue is bound up with complex economic and operational questions that few staff specialists can begin to answer. Yet too many managers still leave the assessment of feasibility to the computer professionals, and neglect their own responsibility for setting the direction of the computer development effort. All this has two principal consequences:

First, current management practices and attitudes are falling short of the demands of today's task. Over the past five years, most computer staffs have doubled, and they may double again by 1975. Yet no overhaul of the management practices of earlier years has taken place. Fourteen of the

36 companies we studied still have no overall plan for computer applications, and the economic and operational feasibility of individual projects is seldom fully explored. Twenty-four companies, including ten with a computer plan, have not established adequate short-term objectives against which to measure the progress of individual computer projects.

Second, the range of such projects now open to many companies has become circumscribed by the limited background of its computer personnel and the limited initiative of its managers. To make better use of computers in the future it will be necessary to expand the horizons of computer professionals and bring managers to a fuller awareness of the computer's vast potential.

The opportunities: near and far-out

The computer's credentials as a cutter of clerical payrolls may now be considered beyond dispute. We have convincing evidence that it can make an equal or greater contribution to corporate profits by reducing the cost of goods sold.

The more successful companies in our study have recognized this potential and are already beginning to exploit it. The dominant lesson of their experience so far: that this second stage of the computer revolution, unlike the first, entails real operational changes—new, perhaps uncomfortable ways of doing business that may well be resisted at the outset.

For companies moving into operating system applications, the feasibility problem becomes more complex. Technical feasibility may again become an issue because marketing, production, and distribution systems are subject to outside influence and are therefore less orderly than accounting systems. Economic feasibility becomes harder to determine since the benefits no longer derive from payroll reductions. Most significant, operational feasibility now depends on the attitude of operating managers.

Teamwork, then, becomes the key. Even a fairly commonplace computer application such as inventory control requires it. Design engineers must give adequate notice of design changes; sales planners must furnish detailed product sales forecasts; and management must give guidance on spares requirements and desired customer service levels. Once established, such cooperation between managers and professional computer staffs becomes a real stimulus to new and profitable applications.

Consider the case of a manufacturer of heavy construction equipment, whose first computer-based inventory control system went into operation well over a decade ago. In this company the computer now plays an integral and indispensable role in production planning and control. These are some of its tasks:

1. Consolidating sales forecasts from 31 countries. Forecast data are

346

consolidated by region, product, and model, then correlated with historical data to establish trends for each product group. The president and the vice president for sales use these staff analyses in their annual budget discussions with division heads.

2. Establishing a quarterly manufacturing plan for each of 13 plants. These plans are updated monthly by reconciling revised sales forecasts with records of finished goods inventory and products in final assembly. The revised manufacturing program may then be exploded into component requirements, and a "net component requirement" analysis prepared. With the help of supplementary manual analysis, lead time between customer order and delivery has been sharply cut and costly reshuffling of finished goods among distribution depots reduced drastically.

3. Maintaining cost schedules in all plants showing the economics of make-or-buy decisions. In conjunction with the "net component requirement" report, these cost schedules make possible intelligent work-load leveling, better allocation among plants, and more soundly based make-or-buy decisions.

4. Central recording of all engineering changes. With changes occurring at a rate of about 2,000 a month, the cost of writing off obsolete stock formerly ran as high as $1.5 million annually. The new system, which allows components in stock to be exhausted before a change is put into effect, has reduced this bill by two-thirds.

5. Maintaining cumulative records on labor efficiency. Besides providing detailed information on direct labor costs and trends, this system analyzes the work content of each component by work center—an invaluable aid to production planners.

The complex network of systems which produces such results has been evolving for 12 years now. Overall, management credits computers with reducing lead time between order receipt and delivery by three to five months for domestic customers, and with cutting direct labor requirements by 2 percent through improved materials availability and better control of work flow. Since direct labor costs amount to approximately $100 million per year, this fractional saving becomes significant both in absolute terms ($2 million) and as a percentage of before-tax profits (5 percent).

Another example of evolutionary development is offered by a giant consumer goods corporation. This company gives its product managers and marketing staffs access to a comprehensive, detailed sales history file in which total U.S. sales over three years are cross-referenced to show product sales data by geographic region, type of outlet, timing with relation to promotions, and packaging. This system, which evolved from a fairly elementary order entry and billing system, is being used today to schedule production at nine plants and to coordinate shipments from 13 warehouses. One gauge of its usefulness may be judged by the willingness of marketing managers to pay the salaries of the programmers who prepare on demand whatever analyses the company requires.

Fast routes to results

Evolutionary development is typical of systems requiring audited data bases, since these cannot be built up overnight. But other systems, equally ambitious, can sometimes be developed quite rapidly where management recognizes that the data-base approach may not be the only, or necessarily the best, route to advanced computer applications.

A manufacturer of high-style clothing, with national outlets and multiple plants, decided two years ago its computers (hitherto used only for accounting purposes) could help forecast sales and establish preliminary cutting schedules at the beginning of each season. The computer forecasting model it adopted has already proved so successful in matching production to demand that the company now plans to put computer forecasting to work in planning purchasing decisions.

Similarly, a couple of oil companies have moved quickly into new fields unrelated to previous computer development work. In a matter of months, one company decided to transfer the production and maintenance records of thousands of domestic oil wells to computer files where they can be correlated and analyzed. This system enables production decline curves of wells and fields to be plotted and future production forecast under various alternative secondary recovery programs. It also calls management's attention to wells that no longer produce enough to cover marginal costs.

The computer systems men and the petroleum engineers brought ideally matched talents to the principal tasks in developing this computer system, namely, data reduction and file design. With the engineers' enthusiastic support, the computer staff has now begun to explore the feasibility of making the same data accessible, through graphic display units, to its engineers in the field, who control expenditures in the hundreds of millions of dollars per year.

Finally, in industry after industry, the science of communications has been wedded to the science of computing in order to centralize record keeping, planning, and control in an ever-more-complex economic environment. Railroads have "control centers" where up-to-the-minute central records are maintained on the movement of freight and rolling stock. Retail chains use teleprinters and central computer-based dispatch systems to reduce branch-store inventories by cutting the stock-replenishment cycle. A wood products company coordinates production at its nine mills to match sales orders transmitted by branch offices throughout the

348

United States directly to a central computer. Banks handle branch accounting centrally. And nearly all the major airlines now have their own versions of the seat reservation system that first proved computers able to control large communications networks on a commercially feasible basis.

It often proves extremely difficult to assess the overall economic effects of these advanced computer applications, simply because no one can say where the corporation would be today *without* its computers. But it would be hard to convince many of these companies that the computer has nothing to do with the edge they have gained on the competition.

The resources—computers, professional computer systems men and programmers, management scientists, and communications experts—are available to all. But something more is required. Advanced computer application concepts, with potential impact on the central activities of a corporation, must have sponsors high in the management pyramid to plead their case. It takes enthusiastic top-management leadership to gain the commitment of operating men—and it takes teamwork between operating men and computer professionals to turn imaginative concepts into practical reality. Indeed, experienced and well-motivated operating managers may well be a better source of profitable ideas than the computer professionals. The most profitable applications uncovered in our study originated with operating executives pondering such ideas as these:

¶ If only we had a way to test the reliability of the sales forecasts made by these regional managers of ours, we might not find ourselves out of manufacturing capacity in Italy at the same time that we're laying off valuable skilled labor in Brazil.

¶ If only we had a way of recording and analyzing all our customer orders in one place, we ought to be able to allocate our production better—improve mill efficiencies and raise the yield from our raw materials.

¶ If only we could easily check out our historical sales performance by product, package, and so on, maybe we could interpret our test marketing results faster and more reliably.

¶ If only we could play with alternatives on our tanker deployment, we might use our capacity better—charter in less and charter out more.

¶ If only we could project our needs for skilled labor three months out, we could save the expense of these crash recruiting and training programs.

For every company, our study suggests, there is a unique set of *feasible and profitable* computer applications, most of them closely related to the sort of strategic opportunities that most vitally concern top executives: marketing and distribution operations in the package goods company, production in the capital equipment concern, planning of facilities for the chemicals maker, exploration and producing in the petroleum company, financial planning in the conglomerate, and so on. And since each corporation has its own unique pattern of problems and opportunities, the computer development strategy that has not worked for one company may work exceedingly well for its competitor.

In almost every industry, at least one company can now be found pioneering in profitable new uses of computers. In such organizations, our findings suggest, the key to success has been a strong thrust of constructive interest from corporate operating executives who have put their own staffs to work on computer development projects. It may soon be a nearly universal practice to transfer operating staff to computer development projects, either by making them members of a project team or by attaching them for a year or two to the corporate computer staff.

In management information and control—another much-discussed area of computer use—a few companies have already succeeded in notably improving the quality and quantity of specific information available to operating managers. Others, as noted earlier, have made profitable use of the computer in decision making through simulation models. A well-known food products company, for example, has constructed and used a computer-based simulation model to assess, under various possible 1970 and 1975 environments: (1) the relative profitability of different product markets, (2) the desirability of investing in new-market development, (3) the impact of investment in added plant capacity, and (4) detailed income statements based on these projections.

Again, computer-based risk analysis techniques have demonstrated their value in a wide range of capital investment situations. The industrial chemicals industry is known for the magnitude of both its investment and its risks. Risk analysis, made practical by computers, has proven invaluable for evaluating alternative strategic plans with the help of simulation models, sometimes even including simulation of alternative competitive responses by the application of game theory. To exploit the potential of these and related techniques, an increasing number of corporations find it necessary to supplement the professional skills of computer men by recruiting specialists in the management sciences.

In recent years, too, much effort and ingenuity have been devoted to the design and promotion of so-called total management information systems. Many executives have understandably become intrigued by the possibilities of such systems, but they are as yet a long way from practical realization in business.

Doubtless the computer's information processing capabilities will one day eliminate the need for large staffs occupied with collecting and interpreting information from various sources for the use of decision makers. But whether the computer will ever be able to evaluate strategic opportunities or indicate the proper timing for corporate actions is by no means assured. Nor will man-machine dialogues via desk-side consoles be likely to become a feature of life in the executive suite any time in the foreseeable future. Top management's principal "interface" with the computer will in all likelihood remain the old-fashioned telephone, with a human information specialist at the other end of the line. What really counts is not the gadgetry but the responsiveness of computer-based systems to management's information needs.

Research on comprehensive computer-based information systems, then, may be a sound investment for some companies, even though the costs of experimentation come high. But no company ought to embark on a program to develop a major management information system except to meet a specific, well-defined need. Even then it should carefully weigh its options —including the option of applying its scarce computer resources to areas where operating success and economic payoff can be predicted with greater confidence.

Keys to the future

In embarking on the present study, we were concerned with measuring the gap between potential and performance, analyzing its background and causes, and synthesizing from the practices of the top performers a few succinct management guidelines for maximizing the computer's effectiveness and unlocking its profit potential.

In the computer field, as in other areas of management, the usefulness of generalizations from successful experience must be sharply limited. We can state *some* of the principles a company must follow to have a reasonable chance of success with the computer. But there will always be certain constraints, needs, and opportunities peculiar to each company which can only be weighed in the light of the individual situation. Hence it will be useful to state general precepts only if their neglect has been widespread and the consequences of that neglect costly. That, unfortunately, is the case with most corporate computer efforts today.

The common denominators of successful computer practice, as seen in the companies we have examined, can be boiled down to three principles: the rule of high expectations, the rule of diversified staffing, and the rule of top-management involvement.

THE RULE OF HIGH EXPECTATIONS. In all of the companies now realizing outstanding *economic* results from computer applications, top management has simply been unwilling to settle for anything less. Departmental and divisional managers have understood that top management will insist on economic results—and that they will be held personally responsible for achieving those results.

The new president of a capital equipment manufacturer, who has succeeded in getting a badly stalled computer program in his company moving again, expresses the prevailing management point of view. Said he: "I ask my department heads to give me regular formal reports on their current successes and failures with computers as well as their future objectives. Right now they're a bunch of sheep with computers. I aim to convert them into computer enthusiasts, so that later I can be jockey, not herdsman."

THE RULE OF DIVERSIFIED STAFFING. Recognizing that computer professionals alone seldom constitute an adequate corporate support staff, the top-performing companies take either of two organizational approaches. Some assign to the corporate computer staff—along with the usual operations research specialists and other professionals—at least one talented individual with experience in each of the major functions of the business. Others, relying on the project approach to computer development, use project teams staffed by temporary transfers from operating departments.

To head up the computer staff and assume responsibility for the implementation of development plans, each of the outstanding companies has taken care to pick a manager who can command respect and confidence throughout the organization. Their experience indicates that this man's effectiveness depends more on his personal stature and professional skills than on the location of his unit in the corporate hierarchy. We found no evidence, statistical or otherwise, to suggest that high organizational status assures effective performance on the part of the corporate computer staff.

THE RULE OF TOP-MANAGEMENT INVOLVEMENT. If any one man can be said to hold the key to the computer's profit potential, it is probably the chief executive. There are five responsibilities that he really cannot delegate if he wants to obtain the best results from his company's computer effort:

1. He must approve objectives, criteria, and priorities for the corporate computer effort, with special attention to the development program.

2. He must decide on the organizational arrangements to carry out these policies and achieve these objectives.

3. He must assign responsibility for results to the line and functional executives served by the computer systems—and see to it that they exercise this responsibility.

4. He must insist that detailed and thorough computer systems plans are made an integral part of operating plans and budgets.

5. He must follow through to see that planned results are achieved.

There is nothing novel in these recommendations; they constitute standard operating practice for the chief executive in most of his traditional areas of responsibility. Yet many otherwise effective top managements find themselves in trouble when it comes to directing their computer efforts because they have abdicated these responsibilities to technicians—men who have neither the operational experience to know the jobs that need doing nor the authority to get them done properly.

Only managers can manage the computer in the best interests of the business. The companies that take this lesson to heart today will be the computer profit leaders of tomorrow.

30. Risk analysis in capital investment

David B. Hertz

Of all the decisions that business executives must make, none is more challenging—and none has received more attention—than choosing among alternative capital investment opportunities. What makes this kind of decision so demanding is not the problem of projecting return on investment under any given set of assumptions. Rather the difficulty lies in arriving at the right assumptions and gauging their probable impact. Each assumption involves its own degree—often a high degree—of uncertainty. Taken together, these combined uncertainties can multiply into a total uncertainty of critical proportions. Here the element of risk enters—and it is in the evaluation of risk that the executive has been able to obtain little help from currently available tools and techniques.

Yet there is a way to help the executive sharpen his key capital investment decisions. This method provides him with a realistic measurement of the risks involved. It evaluates for him the risk at each possible level of return, enabling management to measure alternative courses of action against corporate objectives.

Need for new concept

The evaluation of a capital investment project starts with the principle that the productivity of capital is measured by the rate of return we expect to receive over some future period. A dollar received next year is worth less to us than a dollar in hand today. Expenditures three years hence are less costly than expenditures of equal magnitude two years from now. Hence, we cannot calculate the rate of return realistically unless we take into account (a) when the sums involved in an investment are spent, and (b) when the returns are received.

Comparing alternative investments will thus be complicated by the fact that they usually differ not only in size but also in the length of time over which expenditures will have to be made and benefits returned.

These facts of investment life long ago made apparent the shortcomings of approaches that simply averaged expenditures and benefits, or lumped them together, as in the number-of-years-to-pay-out method. These shortcomings prompted students of decision making to explore more precise methods for determining which of several, or many, possible investments would leave a company better off in the long run.

The early controversy and furor over the most appropriate way of calculating the value of capital investments has largely been resolved. The discounted cash flow method has emerged as a reasonable means of measuring the rate of return that can be expected in the future from an investment made today.

We have methods which, in general, consist of more or less elaborate mathematical formulas for comparing the outcomes of various investments and the combinations of the variables that will affect the investments.[1] As these techniques have evolved, their supporting mathematics has become more and more precise, so that we can now calculate discounted returns to a fraction of a percent.

But the sophisticated businessman knows that less-than-precise data lie behind these precise calculations. At best, the rate-of-return information will be based on an average of different opinions—some reliable, others far less so. When the expected returns on two investments are close, the businessman may well be influenced by "intangibles"—fragile authority for decision, to say the least. Even when the figures for two investments appear quite far apart, and the choice seems clear, there lurk in the back of the businessman's mind memories of the Edsel and other ill-fated ventures.

In short, the decision maker realizes that there must be something more he ought to know, something in addition to the expected rate of return. He suspects that what may be missing relates to the nature of the data on which the expected rate of return has been calculated, and also to the way this information has been processed. It has something to do with uncertainty, with possibilities and probabilities extending across a wide range of rewards and risks.

The weakness of past approaches has nothing to do with the mathematics of rate-of-return calculation in itself. The fact is that, no matter what mathematics may be used, each of the variables involved in calculating rate of return will be subject to a high level of uncertainty. For example:

> The useful life of a new piece of capital equipment can rarely be known in advance with any degree of certainty. It may be affected by variations in obsolescence or deterioration. Relatively small changes in use life can lead to large changes in return. Yet an expected value

---

[1] See for example, Joel Dean, *Capital Budgeting* (Columbia University Press, New York, 1951); "Return on Capital as a Guide to Managerial Decisions," *National Association of Accounts Research Report No. 35*, December 1, 1959; and Bruce F. Young, "Overcoming Obstacles to Use of Discounted Cash Flow for Investment Shares," *NAA Bulletin*, March 1963, p. 15.

for the life of the equipment—based on a great deal of data from which a single best possible forecast has been developed—is entered into the rate-of-return calculation. The same will generally be done for the other factors that have a significant bearing on the decision at hand.

Let us see how this often works out, selecting a case history in which the odds appear to be all in favor of a particular decision:

The executives of a food company must decide whether to launch a new packaged cereal. They have come to the conclusion that five determining variables must be taken into account: *advertising and promotion expense, total cereal market, share of market for this product, operating costs,* and *new capital investment.* On the basis of the "most likely" estimate for each of these variables the picture looks very bright—a healthy 30 percent return. But this future depends on each of the "most likely" estimates actually coming true. If each of these "educated guesses" has, for example, a 60 percent chance of being correct, there can be only an 8 percent chance that *all five* will be correct (.60 × .60 × .60 × .60 × .60). So the "expected" return will actually be dependent on a rather unlikely coincidence. The decision maker needs to know a great deal more about the *other* values used to make each of the five estimates and about what he stands to gain or lose from their various combinations.

Thus, the rate of return actually depends on a combination of values of a great many different variables. But only the expected ranges (e.g., worst, average, best; or pessimistic, most likely, optimistic) of these variables are used in formal mathematical ways to provide the figures given to management. Evidently then, the prediction of a single most likely rate of return depends on supposedly precise numbers that in fact do not tell the whole story.

The "expected" rate of return represents only a few points on a continuous curve of possible combinations of future happenings. It is a bit like trying to predict the outcome of a dice game by saying that the most likely number to come up will be a "7." The description must be seen as incomplete because it does not tell us about all the other things that could happen. For any given throw of two ordinary six-sided dice there are 36 (6 × 6) possible different outcomes—i.e., combinations of sides—but only 11 different possible totals. Thus,

only one outcome will give us a "2";
two outcomes will give us a "3";
three outcomes will give us a "4";
four outcomes will give us a "5";

356

five outcomes will give us a "6";
six outcomes will give us a "7";
five outcomes will give us an "8";
four outcomes will give us a "9";
three outcomes will give us a "10";
two outcomes will give us an "11"; and
only one outcome will give us a "12."

Now suppose that each die has 100 sides and there are eight of them! Here we would have a situation more comparable to business investment: the company's market share might become any one of 100 different sizes, with eight different factors (pricing, promotion, and so on) affecting the outcome.

Nor is this the only trouble. Our willingness to bet on a roll of the dice depends not only on the odds but also on the stakes. Since the probability of rolling a "7" is 1 in 6, we might be quite willing to risk a few dollars on that outcome at suitable odds. But would we be equally willing to wager $10,000 or $100,000 at those same odds, or even at better odds? In short, risk will be influenced both by the odds on various events occurring and by the magnitude of the rewards or penalties involved when they do occur.

> Suppose a company is considering an investment of $1 million. The "best estimate" of the probable return produces the figure of $200,000 a year. It could well be that this estimate comes from the average of three possible returns—a 1-in-3 chance of obtaining no return at all, a 1-in-3 chance of earning $200,000 per year, a 1-in-3 chance of getting back $400,000 per year. Suppose that receiving no return at all would put the company out of business. Then by accepting this proposal management will be taking a 1-in-3 chance of going bankrupt.

> If only the "best estimate" analysis has been used, management might go ahead, unaware that it is taking a big chance. But if *all* of the available information were examined, management might prefer an alternative proposal with a smaller, but more certain (i.e., less variable), expectation.

Such considerations have led nearly all advocates of modern capital-investment-index calculations to plead that the elements of uncertainty be recognized. Perhaps Ross G. Walker sums up current thinking when he speaks of "the almost impenetrable mists of any forecast."[2]

How can the executive penetrate the mists of uncertainty that surround the choices among alternatives?

[2] "The Judgment Factor in Investment Decisions," *Harvard Business Review*, March–April 1961, p. 99.

A number of efforts to cope with uncertainty have been successful up to a point, but all seem to fall short of the mark in one way or another:

1. MORE ACCURATE FORECASTS. Reducing the error in estimates will always be a worthy objective. But no matter how many estimates go into a capital investment decision, when all is said and done, the future remains the future. However well we forecast, we must still be left with the knowledge that we cannot eliminate all uncertainty.

2. EMPIRICAL ADJUSTMENTS. Adjusting the factors influencing the outcome of a decision cannot help but be subject to serious difficulties. We would prefer to adjust them so as to cut down the likelihood that we will make a "bad" investment, but how can we do that without at the same time spoiling our chances to make a "good" one? And in any case, what is the basis for adjustment? We adjust, not for uncertainty, but for bias.

For example, construction estimates are often exceeded. If a company's history of construction costs tells us that 90 percent of its estimates have been exceeded by 15 percent, then in a capital estimate there will be every justification for increasing the value of this factor by 15 percent.

But suppose that new-product sales estimates have been exceeded by more than 75 percent in one-fourth of all historical cases, and have not reached 50 percent of the estimate in one-sixth of all such cases? Penalties for overestimating may be tangible; hence, management is apt to reduce the sales estimate to "cover" the one case in six—thereby reducing the calculated rate of return. In doing so, it may miss some of its best opportunities.

3. REVISING CUTOFF RATES. Selecting higher cutoff rates for protecting against uncertainty represents an attempt to accomplish much the same thing. Management would like to have a possibility of return in proportion to the risk involved. Where uncertainty clouds the various estimates of sales, costs, prices, and so on, a high calculated return from the investment provides some incentive for taking the risk. This is a perfectly sound position. But the decision maker still needs to know explicitly the kind of risks he will be taking—and what the odds may be on achieving the expected return.

4. THREE-LEVEL ESTIMATES. A start at spelling out risks can sometimes be made by taking the high, medium, and low values of the estimated factors and calculating rates of return based on various combinations of the pessimistic, average, and optimistic estimates. These calculations outline the range of possible results, but do not tell the executive whether the pessimistic forecast will be more accurate than the optimistic one—or, in fact, whether the average result is much more likely to occur than either of the extremes. So, although we may have taken a step in the right direction, we do not yet have a clear enough picture for comparing alternatives.

5. SELECTED PROBABILITIES. Various methods have been devised to include

in the return calculation the probabilities of specific factors. L. C. Grant discusses a program to forecast discounted cash flow rates of return where the service life will be subject to obsolescence and deterioration. He calculates the odds that the investment will terminate at any given time after it has been made depending on the probability distribution of the service-life factor. After calculating these factors for each year through maximum service life, he then determines an overall expected rate of return.[3]

Edward G. Bennion suggests the use of game theory to take into account alternative market growth rates as they would determine rate of return for various alternatives. He uses the estimated probabilities that specific growth rates will occur in order to develop the best possible strategies. Bennion points out:

> Forecasting can result in a negative contribution to capital budget decisions unless it goes further than merely providing a single most probable prediction. . . . [With] an estimated probability coefficient for the forecast, plus knowledge of the payoffs for the company's alternative investments and calculation of indifference probabilities . . . the margin of error may be substantially reduced, and the businessman can tell just how far off his forecast may be before it leads him to a wrong decision.[4]

Note that both of these methods yield an expected return, each based on only one uncertain input factor—service life in the first case, market growth in the second. Both are helpful, and both tend to improve the clarity with which the executive can view investment alternatives. But neither sharpens up the range of "risk taken" or "return hoped for" sufficiently to help very much in the complex decisions entailed by capital planning.

Sharpening the picture

Since every one of the many factors that enter into the evaluation of a decision will be subject to some uncertainty, the executive needs a helpful portrayal of the effects that the uncertainty surrounding *each* of the significant factors has on the returns he is likely to achieve. We believe that our method combines the variabilities inherent in all relevant factors. Our objective has been to give a clear picture of the relative risk and the probable odds of coming out ahead or behind in the light of uncertain fore-knowledge.

[3] "Monitoring Capital Investments," *Financial Executive*, April 1963, p. 19.
[4] "Capital Budgeting and Game Theory," *Harvard Business Review*, November–December 1956, p. 123.

A simulation of the ways these factors may combine as the future unfolds has been the key to extracting the greatest possible amount of information from available forecasts. In fact, the approach is very simple, using a computer to do the necessary arithmetic. (A computer program to do this was suggested by S. W. Hess and H. A. Quigley for chemical process investments.[5])

To carry out the analysis, a company must follow three steps:

1. Estimate the range of values for each factor (e.g., range of selling price, sales growth rate, and so on) and within that range the likelihood of occurrence of each value.

2. Select at random from the distribution of values for each factor one particular value. Then combine the values for all of the factors and compute the rate of return (or present value) from that combination. For instance, the lowest in the range of prices might be combined with the highest in the range of growth rate and other factors. (The interdependence of the factors should be taken into account, as we shall see later.)

3. Do this over and over again to define and evaluate the odds governing the occurrence of each possible rate of return. Since the possible combinations of values amount to many millions, we need to test the likelihood that various specific returns on the investment will occur. This is like finding out by recording the results of a great many throws what percent of "7"s or other combinations we may expect in tossing dice. We will list the rates of return we might achieve, ranging from a loss (if the factors go against us) to whatever maximum gain may be possible, given the estimates that have been made.

For each of these rates the chances of occurrence are determined. (Note that a projected return can usually be achieved through more than one combination of events. The more combinations for a given rate, the higher the chances of achieving it—as with "7"s in tossing dice.) The average expectation derives from the average values of all outcomes weighted by the chances that each will occur.

The variability of outcome values from the average is also determined. This is important since, all other factors being equal, management would presumably prefer lower variability for the same return if given the choice. This concept has already been applied to investment portfolios.[6]

When the expected return and variability of each among a series of

[5] "Analysis of Risk in Investment Using Monte Carlo Techniques," *Chemical Engineering Symposium Series 42: Statistics and Numerical Methods in Chemical Engineering* (American Institute of Chemical Engineering, New York, 1963), p. 55.

[6] See Harry Markowitz, *Portfolio Selection, Efficient Diversification of Investments* (John Wiley and Sons, New York, 1959); Donald E. Fararr, *The Investment Decision Under Uncertainty* (Prentice-Hall, Inc., Englewood Cliffs, New Jersey, 1962); William F. Sharpe, "A Simplified Model for Portfolio Analysis," *Management Science*, January 1963, p. 277.

investments have been determined, the same techniques may be used to examine their effectiveness in various combinations, with relation to management objectives.

Practical test

To see how this new approach works in practice, let us take the experience of a management that has already analyzed an investment proposal by conventional techniques. Taking the same investment schedule and the same expected values actually used, we can find what results the new method would produce and compare them with the results obtained when conventional methods were applied.

A medium-size industrial chemical producer has been considering a $10 million extension to its processing plant. The estimated service life of the facility is ten years. Company engineers expect to be able to utilize 250,000 tons of processed material worth $510 per ton at an average processing cost of $435 per ton. Will this investment be a good bet? In fact, what return should the company expect? What are the risks? We will have to make the best and fullest use we can of all the market research and financial analyses that have been developed, in order to give management a clear picture of this project.

As key input factors, management has decided to use:

1. Market size
2. Selling prices
3. Market growth rate
4. Share of market (which results in physical sales volume)
5. Investment required
6. Residual value of investment
7. Operating costs
8. Fixed costs
9. Useful life of facilities.

These elements typify those in many company projects. All of them must be analyzed and combined to obtain a measure of the attractiveness of a proposed capital facilities investment.

How do we analyze this proposal in accordance with our recommended techniques?

Our aim is to develop for each of the nine factors listed a frequency distribution or probability curve. The information will include the possible range of values for each factor, the average, and some idea of the likelihood that the various possible values will be reached. It has been our experience that for major capital proposals managements usually make a significant investment in time and funds to pinpoint information about each of

361

the relevant factors. An objective analysis of the values to be assigned to each can, with little additional effort, yield a subjective probability distribution.

This means probing and questioning each of the experts involved—to find out, for example, whether the estimated cost of production really can be said to be exactly a certain value or whether, as is more likely, it should be estimated to lie within a certain range of values. Range is often ignored in the analysis management usually makes. Yet it may well be relatively easy to determine: if a guess has to be made—as is often the case—it will be easier to guess with some accuracy a *range* rather than a specific single value. Our experience suggests that a series of meetings with management personnel to discuss such distributions will prove most helpful in arriving at realistic answers to *a priori* questions. (The term "realistic answers" implies all the information management does *not* have as well as what it does have.)

The ranges will be directly related to the degree of confidence that the estimator has in his estimate. Certain estimates may be known as quite accurate. They would be represented by probability distributions demonstrating, for instance, that only one chance in ten exists that the actual value will be different from the best estimate by more than 10 percent. Others may have as much as 100 percent ranges above and below the best estimate.

Thus, we treat the factor of selling price for the finished product by asking executives responsible for the original estimates:

1. Given that $510 is the expected sales price, what is the probability that the price will exceed $550?
2. Is there any chance that the price will exceed $650?
3. How likely is it that the price will drop below $475?

Managements must ask similar questions about each of the other elements, until they can construct a curve for each. Experience shows that this is not as difficult as it might sound. Often data on the degree of variation will be readily available: for instance, historical information on variations in the price of a commodity. Similarly, management can estimate the variability of sales from industry sales records. Even for factors that have no history, such as operating costs for a new product, the person who makes the "average" estimate must have some idea of the degree of confidence he has in his prediction, and therefore he is usually only too glad to express his feelings. Likewise, the less confidence he has in his estimate, the greater will be the range of possible values that the variable will assume.

This last point is likely to trouble businessmen. Does it really make sense to seek estimates of variations? It cannot be emphasized too strongly that the less certainty is encountered in an "average" estimate, *the more important it will be to consider the possible variation in that estimate.*

Further, an estimate of how much variation will be possible in a factor, no matter how judgmental it may be, is always better than a simple "average" estimate, since it includes more information about what can be given as the known and unknown. This very *lack* of knowledge may distinguish one investment possibility from another, so that for rational decision making it *must* be taken into account.

This lack of knowledge in itself constitutes important information about the proposed investment. To throw any information away simply because it appears highly uncertain should be understood as a serious error in analysis—an error the new approach has been designed to correct.

The next step in the proposed approach is to determine the returns that will result from random combinations of the factors involved. This calls for realistic restrictions, such as not allowing the total market to vary more than some reasonable amount from year to year. Of course, any method of rating the return may be used at this point, provided that it can be judged suitable to the company. In our case history, management preferred discounted cash flow, so that method will be followed here.

A computer can be used to carry out simulation tests in very little time and at very little expense. Thus, for one trial actually made in this case, 3,600 discounted cash flow calculations—each based on a selection of the nine input factors—were run in two minutes at a cost of $15 for computer time. The resulting rate-of-return probabilities were read out immediately and graphed.

The nine input factors described earlier fall into three categories:

1. MARKET ANALYSES. Included are market size, market growth rate, the firm's share of the market, and selling prices. For a given combination of these factors sales revenue may be determined.

2. INVESTMENT COST ANALYSES. Being tied to the kinds of service-life and operating-cost characteristics expected, these will be subject to various kinds of error and uncertainty; for instance, automation progress makes service life uncertain.

3. OPERATING AND FIXED COSTS. These also are subject to uncertainty, but will perhaps be the easiest to estimate.

The categories are not independent, and for realistic results our approach allows the various factors to be tied together. Thus, if price determines the total market, we first select from a probability distribution the price for the specific computer run. Then for the total market we use a probability distribution logically related to the price selected.

We are now ready to compare the values calculated by the new approach with those obtained under the old. This comparison is shown on page 364.

How do the results under the new and old approaches compare?

In this case, management had been informed, on the basis of the "one best estimate" approach, that the expected return was 25.2 percent before taxes. Running our new set of data through the computer program, we found an expected return of only 14.6 percent before taxes. This surprising

Table 1

Comparison of expected values under old and new approaches

	Conventional "best estimate" approach	New approach
MARKET ANALYSES		
1. *Market size*		
Expected value (in tons)	250,000	250,000
Range	—	100,000–340,000
2. *Selling prices*		
Expected value (in dollars/ton)	$510	$510
Range	—	$385–$575
3. *Market growth rate*		
Expected value	3%	3%
Range	—	0–6%
4. *Eventual share of market*		
Expected value	12%	12%
Range	—	3%–17%
INVESTMENT COST ANALYSES		
5. *Total investment required*		
Expected value (in millions)	$9.5	$9.5
Range	—	$7.0–$10.5
6. *Useful life of facilities*		
Expected value (in years)	10	10
Range	—	5–15
7. *Residual value* (at 10 years)		
Expected value (in millions)	$4.5	$4.5
Range	—	$3.5–$5.0
OTHER COSTS		
8. *Operating costs*		
Expected value (in dollars/ton)	$435	$435
Range	—	$370–$545
9. *Fixed costs*		
Expected value (in thousands)	$300	$300
Range	—	$250–$375

NOTE: Range figures in right-hand column represent approximately 1% to 99% probabilities. That is, there is only a 1 in a 100 chance that the value actually achieved will be respectively greater or less than the range.

difference derives not merely from our use of a range of values under the new approach; it also reflects the fact that we have weighted each value in the range by the chances of its occurrence.

From this it may be seen that our new analysis can help management avoid an unwise investment. If this practice were followed by more companies, much regretted overcapacity might be avoided.

The computer program developed to carry out the simulation allows for easy insertion of new variables. In fact, some programs have previously been suggested that take variability into account.[7] But most programs do not allow for dependence relationships between the various input factors. Further, the procedure employed here permits the choice of a value for price from one distribution. This value in turn determines a particular probability distribution (from among several) that will be used to determine the value for sales volume. To show how this technique works:

> Suppose we have a wheel, as in roulette, with the numbers from 0 to 15 representing one price for the product or material, the numbers 16 to 30 representing a second price, the numbers 31 to 45 a third price, and so on. For each of these segments we would have a different range of expected market volumes; e.g., $150,000–$200,000 for the first, $100,000–$150,000 for the second, $75,000–$100,000 for the third, and so forth. Now suppose that we spin the wheel and the ball falls in 37. This would mean that we pick a sales volume in the $75,000–$100,000 range. If the ball goes in 11, we have a different price and we turn to the $150,000–$200,000 range for a sales volume.

Most significant, the program allows management to ascertain the sensitivity of the results to each or all of the input factors. Simply by running the program with changes in the distribution of an input factor, it is possible to determine the effect of added or changed information (or of the lack of information). It may turn out that fairly large changes in some factors do not significantly affect the outcomes. In the history we have cited here, management was particularly concerned about the difficulty in estimating market growth. Running the program with a series of varying growth possibilities quickly demonstrated that for average annual growths from 3 percent to 5 percent there would be no significant difference in the expected outcome.

In addition, we may observe the implications of the detailed knowledge that the simulation method gives us. Under the method employing single expected values, management arrives at a hoped-for expectation of 25.2 percent after taxes (which, as we have seen, turns out to be wrong unless

[7] See Frederick S. Hillier, "The Derivation of Probabilistic Information for the Evaluation of Risky Investments," *Management Science*, April 1963, p. 443.

there has been no variability in the various input factors—a highly unlikely event). With the method we propose, the uncertainties are clearly portrayed:

Percent return	Probability of achieving at least the return shown
0%	96.5%
5	80.6
10	75.2
15	53.8
20	43.0
25	12.6
30	0

Anticipated rates of return under old and new approaches

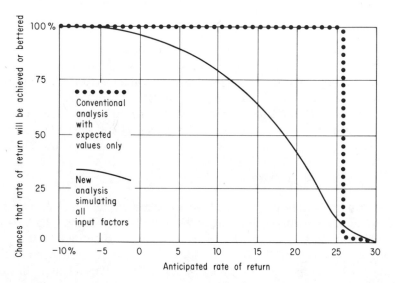

This profile is shown above. Note the contrasting profile obtained under the conventional approach. This concept has also been used for evaluation of new-product introductions, acquisition of new businesses, and plant modernization.

Comparing opportunities

From a decision-making point of view one of the most significant advantages of the new method of determining rate of return is that it allows management to discriminate between measures of (1) expected return based on weighted probabilities of all possible returns, (2) variability of return, and (3) risks.

To visualize this advantage, let us take an example based on another actual case but simplified for purposes of explanation. The example involves two investments under consideration, A and B.

When the investments have been analyzed, the information shown in Table 2 is obtained. We see that:

¶ Investment B has a higher expected return than Investment A.

¶ Investment B also has substantially more variability than Investment A. There is a good chance that Investment B will earn a return quite different from the expected figure of 6.8 percent, possibly as high as 15 percent or as low as a loss of 5 percent. Investment A is not likely to vary greatly from the expected 5 percent return.

¶ Investment B involves far more risk than does Investment A. There will be virtually no chance of incurring a loss on Investment A. But there is one chance in ten of losing money on Investment B. If such a loss occurs, it will amount to an expected $200,000.

Clearly, the new method of evaluating investments provides management with far more information on which to base a decision. Investment decisions made only on the basis of maximum expected return can hardly be the best decisions.

Table 2

Comparison of two investment opportunities

	Investment A	Investment B
Amount of investment	$10,000,000	$10,000,000
Life of investment (in years)	10	10
Expected annual net cash inflow	$1,300,000	$1,400,000
Variability of cash inflow		
1 chance in 50 of being *greater* than	$1,700,000	$3,400,000
1 chance in 50 of being *less* than	$900,000	($600,000)
Expected return on investment	50%	6.8%
Variability of return on investment		
1 chance in 50 of being *greater* than	70%	15.5%
1 chance in 50 of being *less* than	30%	(4.0%)
Risk of investment		
Chances of a loss	Negligible	1 in 10
Expected size of loss		$200,000

Conclusion

The question management faces in selecting capital investments must be first and foremost: What information is needed to clarify the key differences among various alternatives? The basic factors that should be considered—markets, prices, costs, and so on—will generally be agreed upon. And the way the future return on the investment should be calculated, if not agreed on, will at least be limited to a few methods, any of which may be consistently used in a given company. If the input variables turn out as estimated, any of the methods customarily used to rate investments should provide satisfactory (if not necessarily maximum) returns.

But in actual practice the conventional methods do *not* work out satisfactorily. Why? The reason, as every executive and economist knows, is that the estimates used in making the advance calculations come down to just that—estimates. More accurate estimates would be helpful, but at best the residual uncertainty can easily make a mockery of corporate hopes. Even so, there is a solution. To collect realistic estimates for the key factors means to find out a great deal about them. Hence, the kind of uncertainty involved in each estimate can be evaluated ahead of time. Using this knowledge of uncertainty, executives will be able to obtain the best possible value from the information and apply it to decision making.

The value of computer programs in developing clear portrayals of the uncertainty and risk surrounding alternative investments has been proved. Such programs can produce valuable information about the sensitivity of the possible outcomes to the variability of input factors and to the likelihood of achieving various possible rates of return. This information can be extremely important as a backup to management judgment. To have calculations of the odds on all possible outcomes lends some assurance to the decision makers that available information has been used with maximum efficiency.

This simulation approach has the inherent advantage of simplicity. It requires only an extension of the input estimates (to the best of our ability) in terms of probabilities. No projection should be pinpointed unless we are *certain* of it.

The discipline of thinking through the uncertainties of the problem will in itself help to ensure improvement in making investment choices. For to understand uncertainty and risk is to understand the key business problem —and the key business opportunity. Since the new approach can be applied on a continuing basis to each capital alternative as it comes up for consideration and progresses toward fruition, gradual progress may be expected in improving the estimation of the probabilities of variation.

Lastly, the courage to act boldly in the face of apparent uncertainty can be greatly bolstered by the clear portrayal of the risks and possible rewards. To achieve these lasting results requires only a slight effort beyond what most companies already exert in studying capital investments.

31. Business logistics for better profit performance

Alan H. Gepfert

Some years ago a new marketing vice president in a large consumer products company convinced top management that his division should begin a major effort to improve its service to customers. Competitive pressures were mounting, he argued. The only answer would be to cut down on back orders, sharply increase the frequency of deliveries, and reduce stockouts to an absolute minimum.

Most of the vice president's recommendations were carried out. The effect on sales was gratifying—so much so that, one by one, the company's other divisions followed suit. Management opened new field warehouses all around the country. Truck fleets were progressively enlarged, and delivery times cut sharply. Understandably, customers were delighted.

But some members of management were not so happy. They saw that the company had become top-heavy with inventories and that costs of order processing, stock holding, and transportation were creeping steadily higher. Yet they found they could not easily challenge the expanded distribution system. Meaningful cost data seemed difficult to isolate, and marketing men had warned that corrective action would jeopardize the company's market share. Management's customer-service orientation had locked the company into a distribution cost spiral from which there seemed to be no escape.

A host of consumer goods companies have lived through variations of the same story in recent years. Many are still looking for a way out of the spiral of mounting distribution costs and deteriorating profits.

Companies in the extractive and basic processing industries often face profit deterioration for the *opposite* reason. Historically, the conspicuously high cost of transporting bulk raw materials has led them to locate their plants as close as possible to their raw materials sources. At the time the plant location decision is made, this usually entails no competitive penalty. But when a competitor finds a more strategically located source of raw materials or develops a substitute product with different raw materials requirements, the competitive balance is upset and the company that once had an economic edge may find itself with a shrinking share of market and an eroding earnings picture.

Lately there has been evidence that some organizations are becoming alert to the perils of an exclusive raw materials orientation. A number of oil companies, for example, have begun to locate refineries closer to the marketplace. But many other extractive enterprises, still frozen in a production-distribution pattern based on raw materials economics, will soon find themselves vulnerable to change that may come almost overnight.

Such lack of management foresight almost always goes hand in hand with a failure, first, to recognize logistics as a distinct function of the business and, second, to integrate the planning and operating activities of the company's functional divisions in the light of a logistics analysis.

Significance of logistics

Precisely what do we mean by business logistics? What are the benefits of applying a logistics approach to distribution problems? How do the computer and the new quantitative problem-solving methods fit into the picture? And what can chief executives do to ensure effective management of the logistics function in their organizations?

We have no generally accepted definition of the logistics function. I shall use "logistics" to mean the functional bridge that provides for the physical movement of goods from raw materials sources to plants, from plants to warehouses, and from warehouses to customers. This definition may appear broad, but the breadth of perspective is important. If management takes a narrower view of the logistics function, critical problems will be overlooked and significant profit-improvement opportunities missed.

But how is it that significant improvement opportunities can go undetected by normal planning, budgeting, and control processes? A brief review of the basic decisions and decision flows in different types of industries may help make the reason clear.

The basic strategic and interfunctional decisions that shape an enterprise are customarily divided into two major classes: (1) decisions centering on sales and marketing, and (2) decisions centering on manufacturing and production.

In a *consumer*-oriented company, sales and marketing issues dictate strategy. Key decisions relate to the type and mix of products to distribute, the type and location of customers to be served, and the level of service to be provided. Associated with these will be approaches to prices and discount policy, and decisions guiding the makeup of the field sales force. Given this customer-service orientation, the necessary manufacturing decisions then follow.

In a *process*-oriented company, the thrust is reversed. Issues of manufacturing strategy will be settled first. Sales and marketing decisions are then tailored to the manufacturing strategy.

Major decisions of either kind will in effect be the product of a one-way flow. In the consumer-oriented company, feedback from manufacturing to sales and marketing is limited at best. The same may be said of feedback from sales and marketing to manufacturing in the process-oriented company. In fact, one well-known mining corporation bases its long-range planning on a policy of exploring for and developing all possible mineral reserves; it assumes that profitable markets for the end products will always be found.

This characteristic one-way flow of decision-making logic becomes inevitable when the elements that make up logistics have not been pulled together and declared to be a functional responsibility. Lacking such a focus, sales divisions operate warehouses for their own individual product lines; the manufacturing division plans new warehouse locations as part of its plant construction program; the transportation department plans and operates the truck fleet; staff economists, through their inputs to the sales forecasts, help call the tune on inventory levels; and so on. As a result, these decisions never—unless by accident—mesh into the pattern of an optimally profitable distribution system.

All marketing men know how quickly a shrewd customer will move to take advantage of a change in sales or marketing policy that simplifies his operations. One soft goods manufacturer, for example, decided to provide the fastest and most reliable order processing and distribution service in its industry. Customers with limited receiving and warehousing facilities promptly took advantage of this opportunity. They reduced order size and increased order frequency.

This cut down the size of individual deliveries and the number of different products which they had to handle at any one time, as well as the volume of their aggregate inventories.

Observing how these special services had caught on with the customers, the company's sales and marketing people applied pressure for more of the same. Top management agreed to add eight more warehouses to the logistics network. Later on, to exercise maximum control over service and schedules, the company acquired its own transportation fleet. Pressures thereupon built up to improve traffic routing and scheduling through the use of operations research techniques.

Another consumer goods company, with sales of about $300 million and supply and distribution costs of roughly $11 million, suffered from just this sort of one-way flow in logistics decision making. Additional difficulties were created by failure of the company's accounting system to isolate the net cost impact of policies that cut across division boundaries.

371

But top management eventually took corrective action. It instituted a series of projects embracing the entire logistics function. Thanks to a high degree of interfunctional coordination and cooperation, these projects generated a significant series of improvements. Production assignments and warehouse service areas were realigned, with a resulting annual payoff of $321,000. Among similar corrective actions and payoffs: truck shipments were pooled to decrease less-than-truckload-lot volume ($257,000); split-case orders, special handling of back orders, and frequency of shipping to individual customers were all restricted ($221,000); and minimum order sizes were increased ($176,000). Taken together, these measures resulted in an annual payoff of $975,000.

Savings were made possible by a large-scale operations research and computer-based system in which the logistics network was represented by a three-stage linear programming model. Stage 1 covered the warehouse-to-customer distribution system; Stage 2 covered the manufacturing-to-warehouse supply system; Stage 3 took care of monthly production and inventory planning.

To support the OR-computer model, a massive information system was developed. It incorporated a file of demand data from over 300,000 invoices, freight rates in six commodity classes and 11 shipment weight ranges for 1,500 routes, and standard data on operating rates and costs for all warehouses and machine centers. A computer run of the model, with built-in restrictions to ensure the continued feasibility of two-day delivery service, led to a realignment of production assignments and warehouse service areas that yielded the $321,000 payoff cited above.

Here is another instance. Seeking to improve its crude oil allocations, a large oil company developed a linear programming model. The model indicated that the company's annual worldwide transportation ton-miles could be reduced by 10 percent, provided certain changes were made in refinery product mixes and in the assignments of refineries to sales terminals. Implementing these changes was no easy matter, but the gross annual savings of several million dollars in transportation fleet investment and operating costs have more than justified the effort.

COPING WITH UNCERTAINTY. Companies obliged to make long-term plans for a transportation fleet face a task fraught with uncertainty and risk. This is particularly true when the day comes to decide the timing and specifications of future tanker acquisitions. It may be realistic to assume that an ocean tanker or a railway locomotive will have a ten-year life; but customer demand during this span will necessarily be uncertain, future operating costs are unknown, and continuing technological improvements in the equipment, though inevitable, will not be predictable in detail. Given these imponderables and the high cost of equipment—perhaps $300,000 for a locomotive, easily $8 million for a new ocean tanker—the financial risk of these decisions can be heavy indeed. Understandably, such companies have increasingly turned to OR techniques such as risk analysis.

Another OR technique, queuing, or waiting-line theory, has proved useful (particularly when combined with a simulation program) in planning new maintenance facilities for servicing truck or locomotive fleets. For example, the OR-aided redesign of a locomotive maintenance shop not only helped shorten turnaround time, but permitted optimum balancing of the number of service tracks and the number and size of service crews. Associated improvements in diagnosis and preventive maintenance scheduling helped reduce to a minimum the number of locomotives out of service at any given time. Altogether, net costs were cut by over $400,000 per year. Yet the railroad was able better than ever before to live up to published timetables.

HEURISTIC APPLICATIONS. Another company, engaged in large-scale transportation of raw materials, developed a combined man-computer system to achieve the greatest possible efficiency of scheduling within practical limits of traffic feasibility. The problem, being exceptionally complex, necessitated the development of a special heuristic model based on exhaustive documentation of current decision-making guidelines, identification of the controlling economic features, and formulation of a system of logic. The operational steps in using the man-computer system include: (a) making a first computer run to develop an initial tentative schedule, (b) reviewing the schedule and projected net cost as the basis for revising the specifications of the first run, and (c) making a rerun to develop an improved alternative schedule. The system that was finally developed permitted the simulation of 200,000 to 400,000 decisions in a five-minute computer run. It has yielded a payout of millions of dollars a year.

Similarly, a dairy products company was dissatisfied with its performance in routing and scheduling milk deliveries to wholesale customers. Its route plans, reviewed and revised on an average of every three years by the distribution manager, were often badly out of date. Heuristic scheduling provided the answer. It enabled area managers to update route plans locally at any time. These revisions not only responded to changing local costs and customer demands but also permitted specific shifts in service and delivery patterns recommended by route salesmen. Cost savings exceeded $300,000 a year. Even the designers of the system—knowing that it is often hard to improve on the job done by experienced schedulers working with their own rules of thumb—were surprised at the way it outperformed the old manual scheduling system.

SOLUTIONS BY SIMULATION. Computer models have been successfully applied by several companies to evaluate alternatives in warehouse layout and materials-handling equipment where multiple and often conflicting criteria complicate the decision. One metal fabricating company, for example, wanted to conserve warehouse space and avoid traffic bottlenecks. It also hoped to retain flexibility for future expansion in truck dock facilities, thus upgrading its customer delivery service. A simulation program provided the solution that unaided managerial judgment could never have achieved.

A major public utility used a simulation model to cope with the operating complexity of a central-satellite warehouse system. This meant calculating variations in supplier lead time and, as weather conditions altered construction schedules, anticipating the unpredictable fluctuations of demands on its construction materials inventory. With the help of computer simulation, the utility was able to reduce its inventories of construction materials 20 percent, with savings of $540,000 a year.

The benefits of logistics projects are by no means confined to giant corporations with large OR and computer staffs of their own. Of the two largest projects I have just described, the first was completed in 18 months by three senior analysts and the second in 30 months by a five-man team, at a cost of roughly $100,000 and $200,000 respectively.

One corporation with sales over the $1 billion mark boasts a staff of more than 70 analysts in its systems department. Another company with domestic sales of about $180 million retains four OR men, plus eight systems analysts on its corporate computer staff. A third technology-based company in the $50 million bracket employs only three OR analysts. Yet all three companies realize about the same rate of return on logistics-oriented OR investments.

Today most companies above the $20 million sales level employ computer staff analysts with the technical capability for undertaking logistics projects. True, a broader variety of potential logistics improvements is likely to be present in larger, more complex corporations. Yet, many smaller companies miss out on significant opportunities because managers —wrongly assuming their grasp of logistics operations to be comprehensive —feel they cannot and need not take time off from their market-expansion preoccupations to concern themselves with analyzing the economics of company operations. In this way the cost spiral begins mounting ever more steeply as the corporate orientation toward customer service progressively outweighs logistics considerations.

Management's assignment

As a rule, payoffs of any importance will not be obtained without substantial investment of effort by highly skilled OR personnel. The more ambitious systems we have discussed, for example, took from 5 to 12 man-years of development time. But no top management has yet reaped the benefits of effective logistics applications simply by granting a broad charter to the OR staff in the logistics area and then stepping back to await

374

results. Unless senior executives become actively committed to the logistics orientation, they cannot expect to furnish vigorous top-level leadership for the effort—and without such leadership the operations research staff will be unable to identify major projects, gain the support of line executives for programs involving them, or see them through to successful implementation.

Yet once senior executives learn to think in terms of how their policy decisions affect logistics operations and costs—once they grow accustomed, for example, to the idea that marketing policies governing customer service have their cost impact in the logistics area, not in marketing—then functional managers will begin thinking the same way, and the stage will be set for constructive action.

Obviously, senior executives cannot afford to become too deeply involved in building computer-based models, although the technical background necessary for intelligent participation in the development of such models is easy enough to acquire. Rather, top management's primary aim is to recognize and define the logistics issues and to provide the means for an organized attack on the major improvement opportunities. Then the technical aspects of the projects can be safely left to the OR staff and operating personnel.

The effort must above all be managed as a total system. This may present a policy issue, particularly in companies that have long stressed decentralized management and control. Organizational arrangements will therefore vary accordingly. The point of focus for the logistics function may be a particularly able senior member of the operations research or other staff group. It could equally well be a high-level coordinating committee, or a logistics "czar" with authority to enforce changes affecting more than one division or function.

To implement the logistics orientation effectively, experience indicates that three steps are required of top management.

First, *management must provide a strong OR staff organization.* For the foreseeable future, competent OR analysts and computer staff personnel will be in short supply. These key specialists must be utilized effectively. Every effort must be made to ensure their remaining with their projects— with the guiding assumption that such massive and complex logistics projects never take less than months to complete, and sometimes take years.

Second, *top management must define the logistics function in the company and maintain a firm grasp of logistics costs.* As noted earlier, most corporate accounting systems fail to meet the information needs of business logistics. They readily produce data keyed to the financial accounts, but not the essential data on variable costs. Management can easily determine the total costs for order processing, freight, or warehousing; but when it wants to know how these costs would be affected by a prospective new plant or a realignment of customer service assignments among existing warehouses, the traditional accounting system does not have the answers.

Hence, the company must begin by underwriting a project for developing estimates of logistics costs, in total and by major elements. Data of this kind will be needed to identify key improvement opportunities, to develop new systems, and eventually to follow up on performance.

Third, *top management must put the logistics orientation to work.* The most successful mechanism for problem identification and project selection, judging from the experience of a few farsighted companies, is a permanent team or a task force whose membership—operating personnel from appropriate functions, as well as systems analysts, economists, operations researchers, and computer specialists—will change with the requirements of its successive assignments.

The team's first job will be to make a thoroughgoing conceptual analysis of the company's decision-making and information systems. Typically, the results of this analysis will be embodied in a master flow chart like that shown in the exhibit on page 377. This illustrates how to identify a missing feedback link that would permit a two-way flow in the warehousing decision cycle. Note that the analysis concentrates on decision processes per se. No attempt has been made to portray current organizational units or responsibilities, not merely because they are irrelevant but because they obscure key logistics issues and opportunities.

The team's next task will be to analyze in detail the economics of the various elements making up the logistics function. The results of this step can be graphically represented in an overlay keyed to the individual decisions shown on the master flow chart. If current information systems are keyed to financial accounting, this economic analysis will refine available data to match the specified decision blocks on the chart.

With preliminary analyses completed and the results recorded in graphic form, the team should set about identifying potential logistics improvements. There are four possible ways of going about this:

1. Review the economic leverage of particular logistics decisions, concentrating on the big-dollar areas.

2. Reexamine current decision-making procedures, looking for opportunities to replace judgmental, rule-of-thumb procedures with more advanced (perhaps computer-based) analytical systems.

3. Examine information inputs at various points in the decision system to see where improvements might be effected—by filling in gaps in the information currently supplied for decision making or by providing more timely information.

4. Look over currently available information on the *effects* of decisions to see how the information might be improved to provide a better basis for performance evaluation and control.

Thus identifiable opportunities for improvement in the logistics function will be of three kinds: (a) improved decision processes, notably those resulting from the integration of multiple activities formerly handled separately or from the use of analytical models in joint man-computer systems; (b) better input information to support the decision processes; and (c) better output information to be used in evaluating decision effectiveness.

Schematic of logistics-based decision making and information systems

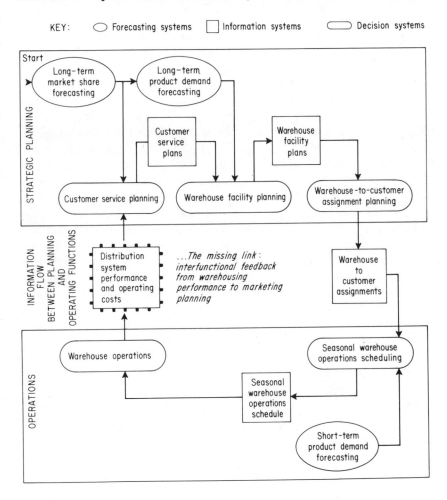

KEY: ◯ Forecasting systems ▢ Information systems ⬭ Decision systems

Each change in the current logistics function should lead to the identification of new improvement opportunities. The identification project selection task, therefore, will not be a one-time effort but a continuing process.

Organizational implications

The logistics orientation I have described is characterized by a systems analysis perspective and by emphasis on operations research approaches. This accords with two clearly evident trends: (1) increasing concern of top management with the structure of decision-making processes, and (2) growing use of quantitative decision-making techniques throughout industry. But the new stress on logistics will also tend to bring serious organizational issues to the surface, especially when top management comes to grips with the problems of coordinating decentralized decision-making processes in a large company.

Problems of coordination will always be present, of course, in decentralized organizations. Though alert to these problems when they occur down the line, top managers often tend to overlook them (or shy away from them) at their own level, particularly when the solution appears to call for a basic reexamination of established organizational structure. Yet the biggest gains in logistics efficiency have demonstrably come about through organization restructuring aimed at increasing the integration of operations.

If a series of improvement opportunities calls for better communication and interaction across an organizational boundary, it is likely that the units concerned should be integrated, or that their components and responsibilities at least should be reshuffled. For example, a hard-goods manufacturer with sales in the $500 million to $600 million range has taken logistics-planning decisions away from the independent operating divisions and centralized them in a new corporate logistics group, headed by a senior vice president. He is charged with all planning for the logistics activities and expected to review all operating division programs that may affect the total logistics function.

To cite another example, a large mining/processing company has now taken its first step toward the centralization of all planning. Eventually, its mining, transportation, and processing functions will be strictly operating divisions. The mining division will develop, but not select, specified mineral properties. The transportation division will implement schedules, but no longer plan the fleet movements or mine-to-mill assignments. The processing division will carry out the mill schedule, but mill schedule planning or mill facility planning will likewise be done at corporate headquarters.

The division managers will naturally be expected to contribute to overall

378

planning, but their line responsibility will be to develop and carry out efficient operating programs within the guidelines laid down by the central planning group. Thus the company will have a mix of centralized strategic planning and decentralized operations. Being a realist, the chief executive anticipates that this reorganization will probably generate a good deal of political maneuvering in the organization. But, for the sake of the economic payoff, he is prepared to see it through.

There can be no way to avoid this; a top management determined to maximize the effectiveness of its logistics operations must be prepared to endure as well as to inflict the discomforts of organizational change. But the rewards of such change may extend beyond the economic benefits of sound logistics management. As readjustments designed to attain these benefits are carried out, the company's formal structure should evolve toward a pattern more closely attuned to the basic economics of its industry. And this will be likely in turn to produce gratifying gains in over-all organizational effectiveness.

32. Management information: the myth of total systems

C. Ridley Rhind

An executive's dependence on information has long been recognized. Speaking of President Franklin D. Roosevelt's approach to the Presidency in the 1930s, Arthur Schlesinger has reported that "the first task of an executive, as he [F.D.R.] evidently saw it, was to guarantee himself an effective flow of information and ideas . . ."[1] Roosevelt made very great efforts to ensure that he received information often from unofficial as well as from official sources, Schlesinger reports.

Although it has not always been so explicitly recognized, the need for information in business must certainly be as great as it is in government, and business executives now universally acknowledge the imperfections of their sources of information. But only recently has it become the height of fashion to look to computers to meet executives' information needs.

Because the computer seems to promise an improvement in the availability and quality of information—which would meet a universal need— computer-based management information systems are much discussed in management journals today. Unhappily, many of the hopes now pinned to such systems seem to be derived from the acuteness of the need rather than any real likelihood of success.

The concept of a computer-based management information system did not spring full-blown from the brain of a single man. Rather, today's management information systems have evolved gradually. Indeed, there is little difference between the advantages we now hope to gain by developing management information systems and those we once (circa 1960) expected to achieve through integrated data processing or management operating systems. These ancestors of management information systems, indispensable as they may be to the running of our businesses, have never really fulfilled their early promise. In fact, management information systems, or MIS for short, sometimes remind me of Oscar Wilde in middle age—a young man with a great future behind him. In fact, the computer does have

---

[1] Quoted in Richard E. Neustadt, *Presidential Power*, John Wiley & Sons, Inc., New York, 1960, p. 149.

a future in MIS, but tight reins must be used to guide its development if it is to fulfill its promise.

Two common misconceptions

Two major errors are commonly encountered in discussions of MIS today: the first error is to forget that every executive in every corporation has an MIS, which may indeed be very well developed and may depend in no way upon a computer; the second error is to forget that an information system may be the source of incorrect information. Let me discuss these errors in some detail.

Obviously, MIS did exist before computers. Every manager has his sources of information, and every manager checks them more or less systematically before he makes his decisions. Managers should not look upon the computer as revolutionary; it is not the first source of comprehensive, accurate, timely information. But they are certainly justified in regarding it as an aggravation, for it does challenge them to change their ways and learn how to use a valuable new source of timely information.

I recently visited the San Francisco Zoo and admired the rhinoceros there, and I read the sign in front of its cage which told me that this was a rhinoceros and that, despite its size, the animal has a very small brain and extremely weak eyesight. However, it is "gifted" (as the sign said) with an extraordinarily acute sense of hearing. All of the rhinoceros' information must therefore come in through its ears. It seems to me that many managers today expect all their information also to come in through their ears: over lunch, in presentations by subordinates, or in conversations with colleagues. Some managers are accustomed to trusting accounting reports as sources of information, but few of them are yet fully aware of the helpful capabilities of the computer in this regard. They need to change their ways, and accept the computer as a colleague.[2]

Let us be clear about the nature of this challenge. It is not a challenge to import revolution, to transform a firm by the injection of something radically new, or to abolish all decision making based on "incomplete, inaccurate, unorganized, or untimely information." To my mind the challenge appears much more manageable: to fit the computer into the communications network that already exists in every firm. This means that the manager must not accept uncritically all that computer systems men tell him about MIS. He is well placed to understand that the computer-based MIS has a *supplementary* role, even though the computer systems man will promote his ideas as revolutionary. It means, too, that the manager must

[2] For an interesting discussion of managers' uses of information, see C. West Churchman, "Managerial Acceptance of Scientific Recommendations," *California Management Review*, Fall 1964, pp. 31–38.

prepare himself to expand his ability to seek information by reducing his dependence on his ears and educating himself in the use of other senses and skills.

The second error into which we commonly fall is that of forgetting that MIS may be quite well developed in a corporation but may give completely wrong information; transferring such a system to a computer will confer little advantage. Professor John Dearden at the Harvard Business School wrote that far too many firms have the very latest in EDP equipment installed but are still relying on accounting systems—and particularly, I would add, upon cost accounting systems—that are at least 20 years behind the times.

It can be very easy to apply the wrong information to the decision at hand, and this most often happens when managers rely on just such accounting systems for a major part of their information, which has not been an uncommon practice. Accounting systems can yield misleading information because even today their principal function is often to provide a clear historical track from individual transactions to the stockholders' annual report. They may be seen as truly democratic systems in which every transaction, large or small, will be treated equally and accounted for. Such systems do not always serve the needs of management decision making. First, accounting systems often do not yield even approximate marginal costs—needed for many decisions. Second, transfer prices are often set either for tax purposes or on a cost basis, and they often become poor guides in make-or-buy decisions. They can cause confusion when, for example, plans to centralize supply and distribution functions are being evaluated, and may seriously muddy the waters when management tries to evaluate the performance of competing divisions. Third, accounting data assembled within organizational or functional lines frequently cannot be correlated with other accounting data for overall business or product-line decisions. Obviously transferring such misleading information into a computer-based MIS will not bring great advantage.

In summary, it seems that managers expect far too much from systems men and far too much from the computer when they pin great hopes on the design of computer-based MIS. Their dissatisfaction with available information will not vanish. I have seen proposals that I can only term visionary and that seem to me to threaten to change the way companies have operated for many years. The systems men responsible for these "revolutionary" proposals seem to have forgotten that managers *do* have information sources, both human beings and accounting systems, to which they are accustomed to turn; and they forget, too, that some of these sources yield misleading information and mislead managers in subtle ways. Despite incompleteness and proneness to mislead, these information systems are not all bad—revolution is not called for.

Managers should look on computer information systems as *supplementary* sources of data and information—and only of "official" information at that. Richard E. Neustadt, writing of Presidents of the United States, notes:

> It is not information of a general sort that helps a President see personal stakes; not summaries, not surveys, not the bland amalgams. Rather . . . it is the odds and ends of tangible detail that pieced together in his mind illuminate the underside of issues put before him. To help himself he must reach out as widely as he can for every scrap of fact, opinion, gossip, bearing on his interests and relationships as President.[3]

The corporate manager, mesmerized by the promise of an encyclopedic computer-based MIS, might profit by reflecting on Neustadt's comments. He should decide for himself the relative importance of official and unofficial information and the extent to which the computer can supply scraps of fact, opinion, or gossip. Furthermore, many managers will find that it can be as difficult for them to seek information from computers as it is for the rhinoceros to gain information through its eyes. A time-consuming process of self-education is needed. Finally, although the easiest option in designing MIS will be to transfer unimproved accounting information systems to ever more sophisticated computer systems, the exercise often proves pointless and may simply perpetuate the inadequacies of a system that, in all probability, could do with a thorough overhaul.

What computers <u>can</u> do

Computers, then, ought not to be considered intrinsic parts of all information systems. But they can play an extremely significant role in making more information available and also in improving the quality of that information.

Computer-based MIS *that work* remain limited in scope today and will almost surely continue to be for many years to come. To me, management means "directing and controlling an enterprise to accomplish an end result," and information encompasses "news, facts, data, and intelligence." Management information, therefore, consists of intelligence or data that enable those who direct an enterprise to achieve the end results they desire. But the management of an enterprise is a complex process occurring on at least three levels, and the *same* MIS cannot serve all levels. In short, "total, integrated management information systems" are a fantasy.

Nor can all levels of corporate management benefit equally from com-

[3] *Presidential Power*, op. cit., p. 147.

puter-based systems. The first level is the strategic management of the corporation, which consists of evaluating the opportunities for profit over the long term. On the basis of its evaluation, management determines corporate policies and objectives, and decides on the deployment of resources necessary to attain these objectives. By definition, many opportunities exist that the company has not seized—and on which there will, therefore, be no internal information.

On the second level of corporate management I would place those managers who divide the strategic plan into logical subdivisions, allocate funds to carry them out, and assign the responsibility for each to one person or group of persons. Performance measurement will also be an important function of managers at this level, and I would say that their overall purpose is to exercise management control.

The third level of management takes in what I shall call the management of operations. This involves determining the specific requirements of men and materials needed for each part of the corporate plan; assigning these resources so that the plan can be carried out in an efficient manner; comparing actual results with plans; and taking corrective action where appropriate. This is a day-to-day process, and many day-to-day problems come down to logistical problems—they have to do with the flow of goods.[4]

What, then, is the potential of computers in serving management information systems? I believe that *their utility will be greatest in aiding the management of operations*. The usefulness of computers in MIS designed to aid in *strategic management* may be judged questionable, and their utility in the *management control* process only slightly less so.

Three success stories

Three recent examples of successful MIS serve to illustrate this point. In the Leatherbee Lectures at the Harvard Business School,[5] Donald I. Lowry of Procter & Gamble described the evolution of what might be called a marketing information system at his company. It started as a transaction-based system handling orders, shipping, and billing. To this was added a system to record daily production, which implied that finished product inventories could be projected. Thus, from all these blocks of data there can be developed an optimum production schedule. According to Lowry, Procter & Gamble's marketing system records orders centrally, assigns them to warehouses for the most economical shipping, and prepares all the necessary paper work. It also—most relevant to a discussion of MIS—automatically creates a sales information base from

[4] This analysis follows that of John Dearden in "Can Management Information Be Automated?" *Harvard Business Review*, March–April 1964, pp. 128–135.

[5] "Leatherbee Lectures," Graduate School of Business, Harvard University, 1967.

384

source data. This is of great usefulness to marketing planners, who can and do call for analyses to aid them in their work.

R. A. Kronenberg of the Weyerhaeuser Company several years ago described his company's attempt to develop an MIS.[6] The objective so far, he said, has been to achieve a centralized system through which sales order and factory production data all flow from the field directly into a computer at Tacoma. This is no mean achievement, since it implies the establishment of exceedingly large product and customer files; Weyerhaeuser's team has also designed a variety of operating reports from these data bases.

Some years ago, the Canadian Pacific Railway Company developed a system for centrally recording and processing complete information on waybills and train and car movements. A daily freight situation report could be made up. *In real time*—as the phrase was then understood—a destination yard would be informed of the makeup of cars in approaching trains. From this, data-based reports to improve control by management were prepared.[7]

These three successful computer-based management information systems have in common a focus on: (1) well-structured operating problems; (2) limited objectives, in the short term at least; (3) high-volume processing of routine transactions. They could equally well be called logistics control systems. Each promises success because, in the company in which it has been installed, logistics determine to a considerable extent the profitability of the corporation as a whole. Thus, the very large expenses incurred in developing the MIS can be justified by the promise that it will make a real contribution toward corporate earnings per share.

The magnitude of development expense has been daunting indeed. Lowry estimates that the systems development costs associated with computerizing the pricing of outbound freight *alone* were $250,000. And as justification for the development of a central information system—not unlike Canadian Pacific's in principle—Greyhound Corporation a few years ago cited an expected 5 or 6 percent improvement in equipment utilization.[8] This represented a considerable payoff, since the company operated over 5,300 buses at that time.

These examples should make clear what I mean by limited scope. The systems described generally have a limited *audience*—operating managers —and concern themselves with limited *activities*—in most cases logistics but sometimes also costs, performance against budget, and certain special

[6] R. A. Kronenberg, "Weyerhaeuser's Management Information System," *Datamation*, May 1967, pp. 28–30.

[7] Alan D. Meacham and Van B. Thompson, eds., *Total Systems*, American Data Processing, Inc., Detroit, 1962.

[8] General Electric Information Systems Group, "Greyhound's 'Magic Memory'," *Information Systems Review*, Winter 1967, pp. 8–9.

projects. One example of what I mean by "special projects": a Department of Defense information system designed to keep track of Defense- and NASA-supported research efforts. The aim has been to make possible better technical coordination and to reduce the duplication of system development expenses.[9]

The dream of omniscience

Some proponents of computer-based MIS appear to regard them as the panacea for *all* management ills. For them, the suggestion that the computer might have limited usefulness would be anathema. For example:

> The goal of . . . the "total systems concept" . . . is nothing less than the complete monitoring of the business enterprise by a computer . . . ; the automatic control by the machines of inventories, production scheduling, shipments, accounting, payrolls and all other operations that can be reduced to mathematical representation; and the limiting of direct human control to such functions as setting overall objectives and reacting to such totally unexpected situations as earthquakes or wars.[10]

In a 1964 *Fortune* article, Gilbert Burck pointed out: "The computer . . . organizes and processes information so swiftly that computerized information systems enable top management to know everything that happens as soon as it happens. . . ."[11]

But a point is being missed here. The key management information problem is to sort the important from the unimportant—and this problem has not yet been solved. Many management information systems aim for comprehensiveness, conferring (or pretending to confer) on the manager a kind of divine omniscience. But would such omniscience guarantee wise decisions? I often wonder.

The implication of articles espousing the comprehensive computer-based MIS is that the author is prepared to unlock all mysteries if only the manager will approve his budget. But to my mind the promises that computers can eliminate shortages, delays, or inaccuracies in available information have been made only by those with a vested interest in computer development work who believe that the more ambitious the system, the greater the status. Some managers have been led to expect great things

[9] See Walter M. Carlson, "A Management Information System Designed by Managers," *Datamation*, May 1967, pp. 37–43.

[10] Herbert E. Klein, "The Office: Management's Billion-Dollar System," *Dun's Review and Modern Industry*, September 1964, p. 134.

[11] Gilbert Burck, "Management Will Never Be The Same Again," *Fortune*, August 1964, p. 126.

and now are urging systems departments to press on with development plans. They would do well to recognize the dreamlike quality of their hopes. Such promises may fulfill wishes for status but they are out of touch with the real world.

To suggest that systems of this kind will be the panacea for all ills to which management is heir implies an assumption that *lack* of information has been the most serious problem facing managers at all levels in the organization. I am speaking of three categories of manager: those charged with strategic planning, those concerned with management control, and those responsible for operating control. The assumption must be considered dubious at best. The type of information provided by computer-based MIS may well offer major advantages to managers charged with operating control. But managers in management control or strategic planning cannot expect to benefit from MIS to the same extent, simply because lack of information is seldom principally to blame when they make poor decisions.

Little help for strategists

Even the most ambitious computer-based information system restricts its field of vision to the history of events occurring *within* the corporation. Strategic management concerns itself with predicting the future and preparing to make the most of the opportunities that it offers. Since these will frequently be opportunities that the company has not yet grasped, an MIS with an internal and historic focus can seldom be of much help.

Nor will a computer-based MIS be likely to prove the salvation of managers administering control systems. The process of control typically relates to the budget system, which may be sketched as follows: In a manufacturing company the annual budget is prepared covering direct and overhead costs. Expenses are divided between fixed and variable costs, so that managers responsible for meeting the budget will not be unjustly held responsible for costs arising from fluctuations in volume. The budget is broken down by department so that each subordinate manager can be held responsible for his portion of the total operation. This annual budget serves as the basis for a monthly report in which the budgeted costs can be adjusted to the actual level of production. Budget figures may then be compared by expense categories to the actual cost. Finally, the resulting variances are analyzed. Management can tell whether costs are in line with the plan. Performance of the factory manager can be evaluated from his response to changing circumstances, and management can move to correct anomalies if they are felt to be of sufficient importance. Thus, the budget becomes the basis of management's control over factory costs. It also represents a communication device through which management tells the factory manager—and he in turn tells his subordinates—what is expected of them.

This sort of management control system can be put on a computer. Indeed, it often is; savings *are* shown in the cost of data handling. But the computer adds nothing to the *quality* of information available to managers within the firm. This is revealed *not* by the computer, but by the budgeting and cost accounting system. Perhaps even more important, it is determined by the care with which management at all levels reviews budgeted figures, and by the effect that the budget has on personal motivation. Although the computer may consolidate performance records, it seems misleading to title the overall system an MIS.

Even timely reporting, which the computer offers, is of no great consequence in management control systems. The budget will commonly be annual, and everyone allows for some flexibility in month-by-month operations. Performance does not normally decline in a matter of days, and if emergency situations arise, managers will not usually rely on the formal information system to bring these to the attention of top management.

Managers charged with strategic planning or the administration of control systems will be unlikely to benefit significantly from the use of the computer to improve the quality of information available to them. The most important reason: they must exercise a great deal of discretion in their work, whereas the information they consider is often relatively basic—some gained from "unofficial" or informal sources, some from the accounting system. Days of deliberation may lead, for example, to the withdrawal of a product, the replacement of a plant manager, the redesigning of a production process, or the revamping of an advertising budget. Such decisions, unlike logistic decisions, will not be made incorrectly for lack of the sort of information you can put on a computer.

Finally, although in a large corporation a great deal of information may be required to administer management control systems, it is nowhere near the volume of information required for operational or logistic control. Since the principal advantage of the computer over other methods of data handling has always been its capacity to handle volume accurately, it has been less useful in management control than in operating control. In operating control systems the computer makes possible what has been impossible hitherto: the correlation of great volumes of detail. This is not so in the administration of management control systems.

Hierarchical data base

The varying information needs of managers at different levels in the organization have been rather generally recognized, but often in a curiously

388

irrelevant way. Management is often pictured as a hierarchy. The purpose of the hierarchy is said to be the delegation of responsibility. In a commercial banking system, for example, it will be necessary for the teller to have access to the details pertaining to each account. This level of detail is not required by middle managers, who may be more interested in such information as summary figures on groups of accounts. Finally, top management must be concerned far more with such things as the loan-to-deposit ratio—an even grosser summary of the information available to the teller. According to this view, the same basic information is seen to be of use to managers at all levels in the corporation. The theory thus conceives of a hierarchical information base, tailored to the hierarchy of management. I believe it has some serious holes in it.

It seems to me that the data collected to assist in the management of daily operations will be of very little interest, even in summary form, to the top management of the corporation. The only action that top managers could take as a result of analyzing such summary information would be to criticize their subordinates, and it is my view that most managers at the top of corporations have a different function in life. Since their primary focus should be on strategic planning, not operational control, they will be far more concerned with the relationship between their company and the outside world than with the daily internal operations of the company itself. Thus, managers charged with strategic planning spend more time thinking about their suppliers and consumers, Wall Street, local government, national government, or the unions than they do about warehousing, manufacturing, and the daily or monthly administration of the selling effort. Yet it is precisely these latter subjects about which computer-based MIS are likely to be able to answer questions in the foreseeable future.

So here we have more evidence that plans to develop a total corporate MIS are based on shaky assumptions. If every manager is to have all the information he wants, there must be *several* information systems within the same corporation. If so, we had better not try to develop all of them at once. Rather, we should begin on just *one* of them—whichever one offers the most incentive, the greatest hope of success, and the most useful role for the computer.

Computers and successful MIS

The key, then, to designing a successful, workable computer-based MIS will be deliberately to limit its scope by restricting the system in two ways. First, in terms of the audience for which it has been designed. In most instances, it should serve managers charged with the smooth daily operation of line departments such as marketing, shipping, warehousing, transportation, or production. Second, it should be restricted in terms of data input and output. The aim should almost always be a well-designed system designed to serve a single function, such as logistics, rather than a complex multipurpose MIS.

If I were asked to work on an information system for executives assigned to the administration of management control systems, I would not turn to computer men for help. I would concentrate far more on systems that related to budgeting, cost control, performance measurement, variance analysis, and so forth, than on the design of computer systems. If I were ordered to start drawing up the specifications for a *total* MIS to serve managers charged with strategic planning—for anything bigger than a grocery store—I would be tempted to argue with my superiors.

We have here one overall implication. Whether information systems will be designed to help in the management of logistics or other activities such as R&D, personnel, or engineering, the team designing the computer-based MIS must include men—preferably managers—professionally qualified in these fields. The objective, after all, must be service, and such men know their own needs best. This was the view expressed by the chairman of A.T.&T., H. I. Romnes, who said that a business information system "must grow out of an organization's own experience"; that it is too important to be left to "experts." "Experts" in this context I take to be computer systems men, and I believe Mr. Romnes was calling on managers to face their responsibilities in this field.

I do not wish to suggest that there can be no uses for computers in strategic management. There are many, but I would class them as unrelated to MIS. Others may not agree. For example, I am optimistic about the computer's capacity to *interpret* data and to help management evaluate strategic opportunities characterized by a mystifying complexity in the number of interacting variables. Simulation and risk analysis, linear programming, regression analysis, and a whole battery of techniques developed by statisticians and management economists have all shown great value and promise. But very often the sort of data required for the type of study in which these techniques are employed will not be the kind that most people envisage putting in their MIS. Furthermore, it will frequently not be the type of data worth collecting regularly month after month. Thus, the usefulness of the computer in MIS seems to be an issue completely separate from the value of the many uses that have been found for it in staff analysis work. Sometimes we need not information but wisdom, and the computer is anything but wise. (I have all the *information* I can use on the state of the economy—rate of inventory accumulation, length of factory workweek, unemployment, strength of wholesale prices, and on and on—but I am not wise enough to predict recessions or stock market movements.)

390

Too many promises

The great power of computers has led many of us—in academic circles, in management, and in the computer systems profession—to dream and speak of ambitious information systems not yet designed or proven. Some have promised a golden future in which lack of information will no longer pose a problem. It has been implied, flatteringly but wrongly, that lack of information constitutes the major obstacle to perfect management today—and that this can be overcome. Such claims are dangerously misleading. To promise what you cannot deliver may win one election or one contract, but it does not win favor, especially from practical managers. I do not think that systems men can deliver some of the unproven systems that have been talked about and which some managers now expect. I think they *can* deliver so much that it seems a pity for anyone to be guilty of overselling. The responsibility for judging between the possible and impossible rests with management.

About the authors

B. CHARLES AMES is Managing Director of the Cleveland office, which he helped found in 1963. A graduate of Illinois Wesleyan University and the Harvard Business School, Mr. Ames was Director of Merchandising at General Telephone & Electronics Corporation before joining McKinsey. Marketing is his area of special interest, and he has served as a consultant to companies in a wide range of industries. His articles on marketing management have been published in the *Harvard Business Review* and *Business Horizons*.

H. IGOR ANSOFF is Dean of the Graduate School of Management at Vanderbilt University in Nashville, Tennessee. Dr. Ansoff, who received his PhD in applied mathematics from Brown University, was formerly a Professor at the Graduate School of Industrial Administration at Carnegie-Mellon University. His articles have appeared in management journals such as the *Harvard Business Review* and *Management Technology*, and his book *Corporate Strategy* (McGraw-Hill, 1965) has been translated into four foreign languages.

MARVIN BOWER, a Director in the New York office, served as Managing Director of the Firm from 1950 to 1967. Mr. Bower's consulting work has included studies of top-management problems for both U.S. and European enterprises. A graduate of Brown University, Harvard Law School, and Harvard Business School, he is the author of *The Will to Manage* (McGraw-Hill, 1966), which has appeared in German, French, and Japanese editions. Mr. Bower is Chairman of the Joint Council on Economic Education, Chairman of the McKinsey Foundation for Management Research, and President of the Institute of Management Consultants. He also serves as Chairman of the Board of Trustees of Case Western Reserve University in Cleveland, Ohio, and is a trustee of Brown University, a member of the visiting committee of Harvard Business School, and Chairman of the Advisory Committee of the Harvard University Program on Technology and Society.

392

The late GILBERT H. CLEE, Chairman of the Firm at the time of his death in 1968, was instrumental in the worldwide expansion of McKinsey & Company, beginning with the opening of the London office in 1959. Mr. Clee served as an adviser on finance and organization to the managements of many international companies. He was president of the board of trustees of his alma mater, Wesleyan University in Middletown, Connecticut, and in 1967 received an honorary LLD from the university. In 1963 he was the recipient of a G. M. Loeb Award for excellence in business and financial writing.

DONALD K. CLIFFORD, JR., a Principal in the New York Office, graduated from Yale University with a BA in American Studies and received his MBA from the Harvard Business School. Before joining McKinsey he was associated with the Cryovac Company, a division of W. R. Grace & Company. A specialist in organization and corporate strategy, Mr. Clifford has worked primarily with clients in the fields of banking and finance.

ALCON C. COPISAROW was Chief Scientific Officer, British Ministry of Technology, before joining McKinsey in 1966 as a Director based in the London office. He had previously been Director of a government research laboratory and the National Economic Development Council. A graduate of Owen's College, University of Manchester, and the Sorbonne, Dr. Copisarow has held a Council of Europe Research Fellowship, and is a Chartered Engineer, a Fellow of the Institution of Electrical Engineering, and a Fellow of the Institute of Physics. He is a frequent contributor to scientific, economic, and engineering journals.

D. RONALD DANIEL, Managing Director of the New York office, has served as a consultant to U.S. companies in many industries on problems of organization and planning and control. His articles have appeared in a variety of business journals. Mr. Daniel is a graduate of Wesleyan University in Middletown, Connecticut, and the Harvard Business School. Before joining McKinsey, he played a key role in developing, implementing, and administering the Navy's first electronic data processing system.

GEORGE H. FOOTE, a Principal in the New York office, has worked with U.S. and Canadian corporations in a wide variety of industries on problems of executive compensation, employee benefits, and manpower planning. A graduate of Harvard College, he also has a CLU degree from the American College of Chartered Life Underwriters. Before joining McKinsey, he was with the Burroughs Corporation and the Canada Life Assurance Company. Mr. Foote has written for a number of management journals, including the *Harvard Business Review* and *Business Horizons*.

PETER P. GABRIEL, is a Principal in the New York office. Before joining McKinsey he was general manager of his own consulting firm in Caracas, Venezuela. Born in Germany, and educated both there and in the United States, Dr. Gabriel received his DBA from the Harvard Business School in 1965. He has written for the *Columbia Journal of World Business* and other management journals, receiving a G. M. Loeb Award in 1968 for financial and business writing. His book *The International Transfer of Corporate Skills* was published by the Division of Research of the Graduate School of Business, Harvard University, in 1967.

ALAN H. GEPFERT, an Associate in the New York office, has specialized in the application of the computer sciences to problems of corporate logistics and finance. A graduate of Case Institute of Technology in Cleveland, Ohio, he was with the Chicago & Northwestern Railroad before joining McKinsey. Mr. Gepfert is a frequent writer and speaker on operations research and management science subjects.

DAVID B. HERTZ, a Director in the New York office, is responsible for the Firm's management sciences, operations research, and computer systems practices. He received his BA, BS, and PhD from Columbia University and is a graduate of the U.S. Navy Postgraduate School. Before joining McKinsey, he was a partner at Arthur Andersen & Co. A former chairman of the Council and president of the Institute of Management Sciences, Dr. Hertz is a member of operations research societies in the U.S. and Europe. A prolific author, he has written widely on computer systems and the management sciences; his latest book, *New Power for Management*, was published last year by McGraw-Hill.

JON R. KATZENBACH, a Director in the San Francisco office, has worked with U.S. clients in a wide range of industries on problems of strategic planning, marketing, profit improvement, organization, and management information. Before joining McKinsey, Mr. Katzenbach was an industrial engineer with U.S. Steel Corporation. He is a graduate of Stanford University and the Harvard Business School, where he was a George F. Baker Scholar.

A. L. MCDONALD, JR., Managing Director of the Firm's Paris office, has worked with the top managements of many European companies since transferring to Europe in 1964. He served for two years as a Principal in the London office, and also for two years as Managing Principal of the Zürich office, before going to Paris. Prior to his move to Europe, Mr. McDonald had specialized in developing marketing strategy and measuring the financial impact of marketing alternatives for U.S. corporations in the insurance, food processing, medical equipment, office machinery, and electrical equipment industries. He received his BA from Emory University in Atlanta, Georgia, and his MBA with distinction from the Harvard Business School.

J. ROGER MORRISON is a Director in the London office. A specialist in business organization, planning and control, and profit improvement, Mr. Morrison has served as a consultant to both U.S. and U.K. corporations in a wide variety of industries. He received a BBA with high distinction from the University of Minnesota and an MBA from the Harvard Business School. Mr. Morrison has written for such periodicals as the *Harvard Business Review* and *Management Today*.

RICHARD F. NEUSCHEL, a Director in the New York office, has worked with U.S. corporations in a wide range of industries on problems of organization and planning and control. He has also directed major studies for governmental agencies, including the Post Office Department and the U.S. Air Force. Mr. Neuschel received his BA from Denison University in Granville, Ohio, and his MBA *cum laude* from the Harvard Business School, where he was a George F. Baker Scholar. He is the author of many articles and three books, including *Management by System* (McGraw-Hill), which will soon appear in its third edition.

ROBERT P. NEUSCHEL, a Director in the Chicago office, has worked with many industrial-oriented companies, chiefly on problems of strategic planning and distribution. Mr. Neuschel is a graduate of Denison University in Granville, Ohio, and the Harvard Business School. Before joining McKinsey he served on the corporate manufacturing staff of Sylvania Electric Products, Inc. His articles have appeared in the *Harvard Business Review*, *Business Horizons*, *Nation's Business*, and *Modern Railroads*.

ARCH PATTON, a Director in the New York office, is widely regarded as a leading authority in the field of executive compensation administration and other aspects of executive manpower management. He has helped the top managements of many U.S. companies to design integrated executive compensation programs and develop improved methods of appraising executive performance. He pioneered the development of executive compensation surveys after World War II. Mr. Patton is a frequent writer and speaker on the various aspects of executive compensation as well as other topics of top-management concern. His book *Men, Money and Motivation* (McGraw-Hill, 1961) has become a classic in its field. Mr. Patton is a graduate of Colgate University and attended the Harvard Business School.

BURTON C. PERSON, formerly an Associate in the New York office, is now Director, Group Product Management at The Singer Company. While with McKinsey he worked with the top managements of many manufacturing companies, chiefly on profit-improvement problems. Mr. Person received his BS in metallurgical engineering and MS in management from the University of Illinois, and his MBA from the Harvard Business School.

C. RIDLEY RHIND, now President of Realtronics, a subsidiary of Cybernetics International, was formerly an Associate in the Firm's San Francisco and Düsseldorf offices. A native of England, he received his BA and MA degrees from Oxford and his MBA from the Harvard Business School. His articles on computer-based management information systems have appeared in *Business Horizons* and *Datamation*.

WILBUR M. SACHTJEN is Director of Business Planning for the American Can Company. A former Associate in the Firm's New York office, he was Vice President—Corporate Development at Pfizer International before joining American Can. Mr. Sachtjen received his BBA from the University of Wisconsin and his MBA from the Harvard Business School.

FREDERICK WRIGHT SEARBY, a Principal in the Paris office, was formerly in the Firm's Chicago and New York offices. A graduate of Dartmouth College and the Harvard Business School, Mr. Searby has done extensive consulting work in the fields of corporate strategy, marketing, and finance. "Controlling Postmerger Change" is the second of his articles to have appeared in the *Harvard Business Review*.

E. EVERETT SMITH is a Director in the New York office. During his 25 years with McKinsey, he has directed major studies for some of the leading corporations in North America and Europe. His experience before entering the consulting profession included commercial and investment banking. Deeply interested in the factors that make one enterprise more competitive than another, Mr. Smith is a frequent writer and speaker on management subjects, particularly in the banking field.

JOHN M. STEWART, a Principal in the New York office, is a graduate of Yale University and the Harvard Business School. Prior to joining McKinsey he was with TRW Inc. in Cleveland, Ohio. Mr. Stewart has worked with technically-oriented clients in the pharmaceutical, electronic, aerospace, and chemical industries on research and development, organization, operations, and marketing problems.

The late ROBERT K. STOLZ was a Senior Consultant in the New York office at the time of his death in 1967. His fields of special interest were organization planning, executive development and compensation, and executive performance appraisal. Mr. Stolz was a graduate of Yale University.

JOHN M. UPDEGRAPH, JR., who was Managing Principal of the Zürich office before taking up his present responsibilities as director of professional staff education at Firm headquarters in New York, has served as a consultant to clients in a variety of industries in the United States and Europe. A graduate of Princeton University and the Harvard Business School, Mr. Updegraph was a group manager at Procter & Gamble before joining McKinsey. He has written for *Business Horizons* and *Chain Store Age*.

Acknowledgments

For permission to reprint, usually in somewhat abridged form, the articles and other writings in this collection, McKinsey & Company extends grateful thanks to the following magazines and publishers:

To the *Harvard Business Review* (Copyright © by the President and Fellows of Harvard College, Cambridge, Mass.) for "Marketing Planning for Industrial Products" by B. Charles Ames (issue of September–October 1968); "Strategies for a Technology-Based Business" by H. Igor Ansoff and John M. Stewart (November–December 1967); "Organizing a Worldwide Business" by Gilbert H. Clee and Wilbur M. Sachtjen (November–December 1964); "Reorganizing for Results" by D. Ronald Daniel (November–December 1966); "Business Logistics for Better Profit Performance" by Alan H. Gepfert (November–December 1968); "Risk Analysis in Capital Investment" by David B. Hertz (January–February 1964); "The Coming Scramble for Executive Talent" by Arch Patton (May–June 1967); "Control Postmerger Change" by Frederick Wright Searby (September–October 1969); "Put the Board of Directors to Work!" by E. Everett Smith (May–June 1958); and "Executive Development—New Perspective" by Robert K. Stolz (May–June 1966).

To *Business Horizons* (Copyright © by the Foundation for the School of Business, Indiana University, Bloomington, Indiana) for "Keys to Better Product Planning" by B. Charles Ames (issue of Summer 1966); "Compensation and the Executive Career Cycle" by George H. Foote (Spring 1965); "Shaping Distribution Channels to Your Needs" by A. L. McDonald, Jr. (Summer 1964); "Presidential Style and Organizational Achievement" by Robert P. Neuschel (June 1969); "Management Information: The Myth of Total Systems" by C. Ridley Rhind (June 1968); "The Promise of Project Management" by John M. Stewart (Fall 1965); and "Rediscovering Profits in Manufacturing" by John M. Updegraph, Jr. and Burton C. Person (Fall 1963).

To *Management Review* (Copyright © by the American Management Association, Inc., New York) for "Can Companies Plan Their Profits?" by Jon R. Katzenbach (issue of July 1967); and "Motivating Tomorrow's Executives" by Arch Patton (January 1968).

To the *Columbia Journal of World Business* (Copyright © by the Trustees of Columbia University, New York) for "New Concepts in Overseas Investment" by Peter P. Gabriel (issue of March–April 1967).

To *European Business* (28, boulevard Raspail, Paris 7e) for "R&D as a Partner in World Enterprise" by David B. Hertz (issue of October 1967).

To *Management Today* (Copyright © by Management Publications, Ltd., London) for "Britain's Quiet Managerial Revolution" by J. Roger Morrison (issue of November 1967).

To McGraw-Hill Book Company, Inc., New York, for Chapter 5 of *The Will to Manage* by Marvin Bower (1966), and for Chapter 12 of *Men, Money and Motivation* by Arch Patton (1961).

* * *

Chapters 1, 12, 13, 19, 24, 26 and 29 first appeared in copyrighted publications of McKinsey & Company, Inc.

Index

Adams, Brooks, quoted, 147
Aharoni, Y., cited, 101*n*.
American Dental Association, 217, 223
American Telephone & Telegraph
    Company, 8, 390
Ash, Roy, quoted, 106–107, 163–164
Avon Products, Inc., 208–209

Barlow, E. R., cited, 103*n*.
Behrman, J. N., cited, 101*n*.
Bennion, Edward G., quoted, 359
Benoit, Emile, cited, 105*n*., 107
Bristol-Myers Company, 6
Brookings Institution, 281
Burck, Gilbert, quoted, 386

Campbell Soup Company, 258
Canadian Pacific Railway Company,
    385
Carlson, Walter M., cited, 386*n*.
Carlyle, Thomas, 40
CBS, 218
Chrysler Corporation, 54
Churchman, C. West, cited, 381*n*.
CIBA Products Company, 317
Clevite Corp., 218
Coca-Cola Company, The, 5
Colgate-Palmolive Company, 310
Communications Satellite Corporation,
    149
Cook, Donald C., quoted, 155
Cordiner, Ralph, quoted, 55
Corning Glass Works, 121–122,
    309

Dean, Joel, cited, 355*n*.
Dearden, John, cited, 382, 384*n*.
Du Pont de Nemours, E. I., &
    Company, Inc., 36, 62, 222–223,
    284, 287, 309, 312–313, 319

Eastern Airlines, 194, 195

Elliott Automation, 284
Executive Peace Corps, 150

Fararr, Donald E., cited, 360*n*.
Fiat S.p.A., 99, 150
Ford Motor Company, 320
Friedmann, W. G., cited, 101

Galbraith, John Kenneth, quoted, 148
Gardner, John, quoted, 152–153
Geigy Chemical Corporation, 317
Geneen, Harold, 194
General Dynamics Corp., 106, 194,
    310
General Electric Company, 36
General Foods International, 74, 184,
    224, 258
General Motors Corporation, 27, 36,
    43, 69
Gillette Company, The, 219
Godfrey, Arthur, 217
Grace, W. R., & Co., 5–6
Grant, L. C., 359
Greyhound Corporation, 385

Haggerty, Patrick, 282–283
Hall, Floyd D., 194
Hemingway, Ernest, quoted, 45
Hess, S. W., cited, 360
Hillier, Frederick S., cited, 365*n*.
Hitachi Ltd., 317
Hoffman-La Roche, Inc., 317

IDEA Corporation, 283
Imperial Chemical Industries, 99, 287
Imperial Smelting Corporation, 322
Indian Head Mills, 77
International Basic Economy Corp.,
    99
International Business Machines Corp.,
    5, 106, 184, 224, 309
International Executive Service Corps,
    150

International Telephone and Telegraph Corp., 194

Jay, Antony, quoted, 47
Jennings, Eugene M., cited, 151, 152n.

Kahn, Herman, quoted, 147–148
Kalmanoff, G., cited, 101n.
Kellogg Company, 5
Kennedy, John F., 56–57
Kitching, John, quoted, 12
Klein, Herbert E., quoted, 386
Kronenberg, R. A., cited, 385n.

Lesch, George H., quoted, 310
Lewis, Roger, 194
Life Insurance Committee on Urban Problems, 149
Lipton Ltd., 217
Litton Industries, 106–107, 150
Lowry, Donald I., cited, 384–385

Markowitz, Harry, cited, 360n.
Marshall, Chief Justice John, quoted, 29
Meacham, Alan D., cited, 385n.
Medicare, 149
Mikesell, R. F., cited, 101n.
Minnesota Mining and Manufacturing Corporation, 309
Montecatini Edison S.p.A., 99
Moreell, Ben, 196

Neustadt, Richard E., quoted, 383

Olivetti & C.S.p.A., 99

Pan American World Airways, 106
Parkinson, C. Northcote, cited, 25, 163n.
Penn Central Company, 15
Phillips Gloeilampen Fabrieken, N.V., 317
Procter & Gamble Co., The, 217, 223, 384–385

402

Quigley, H. A., cited, 360

Rabi, I. I., quoted, 321
Renault (Régie Nationale des Usines Renault), 99
Rhône-Poulenc S. A., 319
Robinson, R. D., cited, 101n.
Rockefeller brothers, 99
Romnes, H. I., quoted, 390
Roosevelt, Franklin D., 380
Royal Dutch/Shell Group, 317

Schlesinger, Arthur, quoted, 380
Sears, Roebuck and Co., 175
Sharpe, William F., cited, 360n.
Sherman, Harvey, quoted, 308–309
Sloan, Alfred P., quoted, 54, 71
Smith, Kline and French Laboratories, 319
Standard Oil Company (New Jersey), 182, 184

Texas Instruments Inc., 282–283, 284–285
Thompson, Van B., cited, 385n.
Thorpe, Jim, quoted, 48
Tower International, Inc., 99
Toynbee, Arnold, quoted, 205

Unilever N. V., 184, 317

Volkswagenwerk A. G., 317

Walker, Ross G., quoted, 357
Wallace, Forrest D., cited, 15n.
Wender, I. T., cited, 103n.
Westinghouse Corporation, 106
Weyerhaeuser Company, 385
Whitehead, Alfred North, quoted, 156

Young, Bruce F., cited, 355n.

Zenith Radio Corporation, 221